JOSEPH CONRAD

HEART OF DARKNESS

Joseph Conrad

HEART OF DARKNESS

[Edited with Biography, Chronology, Character Analysis, Text, Summary and Study Questions]

Aditya Nandwani
B.A. English (Hons), Delhi University;
M.A. (English), IGNOU; Print Journalism (English) YMCA

ANMOL PUBLICATIONS PVT. LTD.
NEW DELHI - 110 002 (INDIA)

ANMOL PUBLICATIONS PVT. LTD.

H.O.: 4374/4B, Ansari Road, Darya Ganj,
New Delhi-110 002 (India)
Ph.: 23278000, 23261597
B.O.: No. 1015, Ist Main Road, BSK IIIrd Stage
IIIrd Phase, IIIrd Block
Bangalore - 560 085 (India)
Visit us at: www.anmolpublications.com

Heart of Darkness

First Published, 2009

PRINTED IN INDIA

Printed at Mehra Offset Press, Delhi.

Contents

Preface ix

1. **Introduction** 1
2. **Biography** 5
3. **Conrad: A Brief Chronology** 16
4. **Historical Context** 20
5. **Character Contrast: Marlow and Mrs. Moore** 33
6. **Narrative Technique: Heart of Darkness** 41
7. **Plot Overview** 49
8. **Major Characters** 56
9. **Complete Text** 62
10. **Summary and Analysis** 160
11. **Study Questions** 168

Q.1. Discuss The Darkness in Heart of Darkness.
Or
Analyse the inner darkness in Heart of Darkness. 168

Q.2. Discuss the major themes in Heart of Darkness.
Or
Analyse the "man's journey into self" with reference to Conrad's Heart of Darkness. 175

Q.3. Discuss the barriers in Heart of Darkness.
Or

How does Marlow becomes an open-minded and loyal human being. 177

Q.4. Analyse the depiction of Africa in Heart of Darkness.
Or
Discuss the racism in Heart of Darkness. 180

Q.5. Discuss the role of Intended in Heart of Darkness.
Or
Analyse the blindfold of the intended. 181

Q.6. Discuss the Post-Colonial Theory and Heart of Darkness.
Or
Analyse the British imperialism portrayed by Conrad in Heart of Darkness. 183

Q.7. Discuss the Spiritual Journey in Heart of Darkness.
Or
Analyse Heart of Darkness as a psychological journey. 185

Q.8. Discuss The Spiritual Voyages of Heart of Darkness.
Or
Critically examine the voyages of Kurtz and Marlow. 187

Q.9. Analyse the Character of Marlow in The Heart of Darkness.
Or
Throughout this story there are many confusing and ever changing sides of Marlow's character and his heart of darkness. Comment 189

Q.10. Discuss the Modernist's Experiments in Heart of Darkness.
Or
Analyse Heart of Darkness as a Modernist text. 191

Q.11. Discuss the theme and setting in Heart of Darkness.
Or
Analyse Heart of Darkness as a novel of a story within a story. 192

Q.12. Write a short note on the Symbol of Ivory in Heart of Darkness.
Or
What is the importance of ivory in Heart of Darkness. 195

Q.13. Analyse Lies in Heart of Darkness.
Or
Critically examine the lies told in Heart of Darkness. 197

Q.14. Examine the role of Women in Heart of Darkness.
Or
Conrad portrays woman as ignorant of truth. Comment. 199

Q.15. Comment on Detachment in Heart of Darkness.
Or
There is a lack of human bonds in Heart of Darkness. Comment. 200

Q.16. Discuss the theme of dark and light in Heart of Darkness
Or
Analyse dark and light as metaphors for European and non European. 203

Q.17. Comment on the role of characters in the Heart of Darkness.
Or
Discuss the importance of characters in the Heart of Darkness. 207

Q.18. Discuss Marlow and the Wilderness in Heart of Darkness. 210

Q.19. Discuss Epiphany in Heart of Darkness. 213
Q.20. Analyse the significance of the Congo River in Heart of Darkness. 214
Q.21. Discuss God and Sin in Heart of Darkness. 216
Q.22. Discuss "White Lies" and "Whited Sepulchres" in Conrad's Heart of Darkness. 220
Q.23. Is Joseph Conrad's Heart of Darkness a Literary Critique of Imperialism? 227
Q.24. What is your impression of these opening pages from Heart of Darkness? Do the Africans seem stereotyped to you? What signs are there that the narrator is sympathetic to them? 238
Q.25. Discuss the Symbolism Motif in Heart of Darkness. 242

12. Further Study Questions **246**

13. Critical Essays **253**

14. Critics Veiws on Conrad **310**

Bibliography **365**

Preface

A novella, Heart of Darkness is Joseph Conrad's most famous work and a foundational text on the subject of colonialism. Heart of Darkness is based in part on a trip that Conrad took through modern-day Congo during his years as a sailor. He captained a ship that sailed down the Congo River. Conrad gave up this mission because an illness forced him to return to England, where he worked on his novella almost a decade later.

The presence of ill characters in the novella illustrates the fact that Heart of Darkness is, at least in part, autobiographical. Many speculations have been made about the identity of various characters, such as the Manager, or Kurtz, most recently and perhaps most accurately in Adam Hochschild's *King Leopold's Ghost*. But the geographical, as well as biographical, vagueness of the novel—which is one of its most artistic, haunting characteristics—make it almost impossible to pin down these details for sure.

Heart of Darkness first appeared in a three-part series in *Blackwood Magazine* in 1899. It was published as a complete novella in 1904. It has since been referred to by many authors and poets. Its most famous lines are both from Kurtz: "exterminate the brutes," and Kurtz's deathbed utterance, "the horror! The horror!"

Author

Chapter 1

Introduction

Heart of Darkness originally appeared serially in *Blackwood's Magazine* in 1899. It was eventually published as a whole in 1902, as the third work in a volume Conrad titled *Youth*. Since its publication in *Youth*, the novel has fascinated numerous readers and critics, almost all of whom regarded the novel as an important one because of the ways it uses ambiguity and (in Conrad's own words), "foggishness" to dramatize Marlow's perceptions of the horrors he encounters. Critics have regarded *Heart of Darkness* as a work that in several important ways broke many narrative conventions and brought the English novel into the twentieth century.

Notable exceptions who didn't receive the novel well were the British novelist E. M. Forster, who disparaged the very ambiguities that other critics found so interesting, and the African novelist Chinua Achebe, who derided the novel and Conrad as examples of European racism.

Conrad voyaged to the Congo in 1890, when he sailed a steamboat up the Congo River just as Marlow does in the novel. As Conrad writes of the novel in his 1917 Introduction, "*Heart of Darkness*... is experience pushed a little (and only very little) beyond the actual facts of the case." Numerous biographical facts find their way into the novel. For example, like Marlow, Conrad had always longed to "follow the sea," the wife of a distant relative (like Marlow's aunt) helped him secure a job with a trading company, the captain who preceded him had been killed by natives in a quarrel (like Fresleven in the novel), and Conrad encountered several men who showed barbaric tendencies similar to the ones exhibited by Kurtz.

What makes *Heart of Darkness* more than an interesting travelogue and shocking account of horrors is the way that it details—in subtle ways—Marlow's gradual understanding of what is happening in this far-off region of the world. Like many Europeans—including his creator—Marlow longed for adventure and devoured accounts such as those offered by Stanley. But once he arrives in the Congo and sees the terrible "work" (as he ironically calls it) taking place, he can no longer hide under the cover of his comfortable civilization. Instead, all the horrors perpetrated by European traders and agents—typified by Kurtz—force him to look into his own soul and find what darkness lies there. In the first half of the novel, Marlow states, "The essentials of this affair lay deep under the surface, beyond my reach"—but by the end of his journey, he will have peeked beneath "the surface" and discovered the inhumanity of which even men such as the once-upstanding Kurtz are capable.

The end of the nineteenth-century brought about one of the most notable examples of imperialism and genocide in modern memory. King Leopold II of Belgium (ruled 1865–1909) possessed an insatiable greed for money, land, and power—and looked to Africa to find them. Like many other Europeans, he was intrigued by reports of Africa made by the famed explorer Henry Morton Stanley (1841–1904), whose books *How I Found Livingstone: Adventures and Discoveries in Central Africa* (1872) and *Through the Dark Continent* (1878) were best-selling accounts of his travels. Through a series of machinations and a deluge of propaganda proclaiming his munificence, Leopold eventually secured the Congo region of Africa as a Belgian colony. On May 20, 1885, Leopold named his new nation the *État Independent du Congo,* or The Congo Free State. This huge area of Africa remained under Belgium control until 1960.

The Congo was a perfect colony for Leopold II for several reasons. First, ivory and rubber were plentiful and could be systematically gathered and shipped to Europe. Second, the only law there was Leopold's: Although he constantly presented himself to his European contemporaries as a philanthropist and humanitarian, Leopold ran the Congo (without ever visiting it) from a distance with an iron hand. Third, labour was plentiful and, more important to Leopold, *free*, because his agents routinely forced the Congolese into slave labour by means of torture or intimidation: Women, for example, were often kidnapped and held until their husbands and sons gathered sufficient quantities of rubber. Forth, there were few operating expenses: Huts and mess-halls were constructed for the agents, and the construction of a railroad system running through the Congo guaranteed that supplies could reach different stations quickly. Finally, the colony was thousands of miles away from sheltered European skies. People could not condemn what they could not see.

Leopold's agents, therefore, comprised a chaotic, unforgiving, and hateful force determined only to make the most money possible by exploiting the natives—often whipping them with a piece of sun-dried hippopotamus hide called a *chicotte,* chopping off their hands and heads, or killing them by dozens at a time. In his recent study of the Congo, *King Leopold's Ghost*, the historian Adam Hochschild estimates that during the period of Leopold's pillage of the Congo, the population dropped by ten million people. Disease, starvation, a low birth rate, and outright murder all combined to turn the Congo into what *Heart of Darkness* later portrayed as a "nightmare." Some observers of the atrocities committed there—such as E. D. Morel and Sir Roger Casement—became noted anti-Leopold activists and launched semi-successful campaigns to end Leopold's rule. Other observers transformed what they saw into art—as did Joseph Conrad when he wrote *Heart of Darkness*.

Leopold's Congo and the people—White and Black—who populated it find their way into the pages of Conrad's novel. The ominous Company that hires Marlow, for example, is a thinly veiled depiction of Leopold's operations in Africa. Leopold's agents become the "faithless pilgrims" looking for riches that Marlow describes once he reaches the Congo, and the chain gang Marlow sees at the Outer Station is a glimpse at the slavery enforced by Leopold's agents. Kurtz, the "first class agent" who commits numerous acts of savagery (including the placing of "rebel" heads upon posts surrounding his hut) is an embodiment of the collective horrors that Conrad witnessed firsthand. As Marlow tells his audience on board the *Nellie,* "In the blinding sunshine of that land I would become acquainted with a flabby, pretending, weak-eyed devil of a rapacious and pitiless folly." The "devil" in this context is the greed that motivated Leopold to continue the systematic ravaging of the Congo and its people for more than twenty years.

Chapter 2

Biography

JOSEPH CONRAD

Family Background and Early Years

Joseph Conrad was born as son of Apollo Korzeniowski and Ewa nee Bobrowska, in Berdyczów (now Berdychiv, Ukraine) on 3 December 1857. Both parents were Polish, members of the local szlachta, landowning gentry-nobility (there was no legal distinction between these two classes in Poland); both were devout Roman Catholics. Until the partition of Poland between Russia, Austria-Hungary and Prussia at the end of the 18th century, Central and Western Ukraine constituted a part of the multinational Polish-Lithuanian Commonwealth; most of the szlachta were ethnic Poles; most of town-dwellers were Jewish; most of the peasantry Ukrainians ("Ruthenians"). Conrad paternal and maternal ancestors settled there in late 17th century.

Conrad's paternal grandfather, Teodor Korzeniowski, captain of the Polish army during the 1830 Insurrection against the Russian rule, lost his estate in the political turbulences of his partitioned country. He had one daughter, Emilia, sent in 1864 to exile in Russia, and three sons: Robert, killed in the 1863 Insurrection, Hilary, who died in 1878 while in compulsory exile to Siberia after the same insurrection, and Apollo, born in 1820. Apollo had a gift for languages and writing. He studied at St Petersburg University and later supported himself by administering landed estates, writing satirical comedies (his satire, tempered by censorship, was patriotic and democratic in spirit and directed against materialism and political opportunism of Polish landowners), and translating from English (Dickens and Shakespeare), French (Victor Hugo and Alfred de Vigny) and German (Heine). He also wrote and circulated in manuscript patriotic and religious poems, in which he expressed his sympathy for oppressed Ukrainian peasantry and exhorted Poles to unswerving fidelity to the cause of their national independence.

Józef Teodor Konrad Korzeniowski (he was to use only his third given name), the only son of Apollo and Ewa, was born in Berdyczów (now Berdychiv) on 3 December 1857.

Apollo wrote his 'Baptismal Poem' for his son:

Baby son, tell yourself
You are without land, without love,
Without country, without people,
While Poland - your Mother is in her grave.

In April 1861 Apollo Korzeniowski moved to Warsaw, ostensibly to start a cultural periodical, but in fact to organise underground resistance to Russian authorities. In October 1861 he formed a clandestine "Committee of the Movement" which was the kernel of the underground National Government of 1863. A few days later he was imprisoned in the Warsaw Citadel.

Ewa Korzeniowska and her son followed Apollo to Warsaw in October 1861, and witnessed his arrest. Ewa was also charged and questioned, but not put in custody. Little Conrad would accompany his grandmother who carried supplies to his imprisoned and ailing father. He wrote later that 'In the courtyard of this [Warsaw] Citadel - characteristically for our nation - my childhood memories begin.' The investigation, by a military tribunal, of the Korzeniowski's lasted till April 1862, but the verdict, issued in fact by the viceroy of Poland, a Russian general, preceded by two weeks the official decision of the court. Although only circumstantial evidence was produced against both Ewa and Apollo, they were sentenced to exile to Northern Russia, "under strict police supervision". The viceroy added in his own hand: "Mind that they do not stop on the way." They were dispatched to Vologda, known for its harsh climate.

In January 1863, for reasons of health, they were allowed to move to Chernihiv, in north-eastern Ukraine. There Ewa Korzeniowska died of tuberculosis in April 1865. Apollo was also gravely ill, and was released from exile in January 1868. He left with his son to Lwów (Lviv), then in Austro-Hungarian Empire, an important Polish cultural centre, and later moved to Cracow, ancient capital of Poland, where he died in May 1869.

Konrad's maternal uncle, Tadeusz Bobrowski, became his guardian and benefactor. Konrad was first educated by his father; a sickly boy, he never regularly attended schools, but couched by tutors passed his formal exams first in Cracow, later in Lviv. In autumn of 1874 he was sent - at least partly for health reasons - to Southern France, with the view of starting a maritime career.

Konrad Korzeniowski becomes Joseph Conrad

Initially Korzeniowski does not seem to have had an intention to leave Poland permanently, and yet in 1883 he assured one of his father's friends of remembering the injunction that "wherever he may sail he is sailing towards Poland". But as a Russian subject and son of convicts he was liable for long military service, and his attempts to be realised from Russian State allegation succeeded only in 1889. By that time he was switched from the French to the British merchant fleet marine (in 1878) and passed his examinations for master mariner (1886); the same year he became a British subject. He never officially changed his original name, and assumed the pen-name of Joseph Conrad only when publishing in 1895 his first novel, Almayer's Folly, dedicated to the memory of T[adeusz] B[obrowski].

He kept up correspondence with his uncle; his letters to him were destroyed during the Bolshevik Revolution, but Bobrowski's letters to Conrad survived and constitute the most important biographical source for Conrad's earlier years. He visited his home country in 1889 and 1893. The following year his uncle died and Korzeniowski's main personal link with Poland ceased to exist.

For the first twenty years of his writing career Conrad struggled with debts: his royalties fell far below his modest expenses. Only in summer 1914 he was able to take a longer vacation, and took his wife and two sons to Poland. The outbreak of the First World War caught them in Cracow; they spent two months in this city and then in the Tatra Mountains to the south of it. While in Cracow and Zakopane, Conrad met several Polish writers, artists and intellectuals. This was to be the last visit to his native country.

The reminiscences of his relatives and friends testify to Conrad's continued emotional involvement in the affairs of Poland and traditions of her culture (e.g., at his country home in Kent he organised private concerts of Chopin's music).

At his funeral (he died in Canterbury on 3 August 1924) the only official present was a representative of Prime Minister of Poland.

Conrad's Polish Cultural Roots

From letters of Apollo Korzeniowski to his friends and other sources we know that young Conrad was an avid reader. He was certainly well acquainted with classical Polish literature, beginning from the work of the great XVIth century poet Jan Kochanowski (whom he mentions in his letters). Most probably the poetry, drama and fiction of Polish romantic writers (of which his father was an epigone) formed the main body of his readings in his native language. 'Polonism I have taken into my works from Mickiewicz and S³owacki', he declared in 1914, mentioning by name the two greatest writers, and also moral and political authorities, of Polish romanticism.

Ideas of moral and national responsibility pervaded this literature. Fidelity and betrayal, honour and shame, duty and escape were frequent subject. The moral problems of an individual were typically posed in terms of communal obligations; and ethical principles, formed under a decisive influence of chivalric ethos, were grounded in the idea that an individual, however exceptional he may be, is always a member of a community. A poet was a typical example of an exceptional individual, burdened with special duties towards his nation. The passage 'from alienation to commitment', recognised as a frequent theme in Conrad's fiction, has been a staple subject in Polish romantic literature.One of the more popular literary forms was the tale (gawêda), a story told by a personal narrator, who often himself is one of the protagonists; it is easy to find a continuation of this form in Conrad's narratives.

Apart from the general presence of important elements of Polish cultural tradition, critics have identified in Conrad's writings many thematic, artistic, and verbal motifs taken from particular works of Polish literature. Polish language itself has also left an imprint on Conrad's prose. Not only in the form of Polonisms (words and idioms used in their Polish rather than English sense), and errors committed here and there in the use of tenses. Occasional looseness of Conrad's syntax and the rhetorical, rolling rhythm of his phrases can be easily traced back to the influence of his native speech.

Polish Themes in His Work

In his essay 'Autocracy and War' (1905), Conrad's most important political statement, Poland is mentioned as a victim of German and Russian imperialism, which links them in their "common guilt".

A Personal Record (1912) contains long and moving fragments telling about his early Polish experiences and about members of his closest family. 'Prince Roman' (1910), included in the posthumous volume Tales of Hearsay) is a tale about Prince Roman S[anguszko] who 'from conviction' joined the forces of Polish uprising against Russian power in November 1830 and, captured, was sentenced to a punishment of hard labour in Siberian mines. We read there about Poland as 'That country which demands to be loved an no other country has even been loved, with the mournful affection one bears for the unforgotten dead and with the inextinguishable fire of a hopeless passion which only a living, breathing, warm ideal can kindle in our breast for our pride, for our weariness, for our exultation, for our undoing.'

In 1914, under the impression of fresh contacts with his compatriots, Conrad wrote a Memorandum outlining his plans of action in the UK in support of Polish interests. His essay 'Poland Revisited' (included later in his Notes on Life and Letters, 1921) describes Conrad's journey to Poland and reflects his depression in face of the British attitude of considering the future of Poland as Russia's internal affair. Two years later in a special 'Note on the Polish Question' (published also in Notes...), addressed to the British Foreign Office, he proposed a reconstruction of Poland under the protectorate of Great Britain and France ('Quite impossible. Russia will never share her interests in Poland with Western Powers' was the negative reply).

Conrad greeted the reconstruction of independent Poland (after 123 years of partitioning) in 1918 with joy, relief, and embarrassment caused by his own lack of faith. He wrote an emotional appeal in support of the new country and in remembrance of its sufferings, 'The Crime of Partition' (1919, included in Notes...). In 1920, while the Polish army was fighting for the survival of the country with a Soviet invasion, he sent a cablegram in support for the Polish Government Loan: 'For Poles the sense of duty and the imperishable feeling of nationality preserved in the hearts and defended by the hands of their immediate ancestors in open struggles against the might of three Powers and in indomitable defiance of crushing oppression for more than a hundred years is sufficient inducement to come forward to assist in reconstructing the independence, dignity and usefulness of the reborn Republic.'

Conrad's Reception in Poland

Some Polish intellectuals accused Conrad of infidelity towards his native country shown by writing in English. The most important expression of such charge was an article, published in 1899 by a well-known and respected Polish woman-novelist, Eliza Orzeszkowa. Conrad took this greatly to heart, and a couple of years later, writing in 1901 to a Cracow librarian Józef Korzeniowski (not a relative of his), he declared: "I have in no way disavowed either my nationality or the name we share It is widely known that I am a Pole and that Józef Konrad are my two Christian names, the latter being used be my as surname so that foreign mouths should not distort my real surname It does not seem to me that I have been unfaithful to my country by having prived to the English that a gentleman from the Ukraine can be as good as sailor as they, and has something to tell them in their own language. I consider such recognition as I have won from this particular point of view, and offer in silent homage where it is due.'

He was by that time becoming known in Poland: the first ever translation of this work (An Outcast of the Islands) was published in a Warsaw periodical in 1897, and other translations followed.

In 1914 he gave his first ever interview, to a Polish journalist Marian D¹browski (husband of Maria D¹browska later one of the most distinguished Polish 20th century novelists and author of a volume of essays on Conrad). He confessed there that his father read to him Mickiewicz's long poem Pan Tadeusz, 'not just once or twice', and made him also read it aloud. He 'used to prefer Konrad Wallenrod and Gra¿yna', Mickiewicz's shorter poetic tales. 'Later I liked S³owacki better. You know why S³owacki? Il est l'ame de toute la Pologne, lui.' [He is the soul of all Poland, he is.]

Conrad's contacts with Polish writers and readers became closer after 1920. He corresponded with several authors and his translators, and in 1921 himself translated from Polish a comedy by Bruno Winawer (The book of Hiob, published posthumously). The most eminent Polish writer of the time,

Stefan ˉeromski, moral authority of Polish liberals and socialists, wrote an enthusiastic introduction to a collected edition of Conrad's works, calling him a 'writer-compatriot'. Conrad responded with a latter, writing: 'I confess that I cannot find words to describe my profound emotion when I read this appreciation from my country, voiced by you, dear Sir - the greatest master of its literature.'

In the 'twenties and 'thirties Conrad became in Poland a very influential writer, much read and discussed both by intellectuals and the broad reading public, with which especially his sea fiction was popular. He reached the peak of his importance in the darkest hours of modern Polish history, during the II World War, in the country invaded again by its German and Soviet neighbours. Conrad, and particularly the Conrad of Lord Jim, became then one of the chief moral authorities for the young members of the Polish underground army and civil resistance.

The first ever full edition of Conrad's works (27 volumes) was published in Poland in 1972-74, with one supplementary volume, containing material confiscated by Communist censors, published by Polish émigrés in London.

Conrad memorabilia in Poland and Ukraine

The hospital in which Conrad was born in Berdychiv does not exist. Opening of a small Joseph Conrad museum in the premises of a magnificent Carmelite Monastery there (a priest from this monastery baptised Conrad) is planned for September 1999. A commemorative plaque in the centre of Warsaw (Nowy Œwiat Street) was placed on the house next to the one in which the Korzeniowski rented their flat in 1862. The cell in Warsaw Citadel in which Conrad's father was imprisoned still exists. So does the house in which he lived with his father in Cracow at the Poselska Street, and the buildings where he stayed as a boarder in Lvov and Cracow (Floriańska Street).

Two volumes of manuscripts of Conrad's father, most of them unpublished, are preserved in the Jagiellonian Library in Cracow. Several important letters and documents concerning Conrad himself are to be found in the PAN Library also in Cracow. The National Library in Warsaw has Tadeusz Bobrowski's letters to Conrad, and several Conrad's letters in Polish. Outside Poland the most important collection of Conrad's MSS connected with his Polish background are kept at the Beinecke Library, Yale University and in the Polish Library in London.

A member of an eminent group of fin de siècle writers that includes Stephen Crane, Robert Louis Stevenson, H. G. Wells, and Henry James, the British short story writer and novelist Joseph Conrad was born in Russian-occupied Polish Ukraine in 1857, the son of Polish aristocrat and militant nationalist Count Apollo Korzeniowski. His father, who translated Victor Hugo's Les Travailleurs de la mer and Dickens into his native tongue, was exiled by the Russians to Vologda in 1862. When the boy was seven his mother died of tuberculosis; his father lived in exile until 1869, when Czarist authorities permitted him to move south; however, after that remove, when young Conrad was just eleven, his father died. He was then adopted by his mother's uncle, the indulgent Tadeusz Bobrowski. At the age of seventeen he began a long period of adventure at sea. As a member of the French merchant marine sailing out of Marseilles, young Conrad was implicated in a Carlist conspiracy to place the Duke of Madrid on the Spanish throne. After a suicide attempt, Conrad joined the British merchant service in 1878.

Not yet twenty-one, he learned English by reading the London Times, Carlyle's Sartor Resartus, and Shakespeare's plays. In 1884, Conrad became a naturalized British subject and gained his master's certificate. In the ten years that followed, he sailed between Singapore and Borneo, voyages that gave him an unrivaled background of mysterious creeks and jungle for the tales that he would write after 1896, when he retired from the sea to settle in Ashford, Kent, with his new wife, Jessie Chambers.

Primarily seen in his own time as a writer of boys' sea stories, Conrad is now highly regarded as a novelist whose work displays a deep moral consciousness and masterful narrative technique. Influenced by Henry James, Conrad's finest works are Nostromo (1904), Heart of Darkness (1899), and Lord Jim (1900). His early novels, including Almayer's Folly (1895), An Outcast of the Islands (1896), and The Nigger of the 'Narcissus' (1897), are full of romantic description in an atmosphere of mystery and brooding. In Tales of Unrest (1898), "Youth" and Other Tales (1902), and Twixt Land and Sea (1912) appeared such outstanding short stories as "Typhoon" and "The Shadow-Line" that describe the testing of human character under conditions of extreme danger and difficulty. Throughout his fiction Conrad is concerned with moral dilemmas, the isolation of the individual to be tested by experience, and the psychology of inner urges in both groups and individuals. His semi-autobiographical The Mirror of The Sea (1906) and Some Reminiscences (1912) (published in the States as A Personal Record) testify to his high artistic aims.

Conrad did not find shore-life easy. His expedition to the Belgian Congo had left him with malarial gout, which afflicted his wrist so much that he often found writing painful. He was never a quick or fluent writer; he thought it a good day when he could produce as little as 350 words with which he was satisfied. After the publication of his first book, which had taken Conrad some five years to write (and which had survived the African jungle, shipwreck, and a Berlin railway cloakroom), Edward Garnett (writer, critic, and publisher's reader) asked, "Why not another?" Gradually Conrad settled down to write for a living. Although perceptive judges such as John Galsworthy and H. G. Wells praised him, the English reading public was slow to recognize the merit of his work.

Conrad uses fiction to analyse the macrocosm (world at large) by presenting objectively and scientifically a microcosm such as a ship's crew. As a young merchant sailor Conrad had been cut off from family, friends, and country; this essential loneliness he conveys in his tales set on the sea and in exotic locales. His sense of isolation stems from the fundamental differences that existed between himself and his fellow seamen—in age, culture, language, education, and experience. However, his remoteness from the British reading public, and his consequent his lack of knowledge about what makes a popular novel, makes his stories all the more real. Conrad often maneuvers to keep the reader at a distance from the characters in order to view them objectively. For example, in writing "The Inn of the Two Witches" in the winter of 1912 for the London Pall Mall (1913) and New York Metropolitan (May, 1913) magazines he resorted to another "Chinese box" narrative technique: an early twentieth-century book-collector recalls some years before having found a manuscript which contained a story (presumably written in the first person).

Here as elsewhere, the world is seen by Conrad as a place of unending contention between the forces of darkness and dissolution on the one hand and those of brotherhood, duty, and bravery on the other; this belief is sometimes referred to as Manichæism, an early Christian heresy. Conrad divides all mankind into two types—the visionaries (who are truly 'young' no matter what their chronological age) and the cynical realists. Conrad implies that a man is already dead if he has lost his ideals and visions. The sea is always present in Conrad's stories; for him, it symbolized the physical, emotional, and mental environment of the individual (as represented by the ship–see, for example, the stories "The Secret Sharer," "Typhoon," and "Youth"). Conrad shows how superficial are rational control and civilisation. Youth, full of romantic visions and idealism, encountering the sheer corruption of the Darwinian jungle, may be overwhelmed by the experience, as Tuan Jim is at the start of Lord Jim on board the Patna.

Chapter 3

Conrad: A Brief Chronology

1857: 3 Dec., Jozef Teodor Konrad Korzeniowski born of Polish aristocratic parents in the Russian occupied Ukraine

1861: Conrad's father, poet and translator Count Apollo Korzeniowski, arrested for patriotic conspiracy

1862: Conrad's parents exiled by Russian authorities to Vologda, Siberia

1865: Conrad's mother dies in bleak climate.

1869: Upon the death of Count Apollo Korzeniowski in Krakow, Poland, Conrad is taken under the protection his maternal uncle, the indulgent Tadeusz Bobrowski.

1874: Conrad leaves his native Poland to avoid Russian conscription; in Marseilles he becomes a trainee seaman with the French Merchant Marine.

1876: As a steward on the Sainte-Antoine, Conrad meets Dominic Cervoni, upon whom he based the protagonist of Nostromo.

1877: Conrad involved in Carlist plot, smuggling arms to the Spanish rebels from Marseilles

1878 March: Conrad attempts suicide, shooting himself in the chest, but recovers. As a result, his uncle clears Conrad's gambling debts. April: Conrad, having lost his French mariner's ticket, joins his first British-registered ship, the ' Mavis', and transfers afterwards to 'The Skimmer of the Sea'.

He would have become liable for Russian military service had he remained in the French merchant service.

1886: Conrad becomes a naturalized British subject, and passes his exam for a British merchant navy Master's certificate, but commands are in short supply.

1887: Conrad involved in accident on 'The Highland Forest' and is hospitalized in Singapore

1887-8: As the first officer on 'The Vidar' Conrad visits numerous ports in the Malay archipelago.

1888: Conrad has his only command as master of the 'Otago'.

1889: Conrad resigns from post on the 'Otago' to return to London, where he begins writing Almayer's Folly.

1890: Conrad, desperate for command, takes a mate's position on a river steamer for the Societe Anonyme pour le Commerce du Haut-Congo, the experience so vividly reflected in Conrad's Congo Journal and eventually in Heart of Darkness.

1891-3: While officer of the clipper 'Torrens' Conrad meets John Galsworthy. In England, Conrad meets Jessie George.

1894 Feb.: death of Tadeusz Bobrowski. Oct.: Unwin agrees to publish Almayer's Folly; in consequence, Conrad meets Unwin's reader, Edward Garnett

1895: Almayer's Folly published by Unwin & Co., London

1896: Outcast of the Islands published. Conrad meets H. G. Wells. 24 March: Conrad marries Jessie George, and begins writing The Rescue.

1897: Conrad publishes The Nigger of the 'Narcissus'. He becomes acquainted with American novelist Henry James and R. B. Cunninghame Graham, upon whom Conrad will base the character of Gould in Nostromo.

1898: Volume of short stories Tales of Unrest, collection of previously published short stories. Conrad collaborates with Ford Madox Ford (Hueffer) and meets American journalist

Stephen Crane. Conrad leases a Kentish farmhouse; his son Borys Conrad is born.

1898-9: Heart of Darkness runs serially in Blackwood's Edinburgh Magazine, which Conrad calls simply " Maga."

1899: J. B. Pinker becomes Conrad's literary agent.

1899-1900: Lord Jim runs serially in Maga.

1900: Stephen Crane, a Conrad intimate, dies; Lord Jim appears in volume form.

1901: Conrad collaborates with Ford to publish The Inheritors.

1902: 'Youth' and Other Stories

1903: 'Typhoon' and Other Stories and, in collaboration with Ford, Romance published

1904: Jessie Conrad, injuring her knees, is disabled for life. Nostromo published

1906: Conrad meets Arthur Marwood. Second son, John, is born. Conrad publishes biography Mirror of the Sea.

1907: The Conrads move to The Someries, Luton Hoo. Conrad publishes The Secret Agent.

1908: The short story collection A Set of Six published

1909: Ford and Conrad argue over C's contributions to The English Review. The Conrads move to a cottage at Aldington.

1910: Conrad completes Under Western Eyes, but suffers a nervous breakdown, lying in bed talking to the characters in the novel. Once recovered, he and Jessie move to Capel House, Orlestone.

1911: Under Western Eyes published

1912: The biographical A Personal Record and short story collection 'Twixt Land and Sea published.

1913: Conrad's first great critical and popular success, Chance, published

1914: Conrad's Chance leads to recognition for his other work and has excellent sales in America. Visiting Poland, the Conrads are nearly trapped there when World War One breaks out in August.

1915: Conrad publishes short story collection Within the Tides, containing the potboiler "The Inn of the Two Witches," published; Victory published

1917: The Shadow Line published. Conrad begins writing notes for a collected edition of his works.

1919: The Arrow of Gold published. The Conrads move to Oswalds, near Canterbury.

1920: The Rescue is completed and published 24 years after Conrad started it.

1921: Conrad visits Corsica to research Suspense. His Notes on Life and Letters published

1923: Visiting America, Conrad is lionized. The Rover is published.

1924: In May, Conrad declines an offered knighthood. On the 3rd of August, Conrad dies of a heart attack. Posthumously, his collaboration with Ford, The Nature of Crime, is published.

Chapter 4

Historical Context

Heart of Darkness originally appeared serially in *Blackwood's Magazine* in 1899. It was eventually published as a whole in 1902, as the third work in a volume Conrad titled *Youth*. Since its publication in *Youth*, the novel has fascinated numerous readers and critics, almost all of whom regarded the novel as an important one because of the ways it uses ambiguity and (in Conrad's own words), "foggishness" to dramatize Marlow's perceptions of the horrors he encounters. Critics have regarded *Heart of Darkness* as a work that in several important ways broke many narrative conventions and brought the English novel into the twentieth century.

Notable exceptions who didn't receive the novel well were the British novelist E. M. Forster, who disparaged the very ambiguities that other critics found so interesting, and the African novelist Chinua Achebe, who derided the novel and Conrad as examples of European racism.

Conrad voyaged to the Congo in 1890, when he sailed a steamboat up the Congo River just as Marlow does in the novel. As Conrad writes of the novel in his 1917 Introduction, "*Heart of Darkness*... is experience pushed a little (and only very little) beyond the actual facts of the case." Numerous biographical facts find their way into the novel. For example, like Marlow, Conrad had always longed to "follow the sea," the wife of a distant relative (like Marlow's aunt) helped him secure a job with a trading company, the captain who preceded him had been killed by natives in a quarrel (like Fresleven in the novel), and Conrad encountered several men who showed barbaric tendencies similar to the ones exhibited by Kurtz.

What makes *Heart of Darkness* more than an interesting travelogue and shocking account of horrors is the way that it details—in subtle ways—Marlow's gradual understanding of what is happening in this far-off region of the world. Like many Europeans—including his creator—Marlow longed for adventure and devoured accounts such as those offered by Stanley. But once he arrives in the Congo and sees the terrible "work" (as he ironically calls it) taking place, he can no longer hide under the cover of his comfortable civilization. Instead, all the horrors perpetrated by European traders and agents—typified by Kurtz—force him to look into his own soul and find what darkness lies there. In the first half of the novel, Marlow states, "The essentials of this affair lay deep under the surface, beyond my reach"—but by the end of his journey, he will have peeked beneath "the surface" and discovered the inhumanity of which even men such as the once-upstanding Kurtz are capable.

The end of the nineteenth-century brought about one of the most notable examples of imperialism and genocide in modern memory. King Leopold II of Belgium (ruled 1865–1909) possessed an insatiable greed for money, land, and power—and looked to Africa to find them. Like many other Europeans, he was intrigued by reports of Africa made by the famed explorer Henry Morton Stanley (1841–1904), whose books *How I Found Livingstone: Adventures and Discoveries in Central Africa* (1872) and *Through the Dark Continent* (1878) were best-selling accounts of his travels. Through a series of machinations and a deluge of propaganda proclaiming his munificence, Leopold eventually secured the Congo region of Africa as a Belgian colony. On May 20, 1885, Leopold named his new nation the *État Independent du Congo,* or The Congo Free State. This huge area of Africa remained under Belgium control until 1960.

The Congo was a perfect colony for Leopold II for several reasons. First, ivory and rubber were plentiful and could be systematically gathered and shipped to Europe. Second, the only law there was Leopold's: Although he constantly presented himself to his European contemporaries as a philanthropist and humanitarian, Leopold ran the Congo (without ever visiting it) from a distance with an iron hand. Third, labour was plentiful and, more important to Leopold, *free*, because his agents routinely forced the Congolese into slave labour by means of torture or intimidation: Women, for example, were often kidnapped and held until their husbands and sons gathered sufficient quantities of rubber. Forth, there were few operating expenses: Huts and mess-halls were constructed for the agents, and the construction of a railroad system running through the Congo guaranteed that supplies could reach different stations quickly. Finally, the colony was thousands of miles away from sheltered European skies. People could not condemn what they could not see.

Leopold's agents, therefore, comprised a chaotic, unforgiving, and hateful force determined only to make the most money possible by exploiting the natives—often whipping them with a piece of sun-dried hippopotamus hide called a *chicotte*, chopping off their hands and heads, or killing them by dozens at a time. In his recent study of the Congo, *King Leopold's Ghost*, the historian Adam Hochschild estimates that during the period of Leopold's pillage of the Congo, the population dropped by ten million people. Disease, starvation, a low birth rate, and outright murder all combined to turn the Congo into what *Heart of Darkness* later portrayed as a "nightmare." Some observers of the atrocities committed there—such as E. D. Morel and Sir Roger Casement—became noted anti-Leopold activists and launched semi-successful campaigns to end Leopold's rule. Other observers transformed what they saw into art—as did Joseph Conrad when he wrote *Heart of Darkness*.

Leopold's Congo and the people—White and Black—who populated it find their way into the pages of Conrad's novel. The ominous Company that hires Marlow, for example, is a thinly veiled depiction of Leopold's operations in Africa. Leopold's agents become the "faithless pilgrims" looking for riches that Marlow describes once he reaches the Congo, and the chain gang Marlow sees at the Outer Station is a glimpse at the slavery enforced by Leopold's agents. Kurtz, the "first class agent" who commits numerous acts of savagery (including the placing of "rebel" heads upon posts surrounding his hut) is an embodiment of the collective horrors that Conrad witnessed firsthand. As Marlow tells his audience on board the *Nellie,* "In the blinding sunshine of that land I would become acquainted with a flabby, pretending, weak-eyed devil of a rapacious and pitiless folly." The "devil" in this context is the greed that motivated Leopold to continue the systematic ravaging of the Congo and its people for more than twenty years.

Due to the controversy generated by postcolonial discourse, and the resultant wealth of material on *Heart of Darkness* it is necessary to narrow down the topic as much as possible, nevertheless that same controversy demands an overview in other to represent the plurality of critical voices, within which mould I shall situate my point and finally examine the question of the author's racism or lack of it.

The critical postcolonial approach to *Heart of Darkness* as a racist text was first pointed out by the Nigerian Writer, Chinua Achebe in a lecture at the university of Massachusetts in 1975. According to Achebe, "*...Heart of Darkness* projects the image of Africa as 'the other world', the antithesis of Europe and therefore of civilisation ". He began with a passing comment on the average westerner's stereotyping of African culture and the informed ignorance of the supposedly enlightened, making an example of the British professor of History, Hugh Trevor-roper, who insisted that Africa had no history and took a swipe at the careful binary pairings in *Heart of Darkness*. The setting of the primordial Congo basin against a tranquil Thames river - the former supposedly bad and the latter good, the evoked African atmosphere of myth and mystery - and thus of the ritualistic and evil, against an enlightened Christian Europe, the 'antithetical' choice of diction and sentences, "steady, ponderous, fake-ritualistic, one about silence and the other about frenzy "; he quoted from pages 103 and 105 of the American Library edition of *Heart of Darkness* to prove his point thus: "It was the stillness of an implacable force brooding over an inscrutable intention" [and] "The steamer toiled along slowly on the edge of a black and incomprehensible frenzy".

Achebe maintained that the "most interesting and revealing passages in *Heart of Darkness* are about people", that is, about characterisation. Although the passage he quoted about Marlow's account of the journey down the Congo river is not explicit on characterisation - which is exactly the point!, I would like to reproduce it in full to examine his implications:

We were wanderers on a prehistoric earth, on an earth that wore the aspect of an unknown planet. We could have fancied ourselves the first of men taking possession of an accursed inheritance, to be subdued at the cost of profound anguish and of excessive toil. But suddenly, as we struggled round a bend, there would be a glimpse of rush walls, of peaked grass-roofs, a burst of yells, a whirl of black limbs a mass of hands clapping, of feet stamping, of bodies swaying, of eyes rolling, under the droop of heavy and motionless foliage. The steamer toiled along slowly on the edge of the black and incomprehensible frenzy. The prehistoric man was cursing us, praying to us welcoming us - who could tell? We were cut off from the comprehension of our surroundings; we glided past like phantoms, wondering secretly appalled, as sane men would be before an enthusiastic outbreak in a madhouse. We could not understand because we were too far and could not remember because we were travelling in the night of first ages, of those ages that are gone, leaving hardly a sign - and no memories.

The earth seemed unearthly. We are accustomed to look upon the shackled form of a conquered monster, but there - there you could look at a thing monstrous and free. It was unearthly, and the men were - No, they were not inhuman. Well, you know, that would come slowly to one. They howled and leaped, and spun, and made horrid faces, but what trilled you was the thought of their humanity - like yours - the thought of your remote kinship with this wild and passionate uproar. Ugly. Yes, it was ugly enough; but if you were man enough you would admit to yourself that there was in you just the faintest trace of a response to the terrible frankness of that noise, a dim suspicion of there being a meaning in it which you - you so remote from the night of first ages - could comprehend.

It is easy to see characterisation in none characterisation in this passage; that is the implicit nature of the kind of characterisation that is carried out here. The African characters are present as a kind of absence. They do not think, speak, do not behave like normal human beings but nevertheless have the physical features of the species - and that is "the fascination it (*Heart of Darkness*) holds over the European mind" that is what troubles Conrad according to Achebe, that is the thrill - this 'ugly' kinship to the human being (there are also passages where Conrad compares them to apes - a popular past-time of imperial Victorian Europe), which is the "horror, the horror" for his early European readers, for whom he confirmed and consolidated the wildest fantasies and myths about Africans. He could be certain of non-contradiction therefore from those readers. And this was why, according to Achebe, the racist nature of the novel was never questioned until he drew attention to it. Further more, if the above passage were to be deconstructed, if we were to 'wayward' the text, it breaks down into subtle binary oppositions and could read something like this: 'we were [modern] wanderers on a prehistoric earth, on an earth that wore the aspect of an unknown planet [as opposed to our civilised world] As we round a bend there would be a glimpse of rush walls, of peaked grass-roofs [as opposed to our sophisticated Victorian architecture]' et cetera. There are also those echoes of meaning which negates the humanity of the Africans in the passage. The Africans were the 'first men' - something baser than human, primordial; a sort of extinct human dinosaur, without a cultural space of their own, re-discovered, categorised and put in their place for their own good; a gelatinous mass of monstrous and senseless limbs, contorted bodies and rolling eyes living partly on trees (in the foliage) and partly in crude lean-tos, which it was fair game to take port-shots at by the colonising imperial power in order to instil a random discipline of hot lead when necessary.

And dragging out the intestines of an earlier stylistic critic of *Heart of Darkness* by F. R. Leavis to the effect that Conrad was woolly and depended on an "adjectival insistence upon inexpressible and incomprehensible mystery", he declared: "When a writer while pretending to record scenes, incidents and their impact is in reality engaged in inducing stupor in his readers through a bombardment of emotive words and other forms of trickery, much more has to be at stake than stylistic felicity". According to him this deliberate stylistic obfuscation merely aided to satisfy the racial sentiments of the day, and Conrad was only acting as the "purveyor of comforting myths". And in pursuing this myths, the African became faceless, insignificant.

Whenever they were given any kind of presence it was only as foils for another European character; i.e. the African woman, who was the savage, inarticulate Other for the Intended. Or if for example they were allowed speech at all it was "a violent babble of uncouth sounds". Conrad could have achieved more verisimilitude for example if he admitted an existence of a form of indigenous linguistic competence among the Africans. Among themselves they also had no means of communication outside of crude grunts. On the matter of speech it is significant that a smattering of English syllables were put into the mouths of one or two savage Congolese. It is in conforming to the hegemonic attitude of the coloniser that he replaced indigenous culture with his own, which he deemed superior. And it is this assumption of a superior humanity which made Achebe finally deem Conrad "a thorough-going racist".

There are those arguments which considers that Conrad is merely ridiculing the 'civilising' mission in Africa, and was concerned with the deterioration of European values in contact with that continent, which is merely a setting for his story, that he is far more less charitable to his European characters (like Kurtz) than to the Africans, towards whom he was sympathetic or that Marlow's opinion, as a fictional character, should not be confused with Conrad's, who was anti-imperialist. Nevertheless it is note-worthy that he took great pains to distance himself from and "set up layers of insulation between himself and the moral universe of his story" [through the framework] of a "narrator behind the narrator". If Africa is merely a setting then Conrad neutralises Africa as a cultural human factor.

That continent becomes a "metaphysical battlefield devoid of all recognisable humanity". For Achebe "the real question is the dehumanisation of Africans which this age-long attitude has fostered and continues to foster in the world". The apparent sympathy in the following passage simply represents that 'bleeding-heart sentiment' reminiscent of "the kind of liberalism espoused by [the] Marlow/Conrad [masquerade] [and which] touched all the best minds of the age in England, Europe and America"

They were all dying slowly - it was very clear. They were not enemies, they were not criminals, they were nothing earthly now - nothing but black shadows of diseases and starvation, lying confusedly in greenish gloom. Brought from all the recesses of the legality of time contracts, lost in uncongenial surroundings fed on unfamiliar food they sickened, became inefficient, and were then allowed to crawl away and rest.

In his critic of Heart of Darkness Patrick Brantlinger compares Achebe's views with those of several critics, who did not agree that Conrad was racist because he was critical of imperialism. An example was Cedric Watts, who insisted that Conrad instead of being a purveyor of racial myths rather "most deliberately and incisively debunks such myths ". Brantlinger then went on to quote from Watts:

Achebe notes with indignation that Conrad (in the "Author's note to *Victory*) speaks of an encounter with a "buck nigger" in Haiti which gave him the impression of mindless violence. Achebe might as well have noted the reference in The Nigger of the "Narcissus"... to a tormented and flattened face - a face pathetic and brutal: the tragic, the mysterious the repulsive mask of a nigger's soul..

The image of the black man drawn here, especially if it refers to personal comments from Conrad is suggestive enough of his racist bias, whether it was conscious or not is another matter. Juxtaposed against Conrad's words in *Personal Records,* describing his first encounter with an English man at the age of sixteen his personal psychology in such matters is made very clear:

His calves exposed to the public gaze...dazzled the beholder by the splendour of their marble-like condition and their rich tone of young ivory... The light of a headlong, exalted satisfaction with the world of men...illumined his face...and triumphant eyes. In passing he cast a glance of kindly curiosity and a friendly gleam of big, sound, shiny teeth...His white calves twinkled sturdily.

Should it then be surprising that in all his novels dealing with black people he never had any redeeming word for these characters. It is instructive that Conrad's letters also carry casual anti-Semitic tones. Perhaps a short biography of Conrad himself might be necessary here but we shall come to that soon enough. According to Bratlinger Conrad was not so much against imperialism out of any sheer moral convictions against it as out of a quarrel with the "lying propaganda used to cover its bloody tracks".

Conrad was more against the high-handed Belgian form of colonialism as practised by King Leopold and *Heart of Darkness* is a about what he saw in Leopold's Congo of 1890, not a general outcry against imperialism in other parts of the World. It is noteworthy that Marlow approves of British imperialism while condemning that variation practised by Belgium and other European conquerors. According to Bratlinger after such a critical passage as "The conquest of the earth [....] the taking of it away from those with slightly flatter noses than ourselves is not a pretty thing." Marlow retirates " one knows that some real work is done in there" i.e. in the British colonies. Or referring also to the differences in British 'efficiency' and Belgian 'sloppiness' Marlow declares: "They were conquerors, and for that what you want is only brute force- nothing to boast of They grabbed what they could get for the sake of what was to be got Just robbery with violence, aggravated murder, and men going at it blind " (.

As for what Conrad saw during his short six months in Congo, it was so little that he had to depend on the "revelations of atrocities that began to appear in the British press as early as 1888". Thus his lurid painting of cannibalism in the *Heart of Darkness* drew heavily on reports of the war between Arab slave traders and Belgians for the control of the Congo, where both sides played on Muslim superstitious fear (of their Congolese troupes) of not attaining paradise if they died mutilated. Thus cannibalism, or the chopping off hands became on both sides a weapon to extract co-operation from them. The characters of Kurtz and Marlow were based on several accounts of men who reported what they went through or from newspaper clippings. For example Bratlinger,quoting Ian Watt, remarked that The Times reported of a certain Hodister and his companions that "their heads were stuck on poles and their bodies eaten". Thus Conrad never personally encountered cannibalism. He was merely playing up to a gallery of pre-conceived ideas about Africans. And although he does show up Kurtz as being evil, it is an evil that was contacted because kurtz "went native" which, for Bratlinger, is as much as saying that "evil is African in Conrad's story". Finally he affirms:

Conrad's stress on cannibalism, his identification of African customs with violence, lust, and madness, his metaphors of bestiality death, and darkness, his suggestion that travelling in Africa is like travelling backward in time to primeval, infantile but also hellish stages of existence - these features of the story are drawn from the repertoire of Victorian imperialism and racism that painted an entire continent dark.

He finally agreed with Achebe that Conrad was a racist.

Hunt Hawkins in *The issue of Racism in Heart of Darkness* refers to the Indian critic Frances B. Singh, who maintained that the story "carries suggestions that the evil which the title refers to is to be associated with Africans, their customs, and their rites [and] "as long as he associates the life of depravity with the life of blacks then he can hardly be called anti-colonial.". Hawkins defends Conrad even while admitting that the accusation of racism should not be dismissed out of hand. He agreed that the limitations of Heart of Darkness as a picture of African colonisation can be readily measured against Achebe's Things fall Apart, which is about the British take-over of an Ibo village at the end of the 19th century. Naturally, in that African novel one would expect a much more balanced character development. We should note that Hawkins agreed Conrad had very little experience of Africa as a continent. He spent less than six months in the Congo acco rding to Hawkins and only in the company of white men.

If Conrad had such little contact to Africa, where did he get the wealth of information on the practices, habits and behaviour of Africans, which forms the setting of the story? Definitely from the hegemonic myths used by Empire to legitimise its political ideology of subjugation and rule. This worked itself out lexically in the text as a binary pairing and in the reducing of other cultures to myths and anthropology. Although, he maintained, Conrad's attitude was complex it was nevertheless critical of racism and sympathetic to non-European peoples.

The word sympathetic itself is condescending. There is the insinuation that 'non-European peoples' should be grateful that they were allowed to breath at all. His arguments is that *Heart of Darkness* makes negative statements about Africans; for example he refers to them as "niggers", "savages" "pre-historic man", "rudimentary souls" but also "praises" them for their "energy, vitality, natural dignity". But in what context? They are praised for their energy, vitality and natural dignity when they appear as a tool towards Malow's ends in, for example, steering the steamboat or defending it against attack. And the only African (a woman) who is a little "visible" is only the noble savage - an inferior Other for the civilised Intended.

In his objective article Robert Burden gives a detailed reception history of Heart of Darkness. The novella is supposed to have derived from the Author's personal experiences in the Congo, particularly as a witness of Belgian brutality there. As we have seen before Conrad's stay in Africa was rather too brief for him to form any meaningful character judgments of the African. This is why he had to depend on myth and prejudiced opinion in his characterization in the fear of losing verisimilitude, which he nevertheless does not achieve. The auto-biographical dimension of *Heart of Darkness* has not been seriously discussed, while its parodying of the European 'scramble for Africa' and its recourse to anthropology in such terms as 'savage' and 'primitive' has necessitated a reading against a transparent historical background, which reading would likely lead to the problematic of imperialism in the early part of the novel and then to the psychological twist in the later sections where power abuse is directly linked to the collapse of civilized values symbolized in the discovery of Kurtz. Burden also argues - quoting several other sources - that the novel should not be seen as necessarily transparent to its historical background but that it should be a many-layered metaphorical continuum. But considering the monumental historical phenomenon of the nineteenth century and since a culture can be readily mapped in its informing historical processes there is no other way of looking at this particular text except against the culture in which it unfolded. A book is ultimately a cultural product.

The proposition that Heart of Darkness is not necessarily racist since Joseph Conrad - through the character of Marlow - is more ironic and criticizes imperialism is what R.G Hampson in *Conrad and the Idea of Empire*, quoting Joyce critics, described as a "reader trap". At the beginning of his 'yarn' Marlow declares - I would like to reproduce it in full for purposes of analysis although it has been hinted at before:

The conquest of the earth, which mostly means the taking it away from those who have a different complexion or slightly flatter noses than ourselves, is not a pretty thing when you look into it too much. What redeems it is the idea only. An idea at the back of it; not a sentimental pretence but an idea; and an unselfish belief in the idea - something you can set up, and bow down before.

Chapter 5

Character Contrast: Marlow and Mrs. Moore

John A. McClure writes in *Kipling and Conrad* that "as the twentieth century opened, the artists and intellectuals of the age increasingly came to believe that imperial rule, if inevitable in the short run, was an inglorious enterprise that deformed both those who ruled and those who submitted". Joseph Conrad and E. M. Forster were among these artists and each expressed their misgivings about the "inglorious enterprise" and its "deforming" effects in *Heart of Darkness* and *A Passage to India* respectively. I will attempt to analyse some of these effects among a range of British characters in both novels in terms of the connections between ideologically motivated cultural assumptions, personal attitudes and behaviour, and psychological crisis.

Vladimir Lenin describes imperialism in his work *Imperialism: The Highest Stage of Capitalism* as the "product of highly developed industrial capitalism. It consists in the striving of every industrial capitalist nation to bring under its control or to annex larger and larger areas of...territory, irrespective of what nations inhabit those regions". When the industrial nation allows its citizens to settle in the conquered territory the area is then a colony and the settlers are colonizers whereas the people native to the area are the colonized. The fundamental motive of imperialism and colonialism is economic: profits are large because investment in the conquered area is nil and native labour is cheap, and this situation is maintained by depriving the colonized peoples of political and economic rights. However, as James Kavanagh points out in his essay "Ideology," such a "social situation embodies an implicit tension that can at any time erupt into open conflict, and thus every class society has certain repressive mechanisms (police, armies, courts)...to force social subjects to accept the relations of subordination and dominance between classes". But ideology, defined by *Webster's Dictionary* as "the integrated assertions, theories, and aims that constitute a sociopolitical programme," is a more efficient way to manage social contradictions because it provides a comprehensive picture of the society in which social and economic inequalities are represented as natural and inevitable. The aim is to make the subordinate classes feel it would be futile to attempt to change their situation and "dominant-class subjects themselves are freer to believe that their wealth and power are after all justified".

Much of the standard British ideology regarding the Empire runs along the lines of 'Britain is the most highly developed civilization in the world and we are actually elevating the people of the regions we control through their exposure to us and our culture,' so that the British and the native peoples are both encouraged to view the imperialistic relationship as good for everyone. Yet, at the same time, a system of cultural assumptions is put forth based on emphasizing and exaggerating the differences between the colonized and colonizer and citing these differences as evidence that the colonizer is "naturally" suited to govern as the colonized is to be governed. This strategy can take the form of racism since ethnicity and/or skin colour are often the most immediately observable differences between the two groups.

The relations between the colonizer and the colonized affect both psychologically. *Heart of Darkness* and *A Passage to India* feature British characters who have internalized the ideological assumptions of their natural superiority to the Africans and Indians respectively yet many, when actually carrying out their imperialistic duties distant from the mother culture, often find their assumptions strained not only because of the stress of the tropics but also because these assumptions are not inherently "true" but are components of a version of reality that justify the British Empire's existence. The characters in both novels deal differently with the fundamental contradiction between systematic dehumanization for economic gain and the ideological justification of "civilizing" the natives. For some, the received cultural assumptions become more entrenched as E. M. Forster so clearly shows in his portraits of the members of the English Club in Chandrapore. Others are not able to resolve the contradictions and sink into madness, as Kurtz does in *Heart of Darkness*, or are not able to recover from disillusion like Mrs. Moore. Still others experience a psychological crisis like Miss Quested and Marlow but learn to live with their revelations.

Many of the novels'characters, under the stress of representing the Empire in a "foreign" culture, take the British cultural assumptions wholly to heart. The brickmaker of the Central Station, in describing Kurtz to Marlow, sums up the British rationale: "He is an emissary of pity and science and progress...the cause intrusted to us by Europe, so to speak, higher intelligence, wide sympathies, a singleness of purpose". Yet, the company Doctor warns Marlow before he leaves for Africa about the way the Europeans in the colonies really behave. The Doctor says those who go to the colonies are changed psychologically, "the changes take place inside, you know", and he warns Marlow to "avoid irritation more than exposure to the sun". Journeying with Marlow up the river, the reader does indeed meet a number of men who lose control and take out their frustration on the natives. Among these is Fresleven, the captain Marlowe replaces, described as "the gentlest, quietest creature that ever walked on two legs" who nevertheless beats a village chief savagely in a minor dispute. McClure concurs that this pattern is typical: "the victims of imperial invasion are made to pay for the frustrations of the invaders". Yet, beyond the physical acts of excessive cruelty, many of the European characters express deep loathing for the natives. The Company's chief accountant, whom Marlow admires for his discipline, exclaims "When one has to make correct entries, one comes to hate those savages-hate them to the death". No one but Marlow questions such sentiments as unjust or questions the assumptions on which they are based, thus the Europeans feel entitled to act cruelly and hate unreservedly.

The psychological stress placed on the British civil servants by the colonial structure is also evident in *A Passage to India.* Ronny Heaslop tells his mother, Mrs. Moore, when she first arrives in Chandrapore that there is a doubleness in everything a native says or thinks, and his mother replies, "You never used to judge people like this at home" to which Ronny responds "India isn't home". Those who occupy the posts of authority like the Callenders and the Turtons epitomize the "ideal" British attitude as when Mrs. Turton reassures Mrs. Moore that "You're superior to everyone in India except one or two of the Ranis, and they're on an equality". The long-time English colonialists continually warn Mrs. Moore, Miss Quested, and Fielding about the dangers of interacting with the natives in any social or intimate way because the contact may contaminate them for, as in *Heart of Darkness,* the implication is that any European who behaves badly must be infected with the native's moral degradation.

All of these attitudes mentioned in both novels wonderfully illustrate two psychological processes. One is examined in detail by Albert Memmi in *The Colonizer and the Colonized.* He explains that " to be a colonizer means to be a nonlegitimate privileged person...[and all actions are geared to]...transforming his usurpation into legitimacy". The way the colonizer does this is to extol his own merits to the skies and "harp on the usurped's demerits, so deep that they cannot help leading to misfortune". And of course, the more the colonizer convinces himself of the despicability of the colonized, the more he himself becomes a tyrant. The second process is really a mirror image of the first but serves to reinforce it. V. G. Kiernan expresses the idea well: "By thinking the worst of their subjects they avoided having to think badly of themselves. Even years later when they were on better terms with their consciences, Englishmen went on thinking of Indians as hopelessly demoralized by climate, or social habits, or ages of Oriental misrule, and therefore permanently in need of foreign tutelage". A cycle is set up in which the native is criticized so that the colonizer must crack down, yet the colonizer can never examine his own cruelty because the colonized is so reprehensible. The original and primary motive of wealth for England gained at the expense of exploiting the natives made such attitudes necessary for the British, to justify their actions to the world but also, and most importantly, to themselves, for to question these received assumptions is to question one's cultural and personal identity.

Kurtz embodies the extreme case of European imperialist motives and thus their most destructive effects. He believes equally in the rhetorical motives of imperialism as well as the actual motives and methods, and the inherent contradictions drive him mad. Kurtz expresses the official ideological line in advocating that the Europeans should appear as Gods to the Africans because "in the simple exercise of our will we can exert a power for good practically unbounded", yet he obviously fully embraces the actual accumulation of raw wealth when he sighs over his "ivory", and he knows the human exploitation such extraction of raw wealth really involves when he writes "Exterminate all the brutes!". Though Kurtz's excessive appetites are continually compared to those of the natives, the reader eventually learns that his appetites actually go beyond all restraint and satisfaction because even the cannibals accompanying Marlow exercise self-control.

Therefore, Kurtz's madness is less brought on by his actual interaction with the natives and due more to the ideological necessity to impugn the colonized with undesirable qualities. Kurtz eventually identifies with this projection until he begins to become the "native" himself, but he is not imitating the native, as I've shown, because the colonial system itself demands that the colonized exaggerate and mislabel the native's "defects" in a degree on level with the intensity of exploitation. Rather, Kurtz imitates the British "idea" of the native; he "goes native" within the darkness projected by the British psyche itself. This process is explained by Francoise Melzter in her interpretation of Lacan's maxim that "the unconscious is the discourse of the Other": "The way the Subject views, and projects upon, an Other will yield a clue concerning the Subject's relationship to his unconscious wishes and desires...[and this is the place]...where the Subject does not recognize himself". McClure agrees with this idea when he writes that the novel suggests the "European characters acquire their lusts for wealth and power in Europe, where these lusts are also contained. Then they come to the colonial world in search of freedom that will allow these lusts to be expressed...[and] they find it", thus "the forces that brutalize [in the novel]...are at the heart of European civilization". When Kurtz psychologically identifies with the Other, the line between the Subject and Object/Other thins out, finally dissolves, and he goes insane.

Other British characters in both novels perceive the dichotomy between the reality and actuality of colonial life and allow the knowledge to change their outlook in more positive ways. Mrs. Moore, Miss Quested, and Marlow all experience a measure of disillusionment when they realise that the professed moral purpose of colonialism conflicts with the actual practices. Mrs. Moore is the least successful of these. Her experience in the Marabar Caves leads to the loss of her Christian optimism and cultural idealism. And since she represents in the novel the "humane" British colonialist, her disillusion with her own personal psychological constructs, which are entwined with British culture and identity, extends to the general insight that Britain is not embarked on a noble, civilizing mission in India and that the exploitation inherent in the colonial system is neither useful for the British nor for the Indians. Yet, her age and health prevent her from adjusting to this psychological blow and she dies soon after.

Miss Quested is not so much radically disillusioned as slowly transformed and the reader senses her transformation continues after she returns to England. What happens to her in the Caves can also be read as an encounter with her subconscious in the form of the projected Other, represented by Aziz, coloured by the ideological assumptions of the British colonialist. The nature of her conversation with Aziz before she enters a Cave indicates anxiety about her upcoming marriage to Ronny and, in fact, she realises she doesn't really love him. There is also the suggestion that she may feel apprehensive about the sexual obligations of marriage. These thoughts are in her mind when she enters the Cave and perhaps the claustrophobic atmosphere inside it leads her to imagine a scenario with Aziz that doesn't really happen. Yet the fact that she mistakenly imagines that Aziz molested her is not only due to her own anxieties regarding sex and marriage but also arises from the European cultural assumption that "the darker races are physically attracted by the fairer, but not vice versa" as McBryde says during Aziz's trial.

Miss Quested has internalized this assumption, as well as being overtly warned by the other colonialists of the untrustworthiness of the Indians, so in a moment of heightened anxiety and disorientation she projects her fear of sexual union and marriage by imagining she must fight off Aziz, a person her culture has taught her will always want her sexually. But as the novel progresses, she sorts out her feelings and not only rightly acquits Aziz but also comes to terms with the realization that she doesn't want to marry Ronny and become what she perceived about the other colonialists from the beginning: They are paranoid, cruel, and misguided. She rejects colonialism not because of a reasoned understanding of its defects but because she realises it hardens and distorts those who maintain it.

Marlow undergoes a similar transformation. His journey up the river to the Central Station to meet Kurtz is a journey to the rotten heart of colonialism. He reexamines every tenet of colonial ideology, going back and forth in arguments with himself between the rhetoric of Europe's "civilizing mission" and the realities of brutality and exploitation. In his internal dialogue, he admits over and over to the realization that the Africans are not beasts but are just as human as he is and Europeans are not morally beyond the level of savagery that they claim of the Africans. McClure writes, "Like those Americans who went to Vietnam out of a mixture of curiosity, idealism, and adventurousness, Marlow finds himself involved in a "conspiracy" that violates every value he respects and does so, incredibly, in the name of these very values...until at last Marlow comes to doubt all assertions of benevolence, all promises of progress". Marlow is disillusioned by his glimpse of the reality behind the pretence but values his insights as important if painful knowledge. He describes his experience to his campanions on the *Nellie*, "It was the farthest point of navigation and the culminating point of my experience.

It seemed somehow to throw a kind of light on everything about me-and into my thoughts". After struggling with the contradictions between "selfish and ruthless economic motives...[and the way they] employ the rhetoric of morality as a mask", Marlow comes to understand both the reality of imperialism beyond the ideology and the corruption of the men who participate in it and he diagnoses the problem in both cases as a lack of restraint. When Kurtz ceases to exercise restraint, he becomes a brute himself, and when Western civilization does not exercise restraint it systematically brutalizes other peoples and cultures. Marlow also hints at the need for a real faith unconnected to economic gain. He is horrified by Kurtz as the "mystery of a soul that knew no restraint, no faith, and no fear". Perhaps it is sincere spiritual striving that really civilizes people.

Ideology is part of everyone's cultural identity and filters our impressions of the world around us. Oftentimes, only when people are in extreme curcumstances that seem to contradict their assumptions do people become conscious of them and sometimes, like Marlow and Miss Quested, realise that these assumptions are wrong. Both Conrad and Forster illustrate in these two novels that when injustice is perpetrated on such a grand scale as was done in the British Empire, everone is affected, everyone is guilty and no one can afford the luxury of an unexamined life.

Chapter 6

Narrative Technique: Heart of Darkness

Heart of Darkness by Joseph Conrad, deals with contentious issues of racism and the questionable validity of policies of colonization employed by European nations during the nineteenth century. In the portrayal of these sensitive issues, Conrad employs a unique narrative point of view in order to manipulate the reader's response to characters, situations, conflicts and issues. The different levels of narration, from the anonymous frame narrator, the first person narration of the protagonist Marlowe, and the limited periods of other first person narrations from the minor characters, at different times add to and contradict the alternative narrations. Through this continual contrast, readers are manipulated and forced to question their own attitudes towards colonization.

The majority of the text is narrated in first person by the character Charles Marlowe. Because of this first person narration, readers are positioned to sympathies with his viewpoints, as the only character for which readers are provided both an exterior and interior. The exterior of Marlowe, how he is perceived by other characters, is provided by the anonymous frame narrator in the opening pages of the novella:

He had sunken cheeks, a yellow complexion, a straight back, an ascetic aspect, and, with his arms dropped, the palms of his hands outwards, resembled an idol.

This is then combined with his own narration, which gives readers an insight into his character's inner thoughts and motivations, his interior. As the two sides of Marlowe are combined in a complete reading of the text, links can be made between Marlowe's emotional development and inner journey through the 'darkness', and the way his character appears externally. The contrasting of these two sides of Marlowe also has ironic implications, as though the frame narrator is led to perceive him as a "...Buddah..." the only enlightenment he has found is one of darkness. In fact, little enlightenment at all, as the novella never affects an adequate closure, posing more questions than answers at its conclusion. As Marlowe is the only character in the text for which both an exterior and interior character is provided, he subsequently seems the most real and readers are manipulated to sympathies with his viewpoint. Readers trace his ideological development as it corresponds with a manipulation of their own attitudes and values. This can be seen in Marlowe's view towards women in the text. It is after speaking to his aunt that Marlowe first makes the statement:

Its queer how out of touch with truth women are:

At first, this seems a rather disconnected comment, yet first person narration allows Marlowe to explain this comment aside from the action of the text. As readers trace Marlowe's physical journey, a move away from Europe to Africa, a similar move can be seen in the text away from female characters to a purely male cast. Women are therefore associated with the supposedly civilized and refined world left behind in Europe, a world ignorant of the evils of colonization, which are to be discovered in Africa. Readers are led through the 'darkness', and as events become more extreme, so does the longing to return to the simpler stages of novella's opening. Readers are even manipulated into a consciousness of this desire when Marlowe confuses his own narration and combines his meeting with Kurtz with the meeting of Kurtz' Intended in Europe. By then, though she is actively marginalized and made "...out of it..." by Marlowe. Readers have reached the same understanding as Marlowe, that her world of untouched

Europe must not be spoilt by the 'darkness' of what the European people have done, if Marlowe is to keep his sanity and any sense of hope. As revealed in the novella's conclusion, to combine these two worlds "...would have been too dark..." It is through the text's unique narrative point of view that readers are manipulated in their attitudes towards the character of Marlowe, and the contrasting situations of untouched Europe and Africa, tainted with colonization.

The focus of Heart of Darkness is undoubtedly the character Kurtz. However, reader understandings of Kurtz are greatly manipulated by the fact that he never presents his own character. Instead, information about him must be gleaned from the narrations of other characters. All characterization of Kurtz is therefore his exterior character, projected in different ways by the narrations of minor characters (each with their own hidden motivations), through the storytelling of Marlowe and the listening ear of the frame narrator. This almost excessive level of separation between reader and character allows readers the distance to reflect objectively on Kurtz' actions and the enterprise of colonization which they represent. Readers are overtly manipulated through a series of different Kurtz exteriors in order to generate a level of understanding of the character. Kurtz is first introduced to Marlowe and readers by the African clerk, who describes him as "...a very remarkable person...".

This minor narrator is the stereotyped Uncle Tom, a character having little respect within both white and black society. Therefore, the assumed white readership of the text does not immediately accept this summation of Kurtz, yet they are led to through its Repetition, a catalogue of Kurtz' praise created in the first chapter of the novella. However this is in stark contrast to the descriptions of Kurtz given in secret conversation by the manager and his nephew in chapter two, of a "...pestilential fellow...". Readers become aware of the fact that different narrators have different motivations for their descriptions of Kurtz, in the specific situation, the manager's jealousy and professional ambition. What is more, it is realised that no information is provided about Kurtz' inner motives:

> They were at a loss for an adequate motive.

Though this breeds curiosity both in Marlowe and readers, it also ensures that Kurtz can never become a fully constructed character, thereby all but preventing any resistant readings that may attempt sympathy for Kurtz. Readers are never given the opportunity to sympathies with the Personification of colonization, as he is only ever an exterior character. In the novella's final chapter, the glorious image of Kurtz from chapter one is confronted with the harsh reality of Kurtz' madness, a contrast made clear through the minor narration of the Russian:

> "Nevertheless, I think Mr. Kurtz is a remarkable man," I said with emphasis. He started, dropped on me a cold heavy glance, said very quietly, "He was," and turned his back on me.

This is the final external description of Kurtz before readers are forced into an awareness of him in his madness. Unfortunately, the Russian provides no insights into Kurtz' inner character and he remains without motivation. On his deathbed, his ramblings are left unexplained to readers. Marlowe poses the burning question in readers' minds to receive a futile response:

> "Do you know what you are doing?" I whispered. "Perfectly," he answered.... (p106)

No explanation or justification is ever provided for the actions of neither Kurtz nor the colonization he embodies. Though readers are made aware of the fact that there is a redeeming 'idea' behind the policy, it is never explicitly expressed in the text. This manipulates readers into an adverse view of colonization. The final descriptions of Kurtz provided by his Intended are known by readers to be a totally unrealistic image of the 'pestilence'. They act to show readers the falsehood of any glorification of colonization governments give to their citizens. In the end, though Kurtz' suffering and

"...horror...." are acknowledged, they remain unexplained. The ambiguous nature of his last words, as it is unsure if the horror is Africa, colonization, or humanity in General, reflect the lack of understanding provided by the text about Kurtz. Throughout Heart of Darkness readers are manipulated by contrasting points of view, into a vision of Kurtz and colonization, already decided by Conrad.

A source of contrast with Marlowe's dominant narration is the anonymous frame narrator. While all other narrators in the text are given clear character outlines, the frame narrator is an unknown while not being omniscient. Both the frame narrator and Marlowe come from the dominant European discourse; however there is a sense of antithesis in their different attitudes towards colonization and imperialism. The text opens with the frame narrator's description of the glory of Europe. The European colonizers are described as "...the great knights-errant of the sea..." (p17) and are combined with light images of fire and a "...spark..." However, these are immediately junta positioned with Marlowe's opening statement:

'And this also,' said Marlowe suddenly, 'has been one of the dark places of the earth.'

The following negative descriptions of the Roman colonisation and imperialism which spawned Europe, combined with the above dark imagery, is a mirror image of the descriptions of the frame narrator. It serves to heighten the contrast and creates an immediate conflict of opinions in the text. Considering the condensed structure of the novella, it is crucial the Conrad uses such stark methods to make readers immediately aware of the issue of the text. This issue being a weighing up of the effects of colonisation with the aim of leading readers to a personal rather than a textual judgement of the policy. The frame narrator is also used at various points in the text to interrupt the narrative flow of Marlowe and focus the discussion on the issue of colonisation. This is done on page 60, where the frame narrator interrupts Marlowe as he begins to digress away from the forward movement of the textual journey. In interrupting, it leads Marlowe to a discussion of cannibals. The presence of cannibalism in the text works to undermine any notions that the superior European culture needs to teach the Africans how to be civilised. In Heart of Darkness it is the cannibals who are the more constrained and civilised, especially when juxta positioned against the "...white, flabby..." European pilgrims, who seem the more irrational and uncivilised in their response to situations. It is the presence of the frame narrator, which focuses the text on this issue, which underpins colonisation. Using an anonymous frame narrator, Conrad keeps a strict focus on the major issues of the text, thereby monitoring the ways in which it is presented to readers.

The final function of the unique narrative structure of Heart of Darkness is that it dictates the overriding message of the text. Because of the extreme similarities between events in Marlowe's constructed life and Conrad's own experiences, there is a danger that readers may fall subject to the intentional fallacy and dismiss the work as autobiographical. Conrad guards against this with his many levels of constructed narration. The character that could be most reasonably attributed to Conrad would be the frame narrator, yet he is most distant from the events of the plot that it becomes unreasonable to draw links between the anonymous narrator and the detailed events. Conrad is thrice separated from the story's focus on Kurtz, a separation through the frame narrator, Marlowe and the minor narrator's. Readers are thereby manipulated so as not to view the text as autobiographical. In fact, the same unique narrative point of view is used to change the novella's message from a didactic judgement of the evils of colonisation to a question, which is left for readers to answer personally.

This is accomplished by contrasting the blurred narrative against distinct dialectic imagery. As discussed, the conflicting representations of Kurtz' exterior lead to a blurred or non-existent understanding of his motives or inner pressures, a blurring which prevents readers from making a clear cut decision as to his character's morality. There are "...shade(s) of Kurtz...". Yet this character understanding is given in a background of dialectic imagery built upon from the novella's opening. Black/white, light/darkness binary opposites are used throughout the text, attempting to simplify the issues into a clear decision of good and evil. Visual imagery creates a stark picture of black and white, examples of which are in the descriptions of African slaves:

He had a tied bit of white worsted round his neck... It looked startling round his black neck, this bit of white thread from beyond the seas.

As the blurred characterisation and starkly clear imagery are superimposed over each other, the effect is a manipulation of readers. This calls on them not to dismiss the issue, but to consider colonisation on a more complex level, with shades of morality, and attempt to answer the novella's questions on that basis. Largely point of view manipulates readers into such an understanding of the issues of the text.

Heart of Darkness, in its portrayal of issues of racism and colonisation, utilises a unique narrative point of view in order to manipulate readers into specific understandings of the characters, their situations, conflicts in the text, and the issue at hand. The first person narration of Marlowe positions readers to sympathise with him, as the only character for which both exterior and interior characterisation is provided. The character of Kurtz, as the personification of colonisation, is barely exposed to readers, to guard against resistant readings of the text. Readers are presented conflicting exteriors of Kurtz, by a number of minor narrators, each colouring his character with their own motivations. The frame narrator, as a contrast to Marlowe, focuses readers on the issues being discussed, a necessary factor in the condensed novella format. By superimposing this blurred narration with clear dialectic imagery, readers are manipulated to have a complex understanding of colonisation and its many shades. As a contentious and sensitive issue in any historical context, it warranted a cautious address, and by utilising such an unusual point of view, Conrad has ensured that his text will respond to any developments in these issues that may arise in the contexts of readers to come.

Chapter 7

Plot Overview

When a yawl called *The Nellie* swings into port along the Thames River within sight of London, the crewmen are as still as the breezeless air. The captain stands on the bow looking out to sea. A deckhand called "The Lawyer" lies on a carpet while one called "The Accountant" arranges dominoes into imaginary buildings. A third man, Marlow, sits back against the mizzenmast.

The unnamed narrator describing the scene says Marlow "had sunken cheeks, a yellow complexion, a straight back, an ascetic aspect, and, with his arms dropped, the palms of hands outward, resembled an idol."

The sun is setting. Marlow observes that the great city they see before them is "one of the dark places of the earth." He then begins telling them a story about another dark place–the very heart of darkness. It is deep within the jungles of the Congo Free State in Africa. (King Leopold II of Belgium established the Congo Free State as a Belgian colony in the late 19th Century.)

Marlow tells the crew that he had been hired at one time by a Belgian company that trades in African ivory at a handsome profit. The company maintained several outposts along a river in the Congo, all of them called "stations." Marlow's mission was to travel more than 200 miles inland, partly on foot but mostly by river steamer, to a company outpost called "the Inner Station" (as opposed to an "Outer" and "Central" stations along the way). Upon his arrival at the Inner Station, he was to reconnoiter the activities of the outpost's manager, a man named Kurtz, who had been incommunicado for some time with his home office in Belgium. Marlow says he was told that it might be necessary for him, depending on what he found in the jungle, to bring Kurtz back to civilization. Kurtz had been running the Inner Station with amazing efficiency, returning tons of ivory to his employers and earning a reputation elevating him to the status of legend.

Here is the story that Marlow narrates about his adventure:

After a month's sea voyage, he arrives on the shore of Africa and must travel the first 30 miles inland, to the company's Outer Station, on a steamer with a Swedish captain. The captain tells Marlow about another man he took inland who hanged himself. When Marlow asks why the man killed himself, the captain says ominously, "Who knows? The sun too much for him, or the country perhaps."

After arriving at the Outer Station, Marlow observes natives building a railroad and setting off dynamite. He is struck by their emaciation.

"I could see every rib, the joints of their limbs were like knobs in a rope; each had an iron collar on his neck, and all were connected together with a chain whose bights swung between them, rhythmically clinking."

They are prisoners. What crime had they committed? Perhaps the crime of simply being available for white Europeans to exploit. "They were not criminals," Marlow says, "they were nothing earthly now–nothing but black shadows of disease and starvation in the greenish gloom."

Marlow must wait 10 days, lodging in a hut, before resuming his trip with 60 hired hands in a tramp through the jungle to reach the Central Station of the Belgian company. There, his own steamer awaits him. During the trek, a few of his men die under the burdens they carry, and at night distant drums pound out strange rhythms. Along the jungle trail, Marlow encounters a native with a bullet hole in his forehead. What happened to him? Why?

Upon arriving at the Central Station, Marlow discovers that the steamboat he is to captain to the Inner Station sits submersed after someone piloted it over stones that ripped out its bottom. The manager of the station has no particular qualities to commend him for his work, except one: He has the uncanny ability to remain healthy while others around him regularly fall victim to tropical diseases. He is jealous of Kurtz's reputation as a master at his trade and claims that Kurtz is conspiring against him, placing his job in jeopardy. Thus, he is all in favor of bringing Kurtz out of the jungle and plans to accompany Marlow to the Inner Station in order to assist in Kurtz's removal.

During his stay at the Central Station, Marlow learns that Kurtz has ceased communicating with the station and has stopped shipping ivory. Moreover, he hears that Kurtz may be sick.

Marlow needs rivets to repair his boat. He had seen endless supplies of them after arriving in Africa. But here, in this godforsaken way station, there is not a single rivet to be found. So, in the next few months, he mends his steamship with any material he can find–a scrap of this, a piece of that. During this time, a gang of men who call themselves the Eldorado Exploring Expedition visits the station. "To tear treasure out of the bowels of the land was their desire," Marlow says, "with no more moral purpose at the back of it than there is in burglars breaking into a safe."

At long last, with the manager of the Outer Station and a crew that includes cannibals as well as white men, Marlow sets out for the Inner Station, navigating the boat deep into the savage beauty of the jungle. It is a primeval world, full of peril and lush with vegetation that thrives in the humid air and heavy silence. The journey challenges Marlow's every navigational talent with twists and turns and shallow water hiding rocks that could once again undo the boat. At night distant drums beat out rhythms of prayer or peace or war. During the day, Marlow occasionally glimpses natives along the shore sometimes shouting or leaping, sometimes frowning or clapping. Eventually, Marlow stops for wood to stoke the steamer's fire and, to his surprise, finds a pile stacked near a hut and a note telling the finder to help himself.

Later, back on the river, the steamer encounters heavy fog, hits a snag, and comes upon hostile natives who shoot arrows and hurl spears at the boat from positions in the dense forest. The white crew members, armed with Winchesters, spray volleys of bullets into the bushes. The boat struggles through the water, brushing overhanging limbs. A black man, Marlow's helmsman, takes a a spear in his side and falls at the feet of Marlow. During all the frenzy, Marlow reaches up and pulls hard on a line that sounds the steam whistle. Again and again he jerks it. Its screeches frighten the natives, who cry out and scramble off into the jungle. The helmsman dies, frowning.

When the boat is under way again, Marlow dumps the body overboard–a callous act, some of the crewmen think, but Marlow worried that the cannibals would have eaten the corpse. Oddly, he learns during the rest of the trip that it is the cannibals who keep their place; the white men, whom he calls "pilgrims," are the ones who are hard to control. They are ever ready to shoot at anything that moves; it is all good sport.

When the steamer arrives at the Inner Station, a talkative Russian trader dressed in motley, like a clown or a jester, greets Marlow. After serving aboard English ships, the Russian had persuaded a Dutch trading company to equip him for a foray into the jungle to reap profits from its riches. He tells Marlow it was he who left the pile of wood along the river.

After almost two years of traipsing through the bush, the Russian ended up at the Inner Station, where he doctored Kurtz through two sick spells. Kurtz maintains a house at the station, but he only recently returned to it after spending time in the interior of the jungle–perhaps taking part in native rituals. He has manipulated the natives into idolizing him, as if he were a god, for his gigantic ego requires homage. But now he is a sick god–"bad, very bad," the Russian says.

Marlow trains a telescope on the house, across a field of high grass. What he sees, he says, surprises him but does not shock him: heads impaled on stakes. All of the heads except one face Kurtz's house, paying homage.

"There was nothing exactly profitable in these heads being there," Marlow says. "They only showed that Mr. Kurtz lacked restraint in the gratification of his various lusts...."

Marlow observes that Kurtz–in spite of his genius as an ivory trader and his ability to dazzle and manipulate the natives–is actually a victim of the jungle, the heart of darkness.

"I think it had whispered to him things about himself which he did not know, things of which he had no conception till he took counsel with this great solitude–and the whisper had proved irresistibly fascinating."

The voice of temptation, perhaps, inviting him to walk on the dark side of his soul, canceling moral law and becoming emperor of all that he sees.

Sometime later, Marlow observes savage-looking natives bearing Kurtz on a stretcher to a cabin at the site.

"I could see the cage of his ribs all astir, the bones of his arm waving," Marlow says. "It was as though an animated image of death carved out of old ivory had been shaking its hand with menaces at a motionless crowd of men made of dark and glittering bronze."

Marlow and his men have a stack of letters for Kurtz–missives which had collected to await delivery–and they take them to the sick man. Kurtz fingers them and acknowledges their receipt in a surprisingly robust voice.

Later, outside, a beautiful native woman appears, then disappears. Days later, she visits Kurtz for an hour while Marlow is nearby. During her conversation with Kurtz, she repeatedly points to Marlow. What she is saying is a mystery to Marlow, for he has no knowledge of native dialects. However, it becomes quite obvious that she has been serving as Kurtz's mistress.

Sometime later, the manager of the Outer Station visits Kurtz and receives a browbeating for saying he wants to "save" Kurtz–that is, take him out of the jungle.

"You are interrupting my plans now," Kurtz tells the manager. "Sick! Sick" Not so sick as you would like to believe."

When the district manager later pulls Marlow aside, he says Kurtz's methods are unsound and is doing more harm than good for the company. Marlow observes that Kurtz is a "remarkable man." The district manager says, "He was."

Marlow learns that it was Kurtz who had ordered the attack on the steamer. He wanted to scare the crew off so that he could remain in the jungle to carry out his enterprises.

Meanwhile, the Russian prepares to return to civilization after receiving ammunition and supplies from Marlow. Before leaving by canoe, he tells Marlow of Kurtz's talent for reciting his own poetry.

After Marlow decides it is time for Kurtz, too, to return to civilization, his crewmen take Kurtz aboard but he later escapes. When Marlow searches for him, he finds him crawling in deep grass. Marlow tells him he will be "lost" if he does not return–although Marlow knows that Kurtz is already lost. Worried that Kurtz will call out to his native friends for help, Marlow threatens to bash his head if he makes a sound.

"I was on the threshold of great things," Kurtz says.

The jungle holds a spell over him; he simply does not want to give up. Kurtz's soul, Marlow says, has gone mad. Yet Marlow manages to prevail.

The next day at noon, he and his crew carry Kurtz into the pilot house of the boat before their trip out of the jungle. When natives gather, Marlow's crewmen begin reaching for their guns as if they are about to have a sporting good time.

So Marlow blows the steam whistle to drive the natives off and, thus, save them from a hale of bullets. The natives run off in a fright–all except for that savagely beautiful woman, who reaches out her arms toward the boat. And then crewmen open fire.

After the boat is on its way, Kurtz speaks out deliriously of all his plans; it seems that the jungle, which had become part of him, is fighting for possession of him. "Oh, I will wring your heart yet," he says, addressing the mysterious wilds. Along the way, the boat lapses into a mechanical problem, and Marlow puts in at an island to effect repairs. While there, Kurtz gives him some papers and a photograph tied together with a shoestring, saying he wants Marlow to keep them away from the meddlesome Outer Station manager. One evening, when Marlow goes into to check on Kurtz, the sick man says, "I am lying here in the dark waiting for death."

Not long after he dies. The last words Marlow hears him speak are "The horror! The horror!"

Apparently, Kurtz is aware of the depth of evil into which he plunged himself. The next day, the crewmen bury him in a "muddy hole."

A year after his return to Belgium, Marlow gives the packet of papers to the person for whom they were intended–Kurtz's fiancée–who mourns his loss, saying he was such a remarkable man, such a good man. "Men looked up to him–his goodness shone in his every act." When she asks Marlow about Kurtz's last moments, he lies: "The last word he pronounced was–your name."

When Marlow ends his story, he resumes his pose–looking like an idol, a Buddha. The unnamed narrator aboard observes at that moment–as black clouds appear in an overcast sky–that the Thames, as it flows out to sea, "seemed to lead into the heart of an immense darkness."

Chapter 8

Major Characters

Charles Marlow

Marlow, who refers to himself as "Charlie," is a pensive but adventurous seaman with a knack for telling a good story. While a small boat on which he is serving sits at anchor near London, he tells his fellow crewmen a harrowing tale about a trip he took up the Congo River in Africa. Marlow represents Joseph Conrad, the author of "Heart of Darkness," who traveled up the Congo in 1890 and witnessed firsthand European exploitation of African natives.

Kurtz

Intelligent, resourceful man who lives in the jungle while harvesting ivory for a Belgian company. In his primitive surroundings, he gives free reign to his dark side, manipulating and controlling the natives and setting himself up as a kind of idol. Eventually, his evildoing and the pestiferous environment sicken him physically and mentally. It is Marlow's mission to bring him out of the jungle and return him to civilization, but he dies on the ride down the river toward the sea.

Unnamed Narrator

Minor character who sets the scene and, from time to time, describes Marlow while the latter tells his story.

District Manager Barely competent manager of the Outer Station whose sole commendable quality is that he remains healthy in the jungle environment. He believes Kurtz is plotting against him.

Swedish Captain

He commands a steamboat that takes Marlow on his first leg of his journey up the Congo River.

Russian Trader

Talkative trader who has made his way into the jungle on his own. He greets Marlow upon the latter's arrival at the Inner Station and updates Marlow on the condition of Kurtz.

Fiancée of Kurtz

Helmsman

Minor Characters Kurtz's native mistress, African tribesmen, cannibals who serve on Marlow's steamboat, white European who serve on the same boat.

Settings

The action takes place in the early 1890's. It begins on a boat anchored within sight of London, England, then shifts to Africa during a flashback in which Charles Marlow, one of the crew members, tells a story about a trip he took up the Congo River to the "heart of darkness."

Climax

The climax occurs when Marlow at long last reaches Kurtz, only to discover that the jungle has corrupted him physically, morally, and mentally. The jungle, of course, is as much the jungle within Kurtz–the tangling undergrowth of evil desires that seize control of his soul–as the jungle without.

Type of Work and Themes

Heart of Darkness is a novella (short novel) that conveys its meaning on symbolic and literal levels. It does not slip neatly into a distinct genre. It is clear, though, that Conrad intended the novel to do the following in revealing his themes:

1. Present an odyssey in which a traveller, Marlow, confronts the dangers of a foreboding wilderness and the people it holds in its grasp. In so doing, he also confronts his own inner self. Like the hero of Homer's *Odyssey*, that ancient tale in which one man becomes every man in the journey through life, Marlow is a curious adventurer who presses on in the face of danger. His journey teaches him that the darkest and most perilous place in the world is not the jungle, but the heart of a human being who succumbs to his evil impulses.
2. Expose the inhumanity of European exploitation of Africa and its people.
3. Call attention to the dark force in the human soul which, when allowed license to express itself, reduces men to atavisms–feral, unfeeling, primeval organisms that feed on others without conscience or moral direction.
4. Present the tragedy of a brilliant and admired man, the Belgian trader Kurtz, who succumbs to this dark force. He is not unlike the hero of a Greek tragedy in that he is a supposedly noble human being who, through self-delusion and repression of his conscience, suffers a downfall. In the end, he understands but fails to subdue the evil within himself.
5. Demonstrate that human beings are complex creatures with manifold motivations and perceptions. Marlow both admires and despises Kurtz, for Kurtz has many sides–some good, some monstrously evil.

Plot Structure: Frame Tale

To tell his story, Conrad uses two narrators, both serving on a small boat, a yawl called *The Nellie*. The first narrator, unidentified, is only a minor character in the story. He sets the scene–a port along the Thames River near London as the sun begins to set–and describes the captain and the crewmen, one of whom is Charles Marlow, the second narrator. Marlow takes over as the main narrator and central character of the story when he begins telling the crew about a journey that took him to Africa and up the Congo River to the "heart of darkness." Marlow's tale continues uninterrupted except at short breaks when the first narrator describes Marlow's demeanor or appearance, or informs the reader of the time of night, as the tale progresses. A literary work with an "outer narrator" who introduces an "inner narrator" (such as Marlow) is often referred to as a frame tale. The outer narrator's story is like the frame around a painting; the inner narrator's story is the painting itself.

Style

Conrad develops Marlow's story with an ingenious mix of elegant imagery and everyday language–the latter including truncated sentences and colloquialisms–expressed through Marlow's intimate first-person narration. Occasionally Marlow addresses the reader with the second-person "you." Overall the writing is first rate, with rich characterization that provides insights into the psychological motivations and moral convictions–or lack of them–of his characters. Descriptions of exploited Africans are striking:

> They were dying slowly–it was very clear. They were not enemies, they were not criminals, they were nothing earthly now–nothing but black shadows of disease and starvation, lying confusedly in the greenish gloom. Brought from all the recesses of the coast in all the legality of time contracts, lost in uncongenial surroundings, fed on unfamiliar food, they sickened, became inefficient, and were then allowed to crawl away and rest.... I began to distinguish the gleam of eyes under the trees. Then, glancing down, I saw a face near my hand. The black bones reclined at full length with one shoulder against the tree, and slowly the eyelids rose and the sunken eyes looked up at me, enormous and vacant, a kind of blind, white flicker in the depths of the orbs, which died out slowly.

The man seemed young–almost a boy–but you know with them it's hard to tell. I found nothing else to do but to offer him one of my good Swede's ship's biscuits I had in my pocket. The fingers closed slowly on it and held–there was no other movement and no other glance.

Marlow often provides brief descriptions of his experiences to supplement detailed descriptions. His abbreviated glimpses of reality are not unlike those of impressionist painters who attempt to capture a moment or a mood in an instantaneous rendering of what they see. Conrad is especially effective when describing the atmosphere of the jungle: dark, forbidding, mysterious, primeval. At times, he waxes into lengthy digressions, but they are often enthralling–building suspense.

The Congo River and the Country in Conrad's Time

The Congo River, one of the longest in the world, forms in central Africa in a country that was known as the Congo Free State in the late 19th Century. The name of the country changed several times in the 20th Century and is known today as the Democratic Republic of the Congo (DRC). From its headwaters, the river flows north in the DRC, then west, then southwest to the Atlantic Ocean. Joseph Conrad traveled up the Congo River in 1890 and later based *Heart of Darkness* on this voyage. Marlow, the main narrator of *Heart of Darkness* arrives on the Atlantic coastline of Africa, then travels up the Congo to several sites in the jungle. (Traveling "up" a river means traveling toward its source, or headwaters; traveling "down" a river means traveling away from its source.) King Leopold II of Belgium established the Congo Free State in the late 19th Century and commissioned the famous Anglo-American explorer Henry Morton Stanley to establish trading posts along the river. Supposedly, these trading posts were set up to civilize and develop the Congo region while ending the slave trade. However, the Belgians exploited the native population while capitalizing on the Congo as a rich source of ivory.

Author Information

Joseph Conrad, one of the most important novelists in English literature, was born in 1857 to Polish parents in Berdichev, Ukraine, a country in eastern Europe that was annexed as part of Poland in 1569 but incorporated into the Russian Empire in the 19th Century. Ukraine is now an independent country. Conrad's birth name was Józef Teodor Konrad Korzeniowski. When he was a child, Conrad learned about the great English authors–including Shakespeare, Dickens, Thackeray, and Sir Walter Scott–from his father, a poet who also translated English books into Polish and French. Young Joseph could read translations of these authors in both of those languages. His parents, devout Roman Catholics, raised him in that religion. When he was still an adolescent, his father and mother died, and thereafter his uncle saw to his upbringing and schooling. In 1874, Conrad abandoned his studies to fulfill a longing to go to sea. Subsequently, he served on French and British merchants ships, sailing around the world. During this time, he became not only a master mariner (acknowledged with a British certificate in 1886) but also a master of the English language. He also became a British subject. In the late 1880's, he began to write. In 1890, he traveled up the Congo River from the Atlantic coast, then back, on a four-month journey. The trip provided him all the background he needed for *Heart of Darkness.* His first novel, *Almayer's Folly,* was published in 1895, marking the first time he used the name "Joseph Conrad" instead of his birth name. Many other distinguished works–including *The Nigger of the Narcissus, Heart of Darkness, Lord Jim, Typhoon,* and *Nostromo*–followed within a decade. The British government invited him to receive knighthood in his later years, but he declined the honour. He died of a heart attack in 1924 at Bishopsbourne, England.

Chapter 9

Complete Text

PART I

The Nellie, a cruising yawl, swung to her anchor without a flutter of the sails, and was at rest. The flood had made, the wind was nearly calm, and being bound down the river, the only thing for it was to come to and wait for the turn of the tide.

The sea-reach of the Thames stretched before us like the beginning of an interminable waterway. In the offing the sea and the sky were welded together without a joint, and in the luminous space the tanned sails of the barges drifting up with the tide seemed to stand still in red clusters of canvas sharply peaked, with gleams of varnished sprits. A haze rested on the low shores that ran out to sea in vanishing flatness. The air was dark above Gravesend, and farther back still seemed condensed into a mournful gloom, brooding motionless over the biggest, and the greatest, town on earth.

The Director of Companies was our captain and our host. We four affectionately watched his back as he stood in the bows looking to seaward. On the whole river there was nothing that looked half so nautical. He resembled a pilot, which to a seaman is trustworthiness personified. It was difficult to realise his work was not out there in the luminous estuary, but behind him, within the brooding gloom.

Between us there was, as I have already said somewhere, the bond of the sea. Besides holding our hearts together through long periods of separation, it had the effect of making us tolerant of each other's yarns—and even convictions. The Lawyer—the best of old fellows—had, because of his many years and many virtues, the only cushion on deck, and was lying on the only rug. The Accountant had brought out already a box of dominoes, and was toying architecturally with the bones. Marlow sat cross-legged right aft, leaning against the mizzen-mast. He had sunken cheeks, a yellow complexion, a straight back, an ascetic aspect, and, with his arms dropped, the palms of hands outwards, resembled an idol.

The director, satisfied the anchor had good hold, made his way aft and sat down amongst us. We exchanged a few words lazily. Afterwards there was silence on board the yacht. For some reason or other we did not begin that game of dominoes. We felt meditative, and fit for nothing but placid staring. The day was ending in a serenity of still and exquisite brilliance. The water shone pacifically; the sky, without a speck, was a benign immensity of unstained light; the very mist on the Essex marsh was like a gauzy and radiant fabric, hung from the wooded rises inland, and draping the low shores in diaphanous folds. Only the gloom to the west, brooding over the upper reaches, became more sombre every minute, as if angered by the approach of the sun.

And at last, in its curved and imperceptible fall, the sun sank low, and from glowing white changed to a dull red without rays and without heat, as if about to go out suddenly, stricken to death by the touch of that gloom brooding over a crowd of men.

Forthwith a change came over the waters, and the serenity became less brilliant but more profound. The old river in its broad reach rested unruffled at the decline of day, after ages of good service done to the race that peopled its banks, spread out in the tranquil dignity of a waterway leading to the uttermost ends of the earth. We looked at the venerable stream not in the vivid flush of a short day that comes and departs for ever, but in the august light of abiding memories. And indeed nothing is easier for a man who has, as the phrase goes, "followed the sea" with reverence and affection, that to evoke the great spirit of the past upon the lower reaches of the Thames. The tidal current runs to and fro in its unceasing service, crowded with memories of men and ships it had borne to the rest of home or to the battles of the sea. It had known and served all the men of whom the nation is proud, from Sir Francis Drake to Sir John Franklin, knights all, titled and untitled—the great knights-errant of the sea. It had borne all the ships whose names are like jewels flashing in the night of time, from the Golden Hind returning with her rotund flanks full of treasure, to be visited by the Queen's Highness and thus pass out of the gigantic tale, to the Erebus and Terror, bound on other conquests— and that never returned. It had known the ships and the men. They had sailed from Deptford, from Greenwich, from Erith— the adventurers and the settlers; kings' ships and the ships of men on 'Change; captains, admirals, the dark "interlopers" of the Eastern trade, and the commissioned "generals" of East India fleets. Hunters for gold or pursuers of fame, they all had gone out on that stream, bearing the sword, and often the torch, messengers of the might within the land, bearers of a spark from the sacred fire. What greatness had not floated on the ebb of that river into the mystery of an unknown earth!... The dreams of men, the seed of commonwealths, the germs of empires.

The sun set; the dusk fell on the stream, and lights began to appear along the shore. The Chapman light-house, a three-legged thing erect on a mud-flat, shone strongly. Lights of ships moved in the fairway—a great stir of lights going up and going down. And farther west on the upper reaches the place of the monstrous town was still marked ominously on the sky, a brooding gloom in sunshine, a lurid glare under the stars.

"And this also," said Marlow suddenly, "has been one of the dark places of the earth."

He was the only man of us who still "followed the sea." The worst that could be said of him was that he did not represent his class. He was a seaman, but he was a wanderer, too, while most seamen lead, if one may so express it, a sedentary life. Their minds are of the stay-at-home order, and their home is always with them—the ship; and so is their country—the sea. One ship is very much like another, and the sea is always the same. In the immutability of their surroundings the foreign shores, the foreign faces, the changing immensity of life, glide past, veiled not by a sense of mystery but by a slightly disdainful ignorance; for there is nothing mysterious to a seaman unless it be the sea itself, which is the mistress of his existence and as inscrutable as Destiny. For the rest, after his hours of work, a casual stroll or a casual spree on shore suffices to unfold for him the secret of a whole continent, and generally he finds the secret not worth knowing. The yarns of seamen have a direct simplicity, the whole meaning of which lies within the shell of a cracked nut. But Marlow was not typical (if his propensity to spin yarns be excepted), and to him the meaning of an episode was not inside like a kernel but outside, enveloping the tale which brought it out only as a glow brings out a haze, in the likeness of one of these misty halos that sometimes are made visible by the spectral illumination of moonshine.

His remark did not seem at all surprising. It was just like Marlow. It was accepted in silence. No one took the trouble to grunt even; and presently he said, very slow—"I was thinking of very old times, when the Romans first came here, nineteen hundred years ago—the other day.... Light came out of this river since—you say Knights? Yes; but it is like a running blaze on a plain, like a flash of lightning in the clouds. We live in the flicker—may it last as long as the old earth keeps rolling! But darkness was here yesterday. Imagine the feelings of a commander of a fine—what d'ye call 'em?—trireme in the Mediterranean, ordered suddenly to the north; run overland across the Gauls in a hurry; put in charge of one of these craft the legionaries—a wonderful lot of handy men they must have been, too—used to build, apparently by the hundred, in a month or two, if we may believe what we read. Imagine him here—the very end of the world, a sea the colour of lead, a sky the colour of smoke, a kind of ship about as rigid as a concertina— and going up this river with stores, or orders, or what you like. Sand-banks, marshes, forests, savages,—precious little to eat fit for a civilized man, nothing but Thames water to drink. No Falernian wine here, no going ashore. Here and there a military camp lost in a wilderness, like a needle in a bundle of hay—cold, fog, tempests, disease, exile, and death—death skulking in the air, in the water, in the bush. They must have been dying like flies here. Oh, yes—he did it. Did it very well, too, no doubt, and without thinking much about it either, except afterwards to brag of what he had gone through in his time, perhaps.

They were men enough to face the darkness. And perhaps he was cheered by keeping his eye on a chance of promotion to the fleet at Ravenna by and by, if he had good friends in Rome and survived the awful climate. Or think of a decent young citizen in a toga—perhaps too much dice, you know—coming out here in the train of some prefect, or tax-gatherer, or trader even, to mend his fortunes. Land in a swamp, march through the woods, and in some inland post feel the savagery, the utter savagery, had closed round him—all that mysterious life of the wilderness that stirs in the forest, in the jungles, in the hearts of wild men. There's no initiation either into such mysteries. He has to live in the midst of the incomprehensible, which is also detestable. And it has a fascination, too, that goes to work upon him. The fascination of the abomination—you know, imagine the growing regrets, the longing to escape, the powerless disgust, the surrender, the hate."

He paused.

"Mind," he began again, lifting one arm from the elbow, the palm of the hand outwards, so that, with his legs folded before him, he had the pose of a Buddha preaching in European clothes and without a lotus-flower—"Mind, none of us would feel exactly like this. What saves us is efficiency—the devotion to efficiency. But these chaps were not much account, really. They were no colonists; their administration was merely a squeeze, and nothing more, I suspect. They were conquerors, and for that you want only brute force— nothing to boast of, when you have it, since your strength is just an accident arising from the weakness of others. They grabbed what they could get for the sake of what was to be got. It was just robbery with violence, aggravated murder on a great scale, and men going at it blind—as is very proper for those who tackle a darkness. The conquest of the earth, which mostly means the taking it away from those who have a different complexion or slightly flatter noses than ourselves, is not a pretty thing when you look into it too much. What redeems it is the idea only. An idea at the back of it; not a sentimental pretence but an idea; and an unselfish belief in the idea—something you can set up, and bow down before, and offer a sacrifice to...."

He broke off. Flames glided in the river, small green flames, red flames, white flames, pursuing, overtaking, joining, crossing each other— then separating slowly or hastily. The traffic of the great city went on in the deepening night upon the sleepless river. We looked on, waiting patiently—there was nothing else to do till the end of the flood; but it was only after a long silence, when he said, in a hesitating voice, "I suppose you fellows remember I did once turn fresh-water sailor for a bit," that we knew we were fated, before the ebb began to run, to hear about one of Marlow's inconclusive experiences.

"I don't want to bother you much with what happened to me personally," he began, showing in this remark the weakness of many tellers of tales who seem so often unaware of what their audience would like best to hear; "yet to understand the effect of it on me you ought to know how I got out there, what I saw, how I went up that river to the place where I first met the poor chap. It was the farthest point of navigation and the culminating point of my experience. It seemed somehow to throw a kind of light on everything about me— and into my thoughts. It was sombre enough, too—and pitiful— not extraordinary in any way—not very clear either. No, not very clear. And yet it seemed to throw a kind of light.

"I had then, as you remember, just returned to London after a lot of Indian Ocean, Pacific, China Seas—a regular dose of the East—six years or so, and I was loafing about, hindering you fellows in your work and invading your homes, just as though I had got a heavenly mission to civilize you. It was very fine for a time, but after a bit I did get tired of resting. Then I began to look for a ship—I should think the hardest work on earth. But the ships wouldn't even look at me. And I got tired of that game, too.

"Now when I was a little chap I had a passion for maps. I would look for hours at South America, or Africa, or Australia, and lose myself in all the glories of exploration. At that time there were many blank spaces on the earth, and when I saw one that looked particularly inviting on a map (but they all look that) I would put my finger on it and say, 'When I grow up I will go there.' The North Pole was one of these places, I remember. Well, I haven't been there yet, and shall not try now. The glamour's off. Other places were scattered about the hemispheres. I have been in some of them, and... well, we won't talk about that. But there was one yet—the biggest, the most blank, so to speak— that I had a hankering after.

"True, by this time it was not a blank space any more. It had got filled since my boyhood with rivers and lakes and names. It had ceased to be a blank space of delightful mystery— a white patch for a boy to dream gloriously over. It had become a place of darkness. But there was in it one river especially, a mighty big river, that you could see on the map, resembling an immense snake uncoiled, with its head in the sea, its body at rest curving afar over a vast country, and its tail lost in the depths of the land. And as I looked at the map of it in a shop-window, it fascinated me as a snake would a bird—a silly little bird. Then I remembered there was a big concern, a Company for trade on that river. Dash it all! I thought to myself, they can't trade without using some kind of craft on that lot of fresh water—steamboats! Why shouldn't I try to get charge of one? I went on along Fleet Street, but could not shake off the idea. The snake had charmed me.

"You understand it was a Continental concern, that Trading society; but I have a lot of relations living on the Continent, because it's cheap and not so nasty as it looks, they say.

"I am sorry to own I began to worry them. This was already a fresh departure for me. I was not used to get things that way, you know. I always went my own road and on my own legs where I had a mind to go. I wouldn't have believed it of myself; but, then—you see—I felt somehow I must get there by hook or by crook. So I worried them. The men said 'My dear fellow,' and did nothing. Then—would you believe it?—I tried the women. I, Charlie Marlow, set the women to work— to get a job. Heavens! Well, you see, the notion drove me. I had an aunt, a dear enthusiastic soul. She wrote: 'It will be delightful. I am ready to do anything, anything for you. It is a glorious idea. I know the wife of a very high personage in the Administration, and also a man who has lots of influence with,' etc. She was determined to make no end of fuss to get me appointed skipper of a river steamboat, if such was my fancy.

"I got my appointment—of course; and I got it very quick. It appears the Company had received news that one of their captains had been killed in a scuffle with the natives. This was my chance, and it made me the more anxious to go. It was only months and months afterwards, when I made the attempt to recover what was left of the body, that I heard the original quarrel arose from a misunderstanding about some hens. Yes, two black hens. Fresleven—that was the fellow's name, a Dane—thought himself wronged somehow in the bargain, so he went ashore and started to hammer the chief of the village with a stick. Oh, it didn't surprise me in the least to hear this, and at the same time to be told that Fresleven was the gentlest, quietest creature that ever walked on two legs. No doubt he was; but he had been a couple of years already out there engaged in the noble cause, you know, and he probably felt the need at last of asserting his self-respect in some way. Therefore he whacked the old nigger mercilessly, while a big crowd of his people watched him, thunderstruck, till some man— I was told the chief's son—in desperation at hearing the old chap yell, made a tentative jab with a spear at the white man— and of course it went quite easy between the shoulder-blades. Then the whole population cleared into the forest, expecting all kinds of calamities to happen, while, on the other hand, the steamer Fresleven commanded left also in a bad panic, in charge of the engineer, I believe. Afterwards nobody seemed to trouble much about Fresleven's remains, till I got out and stepped into his shoes. I couldn't let it rest, though; but when an opportunity offered at last to meet my predecessor, the grass growing through his ribs was tall enough to hide his bones. They were all there. The supernatural being had not been touched after he fell. And the village was deserted, the huts gaped black, rotting, all askew within the fallen enclosures. A calamity had come to it, sure enough. The people had vanished. Mad terror had scattered them, men, women, and children, through the bush, and they had never returned. What became of the hens I don't know either. I should think the cause of progress got them, anyhow. However, through this glorious affair I got my appointment, before I had fairly begun to hope for it.

"I flew around like mad to get ready, and before forty-eight hours I was crossing the Channel to show myself to my employers, and sign the contract. In a very few hours I arrived in a city that always makes me think of a whited sepulchre. Prejudice no doubt. I had no difficulty in finding the Company's offices. It was the biggest thing in the town, and everybody I met was full of it. They were going to run an over-sea empire, and make no end of coin by trade.

"A narrow and deserted street in deep shadow, high houses, innumerable windows with venetian blinds, a dead silence, grass sprouting right and left, immense double doors standing ponderously ajar. I slipped through one of these cracks, went up a swept and ungarnished staircase, as arid as a desert, and opened the first door I came to. Two women, one fat and the other slim, sat on straw-bottomed chairs, knitting black wool. The slim one got up and walked straight at me— still knitting with downcast eyes—and only just as I began to think of getting out of her way, as you would for a somnambulist, stood still, and looked up. Her dress was as plain as an umbrella-cover, and she turned round without a word and preceded me into a waiting-room. I gave my name, and looked about. Deal table in the middle, plain chairs all round the walls, on one end a large shining map, marked with all the colours of a rainbow. There was a vast amount of red—good to see at any time, because one knows that some real work is done in there, a deuce of a lot of blue, a little green, smears of orange, and, on the East Coast, a purple patch, to show where the jolly pioneers of progress drink the jolly lager-beer. However, I wasn't going into any of these. I was going into the yellow. Dead in the centre. And the river was there—fascinating—deadly—like a snake. Ough! A door opened, ya white-haired secretarial head, but wearing a compassionate expression, appeared, and a skinny forefinger beckoned me into the sanctuary. Its light was dim, and a heavy writing-desk squatted in the middle. From behind that structure came out an impression of pale plumpness in a frock-coat. The great man himself. He was five feet six, I should judge, and had his grip on the handle-end of ever so many millions. He shook hands, I fancy, murmured vaguely, was satisfied with my French. Bon Voyage.

"In about forty-five seconds I found myself again in the waiting-room with the compassionate secretary, who, full of desolation and sympathy, made me sign some document. I believe I undertook amongst other things not to disclose any trade secrets. Well, I am not going to.

"I began to feel slightly uneasy. You know I am not used to such ceremonies, and there was something ominous in the atmosphere. It was just as though I had been let into some conspiracy— I don't know—something not quite right; and I was glad to get out. In the outer room the two women knitted black wool feverishly. People were arriving, and the younger one was walking back and forth introducing them. The old one sat on her chair. Her flat cloth slippers were propped up on a foot-warmer, and a cat reposed on her lap. She wore a starched white affair on her head, had a wart on one cheek, and silver-rimmed spectacles hung on the tip of her nose. She glanced at me above the glasses. The swift and indifferent placidity of that look troubled me. Two youths with foolish and cheery countenances were being piloted over, and she threw at them the same quick glance of unconcerned wisdom. She seemed to know all about them and about me, too. An eerie feeling came over me. She seemed uncanny and fateful. Often far away there I thought of these two, guarding the door of Darkness, knitting black wool as for a warm pall, one introducing, introducing continuously to the unknown, the other scrutinizing the cheery and foolish faces with unconcerned old eyes. Ave! Old knitter of black wool. Morituri te salutant. Not many of those she looked at ever saw her again—not half, by a long way.

"There was yet a visit to the doctor. `A simple formality,' assured me the secretary, with an air of taking an immense part in all my sorrows. Accordingly a young chap wearing his hat over the left eyebrow, some clerk I suppose—there must have been clerks in the business, though the house was as still as a house in a city of the dead— came from somewhere upstairs, and led me forth. He was shabby and careless, with inkstains on the sleeves of his jacket, and his cravat was large and billowy, under a chin shaped like the toe of an old boot. It was a little too early for the doctor, so I proposed a drink, and thereupon he developed a vein of joviality. As we sat over our vermouths he glorified the Company's business, and by and by I expressed casually my surprise at him not going out there. He became very cool and collected all at once. `I am not such a fool as I look, quoth Plato to his disciples,' he said sententiously, emptied his glass with great resolution, and we rose.

"The old doctor felt my pulse, evidently thinking of something else the while. `Good, good for there,' he mumbled, and then with a certain eagerness asked me whether I would let him measure my head. Rather surprised, I said Yes, when he produced a thing like calipers and got the dimensions back and front and every way, taking notes carefully. He was an unshaven little man in a threadbare coat like a gaberdine, with his feet in slippers, and I thought him a harmless fool. `I always ask leave, in the interests of science, to measure the crania of those going out there,' he said. `And when they come back, too?' I asked. `Oh, I never see them,' he remarked; `and, moreover, the changes take place inside, you know.' He smiled, as if at some quiet joke. 'So you are going out there. Famous. Interesting, too.' He gave me a searching glance, and made another note. 'Ever any madness in your family?' he asked, in a matter-of-fact tone. I felt very annoyed. 'Is that question in the interests of science, too?' 'It would be,' he said, without taking notice of my irritation, 'interesting for science to watch the mental changes of individuals, on the spot, but...' 'Are you an alienist?' I interrupted. 'Every doctor should be—a little,' answered that original, imperturbably. 'I have a little theory which you messieurs who go out there must help me to prove. This is my share in the advantages my country shall reap from the possession of such a magnificent dependency. The mere wealth I leave to others. Pardon my questions, but you are the first Englishman coming under my observation...' I hastened to assure him I was not in the least typical. 'If I were,' said I, 'I wouldn't be talking like this with you.' 'What you say is rather profound, and probably erroneous,' he said, with a laugh. 'Avoid irritation more than exposure to the sun. Adieu. How do you English say, eh? Good-bye. Ah! Good-bye. Adieu. In the tropics one must before everything keep calm.'... He lifted a warning forefinger.... 'Du calme, du calme. Adieu.'

"One thing more remained to do—say good-bye to my excellent aunt. I found her triumphant. I had a cup of tea—the last decent cup of tea for many days—and in a room that most soothingly looked just as you would expect a lady's drawing-room to look, we had a long quiet chat by the fireside. In the course of these confidences it became quite plain to me I had been represented to the wife of the high dignitary, and goodness knows to how many more people besides, as an exceptional and gifted creature— a piece of good fortune for the Company—a man you don't get hold of every day. Good heavens! and I was going to take charge of a two-penny-half-penny river-steamboat with a penny whistle attached! It appeared, however, I was also one of the Workers, with a capital— you know. Something like an emissary of light, something like a lower sort of apostle. There had been a lot of such rot let loose in print and talk just about that time, and the excellent woman, living right in the rush of all that humbug, got carried off her feet. She talked about 'weaning those ignorant millions from their horrid ways,' till, upon my word, she made me quite uncomfortable. I ventured to hint that the Company was run for profit.

"'You forget, dear Charlie, that the labourer is worthy of his hire,' she said, brightly. It's queer how out of touch with truth women are. They live in a world of their own, and there has never been anything like it, and never can be. It is too beautiful altogether, and if they were to set it up it would go to pieces before the first sunset. Some confounded fact we men have been living contentedly with ever since the day of creation would start up and knock the whole thing over.

"After this I got embraced, told to wear flannel, be sure to write often, and so on—and I left. In the street—I don't know why—a queer feeling came to me that I was an imposter. Odd thing that I, who used to clear out for any part of the world at twenty-four hours' notice, with less thought than most men give to the crossing of a street, had a moment—I won't say of hesitation, but of startled pause, before this commonplace affair. The best way I can explain it to you is by saying that, for a second or two, I felt as though, instead of going to the centre of a continent, I were about to set off for the centre of the earth.

"I left in a French steamer, and she called in every blamed port they have out there, for, as far as I could see, the sole purpose of landing soldiers and custom-house officers. I watched the coast. Watching a coast as it slips by the ship is like thinking about an enigma. There it is before you— smiling, frowning, inviting, grand, mean, insipid, or savage, and always mute with an air of whispering, 'Come and find out.' This one was almost featureless, as if still in the making, with an aspect of monotonous grimness. The edge of a colossal jungle, so dark-green as to be almost black, fringed with white surf, ran straight, like a ruled line, far, far away along a blue sea whose glitter was blurred by a creeping mist.

The sun was fierce, the land seemed to glisten and drip with steam. Here and there greyish-whitish specks showed up clustered inside the white surf, with a flag flying above them perhaps. Settlements some centuries old, and still no bigger than pinheads on the untouched expanse of their background. We pounded along, stopped, landed soldiers; went on, landed custom-house clerks to levy toll in what looked like a God-forsaken wilderness, with a tin shed and a flag-pole lost in it; landed more soldiers—to take care of the custom-house clerks, presumably.

Some, I heard, got drowned in the surf; but whether they did or not, nobody seemed particularly to care. They were just flung out there, and on we went. Every day the coast looked the same, as though we had not moved; but we passed various places—trading places—with names like Gran' Bassam, Little Popo; names that seemed to belong to some sordid farce acted in front of a sinister back-cloth. The idleness of a passenger, my isolation amongst all these men with whom I had no point of contact, the oily and languid sea, the uniform sombreness of the coast, seemed to keep me away from the truth of things, within the toil of a mournful and senseless delusion. The voice of the surf heard now and then was a positive pleasure, like the speech of a brother. It was something natural, that had its reason, that had a meaning.

Now and then a boat from the shore gave one a momentary contact with reality. It was paddled by black fellows. You could see from afar the white of their eyeballs glistening. They shouted, sang; their bodies streamed with perspiration; they had faces like grotesque masks—these chaps; but they had bone, muscle, a wild vitality, an intense energy of movement, that was as natural and true as the surf along their coast. They wanted no excuse for being there. They were a great comfort to look at. For a time I would feel I belonged still to a world of straightforward facts; but the feeling would not last long. Something would turn up to scare it away. Once, I remember, we came upon a man-of-war anchored off the coast. There wasn't even a shed there, and she was shelling the bush. It appears the French had one of their wars going on thereabouts. Her ensign dropped limp like a rag; the muzzles of the long six-inch guns stuck out all over the low hull; the greasy, slimy swell swung her up lazily and let her down, swaying her thin masts. In the empty immensity of earth, sky, and water, there she was, incomprehensible, firing into a continent. Pop, would go one of the six-inch guns; a small flame would dart and vanish, a little white smoke would disappear, a tiny projectile would give a feeble screech—and nothing happened. Nothing could happen. There was a touch of insanity in the proceeding, a sense of lugubrious drollery in the sight; and it was not dissipated by somebody on board assuring me earnestly there was a camp of natives—he called them enemies!— hidden out of sight somewhere.

"We gave her her letters (I heard the men in that lonely ship were dying of fever at the rate of three a day) and went on. We called at some more places with farcical names, where the merry dance of death and trade goes on in a still and earthy atmosphere as of an overheated catacomb; all along the formless coast bordered by dangerous surf, as if Nature herself had tried to ward off intruders; in and out of rivers, streams of death in life, whose banks were rotting into mud, whose waters, thickened into slime, invaded the contorted mangroves, that seemed to writhe at us in the extremity of an impotent despair. Nowhere did we stop long enough to get a particularized impression, but the general sense of vague and oppressive wonder grew upon me. It was like a weary pilgrimage amongst hints for nightmares.

"It was upward of thirty days before I saw the mouth of the big river. We anchored off the seat of the government. But my work would not begin till some two hundred miles farther on. So as soon as I could I made a start for a place thirty miles higher up.

"I had my passage on a little sea-going steamer. Her captain was a Swede, and knowing me for a seaman, invited me on the bridge. He was a young man, lean, fair, and morose, with lanky hair and a shuffling gait. As we left the miserable little wharf, he tossed his head contemptuously at the shore. 'Been living there?' he asked. I said, 'Yes.' 'Fine lot these government chaps—are they not?' he went on, speaking English with great precision and considerable bitterness. 'It is funny what some people will do for a few francs a month. I wonder what becomes of that kind when it goes upcountry?' I said to him I expected to see that soon. 'So-o-o!' he exclaimed. He shuffled athwart, keeping one eye ahead vigilantly. 'Don't be too sure,' he continued. 'The other day I took up a man who hanged himself on the road. He was a Swede, too.' 'Hanged himself! Why, in God's name?' I cried. He kept on looking out watchfully. 'Who knows? The sun too much for him, or the country perhaps.'

"At last we opened a reach. A rocky cliff appeared, mounds of turned-up earth by the shore, houses on a hill, others with iron roofs, amongst a waste of excavations, or hanging to the declivity. A continuous noise of the rapids above hovered over this scene of inhabited devastation. A lot of people, mostly black and naked, moved about like ants. A jetty projected into the river. A blinding sunlight drowned all this at times in a sudden recrudescence of glare. 'There's your Company's station,' said the Swede, pointing to three wooden barrack-like structures on the rocky slope. 'I will send your things up. Four boxes did you say? So. Farewell.'

"I came upon a boiler wallowing in the grass, then found a path leading up the hill. It turned aside for the boulders, and also for an undersized railway-truck lying there on its back with its wheels in the air. One was off. The thing looked as dead as the carcass of some animal. I came upon more pieces of decaying machinery, a stack of rusty rails. To the left a clump of trees made a shady spot, where dark things seemed to stir feebly. I blinked, the path was steep. A horn tooted to the right, and I saw the black people run. A heavy and dull detonation shook the ground, a puff of smoke came out of the cliff, and that was all. No change appeared on the face of the rock. They were building a railway. The cliff was not in the way or anything; but this objectless blasting was all the work going on.

"A slight clinking behind me made me turn my head. Six black men advanced in a file, toiling up the path. They walked erect and slow, balancing small baskets full of earth on their heads, and the clink kept time with their footsteps. Black rags were wound round their loins, and the short ends behind waggled to and fro like tails. I could see every rib, the joints of their limbs were like knots in a rope; each had an iron collar on his neck, and all were connected together with a chain whose bights swung between them, rhythmically clinking. Another report from the cliff made me think suddenly of that ship of war I had seen firing into a continent. It was the same kind of ominous voice; but these men could by no stretch of imagination be called enemies. They were called criminals, and the outraged law, like the bursting shells, had come to them, an insoluble mystery from the sea. All their meagre breasts panted together, the violently dilated nostrils quivered, the eyes stared stonily uphill. They passed me within six inches, without a glance, with that complete, deathlike indifference of unhappy savages. Behind this raw matter one of the reclaimed, the product of the new forces at work, strolled despondently, carrying a rifle by its middle. He had a uniform jacket with one button off, and seeing a white man on the path, hoisted his weapon to his shoulder with alacrity. This was simple prudence, white men being so much alike at a distance that he could not tell who I might be. He was speedily reassured, and with a large, white, rascally grin, and a glance at his charge, seemed to take me into partnership in his exalted trust. After all, I also was a part of the great cause of these high and just proceedings.

"Instead of going up, I turned and descended to the left. My idea was to let that chain-gang get out of sight before I climbed the hill. You know I am not particularly tender; I've had to strike and to fend off. I've had to resist and to attack sometimes—that's only one way of resisting— without counting the exact cost, according to the demands of such sort of life as I had blundered into. I've seen the devil of violence, and the devil of greed, and the devil of hot desire; but, by all the stars! these were strong, lusty, red-eyed devils, that swayed and drove men—men, I tell you. But as I stood on this hillside, I foresaw that in the blinding sunshine of that land I would become acquainted with a flabby, pretending, weak-eyed devil of a rapacious and pitiless folly. How insidious he could be, too, I was only to find out several months later and a thousand miles farther. For a moment I stood appalled, as though by a warning. Finally I descended the hill, obliquely, towards the trees I had seen.

"I avoided a vast artificial hole somebody had been digging on the slope, the purpose of which I found it impossible to divine. It wasn't a quarry or a sandpit, anyhow. It was just a hole. It might have been connected with the philanthropic desire of giving the criminals something to do. I don't know. Then I nearly fell into a very narrow ravine, almost no more than a scar in the hillside. I discovered that a lot of imported drainage-pipes for the settlement had been tumbled in there. There wasn't one that was not broken. It was a wanton smash-up. At last I got under the trees. My purpose was to stroll into the shade for a moment; but no sooner within than it seemed to me I had stepped into the gloomy circle of some Inferno. The rapids were near, and an uninterrupted, uniform, headlong, rushing noise filled the mournful stillness of the grove, where not a breath stirred, not a leaf moved, with a mysterious sound—as though the tearing pace of the launched earth had suddenly become audible.

"Black shapes crouched, lay, sat between the trees leaning against the trunks, clinging to the earth, half coming out, half effaced within the dim light, in all the attitudes of pain, abandonment, and despair. Another mine on the cliff went off, followed by a slight shudder of the soil under my feet. The work was going on. The work! And this was the place where some of the helpers had withdrawn to die.

"They were dying slowly—it was very clear. They were not enemies, they were not criminals, they were nothing earthly now— nothing but black shadows of disease and starvation, lying confusedly in the greenish gloom. Brought from all the recesses of the coast in all the legality of time contracts, lost in uncongenial surroundings, fed on unfamiliar food, they sickened, became inefficient, and were then allowed to crawl away and rest. These moribund shapes were free as air—and nearly as thin. I began to distinguish the gleam of the eyes under the trees.

Then, glancing down, I saw a face near my hand. The black bones reclined at full length with one shoulder against the tree, and slowly the eyelids rose and the sunken eyes looked up at me, enormous and vacant, a kind of blind, white flicker in the depths of the orbs, which died out slowly. The man seemed young— almost a boy—but you know with them it's hard to tell. I found nothing else to do but to offer him one of my good Swede's ship's biscuits I had in my pocket. The fingers closed slowly on it and held—there was no other movement and no other glance. He had tied a bit of white worsted round his neck—Why? Where did he get it? Was it a badge—an ornament—a charm— a propitiatory act? Was there any idea at all connected with it? It looked startling round his black neck, this bit of white thread from beyond the seas.

"Near the same tree two more bundles of acute angles sat with their legs drawn up. One, with his chin propped on his knees, stared at nothing, in an intolerable and appalling manner: his brother phantom rested its forehead, as if overcome with a great weariness; and all about others were scattered in every pose of contorted collapse, as in some picture of a massacre or a pestilence. While I stood horror-struck, one of these creatures rose to his hands and knees, and went off on all-fours towards the river to drink. He lapped out of his hand, then sat up in the sunlight, crossing his shins in front of him, and after a time let his woolly head fall on his breastbone.

"I didn't want any more loitering in the shade, and I made haste towards the station. When near the buildings I met a white man, in such an unexpected elegance of get-up that in the first moment I took him for a sort of vision. I saw a high starched collar, white cuffs, a light alpaca jacket, snowy trousers, a clean necktie, and varnished boots. No hat. Hair parted, brushed, oiled, under a green-lined parasol held in a big white hand. He was amazing, and had a penholder behind his ear.

"I shook hands with this miracle, and I learned he was the Company's chief accountant, and that all the book-keeping was done at this station. He had come out for a moment, he said, 'to get a breath of fresh air. The expression sounded wonderfully odd, with its suggestion of sedentary desk-life. I wouldn't have mentioned the fellow to you at all, only it was from his lips that I first heard the name of the man who is so indissolubly connected with the memories of that time. Moreover, I respected the fellow. Yes; I respected his collars, his vast cuffs, his brushed hair. His appearance was certainly that of a hairdresser's dummy; but in the great demoralization of the land he kept up his appearance. That's backbone. His starched collars and got-up shirt-fronts were achievements of character. He had been out nearly three years; and, later, I could not help asking him how he managed to sport such linen. He had just the faintest blush, and said modestly, 'I've been teaching one of the native women about the station. It was difficult. She had a distaste for the work.' Thus this man had verily accomplished something. And he was devoted to his books, which were in apple-pie order.

"Everything else in the station was in a muddle—heads, things, buildings. Strings of dusty niggers with splay feet arrived and departed; a stream of manufactured goods, rubbishy cottons, beads, and brass-wire set into the depths of darkness, and in return came a precious trickle of ivory.

"I had to wait in the station for ten days—an eternity. I lived in a hut in the yard, but to be out of the chaos I would sometimes get into the accountant's office. It was built of horizontal planks, and so badly put together that, as he bent over his high desk, he was barred from neck to heels with narrow strips of sunlight. There was no need to open the big shutter to see. It was hot there, too; big flies buzzed fiendishly, and did not sting, but stabbed. I sat generally on the floor, while, of faultless appearance (and even slightly scented), perching on a high stool, he wrote, he wrote. Sometimes he stood up for exercise. When a truckle-bed with a sick man (some invalid agent from upcountry) was put in there, he exhibited a gentle annoyance. `The groans of this sick person,' he said, `distract my attention. And without that it is extremely difficult to guard against clerical errors in this climate.'

"One day he remarked, without lifting his head, `In the interior you will no doubt meet Mr. Kurtz.' On my asking who Mr. Kurtz was, he said he was a first-class agent; and seeing my disappointment at this information, he added slowly, laying down his pen, `He is a very remarkable person.' Further questions elicited from him that Mr. Kurtz was at present in charge of a trading-post, a very important one, in the true ivory-country, at `the very bottom of there. Sends in as much ivory as all the others put together...' He began to write again. The sick man was too ill to groan. The flies buzzed in a great peace.

"Suddenly there was a growing murmur of voices and a great tramping of feet. A caravan had come in. A violent babble of uncouth sounds burst out on the other side of the planks. All the carriers were speaking together, and in the midst of the uproar the lamentable voice of the chief agent was heard `giving it up' tearfully for the twentieth time that day.... He rose slowly. `What a frightful row,' he said. He crossed the room gently to look at the sick man, and returning, said to me, `He does not hear.' `What! Dead?' I asked, startled. `No, not yet,' he answered, with great composure. Then, alluding with a toss of the head to the tumult in the station-yard, `When one has got to make correct entries, one comes to hate those savages—hate them to the death.'

He remained thoughtful for a moment. `When you see Mr. Kurtz' he went on, `tell him from me that everything here'— he glanced at the deck—' is very satisfactory. I don't like to write to him—with those messengers of ours you never know who may get hold of your letter—at that Central Station.' He stared at me for a moment with his mild, bulging eyes.

'Oh, he will go far, very far,' he began again. 'He will be a somebody in the Administration before long. They, above—the Council in Europe, you know—mean him to be.'

"He turned to his work. The noise outside had ceased, and presently in going out I stopped at the door. In the steady buzz of flies the homeward-bound agent was lying finished and insensible; the other, bent over his books, was making correct entries of perfectly correct transactions; and fifty feet below the doorstep I could see the still tree-tops of the grove of death.

"Next day I left that station at last, with a caravan of sixty men, for a two-hundred-mile tramp.

"No use telling you much about that. Paths, paths, everywhere; a stamped-in network of paths spreading over the empty land, through the long grass, through burnt grass, through thickets, down and up chilly ravines, up and down stony hills ablaze with heat; and a solitude, a solitude, nobody, not a hut. The population had cleared out a long time ago. Well, if a lot of mysterious niggers armed with all kinds of fearful weapons suddenly took to travelling on the road between Deal and Gravesend, catching the yokels right and left to carry heavy loads for them, I fancy every farm and cottage thereabouts would get empty very soon. Only here the dwellings were gone, too. Still I passed through several abandoned villages. There's something pathetically childish in the ruins of grass walls. Day after day, with the stamp and shuffle of sixty pair of bare feet behind me, each pair under a 60-lb. load. Camp, cook, sleep, strike camp, march. Now and then a carrier dead in harness, at rest in the long grass near the path, with an empty water-gourd and his long staff lying by his side. A great silence around and above. Perhaps on some quiet night the tremor of far-off drums, sinking, swelling, a tremor vast, faint; a sound weird, appealing, suggestive, and wild—and perhaps with as profound a meaning as the sound of bells in a Christian country. Once a white man in an unbuttoned uniform, camping on the path with an armed escort of lank Zanzibaris, very hospitable and festive— not to say drunk. Was looking after the upkeep of the road, he declared. Can't say I saw any road or any upkeep, unless the body of a middle-aged negro, with a bullet-hole in the forehead, upon which I absolutely stumbled three miles farther on, may be considered as a permanent improvement. I had a white companion, too, not a bad chap, but rather too fleshy and with the exasperating habit of fainting on the hot hillsides, miles away from the least bit of shade and water. Annoying, you know, to hold your own coat like a parasol over a man's head while he is coming to.

I couldn't help asking him once what he meant by coming there at all. 'To make money, of course. What do you think?' he said, scornfully. Then he got fever, and had to be carried in a hammock slung under a pole. As he weighed sixteen stone I had no end of rows with the carriers. They jibbed, ran away, sneaked off with their loads in the night—quite a mutiny. So, one evening, I made a speech in English with gestures, not one of which was lost to the sixty pairs of eyes before me, and the next morning I started the hammock off in front all right. An hour afterwards I came upon the whole concern wrecked in a bush—man, hammock, groans, blankets, horrors. The heavy pole had skinned his poor nose. He was very anxious for me to kill somebody, but there wasn't the shadow of a carrier near. I remembered the old doctor—'It would be interesting for science to watch the mental changes of individuals, on the spot.'

I felt I was becoming scientifically interesting. However, all that is to no purpose. On the fifteenth day I came in sight of the big river again, and hobbled into the Central Station. It was on a back water surrounded by scrub and forest, with a pretty border of smelly mud on one side, and on the three others enclosed by a crazy fence of rushes. A neglected gap was all the gate it had, and the first glance at the place was enough to let you see the flabby devil was running that show. White men with long staves in their hands appeared languidly from amongst the buildings, strolling up to take a look at me, and then retired out of sight somewhere. One of them, a stout, excitable chap with black moustaches, informed me with great volubility and many digressions, as soon as I told him who I was, that my steamer was at the bottom of the river. I was thunderstruck. What, how, why? Oh, it was `all right.' The `manager himself' was there. All quite correct. `Everybody had behaved splendidly! splendidly!'—'you must,' he said in agitation, `go and see the general manager at once. He is waiting!'

"I did not see the real significance of that wreck at once. I fancy I see it now, but I am not sure—not at all. Certainly the affair was too stupid—when I think of it— to be altogether natural. Still... But at the moment it presented itself simply as a confounded nuisance. The steamer was sunk. They had started two days before in a sudden hurry up the river with the manager on board, in charge of some volunteer skipper, and before they had been out three hours they tore the bottom out of her on stones, and she sank near the south bank. I asked myself what I was to do there, now my boat was lost. As a matter of fact, I had plenty to do in fishing my command out of the river. I had to set about it the very next day. That, and the repairs when I brought the pieces to the station, took some months.

"My first interview with the manager was curious. He did not ask me to sit down after my twenty-mile walk that morning. He was commonplace in complexion, in features, in manners, and in voice. He was of middle size and of ordinary build. His eyes, of the usual blue, were perhaps remarkably cold, and he certainly could make his glance fall on one as trenchant and heavy as an axe. But even at these times the rest of his person seemed to disclaim the intention. Otherwise there was only an indefinable, faint expression of his lips, something stealthy— a smile—not a smile—I remember it, but I can't explain. It was unconscious, this smile was, though just after he had said something it got intensified for an instant. It came at the end of his speeches like a seal applied on the words to make the meaning of the commonest phrase appear absolutely inscrutable. He was a common trader, from his youth up employed in these parts—nothing more. He was obeyed, yet he inspired neither love nor fear, nor even respect. He inspired uneasiness. That was it! Uneasiness. Not a definite mistrust—just uneasiness—nothing more. You have no idea how effective such a... a.... faculty can be. He had no genius for organizing, for initiative, or for order even. That was evident in such things as the deplorable state of the station. He had no learning, and no intelligence. His position had come to him—why? Perhaps because he was never ill... He had served three terms of three years out there... Because triumphant health in the general rout of constitutions is a kind of power in itself. When he went home on leave he rioted on a large scale—pompously. Jack ashore—with a difference— in externals only.

This one could gather from his casual talk. He originated nothing, he could keep the routine going—that's all. But he was great. He was great by this little thing that it was impossible to tell what could control such a man. He never gave that secret away. Perhaps there was nothing within him. Such a suspicion made one pause—for out there there were no external checks. Once when various tropical diseases had laid low almost every `agent' in the station, he was heard to say, `Men who come out here should have no entrails.' He sealed the utterance with that smile of his, as though it had been a door opening into a darkness he had in his keeping. You fancied you had seen things—but the seal was on. When annoyed at meal-times by the constant quarrels of the white men about precedence, he ordered an immense round table to be made, for which a special house had to be built. This was the station's mess-room. Where he sat was the first place—the rest were nowhere. One felt this to be his unalterable conviction. He was neither civil nor uncivil. He was quiet. He allowed his `boy'—an overfed young negro from the coast—to treat the white men, under his very eyes, with provoking insolence.

"He began to speak as soon as he saw me. I had been very long on the road. He could not wait. Had to start without me. The up-river stations had to be relieved. There had been so many delays already that he did not know who was dead and who was alive, and how they got on—and so on, and so on. He paid no attention to my explanations, and, playing with a stick of sealing-wax, repeated several times that the situation was 'very grave, very grave.' There were rumours that a very important station was in jeopardy, and its chief, Mr. Kurtz, was ill. Hoped it was not true. Mr. Kurtz was... I felt weary and irritable. Hang Kurtz, I thought. I interrupted him by saying I had heard of Mr. Kurtz on the coast. 'Ah! So they talk of him down there,' he murmured to himself. Then he began again, assuring me Mr. Kurtz was the best agent he had, an exceptional man, of the greatest importance to the Company; therefore I could understand his anxiety. He was, he said, 'very, very uneasy.'

Certainly he fidgeted on his chair a good deal, exclaimed, 'Ah, Mr. Kurtz!' broke the stick of sealing-wax and seemed dumfounded by the accident. Next thing he wanted to know 'how long it would take to'... I interrupted him again. Being hungry, you know, and kept on my feet too. I was getting savage. 'How can I tell?' I said. 'I haven't even seen the wreck yet— some months, no doubt.' All this talk seemed to me so futile. 'Some months,' he said. 'Well, let us say three months before we can make a start. Yes. That ought to do the affair.' I flung out of his hut (he lived all alone in a clay hut with a sort of verandah) muttering to myself my opinion of him. He was a chattering idiot. Afterwards I took it back when it was borne in upon me startlingly with what extreme nicety he had estimated the time requisite for the 'affair.'

"I went to work the next day, turning, so to speak, my back on that station. In that way only it seemed to me I could keep my hold on the redeeming facts of life. Still, one must look about sometimes; and then I saw this station, these men strolling aimlessly about in the sunshine of the yard. I asked myself sometimes what it all meant. They wandered here and there with their absurd long staves in their hands, like a lot of faithless pilgrims bewitched inside a rotten fence. The word 'ivory' rang in the air, was whispered, was sighed. You would think they were praying to it. A taint of imbecile rapacity blew through it all, like a whiff from some corpse. By Jove! I've never seen anything so unreal in my life. And outside, the silent wilderness surrounding this cleared speck on the earth struck me as something great and invincible, like evil or truth, waiting patiently for the passing away of this fantastic invasion.

"Oh, these months! Well, never mind. Various things yhappened. One evening a grass shed full of calico, cotton prints, beads, and I don't know what else, burst into a blaze so suddenly that you would have thought the earth had opened to let an avenging fire consume all that trash. I was smoking my pipe quietly by my dismantled steamer, and saw them all cutting capers in the light, with their arms lifted high, when the stout man with moustaches came tearing down to the river, a tin pail in his hand, assured me that everybody was `behaving splendidly, splendidly,' dipped about a quart of water and tore back again. I noticed there was a hole in the bottom of his pail.

"I strolled up. There was no hurry. You see the thing had gone off like a box of matches. It had been hopeless from the very first. The flame had leaped high, driven everybody back, lighted up everything— and collapsed. The shed was already a heap of embers glowing fiercely. A nigger was being beaten near by. They said he had caused the fire in some way; be that as it may, he was screeching most horribly. I saw him, later, for several days, sitting in a bit of shade looking very sick and trying to recover himself; afterwards he arose and went out— and the wilderness without a sound took him into its bosom again. As I approached the glow from the dark I found myself at the back of two men, talking. I heard the name of Kurtz pronounced, then the words, `take advantage of this unfortunate accident.' One of the men was the manager. I wished him a good evening.

`Did you ever see anything like it— eh? it is incredible,' he said, and walked off. The other man remained. He was a first-class agent, young, gentlemanly, a bit reserved, with a forked little beard and a hooked nose. He was stand-offish with the other agents, and they on their side said he was the manager's spy upon them. As to me, I had hardly ever spoken to him before. We got into talk, and by and by we strolled away from the hissing ruins. Then he asked me to his room, which was in the main building of the station. He struck a match, and I perceived that this young aristocrat had not only a silver-mounted dressing-case but also a whole candle all to himself. Just at that time the manager was the only man supposed to have any right to candles. Native mats covered the clay walls; a collection of spears, assegais, shields, knives was hung up in trophies.

The business intrusted to this fellow was the making of bricks— so I had been informed; but there wasn't a fragment of a brick anywhere in the station, and he had been there more than a year—waiting. It seems he could not make bricks without something, I don't know what—straw maybe. Anyway, it could not be found there and as it was not likely to be sent from Europe, it did not appear clear to me what he was waiting for. An act of special creation perhaps. However, they were all waiting— all the sixteen or twenty pilgrims of them—for something; and upon my word it did not seem an uncongenial occupation, from the way they took it, though the only thing that ever came to them was disease— as far as I could see. They beguiled the time by back-biting and intriguing against each other in a foolish kind of way. There was an air of plotting about that station, but nothing came of it, of course.

It was as unreal as everything else—as the philanthropic pretence of the whole concern, as their talk, as their government, as their show of work. The only real feeling was a desire to get appointed to a trading-post where ivory was to be had, so that they could earn percentages. They intrigued and slandered and hated each other only on that account— but as to effectually lifting a little finger—oh, no. By heavens! there is something after all in the world allowing one man to steal a horse while another must not look at a halter. Steal a horse straight out. Very well. He has done it. Perhaps he can ride. But there is a way of looking at a halter that would provoke the most charitable of saints into a kick.

"I had no idea why he wanted to be sociable, but as we chatted in there it suddenly occurred to me the fellow was trying to get at something— in fact, pumping me. He alluded constantly to Europe, to the people I was supposed to know there—putting leading questions as to my acquaintances in the sepulchral city, and so on. His little eyes glittered like mica discs— with curiosity—though he tried to keep up a bit of superciliousness. At first I was astonished, but very soon I became awfully curious to see what he would find out from me. I couldn't possibly imagine what I had in me to make it worth his while. It was very pretty to see how he baffled himself, for in truth my body was full only of chills, and my head had nothing in it but that wretched steamboat business. It was evident he took me for a perfectly shameless prevaricator. At last he got angry, and, to conceal a movement of furious annoyance, he yawned. I rose. Then I noticed a small sketch in oils, on a panel, representing a woman, draped and blindfolded, carrying a lighted torch. The background was sombre—almost black. The movement of the woman was stately, and the effect of the torchlight on the face was sinister.

"It arrested me, and he stood by civilly, holding an empty half-pint champagne bottle (medical comforts) with the candle stuck in it. To my question he said Mr. Kurtz had painted this—in this very station more than a year ago—while waiting for means to go to his trading post. 'Tell me, pray,' said I, 'who is this Mr. Kurtz?'

"'The chief of the Inner Station,' he answered in a short tone, looking away. 'Much obliged,' I said, laughing. 'And you are the brickmaker of the Central Station. Every one knows that.' He was silent for a while. 'He is a prodigy,' he said at last. 'He is an emissary of pity and science and progress, and devil knows what else. We want,' he began to declaim suddenly, 'for the guidance of the cause intrusted to us by Europe, so to speak, higher intelligence, wide sympathies, a singleness of purpose.' 'Who says that?' I asked. 'Lots of them,' he replied. 'Some even write that; and so he comes here, a special being, as you ought to know.' 'Why ought I to know?'

I interrupted, really surprised. He paid no attention. 'Yes. Today he is chief of the best station, next year he will be assistant-manager, two years more and... but I dare-say you know what he will be in two years' time. You are of the new gang—the gang of virtue. The same people who sent him specially also recommended you. Oh, don't say no. I've my own eyes to trust.' Light dawned upon me. My dear aunt's influential acquaintances were producing an unexpected effect upon that young man. I nearly burst into a laugh. 'Do you read the Company's confidential correspondence?' I asked. He hadn't a word to say. It was great fun. 'When Mr. Kurtz,' I continued, severely, 'is General Manager, you won't have the opportunity.'

"He blew the candle out suddenly, and we went outside. The moon had risen. Black figures strolled about listlessly, pouring water on the glow, whence proceeded a sound of hissing; steam ascended in the moonlight, the beaten nigger groaned somewhere. 'What a row the brute makes!' said the indefatigable man with the moustaches, appearing near us. 'Serve him right. Transgression—punishment—bang! Pitiless, pitiless. That's the only way. This will prevent all conflagrations for the future. I was just telling the manager...' He noticed my companion, and became crestfallen all at once. 'Not in bed yet,' he said, with a kind of servile heartiness; 'it's so natural. Ha! Danger—agitation.' He vanished. I went on to the riverside, and the other followed me. I heard a scathing murmur at my ear, 'Heap of muffs—go to.' The pilgrims could be seen in knots gesticulating, discussing. Several had still their staves in their hands. I verily believe they took these sticks to bed with them. Beyond the fence the forest stood up spectrally in the moonlight, and through that dim stir, through the faint sounds of that lamentable courtyard, the silence of the land went home to one's very heart—its mystery, its greatness, the amazing reality of its concealed life. The hurt nigger moaned feebly somewhere near by, and then fetched a deep sigh that made me mend my pace away from there. I felt a hand introducing itself under my arm. 'My dear sir,' said the fellow, 'I don't want to be misunderstood, and especially by you, who will see Mr. Kurtz long before I can have that pleasure. I wouldn't like him to get a false idea of my disposition....'

"I let him run on, this papier-mache Mephistopheles, and it seemed to me that if I tried I could poke my forefinger through him, and would find nothing inside but a little loose dirt, maybe. He, don't you see, had been planning to be assistant-manager by and by under the present man, and I could see that the coming of that Kurtz had upset them both not a little. He talked precipitately, and I did not try to stop him. I had my shoulders against the wreck of my steamer, hauled up on the slope like a carcass of some big river animal. The smell of mud, of primeval mud, by Jove! was in my nostrils, the high stillness of primeval forest was before my eyes; there were shiny patches on the black creek.

The moon had spread over everything a thin layer of silver— over the rank grass, over the mud, upon the wall of matted vegetation standing higher than the wall of a temple, over the great river I could see through a sombre gap glittering, glittering, as it flowed broadly by without a murmur. All this was great, expectant, mute, while the man jabbered about himself. I wondered whether the stillness on the face of the immensity looking at us two were meant as an appeal or as a menace. What were we who had strayed in here? Could we handle that dumb thing, or would it handle us? I felt how big, how confoundedly big, was that thing that couldn't talk, and perhaps was deaf as well. What was in there? I could see a little ivory coming out from there, and I had heard Mr. Kurtz was in there. I had heard enough about it, too— God knows! Yet somehow it didn't bring any image with it— no more than if I had been told an angel or a fiend was in there. I believed it in the same way one of you might believe there are inhabitants in the planet Mars. I knew once a Scotch sailmaker who was certain, dead sure, there were people in Mars.

If you asked him for some idea how they looked and behaved, he would get shy and mutter something about 'walking on all-fours.' If you as much as smiled, he would— though a man of sixty— offer to fight you. I would not have gone so far as to fight for Kurtz, but I went for him near enough to a lie. You know I hate, detest, and can't bear a lie, not because I am straighter than the rest of us, but simply because it appalls me. There is a taint of death, a flavour of mortality in lies— which is exactly what I hate and detest in the world— what I want to forget. It makes me miserable and sick, like biting something rotten would do. Temperament, I suppose. Well, I went near enough to it by letting the young fool there believe anything he liked to imagine as to my influence in Europe.

I became in an instant as much of a pretence as the rest of the bewitched pilgrims. This simply because I had a notion it somehow would be of help to that Kurtz whom at the time I did not see—you understand. He was just a word for me. I did not see the man in the name any more than you do. Do you see him? Do you see the story? Do you see anything? It seems to me I am trying to tell you ya dream—making a vain attempt, because no relation of a dream can convey the dream-sensation, that commingling of absurdity, surprise, and bewilderment in a tremor of struggling revolt, that notion of being captured by the incredible which is of the very essence of dreams...."

He was silent for a while.

"... No, it is impossible; it is impossible to convey the life-sensation of any given epoch of one's existence—that which makes its truth, its meaning—its subtle and penetrating essence. It is impossible. We live, as we dream—alone...."

He paused again as if reflecting, then added:

"Of course in this you fellows see more than I could then. You see me, whom you know...."

It had become so pitch dark that we listeners could hardly see one another. For a long time already he, sitting apart, had been no more to us than a voice. There was not a word from anybody. The others might have been asleep, but I was awake. I listened, I listened on the watch for the sentence, for the word, that would give me the clue to the faint uneasiness inspired by this narrative that seemed to shape itself without human lips in the heavy night-air of the river.

"... Yes—I let him run on," Marlow began again, "and think what he pleased about the powers that were behind me. I did! And there was nothing behind me! There was nothing but that wretched, old, mangled steamboat I was leaning against, while he talked fluently about 'the necessity for every man to get on.' 'And when one comes out here, you conceive, it is not to gaze at the moon.' Mr. Kurtz was a 'universal genius,' but even a genius would find it easier to work with 'adequate tools—intelligent men.' He did not make bricks—why, there was a physical impossibility in the way—as I was well aware; and if he did secretarial work for the manager, it was because 'no sensible man rejects wantonly the confidence of his superiors.' Did I see it? I saw it. What more did I want? What I really wanted was rivets, by heaven! Rivets. To get on with the work—to stop the hole. Rivets I wanted. There were cases of them down at the coast— cases—piled up—burst—split! You kicked a loose rivet at every second step in that station-yard on the hillside. Rivets had rolled into the grove of death. You could fill your pockets with rivets for the trouble of stooping down— and there wasn't one rivet to be found where it was wanted. We had plates that would do, but nothing to fasten them with. And every week the messenger, a long negro, letter-bag on shoulder and staff in hand, left our station for the coast. And several times a week a coast caravan came in with trade goods—ghastly glazed calico that made you shudder only to look at it, glass beads value about a penny a quart, confounded spotted cotton handkerchiefs. And no rivets. Three carriers could have brought all that was wanted to set that steamboat afloat.

"He was becoming confidential now, but I fancy my unresponsive attitude must have exasperated him at last, for he judged it necessary to inform me he feared neither God nor devil, let alone any mere man. I said I could see that very well, but what I wanted was a certain quantity of rivets—and rivets were what really Mr. Kurtz wanted, if he had only known it. Now letters went to the coast every week.... 'My dear sir,' he cried, 'I write from dictation.' I demanded rivets. There was a way—for an intelligent man. He changed his manner; became very cold, and suddenly began to talk about a hippopotamus; wondered whether sleeping on board the steamer (I stuck to my salvage night and day) I wasn't disturbed. There was an old hippo that had the bad habit of getting out on the bank and roaming at night over the station grounds. The pilgrims used to turn out in a body and empty every rifle they could lay hands on at him. Some even had sat up o' nights for him. All this energy was wasted, though. 'That animal has a charmed life,' he said; 'but you can say this only of brutes in this country. No man—you apprehend me?—no man here bears a charmed life.' He stood there for a moment in the moonlight with his delicate hooked nose set a little askew, and his mica eyes glittering without a wink, then, with a curt Good-night, he strode off.

I could see he was disturbed and considerably puzzled, which made me feel more hopeful than I had been for days. It was a great comfort to turn from that chap to my influential friend, the battered, twisted, ruined, tin-pot steamboat. I clambered on board. She rang under my feet like an empty Huntley & Palmer biscuit-tin kicked along a gutter; she was nothing so solid in make, and rather less pretty in shape, but I had expended enough hard work on her to make me love her. No influential friend would have served me better. She had given me a chance to come out a bit—to find out what I could do. No, I don't like work. I had rather laze about and think of all the fine things that can be done. I don't like work—no man does—but I like what is in the work— the chance to find yourself. Your own reality—for yourself, not for others—what no other man can ever know. They can only see the mere show, and never can tell what it really means.

"I was not surprised to see somebody sitting aft, on the deck, with his legs dangling over the mud. You see I rather chummed with the few mechanics there were in that station, whom the other pilgrims naturally despised—on account of their imperfect manners, I suppose. This was the foreman—a boiler-maker by trade—a good worker. He was a lank, bony, yellow-faced man, with big intense eyes. His aspect was worried, and his head was as bald as the palm of my hand; but his hair in falling seemed to have stuck to his chin, and had prospered in the new locality, for his beard hung down to his waist. He was a widower with six young children (he had left them in charge of a sister of his to come out there), and the passion of his life was pigeon-flying. He was an enthusiast and a connoisseur. He would rave about pigeons. After work hours he used sometimes to come over from his hut for a talk about his children and his pigeons; at work, when he had to crawl in the mud under the bottom of the steamboat, he would tie up that beard of his in a kind of white serviette he brought for the purpose. It had loops to go over his ears. In the evening he could be seen squatted on the bank rinsing that wrapper in the creek with great care, then spreading it solemnly on a bush to dry.

"I slapped him on the back and shouted, 'We shall have rivets!' He scrambled to his feet exclaiming, 'No! Rivets!' as though he couldn't believe his ears. Then in a low voice, 'You... eh?' I don't know why we behaved like lunatics. I put my finger to the side of my nose and nodded mysteriously. 'Good for you!' he cried, snapped his fingers above his head, lifting one foot. I tried a jig. We capered on the iron deck. A frightful clatter came out of that hulk, and the virgin forest on the other bank of the creek sent it back in a thundering roll upon the sleeping station. It must have made some of the pilgrims sit up in their hovels. A dark figure obscured the lighted doorway of the manager's hut, vanished, then, a second or so after, the doorway itself vanished, too. We stopped, and the silence driven away by the stamping of our feet flowed back again from the recesses of the land. The great wall of vegetation, an exuberant and entangled mass of trunks, branches, leaves, boughs, festoons, motionless in the moonlight, was like a rioting invasion of soundless life, a rolling wave of plants, piled up, crested, ready to topple over the creek, to sweep every little man of us out of his little existence. And it moved not. A deadened burst of mighty splashes and snorts reached us from afar, as though an icthyosaurus had been taking a bath of glitter in the great river. `After all,' said the boiler-maker in a reasonable tone, `why shouldn't we get the rivets?' Why not, indeed! I did not know of any reason why we shouldn't. `They'll come in three weeks,' I said confidently.

"But they didn't. Instead of rivets there came an invasion, an infliction, a visitation. It came in sections during the next three weeks, each section headed by a donkey carrying a white man in new clothes and tan shoes, bowing from that elevation right and left to the impressed pilgrims. A quarrelsome band of footsore sulky niggers trod on the heels of the donkey; a lot of tents, camp-stools, tin boxes, white cases, brown bales would be shot down in the courtyard, and the air of mystery would deepen a little over the muddle of the station. Five such instalments came, with their absurd air of disorderly flight with the loot of innumerable outfit shops and provision stores, that, one would think, they were lugging, after a raid, into the wilderness for equitable division. It was an inextricable mess of things decent in themselves but that human folly made look like the spoils of thieving.

"This devoted band called itself the Eldorado Exploring Expedition, and I believe they were sworn to secrecy. Their talk, however, was the talk of sordid buccaneers: it ywas reckless without hardihood, greedy without audacity, and cruel without courage; there was not an atom of foresight or of serious intention in the whole batch of them, and they did not seem aware these things are wanted for the work of the world. To tear treasure out of the bowels of the land was their desire, with no more moral purpose at the back of it than there is in burglars breaking into a safe. Who paid the expenses of the noble enterprise I don't know; but the uncle of our manager was leader of that lot.

"In exterior he resembled a butcher in a poor neighbourhood, and his eyes had a look of sleepy cunning. He carried his fat paunch with ostentation on his short legs, and during the time his gang infested the station spoke to no one but his nephew. You could see these two roaming about all day long with their heads close together in an everlasting confab.

"I had given up worrying myself about the rivets. One's capacity for that kind of folly is more limited than you would suppose. I said Hang!—and let things slide. I had plenty of time for meditation, and now and then I would give some thought to Kurtz. I wasn't very interested in him. No. Still, I was curious to see whether this man, who had come out equipped with moral ideas of some sort, would climb to the top after all and how he would set about his work when there."

PART II

"One evening as I was lying flat on the deck of my steamboat, I heard voices approaching—and there were the nephew and the uncle strolling along the bank. I laid my head on my arm again, and had nearly lost myself in a doze, when somebody said in my ear, as it were: 'I am as harmless as a little child, but I don't like to be dictated to. Am I the manager—or am I not? I was ordered to send him there. It's incredible.'... I became aware that the two were standing on the shore alongside the forepart of the steamboat, just below my head. I did not move; it did not occur to me to move: I was sleepy. 'It is unpleasant,' grunted the uncle. 'He has asked the Administration to be sent there,' said the other, 'with the idea of showing what he could do; and I was instructed accordingly. Look at the influence that man must have. Is it not frightful?' They both agreed it was frightful, then made several bizarre remarks: 'Make rain and fine weather—one man—the Council—by the nose'— bits of absurd sentences that got the better of my drowsiness, so that I had pretty near the whole of my wits about me when the uncle said, 'The climate may do away with this difficulty for you. Is he alone there?' 'Yes,' answered the manager; 'he sent his assistant down the river with a note to me in these terms: "Clear this poor devil out of the country, and don't bother sending more of that sort. I had rather be alone than have the kind of men you can dispose of with me." It was more than a year ago. Can you imagine such impudence!' `Anything since then?' asked the other hoarsely. `Ivory,' jerked the nephew; `lots of it—prime sort—lots—most annoying, from him.' `And with that?' questioned the heavy rumble. `Invoice,' was the reply fired out, so to speak. Then silence. They had been talking about Kurtz.

"I was broad awake by this time, but, lying perfectly at ease, remained still, having no inducement to change my position. `How did that ivory come all this way?' growled the elder man, who seemed very vexed. The other explained that it had come with a fleet of canoes in charge of an English half-caste clerk Kurtz had with him; that Kurtz had apparently intended to return himself, the station being by that time bare of goods and stores, but after coming three hundred miles, had suddenly decided to go back, which he started to do alone in a small dugout with four paddlers, leaving the half-caste to continue down the river with the ivory. The two fellows there seemed astounded at anybody attempting such a thing. They were at a loss for an adequate motive. As to me, I seemed to see Kurtz for the first time.

It was a distinct glimpse: the dugout, four paddling savages, and the lone white man turning his back suddenly on the headquarters, yon relief, on thoughts of home—perhaps; setting his face towards the depths of the wilderness, towards his empty and desolate station. I did not know the motive. Perhaps he was just simply a fine fellow who stuck to his work for its own sake. His name, you understand, had not been pronounced once. He was `that man.' The half-caste, who, as far as I could see, had conducted a difficult trip with great prudence and pluck, was invariably alluded to as `that scoundrel.' The `scoundrel' had reported that the `man' had been very ill—had recovered imperfectly.... The two below me moved away then a few paces, and strolled back and forth at some little distance. I heard: `Military post—doctor—two hundred miles—quite alone now— unavoidable delays—nine months—no news—strange rumours.' They approached again, just as the manager was saying, `No one, as far as I know, unless a species of wandering trader— a pestilential fellow, snapping ivory from the natives.' Who was it they were talking about now? I gathered in snatches that this was some man supposed to be in Kurtz's district, and of whom the manager did not approve. `We will not be free from unfair competition till one of these fellows is hanged for an example,' he said. `Certainly,' grunted the other; `get him hanged! Why not? Anything—anything can be done in this country. That's what I say; nobody here, you understand, here, can endanger your position. And why? You stand the climate—you outlast them all.

The danger is in Europe; but there before I left I took care to—' They moved off and whispered, then their voices rose again. `The extraordinary series of delays is not my fault. I did my best.' The fat man sighed. `Very sad.' `And the pestiferous absurdity of his talk,' continued the other; `he bothered me enough when he was here. "Each station should be like a beacon on the road towards better things, a centre for trade of course, but also for humanizing, improving, instructing." Conceive you—that ass! And he wants to be manager! No, it's—' Here he got choked by excessive indignation, and I lifted my head the least bit. I was surprised to see how near they were—right under me. I could have spat upon their hats. They were looking on the ground, absorbed in thought. The manager was switching his leg with a slender twig: his sagacious relative lifted his head. `You have been well since you came out this time?' he asked. The other gave a start. `Who? I? Oh! Like a charm—like a charm. But the rest—oh, my goodness! All sick. They die so quick, too, that I haven't the time to send them out of the country— it's incredible!' `Hm'm. Just so,' grunted the uncle. `Ah! my boy, trust to this—I say, trust to this.' I saw him extend his short flipper of an arm for a gesture that took in the forest, the creek, the mud, the river— seemed to beckon with a dishonouring flourish before the sunlit face of the land a treacherous appeal to the lurking death, to the hidden evil, to the profound darkness of its heart. It was so startling that I leaped to my feet and looked back at the edge of the forest, as though I had expected an answer of some sort to that black display of confidence. You know the foolish notions that come to one sometimes. The high stillness confronted these two figures with its ominous patience, waiting for the passing away of a fantastic invasion.

"They swore aloud together—out of sheer fright, I believe—then pretending not to know anything of my existence, turned back to the station. The sun was low; and leaning forward side by side, they seemed to be tugging painfully uphill their two ridiculous shadows of unequal length, that trailed behind them slowly over the tall grass without bending a single blade.

"In a few days the Eldorado Expedition went into the patient wilderness, that closed upon it as the sea closes over a diver. Long afterwards the news came that all the donkeys were dead. I know nothing as to the fate of the less valuable animals. They, no doubt, like the rest of us, found what they deserved. I did not inquire. I was then rather excited at the prospect of meeting Kurtz very soon. When I say very soon I mean it comparatively. It was just two months from the day we left the creek when we came to the bank below Kurtz's station.

"Going up that river was like traveling back to the earliest beginnings of the world, when vegetation rioted on the earth and the big trees were kings. An empty stream, a great silence, an impenetrable forest. The air was warm, thick, heavy, sluggish. There was no joy in the brilliance of sunshine. The long stretches of the waterway ran on, deserted, into the gloom of overshadowed distances. On silvery sand-banks hippos and alligators sunned themselves side by side. The broadening waters flowed through a mob of wooded islands; you lost your way on that river as you would in a desert, and butted all day long against shoals, trying to find the channel, till you thought yourself bewitched and cut off for ever from everything you had known once—somewhere—far away—in another existence perhaps. There were moments when one's past came back to one, as it will sometimes when you have not a moment to spare for yourself; but it came in the shape of an unrestful and noisy dream, remembered with wonder amongst the overwhelming realities of this strange world of plants, and water, and silence. And this stillness of life did not in the least resemble a peace. It was the stillness of an implacable force brooding over an inscrutable intention. It looked at you with a vengeful aspect. I got used to it afterwards; I did not see it any more; I had no time.

I had to keep guessing at the channel; I had to discern, mostly by inspiration, the signs of hidden banks; I watched for sunken stones; I was learning to clap my teeth smartly before my heart flew out, when I shaved by a fluke some infernal sly old snag that would have ripped the life out of the tin-pot steamboat and drowned all the pilgrims; I had to keep a lookout for the signs of dead wood we could cut up in the night for next day's steaming. When you have to attend to things of that sort, to the mere incidents of the surface, the reality—the reality, I tell you—fades. The inner truth is hidden—luckily, luckily. But I felt it all the same; I felt often its mysterious stillness watching me at my monkey tricks, just as it watches you fellows performing on your respective tight-ropes for—what is it? half-a-crown a tumble—"

"Try to be civil, Marlow," growled a voice, and I knew there was at least one listener awake besides myself.

"I beg your pardon. I forgot the heartache which makes up the rest of the price. And indeed what does the price matter, if the trick be well done? You do your tricks very well. And I didn't do badly either, since I managed not to sink that steamboat on my first trip. It's a wonder to me yet. Imagine a blindfolded man set to drive a van over a bad road. I sweated and shivered over that business considerably, I can tell you. After all, for a seaman, to scrape the bottom of the thing that's supposed to float all the time under his care is the unpardonable sin. No one may know of it, but you never forget the thump—eh? A blow on the very heart. You remember it, you dream of it, you wake up at night and think of it—years after—and go hot and cold all over. I don't pretend to say that steamboat floated all the time. More than once she had to wade for a bit, with twenty cannibals splashing around and pushing. We had enlisted some of these chaps on the way for a crew. Fine fellows—cannibals—in their place.

They were men one could work with, and I am grateful to them. And, after all, they did not eat each other before my face: they had brought along a provision of hippo-meat which went rotten, and made the mystery of the wilderness stink in my nostrils. Phoo! I can sniff it now. I had the manager on board and three or four pilgrims with their staves— all complete. Sometimes we came upon a station close by the bank, clinging to the skirts of the unknown, and the white men rushing out of a tumble-down hovel, with great gestures of joy and surprise and welcome, seemed very strange— had the appearance of being held there captive by a spell.

The word ivory would ring in the air for a while—and on we went again into the silence, along empty reaches, round the still bends, between the high walls of our winding way, reverberating in hollow claps the ponderous beat of the stern-wheel. Trees, trees, millions of trees, massive, immense, running up high; and at their foot, hugging the bank against the stream, crept the little begrimed steamboat, like a sluggish beetle crawling on the floor of a lofty portico. It made you feel very small, very lost, and yet it was not altogether depressing, that feeling. After all, if you were small, the grimy beetle crawled on—which was just what you wanted it to do. Where the pilgrims imagined it crawled to I don't know. To some place where they expected to get something. I bet! For me it crawled towards Kurtz—exclusively; but when the steam-pipes started leaking we crawled very slow.

The reaches opened before us and closed behind, as if the forest had stepped leisurely across the water to bar the way for our return. We penetrated deeper and deeper into the heart of darkness. It was very quiet there. At night sometimes the roll of drums behind the curtain of trees would run up the river and remain sustained faintly, as if hovering in the air high over our heads, till the first break of day. Whether it meant war, peace, or prayer we could not tell. The dawns were heralded by the descent of a chill stillness; the wood-cutters slept, their fires burned low; the snapping of a twig would make you start. Were were wanderers on a prehistoric earth, on an earth that wore the aspect of an unknown planet.

We could have fancied ourselves the first of men taking possession of an accursed inheritance, to be subdued at the cost of profound anguish and of excessive toil. But suddenly, as we struggled round a bend, there would be a glimpse of rush walls, of peaked grass-roofs, a burst of yells, a whirl of black limbs, a mass of hands clapping. of feet stamping, of bodies swaying, of eyes rolling, under the droop of heavy and motionless foliage. The steamer toiled along slowly on the edge of a black and incomprehensible frenzy. The prehistoric man was cursing us, praying to us, welcoming us—who could tell? We were cut off from the comprehension of our surroundings; we glided past like phantoms, wondering and secretly appalled, as sane men would be before an enthusiastic outbreak in a madhouse. We could not understand because we were too far and could not remember because we were travelling in the night of first ages, of those ages that are gone, leaving hardly a sign— and no memories.

"The earth seemed unearthly. We are accustomed to look upon the shackled form of a conquered monster, but there—there you could look at a thing monstrous and free. It was unearthly, and the men were—No, they were not inhuman. Well, you know, that was the worst of it—this suspicion of their not being inhuman. It would come slowly to one.

They howled and leaped, and spun, and made horrid faces; but what thrilled you was just the thought of their humanity— like yours—the thought of your remote kinship with this wild and passionate uproar. Ugly. Yes, it was ugly enough; but if you were man enough you would admit to yourself that there ywas in you just the faintest trace of a response to the terrible frankness of that noise, a dim suspicion of there being a meaning in it which you—you so remote from the night of first ages—could comprehend. And why not? The mind of man is capable of anything—because everything is in it, all the past as well as all the future. What was there after all? Joy, fear, sorrow, devotion, valour, rage—who can tell?—but truth—truth stripped of its cloak of time. Let the fool gape and shudder—the man knows, and can look on without a wink. But he must at least be as much of a man as these on the shore. He must meet that truth with his own true stuff— with his own inborn strength. Principles won't do. Acquisitions, clothes, pretty rags—rags that would fly off at the first good shake. No; you want a deliberate belief. An appeal to me in this fiendish row—is there? Very well; I hear; I admit, but I have a voice, too, and for good or evil mine is the speech that cannot be silenced. Of course, a fool, what with sheer fright and fine sentiments, is always safe. Who's that grunting? You wonder I didn't go ashore for a howl and a dance? Well, no—I didn't. Fine sentiments, you say? Fine sentiments, be hanged! I had no time.

I had to mess about with white-lead and strips of woolen blanket helping to put bandages on those leaky steam-pipes—I tell you. I had to watch the steering, and circumvent those snags, and get the tin-pot along by hook or by crook. There was surface-truth enough in these things to save a wiser man. And between whiles I had to look after the savage who was fireman. He was an improved specimen; he could fire up a vertical boiler. He was there below me, and, upon my word, to look at him was as edifying as seeing a dog in a parody of breeches and a feather hat, walking on his hind-legs.

A few months of training had done for that really fine chap. He squinted at the steam-gauge and at the water-gauge with an evident effort of intrepidity—and he had filed teeth, too, the poor devil, and the wool of his pate shaved into queer patterns, and three ornamental scars on each of his cheeks. He ought to have been clapping his hands and stamping his feet on the bank, instead of which he was hard at work, a thrall to strange witchcraft, full of improving knowledge. He was useful because he had been instructed; and what he knew was this—that should the water in that transparent thing disappear, the evil spirit inside the boiler would get angry through the greatness of his thirst, and take a terrible vengeance. So he sweated and fired up and watched the glass fearfully (with an impromptu charm, made of rags, tied to his arm, and a piece of polished bone, as big as a watch, stuck flatways through his lower lip), while the wooded banks slipped past us slowly, the short noise was left behind, the interminable miles of silence—and we crept on, towards Kurtz. But the snags were thick, the water was treacherous and shallow, the boiler seemed indeed to have a sulky devil in it, and thus neither that fireman nor I had any time to peer into our creepy thoughts.

"Some fifty miles below the Inner Station we came upon a hut of reeds, an inclined and melancholy pole, with the unrecognizable tatters of what had been a flag of some sort flying from it, and a neatly stacked wood-pile. This was unexpected. We came to the bank, and on the stack of firewood found a flat piece of board with some faded pencil-writing on it. When deciphered it said: `Wood for you. Hurry up. Approach cautiously.' There was a signature, but it was illegible—not Kurtz—a much longer word. `Hurry up.' Where? Up the river? `Approach cautiously.' We had not done so. But the warning could not have been meant for the place where it could be only found after approach. Something was wrong above. But what—and how much? That was the question. We commented adversely upon the imbecility of that telegraphic style. The bush around said nothing, and would not let us look very far, either. A torn curtain of red twill hung in the doorway of the hut, and flapped sadly in our faces. The dwelling was dismantled; but we could see a white man had lived there not very long ago.

There remained a rude table—a plank on two posts; a heap of rubbish reposed in a dark corner, and by the door I picked up a book. It had lost its covers, and the pages had been thumbed into a state of extremely dirty softness; but the back had been lovingly stitched afresh with white cotton thread, which looked clean yet. It was an extraordinary find. Its title was, An Inquiry Into Some Points of Seamanship, by a man Towser, Towson—some such name—Master in his Majesty's

Navy. The matter looked dreary reading enough, with illustrative diagrams and repulsive tables of figures, and the copy was sixty years old. I handled this amazing antiquity with the greatest possible tenderness, lest it should dissolve in my hands. Within, Towson or Towser was inquiring earnestly into the breaking strain of ships' chains and tackle, and other such matters. Not a very enthralling book; but at the first glance you could see there a singleness of intention, an honest concern for the right way of going to work, which made these humble pages, thought out so many years ago, luminous with another than a professional light.

The simple old sailor, with his talk of chains and purchases, made me forget the jungle and the pilgrims in a delicious sensation of having come upon something unmistakably real. Such a book being there was wonderful enough; but still more astounding were the notes pencilled in the margin, and plainly referring to the text. I couldn't believe my eyes! They were in cipher! Yes, it looked like cipher. Fancy a man lugging with him a book of that description into this nowhere and studying it—and making notes—in cipher at that! It was an extravagant mystery.

"I had been dimly aware for some time of a worrying noise, and when I lifted my eyes I saw the wood-pile was gone, and the manager, aided by all the pilgrims, was shouting at me from the riverside. I slipped the book into my pocket. I assure you to leave off reading was like tearing myself away from the shelter of an old and solid friendship.

"I started the lame engine ahead. `It must be this miserable trader-this intruder,' exclaimed the manager, looking back malevolently at the place we had left. `He must be English,' I said. `It will not save him from getting into trouble if he is not careful,' muttered the manager darkly. I observed with assumed innocence that no man was safe from trouble in this world.

"The current was more rapid now, the steamer seemed at her last gasp, the stern-wheel flopped languidly, and I caught myself listening on tiptoe for the next beat of the boat, for in sobre truth I expected the wretched thing to give up every moment. It was like watching the last flickers of a life. But still we crawled. Sometimes I would pick out a tree a little way ahead to measure our progress towards Kurtz by, but I lost it invariably before we got abreast. To keep the eyes so long on one thing was too much for human patience. The manager displayed a beautiful resignation. I fretted and fumed and took to arguing with myself whether or no I would talk openly with Kurtz; but before I could come to any conclusion it occurred to me that my speech or my silence, indeed any action of mine, would be a mere futility. What did it matter what any one knew or ignored? What did it matter who was manager? One gets sometimes such a flash of insight. The essentials of this affair lay deep under the surface, beyond my reach, and beyond my power of meddling.

"Towards the evening of the second day we judged ourselves about eight miles from Kurtz's station. I wanted to push on; but the manager looked grave, and told me the navigation up there was so dangerous that it would be advisable, the sun being very low already, to wait where we were till next morning. Moreover, he pointed out that if the warning to approach cautiously were to be followed, we must approach in daylight— not at dusk or in the dark. This was sensible enough. Eight miles meant nearly three hours' steaming for us, and I could also see suspicious ripples at the upper end of the reach.

Nevertheless, I was annoyed beyond expression at the delay, and most unreasonably, too, since one night more could not matter much after so many months. As we had plenty of wood, and caution was the word, I brought up in the middle of the stream. The reach was narrow, straight, with high sides like a railway cutting. The dusk came gliding into it long before the sun had set. The current ran smooth and swift, but a dumb immobility sat on the banks. The living trees, lashed together by the creepers and every living bush of the undergrowth, might have been changed into stone, even to the slenderest twig, to the lightest leaf. It was not sleep—it seemed unnatural, like a state of trance. Not the faintest sound of any kind could be heard. You looked on amazed, and began to suspect yourself of being deaf— then the night came suddenly, and struck you blind as well. About three in the morning some large fish leaped, and the loud splash made me jump as though a gun had been fired. When the sun rose there was a white fog, very warm and clammy, and more blinding than the night. It did not shift or drive; it was just there, standing all round you like something solid. At eight or nine, perhaps, it lifted as a shutter lifts. We had a glimpse of the towering multitude of trees, of the immense matted jungle, with the blazing little ball of the sun hanging over it—all perfectly still—and then the white shutter came down again, smoothly, as if sliding in greased grooves.

I ordered the chain, which we had begun to heave in, to be paid out again. Before it stopped running with a muffled rattle, a cry, a very loud cry, as of infinite desolation, soared slowly in the opaque air. It ceased. A complaining clamour, modulated in savage discords, filled our ears. The sheer unexpectedness of it made my hair stir under my cap. I don't know how it struck the others: to me it seemed as though the mist itself had screamed, so suddenly, and apparently from all sides at once, did this tumultuous and mournful uproar arise. It culminated in a hurried outbreak of almost intolerably excessive shrieking, which stopped short, leaving us stiffened in a variety of silly attitudes, and obstinately listening to the nearly as appalling and excessive silence. 'Good God! What is the meaning—' stammered at my elbow one of the pilgrims—a little fat man, with sandy hair and red whiskers, who wore sidespring boots, and pink pyjamas tucked into his socks. Two others remained open-mouthed a while minute, then dashed into the little cabin, to rush out incontinently and stand darting scared glances, with Winchesters at 'ready' in their hands. What we could see was just the steamer we were on, her outlines blurred as though she had been on the point of dissolving, and a misty strip of water, perhaps two feet broad, around her— and that was all.

The rest of the world was nowhere, as far as our eyes and ears were concerned. Just nowhere. Gone, disappeared; swept off without leaving a whisper or a shadow behind.

"I went forward, and ordered the chain to be hauled in short, so as to be ready to trip the anchor and move the steamboat at once if necessary. 'Will they attack?' whispered an awed voice. 'We will be all butchered in this fog,' murmured another. The faces twitched with the strain, the hands trembled slightly, the eyes forgot to wink. It was very curious to see the contrast of expressions of the white men and of the black fellows of our crew, who were as much strangers to that part of the river as we, though their homes were only eight hundred miles away. The whites, of course greatly discomposed, had besides a curious look of being painfully shocked by such an outrageous row.

The others had an alert, naturally interested expression; but their faces were essentially quiet, even those of the one or two who grinned as they hauled at the chain. Several exchanged short, grunting phrases, which seemed to settle the matter to their satisfaction. Their headman, a young, broad-chested black, severely draped in dark-blue fringed cloths, with fierce nostrils and his hair all done up artfully in oily ringlets, stood near me. 'Aha!' I said, just for good fellowship's sake. 'Catch 'im,' he snapped, with a bloodshot widening of his eyes and a flash of sharp teeth—'catch 'im. Give 'im to us.' 'To you, eh?' I asked; 'what would you do with them?' 'Eat 'im!' he said curtly, and, leaning his elbow on the rail, looked out into the fog in a dignified and profoundly pensive attitude. I would no doubt have been properly horrified, had it not occurred to me that he and his chaps must be very hungry: that they must have been growing increasingly hungry for at least this month past.

They had been engaged for six months (I don't think a single one of them had any clear idea of time, as we at the end of countless ages have. They still belonged to the beginnings of time—had no inherited experience to teach them as it were), and of course, as long as there was a piece of paper written over in accordance with some farcical law or other made down the river, it didn't enter anybody's head to trouble how they would live. Certainly they had brought with them some rotten hippo-meat, which couldn't have lasted very long, anyway, even if the pilgrims hadn't, in the midst of a shocking hullabaloo, thrown a considerable quantity of it overboard. It looked like a high-handed proceeding; but it was really a case of legitimate self-defence. You can't breathe dead hippo waking, sleeping, and eating, and at the same time keep your precarious grip on existence. Besides that, they had given them every week three pieces of brass wire, each about nine inches long; and the theory was they were to buy their provisions with that currency in riverside villages. You can see how that worked.

There were either no villages, or the people were hostile, or the director, who like the rest of us fed out of tins, with an occasional old he-goat thrown in, didn't want to stop the steamer for some more or less recondite reason. So, unless they swallowed the wire itself, or made loops of it to snare the fishes with, I don't see what good their extravagant salary could be to them. I must say it was paid with a regularity worthy of a large and honourable trading company. For the rest, the only thing to eat—though it didn't look eatable in the least—I saw in their possession was a few lumps of some stuff like half-cooked dough, of a dirty lavender colour, they kept wrapped in leaves, and now and then swallowed a piece of, but so small that it seemed done more for the looks of the thing than for any serious purpose of sustenance. Why in the name of all the gnawing devils of hunger they didn't go for us—they were thirty to five—and have a good tuck-in for once, amazes me now when I think of it.

They were big powerful men, with not much capacity to weigh the consequences, with courage, with strength, even yet, though their skins were no longer glossy and their muscles no longer hard. And I saw that something restraining, one of those human secrets that baffle probability, had come into play there. I looked at them with a swift quickening of interest—

not because it occurred to me I might be eaten by them before very long, though I own to you that just then I perceived— in a new light, as it were—how unwholesome the pilgrims looked, and I hoped, yes, I positively hoped, that my aspect was not so— what shall I say?—so—unappetizing: a touch of fantastic vanity which fitted well with the dream-sensation that pervaded all my days at that time.

Perhaps I had a little fever, too. One can't live with one's finger everlastingly on one's pulse. I had often 'a little fever,' or a little touch of other things— the playful paw-strokes of the wilderness, the preliminary trifling before the more serious onslaught which came in due course. Yes; I looked at them as you would on any human being, with a curiosity of their impulses, motives, capacities, weaknesses, when brought to the test of an inexorable physical necessity. Restraint! What possible restraint? Was it superstition, disgust, patience, fear— or some kind of primitive honour? No fear can stand up to hunger, no patience can wear it out, disgust simply does not exist where hunger is; and as to superstition, beliefs, and what you may call principles, they are less than chaff in a breeze. Don't you know the devilry of lingering starvation, its exasperating torment, its black thoughts, its sombre and brooding ferocity? Well, I do.

It takes a man all his inborn strength to fight hunger properly. It's really easier to face bereavement, dishonour, and the perdition of one's soul—than this kind of prolonged hunger. Sad, but true. And these chaps, too, had no earthly reason for any kind of scruple. Restraint! I would just as soon have expected restraint from a hyena prowling amongst the corpses of a battlefield. But there was the fact facing me—the fact dazzling, to be seen, like the foam on the depths of the sea, like a ripple on an unfathomable enigma, a mystery greater—when I thought of it— than the curious, inexplicable note of desperate grief in this savage clamour that had swept by us on the river-bank, behind the blind whiteness of the fog.

"Two pilgrims were quarrelling in hurried whispers as to which bank. `Left.' "no, no; how can you? Right, right, of course.' 'It is very serious,' said the manager's voice behind me; 'I would be desolated if anything should happen to Mr. Kurtz before we came up.' I looked at him, and had not the slightest doubt he was sincere. He was just the kind of man who would wish to preserve appearances. That was his restraint. But when he muttered something about going on at once, I did not even take the trouble to answer him. I knew, and he knew, that it was impossible. Were we to let go our hold of the bottom, we would be absolutely in the air—in space. We wouldn't be able to tell where we were going to—whether up or down stream, or across—till we fetched against one bank or the other—and then we wouldn't know at first which it was. Of course I made no move.

I had no mind for a smash-up. You couldn't imagine a more deadly place for a shipwreck. Whether we drowned at once or not, we were sure to perish speedily in one way or another. 'I authorize you to take all the risks,' he said, after a short silence. 'I refuse to take any,' I said shortly; which was just the answer he expected, though its tone might have surprised him. 'Well, I must defer to your judgment. You are captain,' he said with marked civility. I turned my shoulder to him in sign of my appreciation, and looked into the fog. How long would it last? It was the most hopeless lookout. The approach to this Kurtz grubbing for ivory in the wretched bush was beset by as many dangers as though he had been an enchanted princess sleeping in a fabulous castle. 'Will they attack, do you think?' asked the manager, in a confidential tone.

"I did not think they would attack, for several obvious reasons. The thick fog was one. If they left the bank in their canoes they would get lost in it, as we would be if we attempted to move. Still, I had also judged the jungle of both banks quite impenetrable— and yet eyes were in it, eyes that had seen us. The riverside bushes were certainly very thick; but the undergrowth behind was evidently penetrable. However, during the short lift I had seen no canoes anywhere in the reach—certainly not abreast of the steamer. But what made the idea of attack inconceivable to me was the nature of the noise—of the cries we had heard. They had not the fierce character boding immediate hostile intention. Unexpected, wild, and violent as they had been, they had given me an irresistible impression of sorrow. The glimpse of the steamboat had for some reason filled those savages with unrestrained grief. The danger, if any, I expounded, was from our proximity to a great human passion let loose. Even extreme grief may ultimately vent itself in violence—but more generally takes the form of apathy....

"You should have seen the pilgrims stare! They had no heart to grin, or even to revile me: but I believe they thought me gone mad— with fright, maybe. I delivered a regular lecture. My dear boys, it was no good bothering. Keep a lookout? Well, you may guess I watched the fog for the signs of lifting as a cat watches a mouse; but for anything else our eyes were of no more use to us than if we had been buried miles deep in a heap of cotton-wool. It felt like it, too—choking, warm, stifling. Besides, all I said, though it sounded extravagant, was absolutely true to fact. What we afterwards alluded to as an attack was really an attempt at repulse. The action was very far from being aggressive—it was not even defensive, in the usual sense: it was undertaken under the stress of desperation, and in its essence was purely protective.

"It developed itself, I should say, two hours after the fog lifted, and its commencement was at a spot, roughly speaking, about a mile and a half below Kurtz's station. We had just floundered and flopped round a bend, when I saw an islet, a mere grassy hummock of bright green, in the middle of the stream. It was the ony thing of the kind; but as we opened the reach more, I perceived it was the head of a long sand-bank, or rather of a chain of shallow patches stretching down the middle of the river. They were discoloured, just awash, and the whole lot was seen just under the water, exactly as a man's backbone is seen running down the middle of his back under the skin. Now, as far as I did see, I could go to the right or to the left of this. I didn't know either channel, of course. The banks looked pretty well alike, the depth appeared the same; but as I had been informed the station was on the west side, I naturally headed for the western passage.

"No sooner had we fairly entered it than I became aware it was much narrower than I had supposed. To the left of us there was the long uninterrupted shoal, and to the right a high, steep bank heavily overgrown with bushes. Above the bush the trees stood in serried ranks. The twigs overhung the current thickly, and from distance to distance a large limb of some tree projected rigidly over the stream. It was then well on in the afternoon, the face of the forest was gloomy, and a broad strip of shadow had already fallen on the water. In this shadow we steamed up—very slowly, as you may imagine. I sheered her well inshore—the water being deepest near the bank, as the sounding-pole informed me.

"One of my hungry and forbearing friends was sounding in the bows just below me. This steamboat was exactly like a decked scow. On the deck, there were two little teakwood houses, with doors and windows. The boiler was in the fore-end, and the machinery right astern. yOver the whole there was a light roof, supported on stanchions. The funnel projected through that roof, and in front of the funnel a small cabin built of light planks served for a pilot-house. It contained a couch, two camp-stools, a loaded Martini-Henry leaning in one corner, a tiny table, and the steering-wheel. It had a wide door in front and a broad shutter at each side. All these were always thrown open, of course. I spent my days perched up there on the extreme fore-end of that roof, before the door. At night I slept, or tried to, on the couch. An athletic black belonging to some coast tribe and educated by my poor predecessor, was the helmsman. He sported a pair of brass earrings, wore a blue cloth wrapper from the waist to the ankles, and thought all the world of himself. He was the most unstable kind of fool I had ever seen. He steered with no end of a swagger while you were by; but if he lost sight of you, he became instantly the prey of an abject funk, and would let that cripple of a steamboat get the upper hand of him in a minute.

"I was looking down at the sounding-pole, and feeling much annoyed to see at each try a little more of it stick out of that river, when I saw my poleman give up on the business suddenly, and stretch himself flat on the deck, without even taking the trouble to haul his pole in. He kept hold on it though, and it trailed in the water. At the same time the fireman, whom I could also see below me, sat down abruptly before his furnace and ducked his head. I was amazed. Then I had to look at the river mighty quick, because there was a snag in the fairway. Sticks, little sticks, were flying about—thick: they were whizzing before my nose, dropping below me, striking behind me against my pilot-house.

All this time the river, the shore, the woods, were very quiet— perfectly quiet. I could only hear the heavy splashing thump of the stern-wheel and the patter of these things. We cleared the snag clumsily. Arrows, by Jove! We were being shot at! I stepped in quickly to close the shutter on the landside. That fool-helmsman, his hands on the spokes, was lifting his knees high, stamping his feet, champing his mouth, like a reined-in horse. Confound him! And we were staggering within ten feet of the bank. I had to lean right out to swing the heavy shutter, and I saw a face amongst the leaves on the level with my own, looking at me very fierce and steady; and then suddenly, as though a veil had been removed from my eyes, I made out, deep in the tangled gloom, naked breasts, arms, legs, glaring eyes— the bush was swarming with human limbs in movement, glistening. of bronze colour.

The twigs shook, swayed, and rustled, the arrows flew out of them, and then the shutter came to. `Steer her straight,' I said to the helmsman. He held his head rigid, face forward; but his eyes rolled, he kept on lifting and setting down his feet gently, his mouth foamed a little. `Keep quiet!' I said in a fury. I might just as well have ordered a tree not to sway in the wind. I darted out. Below me there was a great scuffle of feet on the iron deck; confused exclamations; a voice screamed, `Can you turn back?' I caught sight of a V-shaped ripple on the water ahead. What? Another snag! A fusillade burst out under my feet. The pilgrims had opened with their Winchesters, and were simply squirting lead into that bush. A deuce of a lot of smoke came up and drove slowly forward. I swore at it. Now I couldn't see the ripple or the snag either. I stood in the doorway, peering, and the arrows came in swarms.

They might have been poisoned, but they looked as though they wouldn't kill a cat. The bush began to howl. Our wood-cutters raised a warlike whoop; the report of a rifle just at my back deafened me. I glanced over my shoulder, and the pilot-house was yet full of noise and smoke when I made a dash at the wheel. The fool-nigger had dropped everything, to throw the shutter open and let off that Martini-Henry. He stood before the wide opening, glaring, and I yelled at him to come back, while I straightened the sudden twist out of that steamboat. There was no room to turn even if I had wanted to, the snag was somewhere very near ahead in that confounded smoke, there was no time to lose, so I just crowded her into the bank— right into the bank, where I knew the water was deep.

"We tore slowly along the overhanging bushes in a whirl of broken twigs and flying leaves. The fusillade below stopped short, as I had foreseen it would when the squirts got empty. I threw my head back to a glinting whizz that traversed the pilot-house, in at one shutter-hole and out at the other. Looking past that mad helmsman, who was shaking the empty rifle and yelling at the shore, I saw vague forms of men running bent double, leaping, gliding, distinct, incomplete, evanescent. Something big appeared in the air before the shutter, the rifle went overboard, and the man stepped back swiftly, looked at me over his shoulder in an extraordinary, profound, familiar manner, and fell upon my feet. The side of his head hit the wheel twice, and the end of what appeared a long cane clattered round and knocked over a little camp-stool. It looked as though after wrenching that thing from somebody ashore he had lost his balance in the effort. The thin smoke had blown away, we were clear of the snag, and looking ahead I could see that in another hundred yards or so I would be free to sheer off, away from the bank; but my feet felt so very warm and wet that I had to look down.

The man had rolled on his back and stared straight up at me; both his hands clutched that cane. It was the shaft of a spear that, either thrown or lunged through the opening, had caught him in the side, just below the ribs; the blade had gone in out of sight, after making a frightful gash; my shoes were full; a pool of blood lay very still, gleaming dark-red under the wheel; his eyes shone with an amazing lustre. The fusillade burst out again. He looked at me anxiously, gripping the spear like something precious, with an air of being afraid I would try to take it away from him. I had to make an effort to free my eyes from his gaze and attend to the steering. With one hand I felt above my head for the line of the steam whistle, and jerked out screech after screech hurriedly.

The tumult of angry and warlike yells was checked instantly, and then from the depths of the woods went out such a tremulous and prolonged wail of mournful fear and utter despair as may be imagined to follow the flight of the last hope from the earth. There was a great commotion in the bush; the shower of arrows stopped, a few dropping shots rang out sharply—then silence, in which the languid beat of the stern-wheel came plainly to my ears. I put the helm hard a-starboard at the moment when the pilgrim in pink pyjamas, very hot and agitated, appeared in the doorway. 'The manager sends me—' he began in an official tone, and stopped short. 'Good God!' he said, glaring at the wounded man.

"We two whites stood over him, and his lustrous and inquiring glance enveloped us both. I declare it looked as though he would presently put to us some questions in an understandable language; but he died without uttering a sound, without moving a limb, without twitching a muscle. Only in the very last moment, as though in response to some sign we could not see, to some whisper we could not hear, he frowned heavily, and that frown gave to his black death-mask an inconeivably sombre, brooding, and menacing expression.

The lustre of inquiring glance faded swiftly into vacant glassiness. `Can you steer?' I asked the agent eagerly. He looked very dubious; but I made a grab at his arm, and he understood at once I meant him to steer whether or no. To tell you the truth, I was morbidly anxious to change my shoes and socks. `He is dead,' murmured the fellow, immensely impressed. `No doubt about it,' said I, tugging like mad at the shoe-laces. `And by the way, I suppose Mr. Kurtz is dead as well by this time.'

"For the moment that was the dominant thought. There was a sense of extreme disappointment, as though I had found out I had been striving after something altogether without a substance. I couldn't have been more disgusted if I had travelled all this way for the sole purpose of talking with Mr. Kurtz. Talking with... I flung one shoe overboard, and became aware that that was exactly what I had been looking forward to— a talk with Kurtz. I made the strange discovery that I had never imagined him as doing, you know, but as discoursing. I didn't say to myself, `Now I will never see him,' or `Now I will never shake him by the hand,' but, `Now I will never hear him.' The man presented himself as a voice. Not of course that I did not connect him with some sort of action. Hadn't I been told in all the tones of jealousy and admiration that he had collected, bartered, swindled, or stolen more ivory than all the other agents together? That was not the point. The point was in his being a gifted creature, and that of all his gifts the one that stood out preeminently, that carried with it a sense of real presence, was his ability to talk, his words— the gift of expression, the bewildering, the illuminating, the most exalted and the most contemptible, the pulsating stream of light, or the deceitful flow from the heart of an impenetrable darkness.

"The other shoe went flying unto the devil-god of that river. I thought, `By Jove! it's all over. We are too late; he has vanished— the gift has vanished, by means of some spear, arrow, or club. I will never hear that chap speak after all'— and my sorrow had a startling extravagance of emotion, even such as I had noticed in the howling sorrow of these savages in the bush. I couldn't have felt more of lonely desolation somehow, had I been robbed of a belief or had missed my destiny in life.... Why do you sigh in this beastly way, somebody? Absurd? Well, absurd. Good Lord! mustn't a man ever—Here, give me some tobacco."...

There was a pause of profound stillness, then a match flared, and Marlow's lean face appeared, worn, hollow, with downward folds and dropped eyelids, with an aspect of concentrated attention; and as he took vigourous draws at his pipe, it seemed to retreat and advance out of the night in the regular flicker of tiny flame. The match went out.

"Absurd!" he cried. "This is the worst of trying to tell.... Here you all are, each moored with two good addresses, like a hulk with two anchors, a butcher round one corner, a policeman round another, excellent appetites, and temperature normal—you hear—normal from year's end to year's end. And you say, Absurd! Absurd be—exploded! Absurd! My dear boys, what can you expect from a man who out of sheer nervousness had just flung overboard a pair of new shoes! Now I think of it, it is amazing I did not shed tears. I am, upon the whole, proud of my fortitude. I was cut to the quick at the idea of having lost the inestimable privilege of listening to the gifted Kurtz. Of course I was wrong. The privilege was waiting for me. Oh, yes, I heard more than enough. And I was right, too. A voice. He was very little more than a voice. And I heard—him—it—this voice—other voices—all of them were so little more than voices—and the memory of that time itself lingers around me, impalpable, like a dying vibration of one immense jabber, silly, atrocious, sordid, savage, or simply mean, without any kind of sense. Voices, voices—even the girl herself—now—"

He was silent for a long time.

"I laid the ghost of his gifts at last with a lie," he began, suddenly. "Girl! What? Did I mention a girl? Oh, she is out of it—completely. They—the women, I mean— are out of it—should be out of it. We must help them to stay in that beautiful world of their own, lest ours gets worse. Oh, she had to be out of it. You should have heard the disinterred body of Mr. Kurtz saying, 'My Intended.' You would have perceived directly then how completely she was out of it. And the lofty frontal bone of Mr. Kurtz! They say the hair goes on growing sometimes, but this— ah—specimen, was impressively bald. The wilderness had patted him on the head, and, behold, it was like a ball— an ivory ball; it had caressed him, and—lo!—he had withered; it had taken him, loved him, embraced him, got into his veins, consumed his flesh, and sealed his soul to its own by the inconceivable ceremonies of some devilish initiation. He was its spoiled and pampered favourite. Ivory? I should think so. Heaps of it, stacks of it.

The old mud shanty was bursting with it. You would think there was not a single tusk left either above or below the ground in the whole country. 'Mostly fossil,' the manager had remarked, disparagingly. It was no more fossil than I am; but they call it fossil when it is dug up. It appears these niggers do bury the tusks sometimes— but evidently they couldn't bury this parcel deep enough to save the gifted Mr. Kurtz from his fate. We filled the steamboat with it, and had to pile a lot on the deck. Thus he could see and enjoy as long as he could see, because the appreciation of this favour had remained with him to the last. You should have heard him say, 'My ivory.' Oh, yes, I heard him. 'My Intended, my ivory, my station, my river, my—' everything belonged to him. It made me hold my breath in expectation of hearing the wilderness burst into a prodigious peal of laughter that would shake the fixed stars in their places. Everything belonged to him— but that was a trifle. The thing was to know what he belonged to, how many powers of darkness claimed him for their own. That was the reflection that made you creepy all over. It was impossible— it was not good for one either—trying to imagine. He had taken a high seat amongst the devils of the land— I mean literally. You can't understand. How could you?— with solid pavement under your feet, surrounded by kind neighbours ready to cheer you or to fall on you, stepping delicately between the butcher and the policeman, in the holy terror of scandal and gallows and lunatic asylums—how can you imagine what particular region of the first ages a man's untrammelled feet may take him into by the way of solitude—utter solitude without a policeman— by the way of silence—utter silence, where no warning voice of a kind neighbour can be heard whispering of public opinion?

These little things make all the great difference. When they are gone you must fall back upon your own innate strength, upon your own capacity for faithfulness. Of course you may be too much of a fool to go wrong— too dull even to know you are being assaulted by the powers of darkness. I take it, no fool ever made a bargain for his soul with the devil; the fool is too much of a fool, or the devil too much of a devil—I don't know which. Or you may be such a thunderingly exalted creature as to be altogether deaf and blind to anything but heavenly sights and sounds. Then the earth for you is only a standing place—and whether to be like this is your loss or your gain I won't pretend to say. But most of us are neither one nor the other. The earth for us is a place to live in, where we must put up with sights, with sounds, with smells, too, by Jove!—breathe dead hippo, so to speak, and not be contaminated. And there, don't you see? Your strength comes in, the faith in your ability for the digging of unostentatious holes to bury the stuff in— your power of devotion, not to yourself, but to an obscure, back-breaking business. And that's difficult enough. Mind, I am not trying to excuse or even explain—I am trying to account to myself for—for—Mr. Kurtz—for the shade of Mr. Kurtz. This initiated wraith from the back of Nowhere honoured me with its amazing confidence before it vanished altogether. This was because it could speak English to me. The original Kurtz had been educated partly in England, and—as he was good enough to say himself—his sympathies were in the right place. His mother was half-English, his father was half-French.

All Europe contributed to the making of Kurtz; and by and by I learned that, most appropriately, the International Society for the Suppression of Savage Customs had intrusted him with the making of a report, for its future guidance. And he had written it, too. I've seen it. I've read it. It was eloquent, vibrating with eloquence, but too high-strung, I think. Seventeen pages of close writing he had found time for! But this must have been before his—let us say—nerves, went wrong, and caused him to preside at certain midnight dances ending with unspeakable rites, which—as far as I reluctantly gathered from what I heard at various times—were offered up to him— do you understand?—to Mr. Kurtz himself. But it was a beautiful piece of writing.

The opening paragraph, however, in the light of later information, strikes me now as ominous. He began with the argument that we whites, from the point of development we had arrived at, `must necessarily appear to them [savages] in the nature of supernatural beings— we approach them with the might of a deity,' and so on, and so on. `By the simple exercise of our will we can exert a power for good practically unbounded,' etc., etc. From that point he soared and took me with him. The peroration was magnificent, though difficult to remember, you know.

It gave me the notion of an exotic Immensity ruled by an august Benevolence. It made me tingle with enthusiasm. This was the unbounded power of eloquence—of words—of burning noble words. There were no practical hints to interrupt the magic current of phrases, unless a kind of note at the foot of the last page, scrawled evidently much later, in an unsteady hand, may be regarded as the exposition of a method. It was very simple, and at the end of that moving appeal to every altruistic sentiment it blazed at you, luminous and terrifying, like a flash of lightning in a serene sky: `Exterminate all the brutes!' The curious part was that he had apparently forgotten all about that valuable postscriptum, because, later on, when he in a sense came to himself, he repeatedly entreated me to take good care of `my pamphlet' (he called it), as it was sure to have in the future a good influence upon his career. I had full information about all these things, and, besides, as it turned out, I was to have the care of his memory. I've done enough for it to give me the indisputable right to lay it, if I choose, for an everlasting rest in the dust-bin of progress, amongst all the sweepings and, figuratively speaking, all the dead cats of civilization. But then, you see, I can't choose. He won't be forgotten. Whatever he was, he was not common.

He had the power to charm or frighten rudimentary souls into an aggravated witch-dance in his honour; he could also fill the small souls of the pilgrims with bitter misgivings: he had one devoted friend at least, and he had conquered one soul in the world that was neither rudimentary nor tainted with self-seeking. No; I can't forget him, though I am not prepared to affirm the fellow was exactly worth the life we lost in getting to him. I missed my late helmsman awfully— I missed him even while his body was still lying in the pilot-house. Perhaps you will think it passing strange this regret for a savage who was no more account than a grain of sand in a black Sahara. Well, don't you see, he had done something, he had steered; for months I had him at my back— a help—an instrument. It was a kind of partnership. He steered for me— I had to look after him, I worried about his deficiencies, and thus a subtle bond had been created, of which I only became aware when it was suddenly broken. And the intimate profundity of that look he gave me when he received his hurt remains to this day in my memory— like a claim of distant kinship affirmed in a supreme moment.

"Poor fool! If he had only left that shutter alone. He had no restraint, no restraint—just like Kurtz—a tree swayed by the wind. As soon as I had put on a dry pair of slippers, I dragged him out, after first jerking the spear out of his side, which operation I confess I performed with my eyes shut tight. His heels leaped together over the little doorstep; his shoulders were pressed to my breast; I hugged him from behind desperately. Oh! he was heavy, heavy; heavier than any man on earth, I should imagine. Then without more ado I tipped him overboard. The current snatched him as though he had been a wisp of grass, and I saw the body roll over twice before I lost sight of it for ever. All the pilgrims and the manager were then congregated on the awning-deck about the pilot-house, chattering at each other like a flock of excited magpies, and there was a scandalized murmur at my heartless promptitude. What they wanted to keep that body hanging about for I can't guess. Embalm it, maybe. But I had also heard another, and a very ominous, murmur on the deck below. My friends the wood-cutters were likewise scandalized, and with a better show of reason— though I admit that the reason itself was quite inadmissible. Oh, quite! I had made up my mind that if my late helmsman was to be eaten, the fishes alone should have him. He had been a very second-rate helmsman while alive, but now he was dead he might have become a first-class temptation, and possibly cause some startling trouble. Besides, I was anxious to take the wheel, the man in pink pyjamas showing himself a hopeless duffer at the business.

"This I did directly the simple funeral was over. We were going half-speed, keeping right in the middle of the stream, and I listened to the talk about me. They had given up Kurtz, they had given up the station; Kurtz was dead, and the station had been burnt—and so on—and so on. The red-haired pilgrim was beside himself with the thought that at least this poor Kurtz had been properly avenged. 'Say! We must have made a glorious slaughter of them in the bush. Eh? What do you think? Say?' He positively danced, the bloodthirsty little gingery beggar. And he had nearly fainted when he saw the wounded man! I could not help saying, 'You made a glorious lot of smoke, anyhow.' I had seen, from the way the tops of the bushes rustled and flew, that almost all the shots had gone too high. You can't hit anything unless you take aim and fire from the shoulder; but these chaps fired from the hip with their eyes shut. The retreat, I maintained—and I was right—was caused by the screeching of the steam whistle. Upon this they forgot Kurtz, and began to howl at me with indignant protests.

"The manager stood by the wheel murmuring confidentially about the necessity of getting well away down the river before dark at all events, when I saw in the distance a clearing on the riverside and the outlines of some sort of building. 'What's this?' I asked. He clapped his hands in wonder. 'The station!' he cried. I edged in at once, still going half-speed.

"Through my glasses I saw the slope of a hill interspersed with rare trees and perfectly free from undergrowth. A long decaying building on the summit was half buried in the high grass; the large holes in the peaked roof gaped black from afar; the jungle and the woods made a background. There was no enclosure or fence of any kind; but there had been one apparently, for near the house half-a-dozen slim posts remained in a row, roughly trimmed, and with their upper ends ornamented with round carved balls. The rails, or whatever there had been between, had disappeared. Of course the forest surrounded all that. The river-bank was clear, and on the waterside I saw a white man under a hat like a cart-wheel beckoning persistently with his whole arm. Examining the edge of the forest above and below, I was almost certain I could see movements—human forms gliding here and there. I steamed past prudently, then stopped the engines and let her drift down. The man on the shore began to shout, urging us to land. 'We have been attacked,' screamed the manager. 'I know—I know. It's all right,' yelled back the other, as cheerful as you please. 'Come along. It's all right. I am glad.'

"His aspect reminded me of something I had seen—something funny I had seen somewhere. As I manoeuvred to get alongside, I was asking myself, 'What does this fellow look like?' Suddenly I got it. He looked like a harlequin. His clothes had been made of some stuff that was brown holland probably, but it was covered with patches all over, with bright patches, blue, red, and yellow—patches on the back, patches on the front, patches on elbows, on knees; coloured binding around his jacket, scarlet edging at the bottom of his trousers; and the sunshine made him look extremely gay and wonderfully neat withal, because you could see how beautifully all this patching had been done. A beardless, boyish face, very fair, no features to speak of, nose peeling, little blue eyes, smiles and frowns chasing each other over that open countenance like sunshine and shadow on a wind-swept plain. 'Look out, captain!' he cried; 'there's a snag lodged in here last night.' What! Another snag? I confess I swore shamefully. I had nearly holed my cripple, to finish off that charming trip. The harlequin on the bank turned his little pug-nose up to me. 'You English?' he asked, all smiles. 'Are you?' I shouted from the wheel. The smiles vanished, and he shook his head as if sorry for my disappointment. Then he brightened up. 'Never mind!' he cried encouragingly. 'Are we in time?' I asked. 'He is up there,' he replied, with a toss of the head up the hill, and becoming gloomy all of a sudden. His face was like the autumn sky, overcast one moment and bright the next.

"When the manager, escorted by the pilgrims, all of them armed to the teeth, had gone to the house this chap came on board. 'I say, I don't like this. These natives are in the bush,' I said. He assured me earnestly it was all right. 'They are simple people,' he added; 'well, I am glad you came. It took me all my time to keep them off.' 'But you said it was all right,' I cried. 'Oh, they meant no harm,' he said; and as I stared he corrected himself, 'Not exactly.' Then vivaciously, 'My faith, your pilot-house wants a clean-up!' In the next breath he advised me to keep enough steam on the boiler to blow the whistle in case of any trouble. 'One good screech will do more for you than all your rifles. They are simple people,' he repeated. He rattled away at such a rate he quite overwhelmed me. He seemed to be trying to make up for lots of silence, and actually hinted, laughing, that such was the case. 'Don't you talk with Mr. Kurtz?' I said. 'You don't talk with that man—you listen to him,' he exclaimed with severe exaltation. 'But now—' He waved his arm, and in the twinkling of an eye was in the uttermost depths of despondency. In a moment he came up again with a jump, possessed himself of both my hands, shook them continuously, while he gabbled: 'Brother sailor... honour... pleasure... delight... introduce myself... Russian... son of an arch-priest... Government of Tambov... What? Tobacco! English tobacco; the excellent English tobacco! Now, that's brotherly. Smoke? Where's a sailor that does not smoke?"

"The pipe soothed him, and gradually I made out he had run away from school, had gone to sea in a Russian ship; ran away again; served some time in English ships; was now reconciled with the arch-priest. He made a point of that. 'But when one is young one must see things, gather experience, ideas; enlarge the mind.' 'Here!' I interrupted. 'You can never tell! Here I met Mr. Kurtz,' he said, youthfully solemn and reproachful. I held my tongue after that. It appears he had persuaded a Dutch trading-house on the coast to fit him out with stores and goods, and had started for the interior with a light heart and no more idea of what would happen to him than a baby. He had been wandering about that river for nearly two years alone, cut off from everybody and everything. 'I am not so young as I look. I am twenty-five,' he said. 'At first old Van Shuyten would tell me to go to the devil,' he narrated with keen enjoyment; 'but I stuck to him, and talked and talked, till at last he got afraid I would talk the hind-leg off his favourite dog, so he gave me some cheap things and a few guns, and told me he hoped he would never see my face again. Good old Dutchman, Van Shuyten. I've sent him one small lot of ivory a year ago, so that he can't call me a little thief when I get back. I hope he got it. And for the rest I don't care. I had some wood stacked for you. That was my old house. Did you see?'

"I gave him Towson's book. He made as though he would kiss me, but restrained himself. 'The only book I had left, and I thought I had lost it,' he said, looking at it ecstatically. 'So many accidents happen to a man going about alone, you know. Canoes get upset sometimes—and sometimes you've got to clear out so quick when the people get angry.' He thumbed the pages. 'You made notes in Russian?' I asked. He nodded. 'I thought they were written in cipher,' I said. He laughed, then became serious. 'I had lots of trouble to keep these people off,' he said. 'Did they want to kill you?' I asked. 'Oh, no!' he cried, and checked himself. 'Why did they attack us?' I pursued. He hesitated, then said shamefacedly, 'They don't want him to go.' 'Don't they?' I said curiously. He nodded a nod full of mystery and wisdom. 'I tell you,' he cried, 'this man has enlarged my mind.' He opened his arms wide, staring at me with his little blue eyes that were perfectly round."

PART III

"I looked at him, lost in astonishment. There he was before me, in motley, as though he had absconded from a troupe of mimes, enthusiastic, fabulous. His very existence was improbable, inexplicable, and altogether bewildering. He was an insoluble problem. It was inconceivable how he had existed, how he had succeeded in getting so far, how he had managed to remain— why he did not instantly disappear. 'I went a little farther,' he said, 'then still a little farther—till I had gone so far that I don't know how I'll ever get back. Never mind. Plenty time. I can manage. You take Kurtz away quick—quick—I tell you.' The glamour of youth enveloped his parti-coloured rags, his destitution, his loneliness, the essential desolation of his futile wanderings. For months—for years—his life hadn't been worth a day's purchase; and there he was gallantly, thoughtlessly alive, to all appearances indestructible solely by the virtue of his few years and of his unreflecting audacity. I was seduced into something like admiration— like envy. Glamour urged him on, glamour kept him unscathed. He surely wanted nothing from the wilderness but space to breathe in and to push on through. His need was to exist, and to move onwards at the greatest possible risk, and with a maximum of privation. If the absolutely pure, uncalculating, unpractical spirit of adventure had ever ruled a human being, it ruled this bepatched youth. I almost envied him the possession of this modest and clear flame. It seemed to have consumed all thought of self so completely, that even while he was talking to you, you forgot that it was he— the man before your eyes—who had gone through these things. I did not envy him his devotion to Kurtz, though. He had not meditated over it. It came to him, and he accepted it with a sort of eager fatalism. I must say that to me it appeared about the most dangerous thing in every way he had come upon so far.

"They had come together unavoidably, like two ships becalmed near each other, and lay rubbing sides at last. I suppose Kurtz wanted an audience, because on a certain occasion, when encamped in the forest, they had talked all night, or more probably Kurtz had talked. 'We talked of everything,' he said, quite transported at the recollection. 'I forgot there was such a thing as sleep. The night did not seem to last an hour. Everything! Everything!... Of love, too.' 'Ah, he talked to you of love!' I said, much amused. 'It isn't what you think,' he cried, almost passionately. 'It was in general. He made me see things—things.'

"He threw his arms up. We were on deck at the time, and the headman of my wood-cutters, lounging near by, turned upon him his heavy and glittering eyes. I looked around, and I don't know why, but I assure you that never, never before, did this land, this river, this jungle, the very arch of this blazing sky, appear to me so hopeless and so dark, so impenetrable to human thought, so pitiless to human weakness. 'And, ever since, you have been with him, of course?' I said.

"On the contrary. It appears their intercourse had been very much broken by various causes. He had, as he informed me proudly, managed to nurse Kurtz through two illnesses (he alluded to it as you would to some risky feat), but as a rule Kurtz wandered alone, far in the depths of the forest. 'Very often coming to this station, I had to wait days and days before he would turn up,' he said. 'Ah, it was worth waiting for!—sometimes.' 'What was he doing? exploring or what?' I asked. 'Oh, yes, of course'; he had discovered lots of villages, a lake, too—he did not know exactly in what direction; it was dangerous to inquire too much—but mostly his expeditions had been for ivory. 'But he had no goods to trade with by that time,' I objected. 'There's a good lot of cartridges left even yet,' he answered, looking away. 'To speak plainly, he raided the country,' I said. He nodded. 'Not alone, surely!' He muttered something about the villages round that lake. 'Kurtz got the tribe to follow him, did he?' I suggested. He fidgeted a little. 'They adored him,' he said.

The tone of these words was so extraordinary that I looked at him searchingly. It was curious to see his mingled eagerness and reluctance to speak of Kurtz. The man filled his life, occupied his thoughts, swayed his emotions. 'What can you expect?' he burst out; 'he came to them with thunder and lightning, you know— and they had never seen anything like it—and very terrible. He could be very terrible. You can't judge Mr. Kurtz as you would an ordinary man. No, no, no! Now—just to give you an idea— I don't mind telling you, he wanted to shoot me, too, one day— but I don't judge him.' `Shoot you!' I cried `What for?' `Well, I had a small lot of ivory the chief of that village near my house gave me. You see I used to shoot game for them. Well, he wanted it, and wouldn't hear reason. He declared he would shoot me unless I gave him the ivory and then cleared out of the country, because he could do so, and had a fancy for it, and there was nothing on earth to prevent him killing whom he jolly well pleased. And it was true, too. I gave him the ivory. What did I care! But I didn't clear out. No, no. I couldn't leave him. I had to be careful, of course, till we got friendly again for a time. He had his second illness then. Afterwards I had to keep out of the way; but I didn't mind. He was living for the most part in those villages on the lake. When he came down to the river, sometimes he would take to me, and sometimes it was better for me to be careful.

This man suffered too much. He hated all this, and somehow he couldn't get away. When I had a chance I begged him to try and leave while there was time; I offered to go back with him. And he would say yes, and then he would remain; go off on another ivory hunt; disappear for weeks; forget himself amongst these people— forget himself—you know.' `Why! he's mad,' I said. He protested indignantly. Mr. Kurtz couldn't be mad. If I had heard him talk, only two days ago, I wouldn't dare hint at such a thing.... I had taken up my binoculars while we talked, and was looking at the shore, sweeping the limit of the forest at each side and at the back of the house. The consciousness of there being people in that bush, so silent, so quiet—as silent and quiet as the ruined house on the hill— made me uneasy.

There was no sign on the face of nature of this amazing tale that was not so much told as suggested to me in desolate exclamations, completed by shrugs, in interrupted phrases, in hints ending in deep sighs. The woods were unmoved, like a mask—heavy, like the closed door of a prison—they looked with their air of hidden knowledge, of patient expectation, of unapproachable silence. The Russian was explaining to me that it was only lately that Mr. Kurtz had come down to the river, bringing along with him all the fighting men of that lake tribe. He had been absent for several months—getting himself adored, I suppose— and had come down unexpectedly, with the intention to all appearance of making a raid either across the river or down stream. Evidently the appetite for more ivory had got the better of the— what shall I say?—less material aspirations. However he had got much worse suddenly. 'I heard he was lying helpless, and so I came up—took my chance,' said the Russian. 'Oh, he is bad, very bad.' I directed my glass to the house.

There were no signs of life, but there was the ruined roof, the long mud wall peeping above the grass, with three little square window-holes, no two of the same size; all this brought within reach of my hand, as it were. And then I made a brusque movement, and one of the remaining posts of that vanished fence leaped up in the field of my glass. You remember I told you I had been struck at the distance by certain attempts at ornamentation, rather remarkable in the ruinous aspect of the place. Now I had suddenly a nearer view, and its first result was to make me throw my head back as if before a blow. Then I went carefully from post to post with my glass, and I saw my mistake.

These round knobs were not ornamental but symbolic; they were expressive and puzzling, striking and disturbing—food for thought and also for vultures if there had been any looking down from the sky; but at all events for such ants as were industrious enough to ascend the pole. They would have been even more impressive, those heads on the stakes, if their faces had not been turned to the house. Only one, the first I had made out, was facing my way. I was not so shocked as you may think. The start back I had given was really nothing but a movement of surprise. I had expected to see a knob of wood there, you know. I returned deliberately to the first I had seen—and there it was, black, dried, sunken, with closed eyelids—a head that seemed to sleep at the top of that pole, and, with the shrunken dry lips showing a narrow white line of the teeth, was smiling, too, smiling continuously at some endless and jocose dream of that eternal slumber.

"I am not disclosing any trade secrets. In fact, the manager said afterwards that Mr. Kurtz's methods had ruined the district. I have no opinion on that point, but I want you clearly to understand that there was nothing exactly profitable in these heads being there. They only showed that Mr. Kurtz lacked restraint in the gratification of his various lusts, that there was something wanting in him— some small matter which, when the pressing need arose, could not be found under his magnificent eloquence. Whether he knew of this deficiency himself I can't say. I think the knowledge came to him at last— only at the very last. But the wilderness had found him out early, and had taken on him a terrible vengeance for the fantastic invasion. I think it had whispered to him things about himself which he did not know, things of which he had no conception till he took counsel with this great solitude—and the whisper had proved irresistibly fascinating. It echoed loudly within him because he was hollow at the core.... I put down the glass, and the head that had appeared near enough to be spoken to seemed at once to have leaped away from me into inaccessible distance.

"The admirer of Mr. Kurtz was a bit crestfallen. In a hurried, indistinct voice he began to assure me he had not dared to take these—say, symbols—down. He was not afraid of the natives; they would not stir till Mr. Kurtz gave the word. His ascendancy was extraordinary. The camps of these people surrounded the place, and the chiefs came every day to see him. They would crawl.... 'I don't want to know anything of the ceremonies used when approaching Mr. Kurtz,' I shouted. Curious, this feeling that came over me that such details would be more intolerable than those heads drying on the stakes under Mr. Kurtz's windows. After all, that was only a savage sight, while I seemed at one bound to have been transported into some lightless region of subtle horrors, where pure, uncomplicated savagery was a positive relief, being something that had a right to exist—obviously—in the sunshine. The young man looked at me with surprise. I suppose it did not occur to him that Mr. Kurtz was no idol of mine. He forgot I hadn't heard any of these splendid monologues on, what was it? on love, justice, conduct of life—or what not. If it had come to crawling before Mr. Kurtz, he crawled as much as the veriest savage of them all. I had no idea of the conditions, he said: these heads were the heads of rebels. I shocked him excessively by laughing. Rebels! What would be the next definition I was to hear? There had been enemies, criminals, workers—and these were rebels.

Those rebellious heads looked very subdued to me on their sticks. `You don't know how such a life tries a man like Kurtz,' cried Kurtz's last disciple. `Well, and you?' I said. `I! I! I am a simple man. I have no great thoughts. I want nothing from anybody. How can you compare me to... ?' His feelings were too much for speech, and suddenly he broke down. `I don't understand,' he groaned. `I've been doing my best to keep him alive, and that's enough. I had no hand in all this. I have no abilities. There hasn't been a drop of medicine or a mouthful of invalid food for months here. He was shamefully abandoned. A man like this, with such ideas. Shamefully! Shamefully! I—I— haven't slept for the last ten nights...'

"His voice lost itself in the calm of the evening. The long shadows of the forest had slipped downhill while we talked, had gone far beyond the ruined hovel, beyond the symbolic row of stakes. All this was in the gloom, while we down there were yet in the sunshine, and the stretch of the river abreast of the clearing glittered in a still and dazzling splendour, with a murky and overshadowed bend above and below. Not a living soul was seen on the shore. The bushes did not rustle.

"Suddenly round the corner of the house a group of men appeared, as though they had come up from the ground. They waded waist-deep in the grass, in a compact body, bearing an improvised stretcher in their midst. Instantly, in the emptiness of the landscape, a cry arose whose shrillness pierced the still air like a sharp arrow flying straight to the very heart of the land; and, as if by enchantment, streams of human beings—of naked human beings—with spears in their hands, with bows, with shields, with wild glances and savage movements, were poured into the clearing by the dark-faced and pensive forest. The bushes shook, the grass swayed for a time, and then everything stood still in attentive immobility.

"'Now, if he does not say the right thing to them we are all done for,' said the Russian at my elbow. The knot of men with the stretcher had stopped, too, halfway to the steamer, as if petrified. I saw the man on the stretcher sit up, lank and with an uplifted arm, above the shoulders of the bearers. 'Let us hope that the man who can talk so well of love in general will find some particular reason to spare us this time,' I said. I resented bitterly the absurd danger of our situation, as if to be at the mercy of that atrocious phantom had been a dishonouring necessity. I could not hear a sound, but through my glasses I saw the thin arm extended commandingly, the lower jaw moving, the eyes of that apparition shining darkly far in its bony head that nodded with grotesque jerks. Kurtz—Kurtz—that means short in German—don't it? Well, the name was as true as everything else in his life— and death. He looked at least seven feet long. His covering had fallen off, and his body emerged from it pitiful and appalling as from a winding-sheet.

I could see the cage of his ribs all astir, the bones of his arm waving. It was as though an animated image of death carved out of old ivory had been shaking its hand with menaces at a motionless crowd of men made of dark and glittering bronze. I saw him open his mouth wide—it gave him a weirdly voracious aspect, as though he had wanted to swallow all the air, all the earth, all the men before him. A deep voice reached me faintly. He must have been shouting. He fell back suddenly. The stretcher shook as the bearers staggered forward again, and almost at the same time I noticed that the crowd of savages was vanishing without any perceptible movement of retreat, as if the forest that had ejected these beings so suddenly had drawn them in again as the breath is drawn in a long aspiration.

"Some of the pilgrims behind the stretcher carried his arms— two shot-guns, a heavy rifle, and a light revolver-carbine— the thunderbolts of that pitiful Jupiter. The manager bent over him murmuring as he walked beside his head. They laid him down in one of the little cabins—just a room for a bed place and a camp-stool or two, you know. We had brought his belated correspondence, and a lot of torn envelopes and open letters littered his bed. His hand roamed feebly amongst these papers. I was struck by the fire of his eyes and the composed languor of his expression. It was not so much the exhaustion of disease. He did not seem in pain. This shadow looked satiated and calm, as though for the moment it had had its fill of all the emotions.

"He rustled one of the letters, and looking straight in my face said, 'I am glad.' Somebody had been writing to him about me. These special recommendations were turning up again. The volume of tone he emitted without effort, almost without the trouble of moving his lips, amazed me. A voice! a voice! It was grave, profound, vibrating, while the man did not seem capable of a whisper. However, he had enough strength in him— factitious no doubt—to very nearly make an end of us, as you shall hear directly.

"The manager appeared silently in the doorway; I stepped out at once and he drew the curtain after me. The Russian, eyed curiously by the pilgrims, was staring at the shore. I followed the direction of his glance.

"Dark human shapes could be made out in the distance, flitting indistinctly against the gloomy border of the forest, and near the river two bronze figures, leaning on tall spears, stood in the sunlight under fantastic head-dresses of spotted skins, warlike and still in statuesque repose. And from right to left along the lighted shore moved a wild and gorgeous apparition of a woman.

"She walked with measured steps, draped in striped and fringed cloths, treading the earth proudly, with a slight jingle and flash of barbarous ornaments. She carried her head high; her hair was done in the shape of a helmet; she had brass leggings to the knee, brass wire gauntlets to the elbow, a crimson spot on her tawny cheek, innumerable necklaces of glass beads on her neck; bizarre things, charms, gifts of witch-men, that hung about her, glittered and trembled at every step. She must have had the value of several elephant tusks upon her. She was savage and superb, wild-eyed and magnificent; there was something ominous and stately in her deliberate progress. And in the hush that had fallen suddenly upon the whole sorrowful land, the immense wilderness, the colossal body of the fecund and mysterious life seemed to look at her, pensive, as though it had been looking at the image of its own tenebrous and passionate soul.

"She came abreast of the steamer, stood still, and faced us. Her long shadow fell to the water's edge. Her face had a tragic and fierce aspect of wild sorrow and of dumb pain mingled with the fear of some struggling, half-shaped resolve. She stood looking at us without a stir, and like the wilderness itself, with an air of brooding over an inscrutable purpose. A whole minute passed, and then she made a step forward. There was a low jingle, a glint of yellow metal, a sway of fringed draperies, and she stopped as if her heart had failed her. The young fellow by my side growled. The pilgrims murmured at my back. She looked at us all as if her life had depended upon the unswerving steadiness of her glance. Suddenly she opened her bared arms and threw them up rigid above her head, as though in an uncontrollable desire to touch the sky, and at the same time the swift shadows darted out on the earth, swept around on the river, gathering the steamer into a shadowy embrace. A formidable silence hung over the scene.

"She turned away slowly, walked on, following the bank, and passed into the bushes to the left. Once only her eyes gleamed back at us in the dusk of the thickets before she disappeared.

"'If she had offered to come aboard I really think I would have tried to shoot her,' said the man of patches, nervously. 'I have been risking my life every day for the last fortnight to keep her out of the house. She got in one day and kicked up a row about those miserable rags I picked up in the storeroom to mend my clothes with. I wasn't decent. At least it must have been that, for she talked like a fury to Kurtz for an hour, pointing at me now and then. I don't understand the dialect of this tribe. Luckily for me, I fancy Kurtz felt too ill that day to care, or there would have been mischief. I don't understand.... No—it's too much for me. Ah, well, it's all over now.'

"At this moment I heard Kurtz's deep voice behind the curtain: 'Save me!—save the ivory, you mean. Don't tell me. Save me! Why, I've had to save you. You are interrupting my plans now. Sick! Sick! Not so sick as you would like to believe. Never mind. I'll carry my ideas out yet—I will return. I'll show you what can be done. You with your little peddling notions—you are interfering with me. I will return. I....'

"The manager came out. He did me the honour to take me under the arm and lead me aside. 'He is very low, very low,' he said. He considered it necessary to sigh, but neglected to be consistently sorrowful. 'We have done all we could for him—haven't we? But there is no disguising the fact, Mr. Kurtz has done more harm than good to the Company. He did not see the time was not ripe for vigourous action. Cautiously, cautiously—that's my principle. We must be cautious yet. The district is closed to us for a time. Deplorable! Upon the whole, the trade will suffer. I don't deny there is a remarkable quantity of ivory—mostly fossil. We must save it, at all events—but look how precarious the position is—and why? Because the method is unsound.' 'Do you,' said I, looking at the shore, 'call it "unsound method?"' 'Without doubt,' he exclaimed hotly. 'Don't you?'... 'No method at all,' I murmured after a while. 'Exactly,' he exulted. 'I anticipated this. Shows a complete want of judgment. It is my duty to point it out in the proper quarter.' 'Oh,' said I, 'that fellow—what's his name?—the brickmaker, will make a readable report for you.' He appeared confounded for a moment. It seemed to me I had never breathed an atmosphere so vile, and I turned mentally to Kurtz for relief—positively for relief. 'Nevertheless I think Mr. Kurtz is a remarkable man,' I said with emphasis. He started, dropped on me a heavy glance, said very quietly, `he was,' and turned his back on me. My hour of favour was over; I found myself lumped along with Kurtz as a partisan of methods for which the time was not ripe: I was unsound! Ah! but it was something to have at least a choice of nightmares.

"I had turned to the wilderness really, not to Mr. Kurtz, who, I was ready to admit, was as good as buried. And for a moment it seemed to me as if I also were buried in a vast grave full of unspeakable secrets. I felt an intolerable weight oppressing my breast, the smell of the damp earth, the unseen presence of victorious corruption, the darkness of an impenetrable night.... The Russian tapped me on the shoulder. I heard him mumbling and stammering something about `brother seaman—couldn't conceal— knowledge of matters that would affect Mr. Kurtz's reputation.' I waited. For him evidently Mr. Kurtz was not in his grave; I suspect that for him Mr. Kurtz was one of the immortals. `Well!' said I at last, `speak out. As it happens, I am Mr. Kurtz's friend—in a way.'

"He stated with a good deal of formality that had we not been `of the same profession,' he would have kept the matter to himself without regard to consequences. `He suspected there was an active ill-will towards him on the part of these white men that—' `You are right,' I said, remembering a certain conversation I had overheard. `The manager thinks you ought to be hanged.' He showed a concern at this intelligence which amused me at first. `I had better get out of the way quietly,' he said earnestly. `I can do no more for Kurtz now, and they would soon find some excuse. What's to stop them? There's a military post three hundred miles from here.' `Well, upon my word,' said I, `perhaps you had better go if you have any friends amongst the savages near by.' `Plenty,' he said. `They are simple people—and I want nothing, you know.' He stood biting his lip, then: `I don't want any harm to happen to these whites here, but of course I was thinking of Mr. Kurtz's reputation—but you are a brother seaman and—' `All right,' said I, after a time. `Mr. Kurtz's reputation is safe with me.' I did not know how truly I spoke.

"He informed me, lowering his voice, that it was Kurtz who had ordered the attack to be made on the steamer. `He hated sometimes the idea of being taken away—and then again.... But I don't understand these matters. I am a simple man. He thought it would scare you away—that you would give it up, thinking him dead. I could not stop him. Oh, I had an awful time of it this last month.' `Very well,' I said. `He is all right now.' `Ye-e-es,' he muttered, not very convinced apparently. `Thanks,' said I; `I shall keep my eyes open.' `But quiet-eh?' he urged anxiously. `It would be awful for his reputation if anybody here—' I promised a complete discretion with great gravity. `I have a canoe and three black fellows waiting not very far. I am off.

Could you give me a few Martini-Henry cartridges?' I could, and did, with proper secrecy. He helped himself, with a wink at me, to a handful of my tobacco. `Between sailors—you know—good English tobacco.' At the door of the pilot-house he turned round—`I say, haven't you a pair of shoes you could spare?' He raised one leg. `Look.' The soles were tied with knotted strings sandalwise under his bare feet. I rooted out an old pair, at which he looked with admiration before tucking it under his left arm. One of his pockets (bright red) was bulging with cartridges, from the other (dark blue) peeped `Towson's Inquiry,' etc., etc. He seemed to think himself excellently well equipped for a renewed encounter with the wilderness. `Ah! I'll never, never meet such a man again. You ought to have heard him recite poetry— his own, too, it was, he told me. Poetry!' He rolled his eyes at the recollection of these delights. `Oh, he enlarged my mind!' `Good-bye,' said I. He shook hands and vanished in the night. Sometimes I ask myself whether I had ever really seen him—whether it was possible to meet such a phenomenon!...

"When I woke up shortly after midnight his warning came to my mind with its hint of danger that seemed, in the starred darkness, real enough to make me get up for the purpose of having a look round. On the hill a big fire burned, illuminating fitfully a crooked corner of the station-house. One of the agents with a picket of a few of our blacks, armed for the purpose, was keeping guard over the ivory; but deep within the forest, red gleams that wavered, that seemed to sink and rise from the ground amongst confused columnar shapes of intense blackness, showed the exact position of the camp where Mr. Kurtz's adorers were keeping their uneasy vigil. The monotonous beating of a big drum filled the air with muffled shocks and a lingering vibration. A steady droning sound of many men chanting each to himself some weird incantation came out from the black, flat wall of the woods as the humming of bees comes out of a hive, and had a strange narcotic effect upon my half-awake senses. I believe I dozed off leaning over the rail, till an abrupt burst of yells, an overwhelming outbreak of a pent-up and mysterious frenzy, woke me up in a bewildered wonder. It was cut short all at once, and the low droning went on with an effect of audible and soothing silence. I glanced casually into the little cabin. A light was burning within, but Mr. Kurtz was not there.

"I think I would have raised an outcry if I had believed my eyes. But I didn't believe them at first—the thing seemed so impossible. The fact is I was completely unnerved by a sheer blank fright, pure abstract terror, unconnected with any distinct shape of physical danger. What made this emotion so overpowering was— how shall I define it?—the moral shock I received, as if something altogether monstrous, intolerable to thought and odious to the soul, had been thrust upon me unexpectedly. This lasted of course the merest fraction of a second, and then the usual sense of commonplace, deadly danger, the possibility of a sudden onslaught and massacre, or something of the kind, which I saw impending, was positively welcome and composing. It pacified me, in fact, so much that I did not raise an alarm.

"There was an agent buttoned up inside an ulster and sleeping on a chair on deck within three feet of me. The yells had not awakened him; he snored very slightly; I left him to his slumbers and leaped ashore. I did not betray Mr. Kurtz—it was ordered I should never betray him— it was written I should be loyal to the nightmare of my choice. I was anxious to deal with this shadow by myself alone—and to this day I don't know why I was so jealous of sharing with any one the peculiar blackness of that experience.

"As soon as I got on the bank I saw a trail—a broad trail through the grass. I remember the exultation with which I said to myself, 'He can't walk—he is crawling on all-fours—I've got him.' The grass was wet with dew. I strode rapidly with clenched fists. I fancy I had some vague notion of falling upon him and giving him a drubbing. I don't know. I had some imbecile thoughts. The knitting old woman with the cat obtruded herself upon my memory as a most improper person to be sitting at the other end of such an affair. I saw a row of pilgrims squirting lead in the air out of Winchesters held to the hip. I thought I would never get back to the steamer, and imagined myself living alone and unarmed in the woods to an advanced age. Such silly things—you know. And I remember I confounded the beat of the drum with the beating of my heart, and was pleased at its calm regularity.

"I kept to the track though—then stopped to listen. The night was very clear; a dark blue space, sparkling with dew and starlight, in which black things stood very still. I thought I could see a kind of motion ahead of me. I was strangely cocksure of everything that night. I actually left the track and ran in a wide semicircle (I verily believe chuckling to myself) so as to get in front of that stir, of that motion I had seen—if indeed I had seen anything. I was circumventing Kurtz as though it had been a boyish game.

"I came upon him, and, if he had not heard me coming, I would have fallen over him, too, but he got up in time. He rose, unsteady, long, pale, indistinct, like a vapour exhaled by the earth, and swayed slightly, misty and silent before me; while at my back the fires loomed between the trees, and the murmur of many voices issued from the forest. I had cut him off cleverly; but when actually confronting him I seemed to come to my senses, I saw the danger in its right proportion. It was by no means over yet. Suppose he began to shout? Though he could hardly stand, there was still plenty of vigour in his voice. `Go away—hide yourself,' he said, in that profound tone. It was very awful. I glanced back. We were within thirty yards from the nearest fire. A black figure stood up, strode on long black legs, waving long black arms, across the glow. It had horns—antelope horns, I think—on its head. Some sorcerer, some witch-man, no doubt: it looked fiendlike enough. `Do you know what you are doing?' I whispered. `Perfectly,' he answered, raising his voice for that single word: it sounded to me far off and yet loud, like a hail through a speaking-trumpet. `If he makes a row we are lost,' I thought to myself. This clearly was not a case for fisticuffs, even apart from the very natural aversion I had to beat that Shadow—this wandering and tormented thing. `You will be lost,' I said—'utterly lost.' One gets sometimes such a flash of inspiration, you know. I did say the right thing, though indeed he could not have been more irretrievably lost than he was at this very moment, when the foundations of our intimacy were being laid—to endure— to endure—even to the end—even beyond.

"`I had immense plans,' he muttered irresolutely. `Yes,' said I; `but if you try to shout I'll smash your head with—' There was not a stick or a stone near. `I will throttle you for good,' I corrected myself. `I was on the threshold of great things,' he pleaded, in a voice of longing, with a wistfulness of tone that made my blood run cold. `And now for this stupid scoundrel—' `Your success in Europe is assured in any case,' I affirmed steadily. I did not want to have the throttling of him, you understand—and indeed it would have been very little use for any practical purpose. I tried to break the spell—the heavy, mute spell of the wilderness— that seemed to draw him to its pitiless breast by the awakening of forgotten and brutal instincts, by the memory of gratified and monstrous passions. This alone, I was convinced, had driven him out to the edge of the forest, to the bush, towards the gleam of fires, the throb of drums, the drone of weird incantations; this alone had beguiled his unlawful soul beyond the bounds of permitted aspirations. And, don't you see, the terror of the position was not in being knocked on the head— though I had a very lively sense of that danger, too—but in this, that I had to deal with a being to whom I could not appeal in the name of anything high or low. I had, even like the niggers, to invoke him—himself—his own exalted and incredible degradation. There was nothing either above or below him, and I knew it. He had kicked himself loose of the earth. Confound the man! he had kicked the very earth to pieces. He was alone, and I before him did not know whether I stood on the ground or floated in the air. I've been telling you what we said—repeating the phrases we pronounced—but what's the good? They were common everyday words—the familiar, vague sounds exchanged on every waking day of life. But what of that? They had behind them, to my mind, the terrific suggestiveness of words heard in dreams, of phrases spoken in nightmares. Soul! If anybody ever struggled with a soul, I am the man. And I wasn't arguing with a lunatic either. Believe me or not, his intelligence was perfectly clear—concentrated, it is true, upon himself with horrible intensity, yet clear; and therein was my only chance—barring, of course, the killing him there and then, which wasn't so good, on account of unavoidable noise. But his soul was mad. Being alone in the wilderness, it had looked within itself, and, by heavens! I tell you, it had gone mad.

I had—for my sins, I suppose—to go through the ordeal of looking into it myself. No eloquence could have been so withering to one's belief in mankind as his final burst of sincerity. He struggled with himself, too. I saw it—I heard it. I saw the inconceivable mystery of a soul that knew no restraint, no faith, and no fear, yet struggling blindly with itself. I kept my head pretty well; but when I had him at last stretched on the couch, I wiped my forehead, while my legs shook under me as though I had carried half a ton on my back down that hill. And yet I had only supported him, his bony arm clasped round my neck—and he was not much heavier than a child.

"When next day we left at noon, the crowd, of whose presence behind the curtain of trees I had been acutely conscious all the time, flowed out of the woods again, filled the clearing, covered the slope with a mass of naked, breathing, quivering, bronze bodies. I steamed up a bit, then swung down stream, and two thousand eyes followed the evolutions of the splashing, thumping, fierce river-demon beating the water with its terrible tail and breathing black smoke into the air. In front of the first rank, along the river, three men, plastered with bright red earth from head to foot, strutted to and fro restlessly. When we came abreast again, they faced the river, stamped their feet, nodded their horned heads, swayed their scarlet bodies; they shook towards the fierce river-demon a bunch of black feathers, a mangy skin with a pendent tail—something that looked a dried gourd; they shouted periodically together strings of amazing words that resembled no sounds of human language; and the deep murmurs of the crowd, interrupted suddenly, were like the responses of some satanic litany.

"We had carried Kurtz into the pilot-house: there was more air there. Lying on the couch, he stared through the open shutter. There was an eddy in the mass of human bodies, and the woman with helmeted head and tawny cheeks rushed out to the very brink of the stream. She put out her hands, shouted something, and all that wild mob took up the shout in a roaring chorus of articulated, rapid, breathless utterance.

"'Do you understand this?' I asked.

"He kept on looking out past me with fiery, longing eyes, with a mingled expression of wistfulness and hate. He made no answer, but I saw a smile, a smile of indefinable meaning, appear on his colourless lips that a moment after twitched convulsively. 'Do I not?' he said slowly, gasping, as if the words had been torn out of him by a supernatural power.

"I pulled the string of the whistle, and I did this because I saw the pilgrims on deck getting out their rifles with an air of anticipating a jolly lark. At the sudden screech there was a movement of abject terror through that wedged mass of bodies. 'Don't! don't you frighten them away,' cried some one on deck disconsolately. I pulled the string time after time. They broke and ran, they leaped, they crouched, they swerved, they dodged the flying terror of the sound. The three red chaps had fallen flat, face down on the shore, as though they had been shot dead. Only the barbarous and superb woman did not so much as flinch, and stretched tragically her bare arms after us over the sombre and glittering river.

"And then that imbecile crowd down on the deck started their little fun, and I could see nothing more for smoke.

"The brown current ran swiftly out of the heart of darkness, bearing us down towards the sea with twice the speed of our upward progress; and Kurtz's life was running swiftly, too, ebbing, ebbing out of his heart into the sea of inexorable time. The manager was very placid, he had no vital anxieties now, he took us both in with a comprehensive and satisfied glance: the 'affair' had come off as well as could be wished. I saw the time approaching when I would be left alone of the party of 'unsound method.' The pilgrims looked upon me with disfavour. I was, so to speak, numbered with the dead. It is strange how I accepted this unforeseen partnership, this choice of nightmares forced upon me in the tenebrous land invaded by these mean and greedy phantoms.

"Kurtz discoursed. A voice! a voice! It rang deep to the very last. It survived his strength to hide in the magnificent folds of eloquence the barren darkness of his heart. Oh, he struggled! he struggled! The wastes of his weary brain were haunted by shadowy images now—images of wealth and fame revolving obsequiously round his unextinguishable gift of noble and lofty expression. My Intended, my station, my career, my ideas— these were the subjects for the occasional utterances of elevated sentiments. The shade of the original Kurtz frequented the bedside of the hollow sham, whose fate it was to be buried presently in the mould of primeval earth. But both the diabolic love and the unearthly hate of the mysteries it had penetrated fought for the possession of that soul satiated with primitive emotions, avid of lying fame, of sham distinction, of all the appearances of success and power.

"Sometimes he was contemptibly childish. He desired to have kings meet him at railway-stations on his return from some ghastly Nowhere, where he intended to accomplish great things. `You show them you have in you something that is really profitable, and then there will be no limits to the recognition of your ability,' he would say. `Of course you must take care of the motives— right motives—always.' The long reaches that were like one and the same reach, monotonous bends that were exactly alike, slipped past the steamer with their multitude of secular trees looking patiently after this grimy fragment of another world, the forerunner of change, of conquest, of trade, of massacres, of blessings. I looked ahead—piloting. `Close the shutter,' said Kurtz suddenly one day; `I can't bear to look at this.' I did so. There was a silence. `Oh, but I will wring your heart yet!' he cried at the invisible wilderness.

"We broke down—as I had expected—and had to lie up for repairs at the head of an island. This delay was the first thing that shook Kurtz's confidence. One morning he gave me a packet of papers and a photograph— the lot tied together with a shoe-string. `Keep this for me,' he said. `This noxious fool' (meaning the manager) `is capable of prying into my boxes when I am not looking.' In the afternoon I saw him. He was lying on his back with closed eyes, and I withdrew quietly, but I heard him mutter, `Live rightly, die, die...' I listened. There was nothing more. Was he rehearsing some speech in his sleep, or was it a fragment of a phrase from some newspaper article? He had been writing for the papers and meant to do so again, `for the furthering of my ideas. It's a duty.'

"His was an impenetrable darkness. I looked at him as you peer down at a man who is lying at the bottom of a precipice where the sun never shines. But I had not much time to give him, because I was helping the engine-driver to take to pieces the leaky cylinders, to straighten a bent connecting-rod, and in other such matters. I lived in an infernal mess of rust, filings, nuts, bolts, spanners, hammers, ratchet-drills—things I abominate, because I don't get on with them. I tended the little forge we fortunately had aboard; I toiled wearily in a wretched scrap-heap—unless I had the shakes too bad to stand.

"One evening coming in with a candle I was startled to hear him say a little tremulously, 'I am lying here in the dark waiting for death.' The light was within a foot of his eyes. I forced myself to murmur, 'Oh, nonsense!' and stood over him as if transfixed.

"Anything approaching the change that came over his features I have never seen before, and hope never to see again. Oh, I wasn't touched. I was fascinated. It was as though a veil had been rent. I saw on that ivory face the expression of sombre pride, of ruthless power, of craven terror—of an intense and hopeless despair. Did he live his life again in every detail of desire, temptation, and surrender during that supreme moment of complete knowledge? He cried in a whisper at some image, at some vision—he cried out twice, a cry that was no more than a breath:

"'The horror! The horror!'

"I blew the candle out and left the cabin. The pilgrims were dining in the mess-room, and I took my place opposite the manager, who lifted his eyes to give me a questioning glance, which I successfully ignored. He leaned back, serene, with that peculiar smile of his sealing the unexpressed depths of his meanness. A continuous shower of small flies streamed upon the lamp, upon the cloth, upon our hands and faces. Suddenly the manager's boy put his insolent black head in the doorway, and said in a tone of scathing contempt:

"'Mistah Kurtz—he dead.'

"All the pilgrims rushed out to see. I remained, and went on with my dinner. I believe I was considered brutally callous. However, I did not eat much. There was a lamp in there—light, don't you know—and outside it was so beastly, beastly dark. I went no more near the remarkable man who had pronounced a judgment upon the adventures of his soul on this earth. The voice was gone. What else had been there? But I am of course aware that next day the pilgrims buried something in a muddy hole.

"And then they very nearly buried me.

"However, as you see, I did not go to join Kurtz there and then. I did not. I remained to dream the nightmare out to the end, and to show my loyalty to Kurtz once more. Destiny. My destiny! Droll thing life is— that mysterious arrangement of merciless logic for a futile purpose. The most you can hope from it is some knowledge of yourself—that comes too late—a crop of unextinguishable regrets. I have wrestled with death. It is the most unexciting contest you can imagine. It takes place in an impalpable greyness, with nothing underfoot, with nothing around, without spectators, without clamour, without glory, without the great desire of victory, without the great fear of defeat, in a sickly atmosphere of tepid scepticism, without much belief in your own right, and still less in that of your adversary. If such is the form of ultimate wisdom, then life is a greater riddle than some of us think it to be. I was within a hair's breadth of the last opportunity for pronouncement, and I found with humiliation that probably I would have nothing to say.

This is the reason why I affirm that Kurtz was a remarkable man. He had something to say. He said it. Since I had peeped over the edge myself, I understand better the meaning of his stare, that could not see the flame of the candle, but was wide enough to embrace the whole universe, piercing enough to penetrate all the hearts that beat in the darkness. He had summed up—he had judged. 'The horror!' He was a remarkable man. After all, this was the expression of some sort of belief; it had candour, it had conviction, it had a vibrating note of revolt in its whisper, it had the appalling face of a glimpsed truth—the strange commingling of desire and hate. And it is not my own extremity I remember best— a vision of greyness without form filled with physical pain, and a careless contempt for the evanescence of all things—even of this pain itself. No! It is his extremity that I seem to have lived through. True, he had made that last stride, he had stepped over the edge, while I had been permitted to draw back my hesitating foot. And perhaps in this is the whole difference; perhaps all the wisdom, and all truth, and all sincerity, are just compressed into that inappreciable moment of time in which we step over the threshold of the invisible. Perhaps! I like to think my summing-up would not have been a word of careless contempt. Better his cry—much better. It was an affirmation, a moral victory paid for by innumerable defeats, by abominable terrors, by abominable satisfactions. But it was a victory! That is why I have remained loyal to Kurtz to the last, and even beyond, when a long time after I heard once more, not his own voice, but the echo of his magnificent eloquence thrown to me from a soul as translucently pure as a cliff of crystal.

"No, they did not bury me, though there is a period of time which I remember mistily, with a shuddering wonder, like a passage through some inconceivable world that had no hope in it and no desire. I found myself back in the sepulchral city resenting the sight of people hurrying through the streets to filch a little money from each other, to devour their infamous cookery, to gulp their unwholesome beer, to dream their insignificant and silly dreams. They trespassed upon my thoughts. They were intruders whose knowledge of life was to me an irritating pretence, because I felt so sure they could not possibly know the things I knew. Their bearing, which was simply the bearing of commonplace individuals going about their business in the assurance of perfect safety, was offensive to me like the outrageous flauntings of folly in the face of a danger it is unable to comprehend. I had no particular desire to enlighten them, but I had some difficulty in restraining myself from laughing in their faces so full of stupid importance. I dareway I was not very well at that time. I tottered about the streets—there were various affairs to settle—grinning bitterly at perfectly respectable persons.

I admit my behaviour was inexcusable, but then my temperature was seldom normal in these days. My dear aunt's endeavours to `nurse up my strength' seemed altogether beside the mark. It was not my strength that wanted nursing, it was my imagination that wanted soothing. I kept the bundle of papers given me by Kurtz, not knowing exactly what to do with it. His mother had died lately, watched over, as I was told, by his Intended. A clean-shaved man, with an official manner and wearing gold-rimmed spectacles, called on me one day and made inquiries, at first circuitous, afterwards suavely pressing, about what he was pleased to denominate certain 'documents.' I was not surprised, because I had had two rows with the manager on the subject out there.

I had refused to give up the smallest scrap out of that package, and I took the same attitude with the spectacled man. He became darkly menacing at last, and with much heat argued that the Company had the right to every bit of information about its 'territories.' And said he, 'Mr. Kurtz's knowledge of unexplored regions must have been necessarily extensive and peculiar— owing to his great abilities and to the deplorable circumstances in which he had been placed: therefore—' I assured him Mr. Kurtz's knowledge, however extensive, did not bear upon the problems of commerce or administration. He invoked then the name of science.

'It would be an incalculable loss if,' etc., etc. I offered him the report on the 'Suppression of Savage Customs,' with the postscriptum torn off. He took it up eagerly, but ended by sniffing at it with an air of contempt. 'This is not what we had a right to expect,' he remarked. 'Expect nothing else,' I said. 'There are only private letters.' He withdrew upon some threat of legal proceedings, and I saw him no more; but another fellow, calling himself Kurtz's cousin, appeared two days later, and was anxious to hear all the details about his dear relative's last moments. Incidentally he gave me to understand that Kurtz had been essentially a great musician. 'There was the making of an immense success,' said the man, who was an organist, I believe, with lank grey hair flowing over a greasy coat-collar. I had no reason to doubt his statement; and to this day I am unable to say what was Kurtz's profession, whether he ever had any—which was the greatest of his talents. I had taken him for a painter who wrote for the papers, or else for a journalist who could paint—but even the cousin (who took snuff during the interview) could not tell me what he had been—exactly.

He was a universal genius—on that point I agreed with the old chap, who thereupon blew his nose noisily into a large cotton handkerchief and withdrew in senile agitation, bearing off some family letters and memoranda without importance. Ultimately a journalist anxious to know something of the fate of his `dear colleague' turned up. This visitor informed me Kurtz's proper sphere ought to have been politics `on the popular side.' He had furry straight eyebrows, bristly hair cropped short, an eyeglass on a broad ribbon, and, becoming expansive, confessed his opinion that Kurtz really couldn't write a bit—'but heavens! how that man could talk. He electrified large meetings. He had faith—don't you see?—he had the faith. He could get himself to believe anything—anything. He would have been a splendid leader of an extreme party.' `What party?' I asked. `Any party,' answered the other. `He was an—an—extremist.' Did I not think so? I assented. Did I know, he asked, with a sudden flash of curiosity, `what it was that had induced him to go out there?' `Yes,' said I, and forthwith handed him the famous Report for publication, if he thought fit. He glanced through it hurriedly, mumbling all the time, judged `it would do,' and took himself off with this plunder.

"Thus I was left at last with a slim packet of letters and the girl's portrait. She struck me as beautiful— I mean she had a beautiful expression. I know that the sunlight ycan be made to lie, too, yet one felt that no manipulation of light and pose could have conveyed the delicate shade of truthfulness upon those features. She seemed ready to listen without mental reservation, without suspicion, without a thought for herself. I concluded I would go and give her back her portrait and those letters myself. Curiosity? Yes; and also some other feeling perhaps. All that had been Kurtz's had passed out of my hands: his soul, his body, his station, his plans, his ivory, his career. There remained only his memory and his Intended— and I wanted to give that up, too, to the past, in a way— to surrender personally all that remained of him with me to that oblivion which is the last word of our common fate. I don't defend myself. I had no clear perception of what it was I really wanted. Perhaps it was an impulse of unconscious loyalty, or the fulfilment of one of those ironic necessities that lurk in the facts of human existence. I don't know. I can't tell. But I went.

"I thought his memory was like the other memories of the dead that accumulate in every man's life—a vague impress on the brain of shadows that had fallen on it in their swift and final passage; but before the high and ponderous door, between the tall houses of a street as still and decorous as a well-kept alley in a cemetery, I had a vision of him on the stretcher, opening his mouth voraciously, as if to devour all the earth with all its mankind. He lived then before me; he lived as much as he had ever lived—a shadow insatiable of splendid appearances, of frightful realities; a shadow darker than the shadow of the night, and draped nobly in the folds of a gorgeous eloquence. The vision seemed to enter the house with me—the stretcher, the phantom-bearers, the wild crowd of obedient worshippers, the gloom of the forests, the glitter of the reach between the murky bends, the beat of the drum, regular and muffled like the beating of a heart—the heart of a conquering darkness.

It was a moment of triumph for the wilderness, an invading and vengeful rush which, it seemed to me, I would have to keep back alone for the salvation of another soul. And the memory of what I had heard him say afar there, with the horned shapes stirring at my back, in the glow of fires, within the patient woods, those broken phrases came back to me, were heard again in their ominous and terrifying simplicity. I remembered his abject pleading, his abject threats, the colossal scale of his vile desires, the meanness, the torment, the tempestuous anguish of his soul. And later on I seemed to see his collected languid manner, when he said one day, 'This lot of ivory now is really mine. The Company did not pay for it. I collected it myself at a very great personal risk. I am afraid they will try to claim it as theirs though. H'm. It is a difficult case. What do you think I ought to do—resist? Eh? I want no more than justice.'... He wanted no more than justice—no more than justice. I rang the bell before a mahogany door on the first floor, and while I waited he seemed to stare at me out of the glassy panel— stare with that wide and immense stare embracing, condemning, loathing all the universe. I seemed to hear the whispered cry, "The horror! The horror!"

"The dusk was falling. I had to wait in a lofty drawing-room with three long windows from floor to ceiling that were like three luminous and bedraped columns. The bent gilt legs and backs of the furniture shone in indistinct curves. The tall marble fireplace had a cold and monumental whiteness. A grand piano stood massively in a corner; with dark gleams on the flat surfaces like a sombre and polished sarcophagus. A high door opened—closed. I rose.

"She came forward, all in black, with a pale head, floating towards me in the dusk. She was in mourning. It was more than a year since his death, more than a year since the news came; she seemed as though she would remember and mourn forever. She took both my hands in hers and murmured, 'I had heard you were coming.' I noticed she was not very young—I mean not girlish. She had a mature capacity for fidelity, for belief, for suffering. The room seemed to have grown darker, as if all the sad light of the cloudy evening had taken refuge on her forehead. This fair hair, this pale visage, this pure brow, seemed surrounded by an ashy halo from which the dark eyes looked out at me. Their glance was guileless, profound, confident, and trustful. She carried her sorrowful head as though she were proud of that sorrow, as though she would say, 'I—I alone know how to mourn for him as he deserves.' But while we were still shaking hands, such a look of awful desolation came upon her face that I perceived she was one of those creatures that are not the playthings of Time. For her he had died only yesterday. And, by Jove! the impression was so powerful that for me, too, he seemed to have died only yesterday—nay, this very minute. I saw her and him in the same instant of time—his death and her sorrow—I saw her sorrow in the very moment of his death. Do you understand? I saw them together—I heard them together. She had said, with a deep catch of the breath, 'I have survived' while my strained ears seemed to hear distinctly, mingled with her tone of despairing regret, the summing up whisper of his eternal condemnation. I asked myself what I was doing there, with a sensation of panic in my heart as though I had blundered into a place of cruel and absurd mysteries not fit for a human being to behold. She motioned me to a chair. We sat down. I laid the packet gently on the little table, and she put her hand over it.... 'You knew him well,' she murmured, after a moment of mourning silence.

"'Intimacy grows quickly out there,' I said. 'I knew him as well as it is possible for one man to know another.'

"'And you admired him,' she said. 'It was impossible to know him and not to admire him. Was it?'

"'He was a remarkable man,' I said, unsteadily. Then before the appealing fixity of her gaze, that seemed to watch for more words on my lips, I went on, 'It was impossible not to—'

"'Love him,' she finished eagerly, silencing me into an appalled dumbness. 'How true! how true! But when you think that no one knew him so well as I! I had all his noble confidence. I knew him best.'

"'You knew him best,' I repeated. And perhaps she did. But with every word spoken the room was growing darker, and only her forehead, smooth and white, remained illumined by the inextinguishable light of belief and love.

"'You were his friend,' she went on. 'His friend,' she repeated, a little louder. 'You must have been, if he had given you this, and sent you to me. I feel I can speak to you—and oh! I must speak. I want you—you who have heard his last words— to know I have been worthy of him.... It is not pride.... Yes! I am proud to know I understood him better than any one on earth— he told me so himself. And since his mother died I have had no one— no one—to—to—'

"I listened. The darkness deepened. I was not even sure whether he had given me the right bundle. I rather suspect he wanted me to take care of another batch of his papers which, after his death, I saw the manager examining under the lamp. And the girl talked, easing her pain in the certitude of my sympathy; she talked as thirsty men drink. I had heard that her engagement with Kurtz had been disapproved by her people. He wasn't rich enough or something. And indeed I don't know whether he had not been a pauper all his life. He had given me some reason to infer that it was his impatience of comparative poverty that drove him out there.

"`... Who was not his friend who had heard him speak once?' she was saying. `He drew men towards him by what was best in them.' She looked at me with intensity. `It is the gift of the great,' she went on, and the sound of her low voice seemed to have the accompaniment of all the other sounds, full of mystery, desolation, and sorrow, I had ever heard—the ripple of the river, the soughing of the trees swayed by the wind, the murmurs of the crowds, the faint ring of incomprehensible words cried from afar, the whisper of a voice speaking from beyond the threshold of an eternal darkness. `But you have heard him! You know!' she cried.

"`Yes, I know,' I said with something like despair in my heart, but bowing my head before the faith that was in her, before that great and saving illusion that shone with an unearthly glow in the darkness, in the triumphant darkness from which I could not have defended her— from which I could not even defend myself.

"`What a loss to me—to us!'—she corrected herself with beautiful generosity; then added in a murmur, `To the world.' By the last gleams of twilight I could see the glitter of her eyes, full of tears—of tears that would not fall.

"`I have been very happy—very fortunate—very proud,' she went on. `Too fortunate. Too happy for a little while. And now I am unhappy for—for life.'

"She stood up; her fair hair seemed to catch all the remaining light in a glimmer of gold. I rose, too.

"`And of all this,' she went on mournfully, `of all his promise, and of all his greatness, of his generous mind, of his noble heart, nothing remains—nothing but a memory. You and I—'

"`We shall always remember him,' I said hastily.

"`No!' she cried. `It is impossible that all this should be lost— that such a life should be sacrificed to leave nothing— but sorrow. You know what vast plans he had. I knew of them, too—I could not perhaps understand—but others knew of them. Something must remain. His words, at least, have not died.'

"`His words will remain,' I said.

"`And his example,' she whispered to herself. `Men looked up to him— his goodness shone in every act. His example—'

"`True,' I said; `his example, too. Yes, his example. I forgot that.'

"But I do not. I cannot—I cannot believe—not yet. I cannot believe that I shall never see him again, that nobody will see him again, never, never, never.'

"She put out her arms as if after a retreating figure, stretching them back and with clasped pale hands across the fading and narrow sheen of the window. Never see him! I saw him clearly enough then. I shall see this eloquent phantom as long as I live, and I shall see her, too, a tragic and familiar Shade, resembling in this gesture another one, tragic also, and bedecked with powerless charms, stretching bare brown arms over the glitter of the infernal stream, the stream of darkness. She said suddenly very low, `He died as he lived.'

"`His end,' said I, with dull anger stirring in me, `was in every way worthy of his life.'

"`And I was not with him,' she murmured. My anger subsided before a feeling of infinite pity.

"'Everything that could be done—' I mumbled.

"'Ah, but I believed in him more than any one on earth—more than his own mother, more than—himself. He needed me! Me! I would have treasured every sigh, every word, every sign, every glance.'

"I felt like a chill grip on my chest. 'Don't,' I said, in a muffled voice.

"'Forgive me. I—I have mourned so long in silence—in silence.... You were with him—to the last? I think of his loneliness. Nobody near to understand him as I would have understood. Perhaps no one to hear....'

"'To the very end,' I said, shakily. 'I heard his very last words....' I stopped in a fright.

"'Repeat them,' she murmured in a heart-broken tone. 'I want—I want—something—something—to—to live with.'

"I was on the point of crying at her, 'Don't you hear them?' The dusk was repeating them in a persistent whisper all around us, in a whisper that seemed to swell menacingly like the first whisper of a rising wind. 'The horror! The horror!'

"'His last word—to live with,' she insisted. 'Don't you understand I loved him—I loved him—I loved him!'

"I pulled myself together and spoke slowly.

"'The last word he pronounced was—your name.'

"I heard a light sigh and then my heart stood still, stopped dead short by an exulting and terrible cry, by the cry of inconceivable triumph and of unspeakable pain. 'I knew it—I was sure!'... She knew. She was sure. I heard her weeping; she had hidden her face in her hands. It seemed to me that the house would collapse before I could escape, that the heavens would fall upon my head. But nothing happened. The heavens do not fall for such a trifle. Would they have fallen, I wonder, if I had rendered Kurtz that justice which was his due? Hadn't he said he wanted only justice? But I couldn't. I could not tell her. It would have been too dark—too dark altogether...."

Marlow ceased, and sat apart, indistinct and silent, in the pose of a meditating Buddha. Nobody moved for a time. "We have lost the first of the ebb," said the Director suddenly. I raised my head. The offing was barred by a black bank of clouds, and the tranquil waterway leading to the uttermost ends of the earth flowed sombre under an overcast sky—seemed to lead into the heart of an immense darkness.

Chapter 10

Summary and Analysis

Part 1

Heart of Darkness begins on board the *Nellie*, a small ship moored on the Thames River in London. After describing the river and its slow-moving traffic, the unnamed narrator offers short descriptions of London's history to his companions who, with him, lazily lounge on the deck, waiting for the tide to turn. With him are the Director of Companies (their Captain), a lawyer, an accountant, and Marlow, the novel's protagonist. As the sun sets, the four men become contemplative and brooding; eventually, Marlow breaks the spell of silence by beginning his tale about his voyage to the Congo.

The other men remain silent while Marlow collects his ideas, after which he begins the story proper. The remainder of the novel becomes (with a few exceptions) the narrator's report of what Marlow tells him and the others on board the *Nellie*. Conrad's novel is thus a *frame tale*, or story-within-a-story.

As a boy, Marlow was fascinated by maps and yearned to become a seaman or explorer who could visit the most remote parts of the earth. As a young man, Marlow spent approximately six years sailing in the Pacific before returning to London—where he then saw, in a shop window, a map of Africa and the Congo River. Recalling the news of a Continental trading Company operating in the Congo, Marlow became determined to pilot a steamboat to find adventure in Africa. He asked his aunt, who knew the wife of a Company official to assist him in getting a job as a pilot; she happily complied.

Marlow hurried across the English Channel to sign his contracts at the Company's headquarters in Brussels. Passing through an office with two women who are knitting, Marlow spoke with the Company's director for less than a minute; after being dismissed, he was asked to sign a number of papers in which he promised not to divulge any trade secrets. Marlow finally reached the mouth of the Congo. Finding passage on a little sea-bound steamer to take him where his steamboat awaited him, Marlow spoke with its Swedish captain about the Company and the effects of the jungle on Europeans. The Swede then told Marlow a short yet ominous story about a man he took upriver who hanged himself on the road. Shocked, Marlow asked why, only to be told that perhaps the "sun" or the "country" were too much for him. Eventually, they reached the Company's Outer Station, which amounted to three wooden buildings on the side of a rocky slope. Out of this station was shipped the Company's most important and lucrative commodity: ivory.

Marlow spent the next ten days waiting for the caravan to conduct him to the Central Station (and his steamboat), during which time he saw more of the Accountant. On some days, Marlow would sit in his office, trying to avoid the giant "stabbing" flies. When a stretcher with a sick European was put in the office temporarily, the Accountant became annoyed with his groans, complaining that they distracted him and increased the chances for clerical errors. Noting Marlow's ultimate destination in the interior region of the Congo, the Accountant hinted that Marlow would "no doubt meet Mr. Kurtz," a Company agent in charge of an incredibly lucrative ivory-post deep in the interior. The Accountant described Kurtz as a "first class agent" and "remarkable person" whose station brought in more ivory than all the other stations combined. He asked Marlow to tell Kurtz that everything at the Outer Station was satisfactory and then hinted that Kurtz was being groomed for a high position in the Company's Administration.

The day after this conversation, Marlow left the Outer Station with a caravan of sixty men for a two hundred-mile "tramp" to the Central Station. (The men were native porters who carried the equipment, food and water.) Marlow saw innumerable paths cut through the jungle and a number of abandoned villages along the way. He saw a drunken White man, who claimed to be looking after the "upkeep" of a road, and the body of a native who was shot in the head. Marlow's one White companion was an overweight man who kept fainting due to the heat. Eventually, he had to be carried in a hammock, and when the hammock skinned his nose and was dropped by the natives, he demanded that Marlow do something to punish them. Marlow did nothing except press onward until they reached the Central Station, where an "excitable chap" informed him that his steamboat was at the bottom of the river; two days earlier, the bottom of the boat had been torn off when some "volunteer skipper" piloted it upriver to have it ready for Marlow's arrival.

Marlow was therefore forced to spend time at the Central Station. As he did with the Outer Station, he relates to his audience on the *Nellie* his impressions of the place. Marlow met a Brickmaker (although Marlow did not see a brick anywhere) who pressed him for information about the Company's activities in Europe. When Marlow confessed to knowing nothing about the secret intrigues of the Company, the Brickmaker assumed he was lying and became annoyed.

At this point, Marlow breaks off his narrative, explaining to the men on the *Nellie* that he finds it difficult to convey the dream-like quality of his African experiences.

Marlow resumes his tale by continuing the description of his talk with the Brickmaker, who complained to Marlow that he could never find the necessary materials needed to make any bricks. Marlow told of how he needed rivets to repair his steamboat, but none arrived in any of the caravans.

After his conversation with the Brickmaker, Marlow told his mechanic (a boilermaker) that their rivets would be arriving shortly. (Marlow assumed that because the Brickmaker was eager to please him because he assumed Marlow had important friends, he would get him the necessary rivets.) Like the Brickmaker, the mechanic assumed that Marlow had great influence in Europe. However, the rivets did not arrive—instead, a number of White men riding donkeys (and followed by a number of natives) burst into the Central Station. Marlow learned that these men called themselves the Eldorado Exploring Expedition and that they had arrived in search of treasure. The Manager's uncle was the leader of the Expedition, and Marlow saw him and his nephew conspiring on many occasions. At times, Marlow would hear Kurtz's name mentioned and become mildly curious, but he felt a strong desire to repair his steamship and begin his job as a pilot.

Part 2

One evening Marlow eavesdropped on the Manager and his uncle as they discussed Kurtz. Marlow learned that Kurtz asked the Company's Administration to send him into the jungle to show how much ivory he could acquire, and that he sent his assistant back to the Manager because he found him inadequate for the work. Marlow further learned that there were "strange rumours" circulating about Kurtz's behaviour. The Manager insinuated that he hoped Kurtz would die in the jungle. A few days later, the Eldorado Expedition entered the jungle; they had no news except that all the donkeys were dead. His steamboat repaired, Marlow began his voyage to the Inner Station, accompanied by the Manager, the other agents whom Marlow calls "pilgrims," and 20 natives (who were also cannibals).

About fifty miles below the Inner Station, the steamboat came across a hut of reeds; near the hut were the remnants of a flag and a neatly stacked woodpile. Near the woodpile, written on a board, were the words, "Wood for you. Hurry up. Approach cautiously." Inside the hut, Marlow found evidence of a White tenant: a rudely formed table, a heap of rubbish, and a book about seamanship with some sort of code written in the margins. The natives took the wood (to power the steamboat) and Marlow slipped the book in his pocket.

When they were about a mile and a half below the Inner Station, unseen, silent natives who fired small arrows attacked the steamboat. The pilgrims fired their guns into the bush while the attack continued, the helmsman soon being killed by a spear.

Finally, Marlow reached the Inner Station. He first saw a "long, decaying building" with a number of posts around it; each post was topped with a "round curved ball." (Later, Marlow discovered that the building was Kurtz's quarters and that the "balls" were human heads.) A White man met them at the shore and reminded Marlow of a harlequin; he informed them that Kurtz was still alive. The Harlequin then explained that the natives attacked Marlow's steamboat because they did not want anyone to take Kurtz away from them.

Part 3

The Harlequin told Marlow that he had spent many nights listening to Kurtz speak about a variety of subjects. Marlow further learned that Kurtz was prone to wandering into the jungle with his band of native followers on ivory raids. While listening to the Harlequin, Marlow looked through his binoculars at Kurtz's quarters and discovered that the round knobs he previously saw on the posts bordering the house were the heads of native "rebels," turned inward to face Kurtz as he sat inside. Suddenly, Marlow saw a group of natives appear from a corner of the house, bearing Kurtz on a stretcher. Fearing an attack, Marlow, the Harlequin, and everyone on the steamboat stood still—until Marlow saw Kurtz's emaciated arm emerge from the stretcher and order his army to leave. The Manager and other agents laid Kurtz in his bed and delivered his belated pieces of mail.

Marlow left Kurtz's room and saw, on the bank of the river, Kurtz's African mistress, who captivated Marlow with her pride, stature, and appearance. She boarded the steamboat for a minute without speaking, lifted her arms, and then vanished into the bush. Marlow then heard Kurtz speaking derisively to the Manager from inside his room. Trying to appear nonplussed, the Manager came out of the room and told Marlow that, while Kurtz had amassed a remarkable quantity of ivory, he was low and that his ivory district would have to be closed because his method was unsound. Fearful of the Manager's intentions, the Harlequin told Marlow his suspicion that Kurtz's White rescuers were actually trying to hurt him. Recalling the overheard conversation between the Manager and his uncle, Marlow told the Harlequin that he was correct. The Harlequin then revealed that Kurtz had ordered the attack on the steamboat because "he hated the idea of being taken away." The Harlequin asked Marlow to guard Kurtz's reputation once he arrived in Europe, asked him for some rifle cartridges and shoes, and then left the Inner Station.

Shortly after midnight, Marlow awoke to the sounds of a drumbeat and natives reciting incantations. After hearing a "burst of yells," Marlow entered Kurtz's room and found he had escaped. He found Kurtz crawling through the grass and finally approached him. At first, Kurtz told Marlow to run and hide himself—but he then began telling Marlow that he had "immense plans" that were ruined by the Manager. Marlow listened, hoping that Kurtz would make no noise or give no sign for his men to attack. Finally, Marlow led Kurtz back to his room.

They left the Inner Station the next day. As they floated downstream, three natives covered in bright red earth shouted some form of spell; they next saw Kurtz's native mistress run to the riverbank and begin shouting something that the rest of Kurtz's 1,000 followers began repeating. The Whites on the steamboat began pointing their rifles at the shore; to avoid a massacre, Marlow began blowing the whistle to scare the natives away. Many of them ran, but the "wild woman" did not. The Whites on deck then opened fire on Kurtz's followers.

As they made their way to the sea (and Europe), Kurtz continued to talk of his ideas, plans, station, and career. Kurtz gave Marlow a packet of papers and a photograph and asked him to keep it for him, out of reach of the Manager. One evening, after repairing the engine, Marlow entered Kurtz's room and heard him whisper his final words: "The horror! The horror!" Marlow entered the mess-room and refused to meet the inquiring eyes of the Manager. Eventually, the Manager's servant boy peeked into the mess-room and announced, in a contemptuous voice, "Mistah Kurtz—he dead." Kurtz was buried in the jungle the next day. Stricken by Kurtz's death, Marlow almost considered suicide, and the remainder of his journey back to Europe is omitted from his narrative.

Back in Brussels, Marlow's aunt tried to nurse him back to health. An unnamed representative of the Company then visited Marlow and wanted the papers that Kurtz had given to Marlow. As he did when pressed by the Manager on their voyage home, Marlow refused. He eventually gave the man the copy of Kurtz's report on "The Suppression of Savage Customs," but with the postscript ("Exterminate all the brutes!") torn off. Marlow then met Kurtz's cousin, who told Marlow that Kurtz was a great musician and a "universal genius." Marlow gave him some unimportant family letters from the packet. A journalist then accosted Marlow, eager for information about Kurtz. As they talked, the journalist told Marlow that Kurtz could have been a great politician for any party, because he had the charisma and voice to "electrify" large meetings. Marlow gave him Kurtz's report on "Savage Customs" and the journalist said he would print it.

Marlow thought it necessary to visit Kurtz's Intended—his fiancée, whose photograph Kurtz had given Marlow on the voyage home. Marlow waited for her in her drawing room until she entered, dressed in mourning. She immediately struck Marlow as trustworthy, sincere, and innocent. As she told Marlow that no one knew Kurtz as well as she, he struggled to maintain his composure, because he did not want to reveal to her what Kurtz actually became during his time in the jungle. When she asked Marlow to tell her Kurtz's last words, Marlow hesitated—and then lied, saying, "The last word he pronounced was—your name." The Intended sighed and wept. Marlow's tale is over. On board the *Nellie*, the anonymous narrator and the other men sit motionless. The narrator looks at the dark clouds, the overcast sky, and the Thames—which he now sees as flowing "into the heart of an immense darkness."

Chapter 11

Study Questions

Q.1. Discuss The Darkness in Heart of Darkness.
Or
Q. Analyse the inner darkness in Heart Of Darkness.

It can be said that a certain degree of darkness lies within every person, but this darkness will not surface unless given the correct environment. The darkness, however, can emerge and ultimately destroy the person if not checked by reason. If one's inner darkness does surface, the victim then is given the opportunity to reach a point in personal growth, and to gain a sense of self-knowledge from it. That is, when one's darkness appears, one must learn from this experience how he or she can prevent similar results from occurring in the future. It is ultimately through self-knowledge that we gain the power to defeat our inner darkness, and all of its elements. Just as everyone has the potential for evil within themselves, we too have the potential for true goodness. In many literary works the author attempts to exemplify the evil which lies within by showing many characters which have been, or are being overcome by their inner darkness.

In the novel Heart of Darkness by Joseph Conrad we see how Marlow's journey into his ultimate evil, into his inner self, can be a positive experience. By contrasting Marlow with Kurtz, who represents the absolute evil, we can see the two products of an inner evil which has emerged. Marlow, who defeats his evil, and gains self-knowledge, and Kurtz, who is defeated by his darkness and falls prey to its wrath. In William

Golding's Lord of the Flies the author points out how easily people can be over taken by the darkness, how the potential for good can be destroyed by the evil, but ideally how good will triumph. Through an examination of these two works we can see how the darkness within, given the correct environment will surface. The circumstances which eventually cause the appearance of the inner darkness in these two novels stems from the lack of civility, the true test, or journey which every life contains, and finally the product of evil which lies in all of us, either through acts of commission or omission.

When people lack the aspect of civility in their lives they too will lack the restraints and barriers it has on one's inner evil. Civility, in essence, provides the basic structure for good. Through laws, structure, and general order, goodness then, for the most part will be the end product. Therefore a lack of civility would result in a lack of order, morals, and laws, leaving chaos to over power. The desolate island in The Lord of the Flies represents a lack of civility. Without parents, law makers, and guardians the darkness which surfaces is inevitable. Piggy said in a feared state upon this realization:

"This is an island? Well I think this is an island! That's a reef out in the sea. That means we are all alone! Perhaps there aren't any grownups anywhere".

It is clear that the civilization of the modern world is unavailable on the island. Although Ralph, who represented the aspect of order, attempts to reach a point of civility, unfortunately was unsuccessful. He said in his struggle: "We've got to have rules and obey them. After all we're not savages. We're English, and the English are the best at everything" Ironically the very group he was talking to broke order and formed the savage group known as the 'hunters'. Similarly Piggy too represents civility.

He incorporates the conch which to aids in the order of the island. He is very fearful of the lack of civility and scared by the hunters. He feels that civility and order, although the ideal route, was going to be crushed, and with it him: "We can't do this, the savages, they would crush us". It is quite obvious how the potential evil in a group of young boys unavoidably arises due to the lack of restraint and order. When the darkness surfaces Jack and his group of hunters gain no self-knowledge, and therefore can not reprieve themselves nor the evil which takes over.

A strong parallel can be drawn between the island in Lord of the Flies and The Congo in The Heart of Darkness. The Congo in is similarly used to represent the absence of restraint and order. The effect which is used exemplifies a lack of civility, which in turn provides the opportunity for the emergence of darkness. At the beginning of the novel Marlow begins his descent into the Congo, which presents a dark image of death and suffering.

It was a thing which looked as dead as the carcass of some strange animal. I came upon more pieces of decaying machinery, and a stack of rusty rails. To the left a clump of trees in a twisted shady spot, the ground shook.

The capacity for evil in the jungle is endless. This is illustrated through the natives which who go mad and begin killing. Marlow struggles but by realizing his potential for good, manages to contain his evil. Unfortunately the result was not the same for many others: "I don't know how this would have struck the others but to me the evil was unspeakable, but not undefeatable".

The Congo and the lack of restraints it represents causes one to lose common sense. Without common sense the mind is deteriorated. It is also left twisted and functionally useless in regards to civilized thought or action. The power of mind in most cases is no match for the lack of order and the lack of reason for most of the Congo's inhabitants. Kurtz fell victim to this and his mind became extremely deteriorated due to the lack of order. He eventually finds his inner darkness come forth and essentially control all his thoughts and actions.

By comparing the two novels it is clear how one's inner darkness will surface without the restraints of civilization. In the case of Jack and the hunters, the children are accustom to civility, laws, and order. The fact that parents and teachers were always placing unwanted rules on them, probably caused an initial enjoyment of the lack of civility so much that the growing savageness within grew blindly. The darkness was being to rise.

This is shown through Jack, when asked about the war paint he was wearing replied: "For hunting! Like in the wars, you know, dazzle paint! We look more savage!" This can be compared to the darkness which surfaced in Kurtz and the natives of the Congo, however their darkness was the result of greed rather than ignorance. Unlike Jack and the hunters, the greed for money and power by Kurtz allowed his darkness, which controlled him in the end, to surface. The on going evil growing in Kurtz was not only a result of the jungle, but it was shown through it as well. As he gained more darkness the jungle thickened and became increasingly dangerous: "...as we crept on closer towards Kurtz the snags were thickining and the water becoming treacherous..." If civilized limits are placed upon society as a whole, the majority of people have the opportunity to contain the darkness within. If and when it occasionally surfaces then the knowledge which is gained through a civilized lifestyle will contain, and defeat the individual's darkness.

It is true that every person must undergo the ultimate test at some point of his or hers life time. The test between good and evil. This test can be as simple as small, daily difficulties, or as large as the general principle in which one bases his or hers life upon. Although many people will fail the test which are given to them, it is better to attempt the test and fail, than it is never to have taken it at all. Ralph and Piggy, who as well as representing civility, now also represent the goodness, or the 'passers' of this test of life.

Through the many altercations with the hunters, those who have failed the test, we can observe the darkness beginning to rise. The ultimate dark figure, Jack, who hasn't even attempted the test, that is to be satisfied with one's dark lifestyle, shows how the journey of life presents us with the tasks and trials which we are tested upon. Piggy perhaps was the character who was presented with the most tests. Many times he almost lost his sense and civility, but he always prevailed. Piggy at the verge of losing his sense murmured: "Nobody knows where we are! Perhaps they knew before but they don't know now 'cos we'll never get there!" Not soon after, however, Piggy regained his sensible approach to the situation. It is impossible for one person to pass every test that life gives them, but the important thing is that you learn from every test, pass or fail, one must gain self-knowledge from each altercation.

When Marlow's time came to take his test, it was not necessarily that he passed it, but more importantly he gains the self-knowledge needed in order to defeat the darkness within him. By containing his darkness and preventing the release of his evil, he allows a certain degree of goodness to surface. The result of one's ability to contain his or her darkness does not always equal goodness, but instead it represents the awareness gained from each test. The natives show through their savagery and murderous ways that they have subsequently failed to gain the desired self-knowledge to maintain their goodness. Kurtz can be viewed as the character in the novel who doesn't attempt to take life's challenges and at length seals his dark fate. Marlow's first view of Kurtz shows how the goodness, and evil fail to co-exist together: Seeing Kurtz for the first time, It was a distant glimpse:

> The dugout, four paddling savages, and the lone white man turning his back suddenly on the headquarters, on relief, on thoughts of home—perhaps; setting his face towards the depths of the wilderness, towards his empty and desolate station.

Had Kurtz even attempted the journey or test he was faced with perhaps he may have seen things in a different light. The natives on the other hand appear ignorant, but at the same time they appear content with their lifestyles.

The two novels can be compared in many ways according to the characters, and the tests they take along the journey of their lives. Piggy and Ralph can be compared to Marlow in the fact that they had either passed the test or clearly gained the self-knowledge to prevent the potential darkness within themselves from escaping. The two groups, the 'hunters' and the 'natives' can be similarly compared in terms regarding the characters who attempted to take the test but failed, an action which can, but not in these two cases, result in self-knowledge. Finally the two symbols of true darkness, Kurtz and Jack. The darkness within them surfaced due to that fact that not only did they fail to take the test of life, but they appeared to be content with the situation that this left them in.

The evil which lies within all of us has a third and final way of showing itself. This is exemplified through acts of commission, and through acts of omission. Edmund Burke was quoted as saying "Evil happens when good men do but nothing".The actions which one commits, or fails to commit, can act as a channel in which evil or darkness will begin show. The dark forces which lay in Jack and his group were confirmed by their final direct actions. The action which reiterated the darkness in Jack was the murder of Piggy. The murder was very brutal, and unnecessary: "The rock that had killed Piggy had bounded into the thicket and bounced there, landing in the middle for all to see".Not only had they committed the murder but they indirectly reinforced their desire to deny civilization, as Piggy represented this. Earlier in the novel when Jack, and the hunters, directly disregarded civilization, they performed their first act of omission. This coupled with the savagery they possessed, showed a distinct lack of reason and reality, two of the key components to maintaining one's inner goodness. Finally the murder of Simon, who represented the Christ figure in the book, was the element which finalized Jack's descent into a irretrievable darkness.

Through the acts of commission and omission in Heart of Darkness, it is clear how the same actions, by separate people, can result in differing consequences. Marlow and Kurtz both live within the treacherous Congo, and are involved in the sales of ivory to gain power and wealth. The greed and stubbornness shown by the two men is very similar, but the result divers. Due to Kurtz's inner darkness which had risen, his downfall was evident. But through Marlow's ability to gain the self-knowledge required he was able to prevent his evil from emerging, which in turn would lead to his eventual demise.

The natives on the other hand represent an indirect act of omission in which they were unable to obtain any knowledge. When the evil within them begins to surface they begin to break down mentally and physically. They become fierce, then eventually cataclysmic. They allow their true inner evil to take over, and they lose all capacity to gain any self-knowledge, which may have averted this catastrophe.

The characters in the novels again are comparative with respect to direct and indirect actions. Marlow and Ralph, through all the hardships and lack of civility, overcome the test of life, and finally prevent their own actions from surfacing their inner darkness. They are alike as they gain the essential knowledge to prevent this potential evil from taking its course. The natives and hunters find themselves in a situation in which, although they have committed few actions, have by-passed the opportunity to gain the smallest amount of knowledge, let alone the amount needed for to prevent future evil occurrences. Finally, Kurtz and Jack through their direct and deliberate actions place themselves in a position where it is obvious that self-knowledge and control is not what they desire, but instead the inner darkness which controls them to surface. When one is in the position of gaining self-knowledge, or materialistic amounts, we are faced with one of the greatest and most true tests of life, it is imperative that one takes the test, for you can not avoid the test by attempting to gain both.

Through examining the many different images which allow one's inner evil to surface, the lack of civility and restraints for good, the test which we must endure through life, and evil through commission and omission, it is evident how evil, if not checked by reality, reason, and imagination can surface in real life situations. Even in today's society with the amount of civility we posses, inner darkness may arise in many ways. This is predominate in direct actions, but appropriately too through those omission. With the potential for evil so great in today's materialistic, difficult society, we find ourselves with the difficult task of taking life's many journeys and tests. Not every journey will result in goodness, and the ones that do not are a learning experience in which must gain the self-knowledge to prevent our inner darkness from emerging. We must also be able to take the knowledge with us through every experience we encounter and incorporate it into our daily lives.

Q.2. Discuss the major themes in Heart of Darkness.
Or
Q. Analyse the "man's journey into self" with reference to Conrad's Heart of Darkness.

There are many themes that run through the novel Heart of Darkness.

There are however two main and significant ones. These are the theme of restraint and man's journey into self.

The importance of restraint is stressed throughout Heart of Darkness. In the novel Marlow is saved by restraint, while Kurtz is doomed by his lack of it.

Marlow felt different about Africa before he went, because the colonization of the Congo had "an idea at the back of it." Despite an uneasiness, he assumed that restraint would operate there. He soon reaches the Company station and receives his first shock, everything there seems meaningless. He sees no evidence here of that "devotion to efficiency" that makes the idea work. In the middle of this, Marlow meets a "miracle".

The chief accountant has the restraint that it takes to get the job done. He keeps up his apearance and his books are in "apple-pie order." Marlow respects this fellow because he has a backbone.

"The cannibals some of those ignorant millions, are almost totally characterized by restraint." They outnumber the whites "thirty to five" and could easily fill their starving bellies. Marlow "would have as soon expected restraint from a hyena prowling amongst the corpses of a battlefield." The cannibals action is "one of those human secrets that baffle probability." This helps Marlow keep his restraint, for if the natives can possess this quality Marlow feels he certainly can.

Kurtz is the essence of the lack of restraint Marlow sees everywhere. Kurtz has "kicked himself loose from the earth." "He owes no allegiance to anything except those animal powers, those various lusts, those unpermitted aspirations lurking in the darkness of his inner station.

Marlow also responds to these dark callings, and he almost becomes their captive. He confuses the beat of the drum (the call to man's primitive side) with his own heartbeat, and is pleased. Yet he does not slip over the edge as Kurtz does. Marlow keeps to the track. When he is confronted with the ultimate evil where a man "must fall back on (his) own innate strength, upon (his) own capacity for faithfulness," he is able to do so, he shows the necessary restraint.

The second theme of course is man's journey into self. During Marlow's mission to find Kurtz, he is also trying to find himself. He, like Kurtz had good intentions upon entering the Congo. Conrad tries to show us that Marlow is what Kurtz had been, and Kurtz is what Marlow could become. Every human has a little of Marlow and Kurtz in them. Marlow says about himself, "I was getting savage," meaning that he was becoming more like Kurtz. Along the trip into the wilderness, they discover their true selves through contact with savage natives.

As Marlow journeys up the Congo, he feels he is travelling back through time. He sees the unsettled wilderness and can feel the darkness of it's solitude. "Marlow comes across simpler cannibalistic cultures along the banks. The deeper into the jungle he goes, the more regressive the inhabitants seem."

Kurtz had lived in the Congo, and was separated from his own culture for quite some time. He had once been considered an honourable man, but the jungle changed him greatly. Here isolated from the rest of his own society, he discovered the evil side and became corrupted by his power and isolation.

Marlow realises that only very near the time of death, does a person grasp the big picture. He describes Kurtz's last moments "as though a veil had been rent." Kurtz's last "supreme moment of complete knowledge," showed him how horrible the human soul really can be. Marlow can only guess as to what Kurtz saw that caused him to exclaim "The horror!

The horror," but later adds that "Since I peeped over the edge myself, I understand better the meaning of his stare... it was wide enough to embrace the whole universe, piercing enough to penetrate all the hearts that beat in the darkness..he had summed up, he had judged." Marlow guesses that Kurtz suddenly knew everything and discovered how horrible the man can be.

Marlow learned through Kurtz's death, and he now knows that inside every human is horrible evil side.

In conclusion the themes of restraint and man's journey into self run through Heart of Darkness and actually become intertwined. It is interesting to note that Marlow and Kurtz coming from the same background do not end up the same in the novel. Kurtz is doomed by his lack of restraint.

Q.3. Discuss the barriers in Heart of Darkness.

Or

Q. How does Marlow becomes an open-minded and loyal human being.

Heart of Darkness is a book that explores many different ideas and philosophies regarding human life. How people see each other and connect with each other is one of the larger aspects of human life covered in this tale. During his journey, Marlowe meets many different types of people that he is able to decipher from the good and bad personal characteristics. These people all contribute to Marlowe's growth as a person as he breaks down barriers inside himself that deal with race, loyalty, and the way people interrelate with each other.

The first site that Marlowe sees on his expedition puts an instant stereotype into his head. The sight is one of skinny, black labourers at the Outer Station. Marlowe sees a young boy who is hungry and feeds him a biscuit. Marlowe sees these images of people and how they're living, and consciously or unconsciously, makes a note in his mind that this is the way Africans are. This initial impression of the Africans had formed a barrier that Marlowe would change within himself by the end of the story.

Immediately after his encounter with the labourers, Marlowe meets the accountant at the station who provides Marlowe with his first real distinction between the races. The accountant presented himself in a gracious manner. He was Caucasian, wore fancy clothes, had oiled hair, sported varnished boots, and he had a starched white collar. This all made the man look oddly out of place given that he was in the middle of the jungle and surrounded by filthy labourers. Marlowe wasn't sure about what to think of this man at first, but when a sick man was brought into the accountant's office, the accountant gripes about the inconvenience to himself. "The groans of a sick person distract my attention, and without that it is extremely difficult to guard against clerical errors in this climate". This cruel and cold side of the typical European ivory trader shows through very clearly to Marlowe. This was his first, but not only experience on the journey with a greedy white male.

The white manager on the boat is another character that speaks to Marlowe's intellect by way of his actions. Marlowe gains some of his most significant self-growth in the story through his encounters and his analyzing of the manager. Marlowe is constantly hearing about ways that the manager and his crew are trying to take over the ivory ring and how they are trying to stop Kurtz from continuing his dominance in this trade. Marlowe is always noting to himself the scheming ways of the white, European manager, and how this way of behaving is one of hollowness. It does not take long for Marlowe to see the actions of this man and dismiss him as a negative force.

Along for the ride on the boat is a couple of other groups of people that help Marlowe find himself. The cannibals, a group of workers that are on the boat to work for a meager wage and little respect, offer Marlowe the best example of self-will that he sees throughout his entire voyage. As the small amount of food brought on board by the cannibals themselves begins to run extremely low, and the eating of members of the crew becomes imminent, the cannibals show extreme restraint by holding back and not attempting in any way to use the white crew members as a source of food. This comes as a complete shock to Marlowe and the rest of his crew because they were extremely out numbered and saw no reason why the cannibals would not take advantage of their situation. Before this incident, Marlowe thought of the Africans as aggressive and wild people, but now he saw that they are capable of acting in a civilized way. Marlowe sees this loyalty in the cannibals and recognizes it as an honourable and courageous action.

The black helmsman on the boat also makes Marlowe realise full circle how important of a trait loyalty really is. When the helmsman dies, Marlowe mourns his lost mate and actually feels a loss for the black man. "...it was a kind of partnership. He steered for me-I looked after him...a subtle bond had been created of which I only became aware when it was suddenly broke". This incident knocks down a wall inside Marlowe. Earlier in the story, Marlowe dismissed one of his black workers as just a pawn in the grand scheme of things. The helmsman dying lets Marlowe realise how vital the black workers on the boat really were, both in their work and the loyalty they exhibited.

The meeting of Kurtz was something that was built up for Marlowe throughout his entire journey down the Congo. When he meets the man, Kurtz was very ill and acting strangely. He had been overcome by his passion for the ivory trade and had let it take over his life to a point where it was going to kill him. Marlowe recognized this, but what he also recognized was although it had gone a little overboard in Kurtz's case, it was the loyalty to his craft that had made Kurtz so successful. Marlowe became friends with Kurtz over the last few days of his life and they had an instant rapport. Kurtz trusted Marlowe and gave him some important items to distribute away from the greedy manager after his own death. "I did not go to join Kurtz there and then. I did not. I remained to dream the nightmare out to the end and to show my loyalty to Kurtz once more".

After his time with Kurtz, Marlowe realised what this whole journey was about. It wasn't about ivory or making money; it was about the pursuit of character that makes people in this world better. Marlowe used what he learned on this journey to break down the barriers inside himself and become a better person. Marlowe was no longer just a naïve European; he was now an open-minded and loyal human being.

Q.4. Analyse the depiction of Africa in Heart of Darkness.
Or
Q. Discuss the racism in Heart of Darkness.

Chinua Achebe believes that Joseph Conrad's Heart Of Darkness is racist based on Conrad's descriptions of Africa and it's people. Achebe, author of Things Fall Apart, stresses Conrad's depiction of Africa as the antithesis of Europe and civilization, and the animal imagery present throughout the novella.

Heart of Darkness, written in 1899 during the period of British Imperialism, concerns a British trading company and their expedition into the Congo for ivory. The African natives are treated brutally by the Europeans, and despite Conrad's casual condescension towards the Africans, one cannot help feeling resentment at the unnecessary cruelty they must endure. The novella stands as a document against the imperialist practices—Conrad was quite liberal for the time.

The natives are referred to as "savages" several times throughout the story, but Conrad is not using any particularly strong words for the time. The European audiences who would be reading would not find anything racist about it. By today's more sensitive standards, such deference is more serious, but turn-of-the-century England was sure to expect far harsher. Educated people reading Conrad's novel should understand the differences between the past and the present, and be forgiving of his language.

The deeper the expedition progressed into the centre of the continent, the more isolation was felt by the crew. In a sense, Central Africa IS the antithesis of Western Europe — it lacks not only the hectic urban structures but also the Social Darwinist attitudes of the time. It is in this remote environment that man must face his true self without any illusions, and the darkness of the human soul is apparent. The uncivilized environment may mock western civilization's refinement, but this is not derogatory towards the jungle, but rather an eye-opener to the European audience.

By exhibiting the deeds of the Europeans, their portrayal becomes so negative that they become the savages. Conrad clearly is sympathetic to the plight of the Africans, and any racial epithets, if not accepted by progressives of the time, are not meant as attacks directed at the natives.

It should be obvious that Conrad is on their side — or is this "undermined by the mindlessness of its context and the pretty explicit animal imagery surrounding it"? I think not. Conrad's animal imagery is used as a metaphor for the human spiritual being, not as a comparison to the natives.

Heart of Darkness is not intended to be a portrait of the African people at all. It is a story of what was inflicted upon them. It is a story of man's introspective into himself when there is nowhere else to turn. It is a story of an obsessed man named Kurtz and what he did for his own gain. It is a strikingly accurate account of a historical period past, and it should not be regarded today as a hateful spew of racism.

Q.5. Discuss the role of Intended in Heart of Darkness.
Or
Q. Analyse the blindfold of the intended.

Heart of Darkness is a novel in which many relatively minor characters serve major functions in the overall meaning of the work. One such character is Kurtz's Intended who starkly contrasts against Kurtz's evil to better show the evil and primal side of man.

The Intended is the embodiment of man's denial of the truth of inner evil. In the painting of the Intended, her blindfold shows her blindness to the truth, symbolized by the torch she holds. The truth of man's evil is within her grasp, but yet she allows herself to be blinded so she cannot accept this to be true. She is in denial – as far as she knows, if she can't see the evil or that it holds a penetrating presence, it does not exist to her.

Ironically, however, Conrad describes the Intended as having "a shade of truthfulness upon [her] features." She is an innocent – the word "halo" compounds that notion; however this too is ironic. She is only a person, just as capable of malevolence as anyone else, which is symbolized by the black she wears. Marlow only lies about Kurtz's life and death to spare the Intended the knowledge of what Kurtz had become – a manifestation of raw human evil. Marlow is the blindfold that shields her from the truth that Kurtz fell to a natural inner compulsion towards iniquity, and that this inner evil exists everywhere.

Because she denies the existence of an inner evil, the Intended is only as innocent as a human being can be. This innocence contrasts severely with Kurtz's own evil. This innocent girl was the fiancee of a murderer "demi-god" who decapitated people. She is the innocent side of the relationship, or the yang. She is pure, but with a spot of darkness being the potential for evil only because she is human. Kurtz is the dark side of the relationship, the yin. He is an "animated figure of death" who once was noble and innocent, like the fiancee. He went to Africa with good intentions, but was corrupted by unadulterated freedom. With no society to tell him how to act, he fell prey to his inner darkness. The Intended is confined by society – another reason why she cannot possibly comprehend or even want to know about the inner evil of man.

When Kurtz's health rapidly starts to deteriorate, he speaks out in delerium about this choking evil and how he feels innocents should be protected from the knowledge of it.

He says "we must help [the women] stay in that beautiful world of their own, lest ours gets worse." He feels that the preservation of ignorance is better than the knowledge of this despotic truth. Once the presence of this natural evil is discovered, a person is nearly always committed to its path. Kurtz's feelings for his intended make him realise that not all truths should be known.

The Intended symbolizes man's denial and unwillingness to learn truths too awful to know. A person should be aware of his own natural malevolence, yet not become evil, finding a balance in between. Conrad shows through the Intended that some truths should never be known.

Q.6. Discuss the Post-Colonial Theory and Heart of Darkness.

Or

Q. Analyse the British imperialism portrayed by Conrad in Heart of Darkness.

"Heart of Darkness" begins and ends in London; on the Nellie on the Thames. The most part, however, takes place in the Congo (now known as the Republic of the Congo). The Congo, as it was originally known, was inhabited first by pygmy tribes and migratory 'Bantus' and was 'discovered' by the Portuguese in the 14th Century. The Portuguese brought with them Catholocism; European missionaries. The Congo was ruled by King Alfonso I from 1506 - 1540 and Shamba Bolongongo from 1600 - 1620. The slave trade was rife in the Congo, from about 1500 until 1830. King Leopold of Belgium ruled, between 1878 and 1908, and would have been King at the time "Heart of Darkness" was set. Conrad himself actually arrived in the Congo on 12 June 1890, and it would be safe to say that he would have used his experience in the Congo when writing "Heart of Darkness".

At its time of writing for Blackwood's Magazine (December 1898), Britain was in its last years of Victorian rule. Queen Victoria was actually the niece of King Leopold of Belgium. Britain was the most powerful and influential nation on Earth; its Empire spread throughout Europe, Asia and

Africa. Joseph Conrad, born in the Ukraine in 1857, as Jozef Teodor Konrad Korzeniowski, as the author, was an outsider looking out. Neither British nor African, he seemed to be the perfect candidate for writing about two countries he had knowledge of - England and the Congo.

African exploration was quite popular; in Conrad's day, Livingstone died in 1873, in Ilala, Africa, and Stanley returned from his final African expedition in 1890. As exploration was popular, so was the adventure story - tales of African exploration were available in abundance. Imperialism was also a popular theme at this point in the late nineteenth Century. Conrad's novella, whilst to contemporary critics (Achebe, for example) may appear racist; at the time was accepted as another piece of work from a very much published genre. The novella is literally filled with literal and metaphoric opposites; the Congo and the Thames, black and white, Europe and Africa, good and evil, purity and corruption, civilisation and 'triumphant bestiality', light and the very 'heart of darkness'.

Conrad portrays British imperialism in the perhaps naive character of Marlow, who is glad to see the "vast amount of red" on the Company's map; signifying the British territory. He is glad that "real work is done there"; meaning salvation, religion, culture and commerce. The reality of the colonialism is portrayed by Conrad in the form of the District Manager; a real imperialist, taking full advantage of his position and that of the colony. Marlow sees the Manager's only positive quality as the fact that he was never ill. From what Marlow knows of Kurtz, it is apparent that Marlow sets Kurtz on a mental pedestal; as the man who is bringing civilisation, through Imperialism, to the savages, and yet still managed to reap more reward, in the shape of ivory.

Marlow's opinion of Imperialism is dented time and again by his witnessing the lengths the Imperialists would go for profit. This opinion is destroyed, totally; when Marlow actually meets Kurtz, and realises that; far from conquering the darkness, Kurtz himself has been conquered by the darkness. The roles of Kurtz's 'Intended' and the African woman who appeared to be his mistress are often noted to be of great importance. The European's pure faith in Kurtz's good nature contrasts with Marlow's knowledge of his corruption.

Conrad sets the Intended up to symbolise the removedness of the British from the events in Africa. She is grief-stricken and full of the dreams of what might have been, had Kurtz not died. Kurtz's 'mistress' shows not grief at Kurtz's departure, but a definite defiance; she being the only native still standing after Marlow sounded the steamer's whistle. The Intended's knowledge of Kurtz, whilst she claimed to have known 'him best' was incomplete, even illusory. The memory she is left with is itself a lie; provided by Marlow.

The women have two sets of characteristics; seemingly the accepted Victorian values and the post-colonial values. The Victorian reading would show the Intended as feminine, beautiful and saintly, rightly in a state of mourning, even a year after Kurtz's death. Her innocence would suggest her purity. The Intended would have symbolised civilisation. The mistress would show as masculine, savage, careless of the fact that her loved one was leaving. The African woman would have symbolised the savage unknown that was Africa. The post-colonial reading would show the Intended as foolish, mourning a man she barely knew. Her innocence would suggest her naivety; her faith based upon a lie. The mistress would show as erotic, living on in independence without Kurtz. The African woman here would have symbolised the fact that Africa did not need Britain's 'salvation', contrary to the British belief, based upon a lie, propaganda symbolised by the Intended's faith.

Q.7. Discuss the Spiritual Journey in Heart of Darkness.
Or
Q. Analyse Heart of Darkness as a psychological journey.

Heart of Darkness by Joseph Conrad may be a narrative about colonisation, revealing its drawbacks and corruption, but it may also be understood as a journey into the depths of one's psyche, if taken at a symbolic level.

At the beginning of the novel the reader is informed that Marlow is "not typical", that he, contrary to stay-at-home-minded seamen, is a "wanderer". He has no home, in a psychological sense of the word. He simply "follows the sea". This may evoke an interpretation that the man is disturbed, that he attempts to find out about the secrets of his soul, to get to know himself. Since boyhood he had been interested in unexplored lands and especially in a long winding snake-like river with the "head" in the sea and the "tail" plunging deeply into the land, which, as Marlow admits, "charmed" him. This image resembles a map of a journey from the dark lands of the soul, the unconstrained, uncivilised core, which may be called a Freudian Id, towards light, that is Superego. Marlow desires to follow this path in the opposite direction to explore the depths of himself.

If the uncivilised land is a dark Id, then Superego is presented as the civilised world, full of light, knowledge, awareness of the self. The light came upon the gloom of London with the Roman conquest, which introduced discipline by force and formed the savages into an orderly society. The Roman conquest symbolises the eternal battle between the Id and the Superego, the latter always struggling to impose rules on the former. This is what is taking place in Congo. The aim of the colonists is to bring Christianity to the black people, but in the end it turns out that it is not the civilisation which wins, but the Id. It rots the soul with corruption, stealing money from the natives. When there is no watch from the society over one's doings, one can do anything they please, like Kurtz, whom Id overtook completely.

What saves Marlow from losing his constraints is that he maintains psychological balance between the two drives. His position is in the sphere of Ego; he sails the grey sea (middle colour between light and darkness) along the shore, occasionally going inland, but never plunging too deep, thus securing himself from the influence of the darkness. He attempts to get to know the primitive, unconscious part of his soul by grasping bits and pieces of it, and finds there a figure of Kurtz who fascinates him but also terrifies by his unpredictability, capability of killing people if he pleased, the danger he poses to his mates. Kurtz had mingled with the natives and the forest too much, and by meeting Kurtz Marlow was able to see what would happen if Id totally possessed him. In fact, Kurtz may be a dark side of Marlow, a projection of his psyche personifying the instinctive drive of human beings.

Having experienced the "darkness" of the soul, Marlow stands out, becomes a different person; he is grey, which indicates that by exploring the instinct he gained some of the darkness of it.

Q.8. Discuss The Spiritual Voyages of Heart of Darkness.

Or

Q. Critically examine the voyages of Kurtz and Marlow.

Heart of Darkness describes an outward journey to the heart of Africa that parallels an inward journey to the heart and depths of man's being. Two spiritual voyages are made by Kurtz and Marlow.

Kurtz was a great man who discovered a flaw in himself while working in Africa. He lacked "restraint" to control the emerging dark side which he found within himself. He plumbs the depths of man's dark side -a side which civilization and culture represses - but is swallowed up, by these forces which eventually overcome him in the isolation of darkest Africa. He falls into unspeakable acts and experiences the primitive power and ecstasy and horror of man's uninhibited darkness. Marlow holds back from "the abyss," although he humbly takes no credit for this achievement, ascribing it to grace. Nonetheless, he comes away changed, even enlightened, by this glimpse into the deeper and darker mysteries of life.

William Blake suggests that the road to heaven leads through hell. Blake also saw the pursuit of truth and self awareness as an effort to combine the Innocence of the Lamb with the darker Passion of the Tyger, the two poles of man's and life's existence. Wisdom and enlightenment come to the one who effectively understands and harmonizes both sides of this human nature.

Few people make the effort because society discourages such knowledge in an effort to protect itself. Most people are ignorant of themselves, blithely self-satisfied in their protected world. Kurtz was one of the great men of Europe, a poetic visionary and promoter of progressive causes. In Africa, repressed urges arose which he could not control. Lost in the darkness of his own being, he defines this new found reality as "the horror." Despite his descent into evil, Marlowe respects Kurtz in comparison to the much more "hollow men" whom he ironically calls "pilgrims." These men operate on the "raw principle of rapacious greed" while pretending to be apostles of progress. Such pyjama-clad, gun waving, slave driving, self righteous fools sicken Marlow and, compared to their nightmare of ignorance, the nightmare of Kurtz commands respect and allegiance. His was a spiritual voyage which failed.

Marlow, we are led to believe, has succeeded. He is five times described by the narrator of this frame story in the posture of a meditating or preaching Buddha. The Buddha is the supreme example of enlightened consciousness and so Marlowe represents a kind of hard won enlightenment. Like the Ancient Mariner, he has made a spiritual voyage and returned to tell his story to ears that will listen. Of the listeners on board the Nellie, only the narrator seems, in spite of himself, to have such ears. On returning to Brussels, Marlow's reaction to the European sophisticates he finds there is revulsion. Never having been tested, their confidence and self control he sees as worthless (as Kurtz's turned out to be). They are protected by the "butcher and policeman." The butcher kills for us and so supports the illusion that life is all sweetness and light; the policeman (neighbours, priests, parents etc.) is a force of repression and inhibition and as such promotes the illusion that mankind is essentially gentle and loving. Shooting on our fellow citizens in the manner of the People's Liberation Army in China was described as "unthinkable" and "beyond belief." Kurtz and Marlow knew better.

Marlow calls Brussels the "sepulchral city" because its citizens are in a tomb. They have not yet begun to live in the sense that they have not yet taken the first step toward self-awareness, a process requiring knowledge of both light and dark. Marlow's first step came physically and symbolically with his first step past the Dantesque black ladies - his first step into hell. His last step comes in his willingness to lie to Kurtz's Intended, breaking a previously held principle. This lie is in defence of the other side of existence, pure innocence, as represented by the unenlightened but pure faith of Kurtz's fiancé.

Marlow is a changed man. Like the mariner and his wedding guest, Marlow and his listener(s) (the narrator/us) have lost the superficial empty happiness of life before Africa and have gained a fuller but more troubling wisdom with his return to Europe. They are "sadder but wiser" men who seem to reflect Joseph Conrad's own words about his trip to Africa that, "before-the Congo, I was a mere animal."

Q.9. Analyse the Character of Marlow in The Heart of Darkness.

Or

Q. Throughout this story there are many confusing and ever changing sides of Marlow's character and his heart of darkness. Comment

Charlie Marlow appeared to be a man of great pride and civilization. He always spoke very proper and was a classic example of a man of his time.

Throughout this novel though, this painted image I have of Marlow begins to slowly drip away.

There were several instances which creates confusion about Marlow. The first one was at the very beginning of the story. Marlow began talking about his childhood and how he had dreamed of becoming a captain or a skipper on one of the glorious steamboats. He went on and on about it in such great detail that you almost began to believe that he was a captain, though he was only a young boy at the time. His determination and love seemed eternal, and nothing was going to take his dream away from him. At least that is what we were lead to believe. Marlow soon grew old and so did his dream.

The determination side of Marlow slipping away into the river along with his childhood vision of being a captain. It didn't seem that something like age would stop Marlow from taking on this challenge. After he talked about it so much you would think only death itself would stop him. Unfortunately, Marlow gave up and decided to move on with his life. That was the way it was going to have to be, or so he thought.

Marlow can be seen as a seemingly comfortable old man now. He didn't have his dream job, but he was still well off. One day though Marlow's fantasy job basically just fell into his lap. A steamboat captain was killed and Marlow was not about to let another soul take this job away from him. He was fixed to get the job, but wasn't sure how to get it himself This is where more confusion starts with Marlow.

Marlow didn't want to have to work to get the job, so he asked his Aunt to get the job for him. This struck me as very odd considering the way that Marlow felt about women. He felt that women should just do there own little house chores and nothing else, for they weren't needed and basically would just be in the way. After asking his Aunt to get him the job he made a comment that really make anyone angry. Marlow stated, "Then-would you believe it?-I tried the women. I, Charlie Marlow set the women to work-to get a job.

Heavens! Well, you see it was the notion that drove me." This is the point in the story that one can find Marlow to be rather lazy. If he had been so manly and wise don't you think that he could have gotten the job himself?. Of course his Aunt came through for him and Marlow was off to roam the river of his desire.

Throughout the rest of this story Marlow just continues to confuse and at some times even frustrate. There was one point in the story that Marlow almost seemed to have a heart. He saw a homeless man and stared at him, started to feel a bit sorry, but quickly caught himself almost as if having a conscience was a bad thing.

This is where a big part of Marlow's heart of darkness can be seen Another thing that really bothered me about Marlow was how he got so caught Up in the image of Kurtz, even though he didn't even know him. A man like Marlow would be a follower, but that just turned out to be another side of Marlow. He began to lose sight of everyone around him and concentrated on just the illusion and image of a man that he had never even seen.

Marlow is a self centred, and cold hearted man. He didn't care about anything or anyone around him, except for the people that could give him something in return.

Marlow is an extremely puzzling character. I know that people have many sides to them, but Marlow seemed to change so fast and drastic.

It was a good decision on Conrad's part to make Marlow so dimensional. It really added a lot of interest to the novel. It almost kept you on your toes, because you never knew what type of character transformation Charlie Marlow was going to under go next.

Q.10. Discuss the Modernist's Experiments in Heart of Darkness.
Or
Q. Analyse Heart of Darkness as a Modernist text.

In Joseph Conrad's Heart of Darkness, a chaotic form of writing takes place which is characteristic of the Modernist's experiments in their style of literature of stream-of-consciousness. Written before WWI took place, he spoke of a different type of chaos and uncertainty present in the world at this time; the issue of slavery.

Heart of Darkness describes a voyage to Africa, common for the British still, despite the horrific treatment which was apparent of colonization. The chaotic, stream-of-consciousness style Conrad took on helped to display the confusion, and made the reader have to interpret for themselves what they thought the writer meant. Conrad experiments with this style, leaving some sentences without ending: "not a sentimental pretense but an idea;...something you can set up...and offer a sacrifice to....", a very choppy form of literature and causes the reader to fill in the holes and interpret themselves, alone. Conrad skips about from talking of the "two women knitted black wool feverishly" at the gate of the city (of hell), to his aunt which he feels women are "out of touch with truth," to how the British are as "weak-eyed devil(s) of a rapacious and pitiless folly". Conrad's mind moves about as ours do along a large duration of literary monologue to convey to the reader the author's ideas, as interpreted by the reader.

Conrad's narrative frame also continues his experimentation with literary form in Modernist style. Two separate monologues are present throughout Heart of Darkness. The first part starts out with an unnamed narrator aboard the ship Nelly, describing to himself, as well as to the reader, those aboard the ship, particularly Marlow. At first, the narrator is not known for sure to be a character aboard the ship until a few paragraphs later identify him as a person observing the others-"Between us there was, as I have already said,". Marlow gradually takes over the narration, beginning "'And this also,' said Marlow suddenly" is the first breaking point in Conrad's Modernist narrative experiment. By page 2195, Conrad has Marlow take over the entire monologue narrative, as the unnamed narrator jumps time after time, but is rarely thought of for the majority of Heart of Darkness.

Q.11. Discuss the theme and setting in Heart of Darkness.
Or

Q. Analyse Heart of Darkness as a novel of a story within a story.

Heart of Darkness is a novella that is one story being told by Marlow within the actual story by Joseph Conrad. The novella is set on a boat, the Nellie, on the Thames river in England, but the story that Marlow tells is set in the Belgian Congo. When relating the theme of this novella to the setting it has to be looked at from both the Thames and Congo rivers. Heart of Darkness shows the superiority of whites over blacks in a context where the blacks are considered to be savages and whites are supposed to be civilized.

Marlow is telling the story to his friends in the dark of night on the Thames river. As he begins the day is just ending "in a serenity of still and exquisite brilliance." It is a very sombre and dull atmosphere and as the calmness begins to fade it becomes more profound. At one point Marlow stops and is interrupted by the unknown narrator who describes the setting on the Nellie. "It had become so pitch dark that we listeners could hardly see one another. For a long time already he, sitting apart, had been no more to us than a voice....I listened, I listened on the watch for the sentence, for the word, that would give me the clew to the faint uneasiness inspired by this narrative that seemed to shape itself without human lips in the heavy nightair of the river."

As the story ends the setting on the Thames river is once again described by the unseen narrator. "The offing was barred by a black bank of clouds, and the tranquil waterway leading to the uttermost ends of the earth flowed somber under an overcast sky-seemed to lead into the heart of an immense darkness."

The superiority of whites over blacks in the novella faces the harsh reality that the whites are there not to colonize the Congo but to conquer it. As Marlow puts it "They were no colonists; their administration was merely a squeeze, and nothing more, I suspect. They were conquerors, and for that you want only brute force-nothing to boast of, when you have it, since your strength is just an accident arising from the weakness of others. They grabbed what they could get for the sake of what was to be got. It was just robbery with violence, aggravated murder on a great scale, and men going at blind-as is very proper for those who tackle a darkness. The conquest of the earth, which mostly means the taking away from those who have a different complexion or slightly flatter noses than ourselves, is not a pretty thing when you look into too much."

In the novella the blacks are described at one point as helpers but, they are not really, they are treated more like slaves. The white men are corrupt and greedy in the Congo, as Marlow states when he is first entering the Congo. "I've seen the devil of violence, and the devil of greed, and the devil of hot desire; but, by all the stars! These were strong, lusty, red-eyed devils that swayed and drove men-men, I tell you. But as I stood on this hillside, I foresaw that in the blinding sunshine of that land I would become acquainted with a flabby, pretending, weak-eyed devil of a rapacious and pitiless folly."

The whites enter the jungle thinking it must be tamed and that its savage, dark natives must become civilized. The white man=s uneasy and disconcerted relations with the barbarism of Africa only makes things worse for the natives. The natives have a relationship with nature where things are still pure and innocent, where they are not exposed to the corruption of the civilized world. The white men conform some natives to live by rules and these natives help to enslave the others. This creates unhappiness and degradation of the blacks where they tend to retreat to the forest to die. "Black shapes crouched, lay, sat between the trees leaning against the trunks, clinging to the earth, half coming out, half effaced within the dim light, in all the attitudes of pain, abandonment, and despair....And this was the place where some of the helpers had withdrawn to die."

The ivory trade in the Congo is very dark and obscure, no one really knows how Kurtz=s gets the ivory he does. Marlow describes Kurtz face just before his death "I saw on that ivory face the expression of somber pride, of ruthless power, of craven terror-of an intense and hopeless despair." Both Kurtz and Marlow found a dark heart of Africa with primeval power that forced them to look at the darkness, hate, fear and evil within themselves. They saw that the white men were not really bringing progress to the darkest Africa but they were deteriorating their own morale.

The blacks in Heart of Darkness have no personal traits or uniqueness, there is no humanity in their characters. Their appearance is never really described the only thing Marlow says about them is that they are black, no details, "Black shapes...black bones...black neck,". But the whites in the novella are described in more detail such as the way Marlow describes the manager, Kurtz, and the girl. "I met a white man, in such an unexpected elegance of get-up that in the first moment I took him for a sort of vision. I saw high starched collar, white cuffs, a light alpaca jacket, snowy trousers, a clean necktie, and varnished bots. No hat. Hair parted, brushed, oiled, under a green-lined parasol held in a big white hand."

As Marlow puts it the whites in the Congo are in a "lightless region of subtle horror, where pure, uncomplicated savagery was a positive relief,". The white men have no escape from the darkness as Kurtz realised a he spoke his last words, "The horror! The horror!", but the blacks can retreat back to their way of life of helpless savages instead of being unhappy slaves.

The theme of Heart of Darkness is evil and mysterious, we never really know how the whites over power the blacks. The theme is very suited to the setting, both have the image of darkness.

The theme and setting are a harsh reality in the Congo where everything is dark in some way, whether it be the darkness of the blacks skin, the dark evilness of the whites or the gloominess of the environment. The theme where the whites have supremacy over the blacks is evil and very dark goes along with the dull and dreary setting, neither has any life to it. The environment is dark and lifeless and the blacks have no freedom due to the manipulation by the whites men.

Q.12. Write a short note on the Symbol of Ivory in Heart of Darkness.

Or

Q. What is the importance of ivory in Heart of Darkness.

In Heart of Darkness Joseph Conrad often uses vague,"muted" descriptions, leaving a melange of possible meanings in the reader's lap.

One exception to this trend is Conrad's symbolic use of ivory. Within the frame of the story, his references to ivory can obviously be seen as a representation of the white man's greed.Towards the end of the book ivory comes to symbolize the oozing evil that drips from the heart of darkness.

It isn't long before Conrad makes a commentary on the greed of the whites.By the thirty-seventh page via Marlow associates them with a "false religion." He says that the men at the Central Station are, "like a lot of faithless pilgrims bewitched inside a rotten fence. Pilgrims are usually people who travel to a holy place, so why the choice of words? Conrad further explains in the following lines when he says, "The word 'ivory' rang in the air, was whispered, was sighed. You would think they were praying to it." In their rapacity the "pilgrims" have placed ivory as their God, a realization that has greater meaning towards the end of the book.

The significance of ivory begins to move away from avarice and takes on a purely evil connotation as Marlow approaches those hearts of darkness: the Inner Station and Kurtz. Kurtz's relationship with ivory seems to have been reiterated by every company member through the course of the story. Of course Kurtz "harvested" more ivory than all the other stations combined, and therefore it almost seems appropriate that Conrad would use extensive ivory imagery in describing Kurtz. Earlier, during his digression on Kurtz, Marlow says, "The wilderness had patted him on the head, and, behold, it was like a ball-an ivory ball".

By the time that Kurtz is carried out on a stretcher the evil has so overtaken him that, "I could see the cage of his ribs all astir, the bones of his arms waving. It was as though an animated image of death carved out of old ivory had been shaking its hand with menaces at a motionless crowd of men made of dark and glittering bronze". The evil has now grown to encompass his entire body, and soul. Kurtz's lust for ivory is recounted by the Russian. Once he threatened to shoot the Russian, who was squirreling a small quantity of ivory- "because he could do so, and had a fancy for it, and there was nothing on earth to prevent him from killing whom he jolly well pleased."

The almost god-like power that Kurtz wields is unchecked, save for disease.

In Heart of Darkness ivory plays a dual role in significance. On one hand it is representative of evil and greed, and on the other, it is representative of the measures taken to acquire it in the first place (i.e. mistreatment of blacks). Conrad's use of ivory in order to symbolize darkness is also in keeping with his occasional reversal of the colours normally associated with good and evil, white and black. Ivory as a material is one of the purest and whitest found in nature, while Kurtz's soul is purely black.

Q.13. Analyse Lies in Heart of Darkness.

Or

Q. Critically examine the lies told in Heart of Darkness.

A lie is an untruth. It can be a false statement or a statement left unsaid that causes someone to be misled. In life, lies are told for many different reasons. In fiction, they thicken the plot. In Conrad's Heart of Darkness, Marlow dislikes lies and therefore only tells two, both in extraordinary circumstances. The lies that Marlow tells show several things about him. For example, even though he has been touched by evil, he is still a good man. He never actually tells a lie, instead he lets others continue to believe what they already believe. This helps him justify his lies.

Marlow, in the middle of his story, interrupts himself to say "You know I hate, detest, and can't bear a lie." He does not think that he is better than the rest of the world. Lies simply appall him. Marlow feels there is a "taint of death, and a flavour of mortality in lies." Lying makes him feel "miserable and sick, like biting something rotten would do." Since he feels this way, he would only tell a lie in extraordinary circumstances.

The first lie that Marlow told was in an extraordinary circumstance. It was told because of a notion that it would somehow be of help to Mr. Kurtz. The lie was told in order to allow the brick maker to think he had more influence in the company than he actually had. This lie would help Kurtz in two ways. Firstly, it would help Marlow to get the rivets he needed to fix the boat, and that would provide Kurtz with either a means of communication or a way out of the jungle. Secondly, it would provide Kurtz with an ally who was perceived as influential. Marlow knew that others were jealous of the Mr. Kurtz's success. Some saw him as the next "Director of the Company," and some were trying to find a reason to hang him. If Marlow was considered powerful, he might be able to help Mr. Kurtz. This was an extraordinary reason for telling a lie.

The second lie was also told in extraordinary circumstances. It is told to "the intended" so that the image of her dead fiancé would not be destroyed. She had waited at least two years for her lover to return from Africa, and during this time had built his image up in her mind. To her, Kurtz was a man to be admired. She felt it would be "impossible not to love him." She was proud to have been engaged to Kurtz, and would be shocked to learn of the things he had done. Marlow had to decide if he should tell her the truth about Kurtz and cause her even greater grief, or let her go on believing that he was a good man. This is an extraordinary circumstance, and thus one in which Marlow could tell a lie. The significance of this lie is that it would serve no purpose to tell the truth, so Marlow did not. Kurtz was dead, and to tell the truth would only hurt an innocent woman. She had no idea that her fiancé had an evil heart. She thought that he was loved and admired by everyone who knew him. If she learned of the things he had done, it would destroy her.

Marlow showed his good side by not telling her the truth about Kurtz. This is a suitable ending to the work because it means that even though Marlow had met a man with a "Heart of Darkness," and that even after facing his own darkness, he could come out of the jungle unchanged for the most part. He is still a good human being with feelings and a sense of right and wrong. Marlow never actually vocalized a lie. He simply allowed others to continue to believe an untruth. First, the brick maker thought Marlow was more influential than he actually was, and Marlow allowed him to continue to believe that. Secondly, the intended thought her fiance was a good man, and Marlow allowed her to continue to believe that. Since he never actually vocalized a lie, he was better able to justify them to himself. Marlow dislikes lies, and only tells them in extraordinary circumstances. When he does lie, it is for the sake of others, not himself. This shows that he is a kind human being. It is unfortunate that all lies are not told with such noble purpose. The world would be a better place if they were.

Q.14. Examine the role of Women in Heart of Darkness.
Or
Q. Conrad portrays woman as ignorant of truth.Comment.

Women seem to be categorized into a separate group, serving as supplements to men's actions, characters and behaviour. All of them seem to live in the realm of their own, built on the idealistic conception of the surrounding world, governed by fair rules and laws.

The two women Marlow encounters in the Company's office knit black wool – they represent the Fates who guard the "door of Darkness" (Hell and Destruction) and to the "house in a city of dead". The black colour may be associated with the Natives on whose destruction and exploitation the Company was based. Black is also equivalent to the Darkness into which Marlow descends (sin and death). The wool may signify the thread of life. Their appearance is foreshadowed by the two black hens which 'decided' about Fresleven's doom.

Marlow's aunt is depicted with an underlying irony ("a dear enthusiastic soul") which points to an illusive existence of a white woman in her civilised imagined world. She was "ready to do anything" for Marlow in the name of a "noble cause", that is, colonising the Blacks and implementing civilisation in the Darkness of Congo. She firmly believes her nephew to be the "emissary of light", overlooking the dark level of exploiting the Natives for financial benefits (ivory).

The painting of a woman who is "blindfolded, carrying a lighted torch" which Marlow admires signifies initial intentions of Kurtz and his beliefs before he was swallowed by the tempting Darkness. He was to have been an emissary of light but remained blindfolded and did not see the consequences leading him to his self-destruction. The painting indicates the original, good nature of Kurtz, lost in the dark of the Congo.

The native woman represents the whole Black community and the beauty of the wilderness, both of which were invaded by the 'civilised' whites. She is the passionate reality, being "savage and superb, wild-eyed and magnificent", reminding the whites of the Black heritage and their own culture (jewellery). The gesture of throwing her arms into the sky may symbolise a dumb outcry to God to restore the original Time when the land was not raided and there was peace and freedom ("wild sorrow...dumb pain"). The lack of words which remain unsaid, only reiterates her appearance and the message sent by her behaviour.

Kurtz's fiancee becomes contrasted with the native woman – the Intended, as signified by the name, will remain the Intended, living with an idealistic image of her husband-to-be whom she unquestionably believed to be of impeccable character and behaviour. The truth about Kurtz would be "too dark" and would destroy her illusive world based on the false image of his greatness.

"Women...we must help them to stay in that beautiful world of their own, lest ours gets worse."

These words uttered by Marlow deny the quest into the Darkness for women – their role is limited to living in their own world because the might be too weak to face all the obstacles and temptations

Q.15. Comment on Detachment in Heart of Darkness.
Or
Q. There is a lack of human bonds in Heart of Darkness. Comment.

In the book Heart of Darkness, Marlowe only allows himself to form only one bond. Marlowe allows himself to form a small "safe" attachment to Kurtz because Kurtz is already very attached. He does not form any other bonds. In fact, he uses his racism to eliminate the possibility of having feelings for about ninety nine percent of the African population.

Marlowe not only looks at the African people as being to different from him to be normal, but he goes so far as to describe Africa as being another world, a world containing savages. He would not let himself become attached to this land, or it's inhabitants. Anytime he feels himself having a relationship with anyone, he purposely stops himself from feeling, fearing that opening himself up may result inrejection and/or heartbreak.

He claimed that he felt a connection with Kurtz this, I believe, is because he knew that this was "safe." This was "safe" because he knew that Kurtz would die before any real attachment could be made. He also knew that Kurtz would not have the same feeling for him as he had for Kurtz. This is because Kurtz already had two girlfriends, and a best friend (the Russian). This was something that Marlowe could deal with because Kurtz was already deeply involved so it held little risk for intense attachment. This is also shown when the helmsman, man who steers the ship, gets killed. Marlowe says that he liked that man because he was reliable, and not mush else. He did not even shed a tear for a man that he worked everyday with for the last six months. He simply threw him overboard, thinking about it for only a few minutes and then, he walked away. The Cannibals on the ship were starving. They had almost no food with them, and were not given the opportunity to buy food. The helmsman body could have been enough food for all of them for awhile. Marlowe, acting in character, did not care about this. He said that it may start a bad chain of events. Because of this all of the Cannibals went hungry for the rest of the trip.

Going along with his inability to have healthy relationships with people and his inability to care, is his racism. This racism acts as a good buffer against attachment. Almost everyone that Marlowe came into contact with was black. Because they were black Marlowe did could not care about them. This drastically reduced his chances of meeting someone that he may care about.

Many of the Europeans that lived in Africa at this time used their racism in this way; they used it to dismiss the Africans. The British did not understand the Africans, and therefore thought them to be savages. In fact, Chinua Achebe says that a British historian and Reguis professor at Oxford believed that African history did not even exist. This, I would assume, is one of the reasons why the British felt that it was not only their right but also, their duty to civilize Africa.

Chinua Achebe writes in his 1977 article Racism in the Heart of Darkness that "The Heart of Darkness projects the image of Africa as "another world". By "another world" I believe that Achebe is talking about what the Europeans believed to be an uncivilized society. Conrad portrays the Africans almost the same way that we would aliens, yet he feels a connection with them. Later Achebe writes "it is not the differences that worry Marlowe, but the lurking hint of kinship, of common ancestry". Marlowe tries to comfort himself by telling himself that Africa simply a different world, but he recognizes their mutual humanness. This frightens Marlowe because he feels a bond with these people. He feels a bond for people who he has been conditioned to believe are lower then him. He feels connected to these savage "criminals." Not only would Marlowe never admit to feeling anything for anyone, but especially not for a black man.

Anytime Marlowe felt himself forming a relationship with anyone, he would purposely stop himself from caring about them. Marlowe only chose to make one friend throughout the whole story. This friend was someone that he know could not return his admiration. He did not even allow himself to see the Africans as equals, much less form an attachment to them. Marlowe used his racism as a barrier against them.

He did not even let himself form any sort of attachment to the new land he was in. He described it as "another world," as if it was too far from "normal" to be lovable. Marlowe was a very lonely man but, he deserves no pity. He set himself up to be lonely.

Light and Dark in Conrad's Heart of Darkness

Q.16. Discuss the theme of dark and light in Heart of Darkness

Or

Q. Analyse dark and light as metaphors for European and non European.

In Joseph Conrad's Heart of Darkness, the author adverts to the idea that the "entrapment of light by darkness [that] is continually suggested" is comparative to Marlow's personality and perspective of his expedition down the Congo River. Light symbolizes any object or concept that is positive while darkness represents anything that elicits malice. The way in which Conrad approaches the novel by using darkness constantly prevail over light shows a continual theme of foreboding and gloom. Everything that shows vibrancy is illuminated through Conrad's words. These symbolisms and representations have a undeviating effect on the personality and perspective of the protagonist, Marlow. Conrad's use of a frame tale is exceedingly important when the character that is sharing his recollections has an altered perception. One may scrutinize the perspective of the African landscape as a natural wonder and not a foreboding nightmare as Marlow illustrates. The altered perception of Marlow, as using darkness as a victor of light, exhibits that Conrad utilizes the frame tale as a scapegoat for his personal perspective. The accounts of the narrative are the actual happenings of Conrad's individual journey up the Congo River. The reader, through Marlow's speech, can visualize any given atmosphere described in the book. Unfortunately, there are not any existing neutral settings throughout the book. The landscapes are either overcome by darkness or light. The effect of this darkness or light has a direct corollary to the reader.

Immediately the reader recognizes a contrast between the peaceful European setting and the disarray of the African atmosphere described later in the novel. The description of the Thames River offers the reader a glimpse into the superlative imagery. Because the Thames river is a favorable location,

Marlow views it as "nearly calm," all is still, the sails do no flutter and the "tide has subsided." Light is the prevalent force within the first section of the novel but as the story progresses and grows nearer the climax, the landscape is invaded with gloom and disgust as seen when Marlow states, "Going up that river was like travelling [sic] back to the earliest beginnings of the world...an empty stream, a great silence, an impenetrable forest...And this stillness of life did not in the least resemble a peace...It was the stillness of an implacable force brooding over an inscrutable intention." In comparison to the portrayal of the European setting, darkness theoretically plagues his story to the extent that an immediate listener is compelled to compose Marlow as one states, "Try to be civil, Marlow."

The voice of this listener is comparable to the voice of the reader displaying that Marlow is displacing the effect of his story on the imagery and that he may be losing control of his mind. This is in compliance with Adelman as he states, "Marlow is described as journeying...into the darkness of the beginnings of time, the darkness of Africa-a regression that threatens his sanity". The contrast of these atmospheres has a clear connection to the insight of Marlow.

The initial paragraph is the first introduction to the masterful and colourful imagery that Conrad utilizes to reflect Marlow's attitude. Marlow's personality is primarily based on the visual characteristics of the atmosphere he is presently located. For example, the first paragraphs refer to a regular day drawing to a close. His interpretation of the sky and weather both suggest beauty and mystery. In the following pages, his overall feeling was of joy as he described his childhood and how he was driven to exploration by a fascination of the remote places on a map, based upon his experiences with nature in the previous pages. If on the other hand, as seen numerously in the book, the setting was ominous and "dark" his overall feeling would be of a pessimistic manner. These feelings and outlooks affect the way the story is retold and this effect has significance to the comprehension of the reader.

The excursion through the Congo is the basis of the novel but Conrad's use of the frame tale allows the reader constant access to Marlow's sentiment. Through the detailed narration, the emotions that Marlow experiences are incorporated into his story. These emotions are directly cast to the two separate listeners, the shipmates and the reader. The reader experiences the entrapment of light by darkness just as Marlow sustains it but, in essence, the reader is at a disadvantage. This disadvantage arises from the fact that Marlow's feelings of anger, gloom and joy are relayed into the comprehension of the reader. The reader is subjected to the personal emotions of Marlow and these sentiments influence the personal views of the actual reader. Marlow's sensations elicit different sentiments of the reader for the reason that it is a natural human trait to identify with someone to arrive at a common understanding of a topic at hand. For instance, the Bible is a difficult book to comprehend but one is able to do so by realizing the nature of the author and identify with her/her. The reader must identify with Marlow and his personal nature to fully grasp the gist of the occurrences throughout the novel.

The method that Marlow tells the story to his shipmates is as important as the contents of the story itself. The darkness that inhabits the setting wherever Marlow is present is directly related to the darkness that metaphorically inhabits his words. For instance, when Marlow describes the setting of Africa as a place of darkness and uncivilized behaviour, the narrator notes a tremble or hesitation in his voice. This hesitation displays the inconsistency with Marlow retelling the story. On the other end of the spectrum, where Marlow describes favorable objects that he takes interest in the reader is fully aware that he is bias to things of such manner. For example, when Marlow speaks of the Thames river as a "venerable stream" that exists to perform "unceasing service" to those who have tamed it, he speaks in an almost glow that shows his interest which gains the reader's attention.

Contrasts between what the narrator describes and Marlow's personality also exist. This is supported through what the narrator speaks of regarding England's glorious past and also of what critics assert, "Marlow...recalls that in Roman times, England itself was a place of darkness, the very end of the world". The narrator describes England as a civilized place where "knight-errants" of the sea have brought that peace. This description by the narrator has intermittent references to civilization and peace which according to critics, "light and civilization are benevolent forces". Marlow's personality and perspective of England's glorious past is, in fact, not glorious at all. He refers to the knight-errant as "faithless pilgrims" that have only brought death, and by no means peace. While exploring Marlow's perspective, the issue of imperialism is raised. Imperialistic views of Marlow are centred around the involvement of the Company and the effect it has on the natives of Africa. According to Adelman, "he [Marlow] associates darkness with...imperialism". This contrast and the manner that Conrad chose to display it shows his purpose in the relationship between light versus darkness and Marlow's personality.

Conrad conducts Marlow's personality according to his description of the setting. Marlow is unconsciously aware of what the narrator describes, as Conrad uses this as a tool to enhance Marlow's personality. To clarify, Conrad could go into fastidious detail of ivory, for example, and its symbolism and Marlow automatically obtains the symbolism, as seen through his speech, "The word 'ivory' rang in the air, was whispered, was sighed. You would think they were praying to it." Note that Conrad chooses ivory to be of rarity which in turn increases the value, and not anything "dark." For example, Conrad would never choose oil to be of necessity because it disrupts the colour association that is integrated throughout the book. Marlow's personality is enhanced through the description of Ivory because it informs the reader that Marlow is interested in a "white" object which signifies an interest in something worthwhile. This displays Marlow's intelligence to the reader.

Marlow is constantly attempting to project an intriguing story for the shipmates, and thus the reader. This statement is supported when Marlow asks rhetorical questions to his shipmates: "Do you see the story? Do you see anything? It seems I am trying to tell you a dream"(24.). Marlow suddenly becomes aware of his immediate listeners and speaks directly to them as individuals. These listeners are, in essence, the reader. Conrad realises that at certain junctures in his story the reader may lose interest. As a repercussion, Conrad institutes particular statements that maintain the intellectual involvement of the reader. Once again when Marlow detects disinterest and fiercely responds to someone sighing he questions the integrity of the listener. He automatically assumes that the listener sighs because of the absurdity of what is being stated: "Why do you sigh in this beastly way, somebody?". As Marlow continues, the intermittent utterances regarding the reader's involvement play a pivotal role in developing the contrast between darkness and light as Marlow nears the actual "heart of darkness."

Q.17. Comment on the role of characters in the Heart of Darkness.

Or

Q. Discuss the importance of characters in the Heart of Darkness.

The characters in the Heart of Darkness, help depict the theme throughout their environment. There must be something distinctive to relate the themes and storyline too, and the characters play that role.

One uniqueness in the novel is that there are only two specific names for all the characters, Kurtz and Marlow. The rest of the characters in the novel follow under general names such as, the manager, the helmsman etc.

This is very interesting because its difficult to determine why Conrad would use this approach. Possibly Conrad takes this approach to express the theme of lost identity. This proves that the journey to find one's self, is one where not everything appears to be what it seems. In this long process one can change very much. Kurtz is a great example, he changed from being a painter and "essentially a great musician, to becoming corrupt by being swept up and digested by the darkness.

Kurtz went past the point of no return, he was to corrupted to know he was being assaulted by the powers of darkness. Finding one's self is a dangerous journey. There are many distractions along the way that deal with temptation. These 'temptations' are deadly and can lead to a great deal of horror and suffering. This proves that the journey to the soul is not a pleasant journey. Marlow "saw the inconceivable mystery of a soul that knew no restraint, no faith, no fear, yet struggling blindly with itself."

Anyone who read Heart of Darkness can go back and take a look at the character Kurtz and relate themselves to a moment in their life that they had fallen into the binding grip of the darkness.

The mood of a story reflects the way the author makes the reader feel. In Heart of Darkness the reader acknowledges three main moods while reading. These moods can be associated with the journey to the soul. The first mood that the reader should acknowledge is the awareness of the unknown. The unknown is a very frightful aberration, but to be aware of 'it' makes it a morbid ambience. Marlow's journey to find his soul, is filled with danger and a foul smell, the stench of not knowing the area, the people or himself. The unknown is "the lurking death, to the hidden evil, to the profound darkness of its heart." Marlow begins his journey by meeting the crew of the ship. He meets and becomes friends with them. "Going up that river was like travelling back to the earliest beginnings of the world, when vegetation rioted on the earth and the big trees were kings." His experiences with them are significant in finding himself but no one really knows where they are. The entrance into the enigmatical jungle is significant, because it demonstrates how one first begins their journey, there is only the unknown which is present.

One must face their unknown side to find themselves and their soul. The gut feeling or instinct of being aware that something is approaching and not knowing what it is creates a warning that makes one aware of the risks involved in searching for the soul.

The fear of the unknown is something everyone can relate to, especially at a young age. Youths, often when asked to think of something scary, mention the Bogeyman or Freddy Cougar.

Children really do not have a concept of the unknown and it's the same with adults. It is a formidable place, where anything can happen. It is a vast void, filled with billions of possibilities, both negative and positive. The fear of the unknown represented in Heart of Darkness deals with the journey into the unknown in search of the soul. "Kurtz who embarks on a harrowing 'night journey' into the savage heart of Africa, only finds his dark and evil soul."

"The wilderness had patted him on the head, and, behold, it was like a ball-an ivory ball; it had caressed him, and-lo!-he had withered; it had taken him, loved him, embraced him, got into his veins, consumed his flesh, and sealed his soul to its own by the inconceivable ceremonies of some devilish initiation."

Marlow with his descriptions of the jungle, probably thought the jungle was a living thing. "An empty stream, a great silence, an impenetrable forest." The fear of entering such a terrible place, but how could he know it was terrible unless he entered it? The answer is simple, the only way Marlow can be scared is if he can already identify fear. Fear is unknown just like the soul until it is found, and can be meddled with.

The faint and entangled environs of the jungle create this fear of the unknown in search of the soul.

The fear of disappointment is another factor which involves the journey to the soul, because one may not always like what they find.

Marlow wants to see the 'great' godlike Kurtz. but is he really that great?

Marlow's quest was to find Kurtz and that he did, but by doing this he saw the horror and managed to save himself and his soul. Marlow has already seen men go time and time through "the door of Darkness," and knows the esoteric circumstances that lay ahead for these ignorant, blind men.

"Making a vain attempt, because no relation of a dream can convey the dream-sensation, that commingling of absurdity, surprise, and bewilderment in a tremor of struggling revolt, that notion of being captured by the incredible which is of the very essence of dreams...." Marlow realises that in the end everything turned out for the best. His experience will linger on with his life and the fear of disappointment would part.

Finding one's self in Heart of Darkness is created by mood and atmosphere. The ideas and mood behind the atmosphere brush off against the state of the reader. While reading the novel I was able to reflect on my own journey to the soul. Any reader can reflect and realise the inevitable.

The journey is not a pleasant one, it is a very difficult task, where evil lurks in the smallest of places. These places could be anywhere including the soul and the soul is one of man's most unique qualities. It determines who we are and how we treat everyone surrounding our presence. In this universe people live and die but a soul is immortal and will undertake an eternity.

Q.18. Discuss Marlow and the Wilderness in Heart of Darkness.

Marlow has always been mystified and curious about the parts of the world that have been relatively unexplored by the white race. Ever since he was a little kid he used to look at many maps and wonder just what laid in the big holes that were unmapped. Eventually one of these holes was filled up with the continent of Africa, but he was still fascinated especially by this filled in hole. When he found out that he could maybe get a job with a company that explored the Congo area in Africa he sought after it and got it. After all, it was as a steamship captain on the mighty Congo river. This was "a mighty big river...resembling an immense snake uncoiled, with its head in the sea, its body at rest curving afar over a vast country, and its tail in the depths of the land". This snake like river was full of mystery to the adult Marlow and seemed to call him to it.

The wildness that the African wilderness seems to promote is foreshadowed right away to Marlow before his journey gets going. He finds out that the captain he is replacing was killed over a trading disagreement between him and a chief. It turns out that the caption thought he got a raw deal and then proceeded to hit the chief on the head with a stick, whereupon the chiefs son then stuck him with a spear and killed him. This promoting of wildness comes out in the fact that this captain "was the gentlest, quietest creature ever walked on two legs...but he had been a couple of years already out there".

Marlow then proceeds to head for the Congo, and when he finally reaches the company's lower station he begins to see how the white man has come to try and civilize and control the wildness of Africa and its inhabitants. The blacks were being used as slaves at the station to build railroads. The scene left Marlow feeling that the blacks "were not enemies, they were not criminals, they were nothing earthly now,—nothing but black shadows of disease and starvation". Marlow sees how the asserted superiority of the white man has led to the devastation of the black natives in both spirit and body.

Marlow then heads out of the lower station towards the company's central station by foot. He notices on his journey the fact that there were "paths everywhere; a stamped-in network of paths spreading over the empty land. The population had cleared out a long time ago." There were "several abandoned villages". This again shows how the white men have affected the way of Africa and it's inhabitants. They forced the Africans out of their homes to recede deeper into the wilderness.

Once he reaches the central station Marlow begins to come to terms with more of what is Africa, as he is getting deeper in the heart of it. He notices that there is "a great silence around and above." This signifies the fact that it is uncivilized, and thus there is none of the hub-bub of traffic and industry that pollutes the civilized countries with noise. Africa is just the wilderness and its inhabitants in harmony with one another. The only noise heard is every once in a while "the tremor of far-off drums...a sound weird, appealing, suggestive, and wild". Maslow notices how this very primitive sound is very powerful and appeals to the primitive emotions found inside himself. He is beginning to understand that he might have come from a place like this once, and can still somehow feel it in his inheritance.

He begins to understand this primitive past contained within the inner walls of Africa when he begins traveling once again further up the Congo River. "Going up the river arms was like traveling back to the earliest beginnings of the world, when vegetation rioted on the earth and the big trees were kings. An empty stream, a great silence, and impenetrable forest. The long stretches of the waterway ran on, deserted, into the gloom of the overshadowed distances". Marlow can feel the landscape begin to pull at the primitive man found within his civilized shell. It is trying to bring it back out. Marlow and the others were going into this primitive self because they were "accustomed to look on the shackled form of a conquered monster, but there [the Congo River in Africa] you could look at a thing monstrous and free". Africa was indeed free of the restraints placed upon man and the earth in an industrialized and civilized world. Here, in Africa, man was free to be the very core of himself in a free, living, breathing wilderness.

Marlow does describe the land as darkness a lot, as the title Heart Of Darkness implies, but I feel it is only the darkness of what once used to be for the white man. I believe this darkness was put there to show the vanity of the white conquerors. It was put there to show their untrue belief of superiority to the black man because they were "civilized" and the blacks were "uncivilized" like men in the dark ages. I don't believe the intention of the author was to paint Africa as a place of hidden evil and savagery. He was just trying to show that this might have been where the white man once came from, but had long ago forgotten, and thus the memory is a very faint memory lost in the darkness of a very distant past in the white man's culture. In Africa, however, the White Man confronts his primitive nature once again as he once again re-enters into this long forgotten darkness and finds his true inner nature. He is not unlike the black man when it comes down to it. The situation has the only real difference in their conduct, not the nature of the people. The white man has the civilized environment as his influence while the Africans have the wilderness as their environment. Marlow and Kurtz are the ones in the story who truly realise this fact, and it shows in their behaviour and actions, and it shows in their descriptions of the landscape and the African people.

Q.19. Discuss Epiphany in Heart of Darkness.

Marlow, in the novel "The Heart of Darkness," experiences an epiphany, or a dramatic moment in which a character intuitively grasps the essential nature or meaning of some situation.

The moment in which Marlow experiences his epiphany is right after the helmsman gets killed by natives, which are associated with Kurtz. The thing that Marlow realises is the savagery of man and the corruption of the ivory trade. The actual change takes place when Marlow sees the helmsman die. Marlow sees the death take place and is shocked. "The side of his head hit the wheel twice, and the end of what appeared a long cane clattered round and knocked over a little campstool.... my feet felt so very warm and wet that I had to look down.... It was the shaft of a spear that...had caught him in the side just below the ribs. I had to make and effort to free my eyes from his gaze and attend to the steering.... I declare it looked as though he would presently put to us some question in an understandable language; but he died without uttering a sound, without moving a limb, without twitching a muscle.... 'He is dead,' murmured the fellow, immensely impressed. 'No doubt about it,' said I." When this happened, Marlow realised the savagery of man, horror of death, and the corruption of the ivory trade. He realises that in the ivory trade, that the ivory is more valuable than human life and that traders will do almost anything to get it. Marlow also realises man's savagery in the event that man puts greater value on riches than on human life. This is the epiphany of Marlow in "The Heart of Darkness."

The epiphany of Marlow in "The Heart of Darkness" has significance in the overall story. The theme of the story is how every man has inside himself a heart of darkness and that a person, being alienated like Kurtz, will become more savage. Marlow, in his epiphany, realises the savagery of man and how being alienated from modern civilization causes one to be savage and raw. This savagery is shown especially in the death of the helmsman, which is where Marlow's epiphany takes place, but the savagery is also show in Kurtz. The link that Kurtz has to the natives and the death of the helmsman is that the natives work for Kurtz. This also shows how Kurtz has become more savage—that killing and death has no effect on him anymore. His savagery is shown by how the natives will kill to get what they want and Kurtz wants. This savagery shown by the natives and Kurtz in the death of the helmsman, links both Marlow's epiphany and the theme of "The Heart of Darkness" together.

This, overall, explains the significance of the epiphany and the theme of "The Heart of Darkness" and how they are linked to one another.

Q.20. Analyse the significance of the Congo River in Heart of Darkness.

The Significance of the Congo River For Marlow, the journey on the Congo River is one of the most difficult and ominous journeys he will ever take. The fact that it takes him around and not completely into the jungle is significant of Marlow's psychological journey as well. He never really goes on land but watches the shore from the outside. The only time he goes on shore he finds a wasteland. For Marlow the jungle of the Congo is representative of evil that man is capable of. In Heart of Darkness, it seems that the further Marlow travels into the jungle, the deeper he looks into himself. All this time is spent on the Congo River as he looks from the outside. This is symbolic as he is looking at his soul from the outside but never really sees himself until he goes on land to get Kurtz. When he arrives on land is symbolic of when he looks the deepest into himself. He goes to find Kurtz on his deathbed and is given he choice to take over for him as a god among an African tribe. Marlow is faced with the ultimate choice between good and evil. For a moment it is uncertain what choice Marlow will make. But, unlike Kurtz, Marlow picks the good over evil, as he rescues Kurtz back to the steamer. The fact that Marlow sailed along the Congo River, around the jungle, and not actually into the jungle is an important symbol also. Marlow never walks the path that Kurtz did to self-destruction. He went around the jungle to avoid getting captured by evil. Kurtz was a decent Englishman until he gave into the desires of his heart of darkness. Kurtz spent all his time in the jungle and eventually forgot all of his self-control, manners, and upbringing.

He truly looked in the deepest part of himself and found that his evil desires would reign. This is symbolic because he was deep inside the jungle. In this respect Conrad uses to men to show the reader both the good and bad of humankind. He shows the true evil and good that man is capable of If proper restraints had been there would Kurtz have done things differently? The fact that no one was around to keep Kurtz in check helped him succeed in becoming capable of the immense evil he became. Marlow had his shipmates there to keep him responsible. When he left the steamboat there wasn't anyone to restrain Marlow. He was face to face with himself and his human desires, but as he looked at Kurtz and what the evil had done to him he saw the consequences of choosing evil. If Marlow hadn't seen the consequences would he have acted differently? In the beginning of the novel, Marlow talks of things as if they are happening far away from him and not actually happening close by which represents that he is on the outside looking in. He also talks about a fog that settles over the river. This fog represents a distortion of what lies ahead. As he makes his decisions based on what he thinks is right but really he has no idea of what will happen to him or his crew. As the novel progresses the reader will start to understand all of these themes and symbols that the Congo River represents.

Q.21. Discuss God and Sin in Heart of Darkness.

A long debated issue that has plagued human beings since the fall of man is what leads people to commit evil actions and whether evil is inherent in all people. In the literary work of Joseph Conrad's Heart of Darkness, Marlow grapples with those two similar issues. They way in which Charlie Marlow, the protagonist and skipper, goes about determining the answers are by observing his and other people's goals and motivations throughout his voyage of discovery and self-enlightenment in the Congo of Africa.

In the novel Heart of Darkness Joseph Conrad seems to be suggesting that the environment pushes people to their extremes, so they commit evil actions. I agree with this idea because in the Bible it says; "...bad company corrupts good character." Anybody can look around and see that the world is evil. You may see people like politicians doing good for the community on the news, but you know that they are truly looking out for their own self-benefit, more money and publicity. Or even in the novel where it tells about Kurtz having the most successful ivory station in Africa, the way in which he achieved this is by raiding other tribes of their possessions. The Bible states that in ", For the world offers only the lust for physical pleasure, the lust for everything we see, and pride in our possessions. These are not from the Father. They are from this evil world." There are several cases of people having mental breakdowns because of stress from the world's imperfectness. This mental collapse sometimes results in them attempting to, or actually murdering others, or even committing suicide., The Heart is more deceitful that all else and is desperately sick; Who can understand it?" This verse gives proof that our hearts are sick from the evil in them, which corrupts good judgment and self-restraint. For another example the character Kurtz, the owner of the inner station, which is the most successful station, turned his back on his European roots. Kurtz became a god to the natives, and killed people who displeased him. Evidently, one has to admit, whether or not they believe in God, that the world is evil, corrupt, and man is prone to react abnormally to a difference of environment.

When Adam sinned, sin entered the entire human race. Adam's sin brought death, so death spread to everyone, for everyone sinned." An example of this in general would be as Michael Roy Luce, my youth pastor, says; "a chicken is a chicken and a person is a person." Meaning, a chicken cannot do or be anything more than a chicken can be. The chicken can try to fly or pretend to fly but he will never truly fly. Just like a person can try to be, but cannot truly be perfect because he is not God, he is merely a human being. In the Heart of Darkness, Kurtz was not born a murder but he was born with the capacity to murder and to commit other sins. The only difference is that he hardens himself towards the guilt of murder, instead of lying or cheating, which would seem like the lesser evil to the world. Yet they are all equally detestable in God's eyes but we still try to justify our sins.

The Bible talks about this very topic... "But God shows his anger from heaven against all sinful, wicked people who push the truth away from themselves. For the truth about God is known to them instinctively. God has put this knowledge in their hearts. From the time the world was created, people have seen the earth and sky and all that God made. They can clearly see his invisible qualities - his eternal power and divine nature. So they have no excuse whatsoever for not knowing God. Yes, they knew God, but they wouldn't worship him as God or even give him thanks. And they began to think up foolish ideas of what God was like. The result was that their minds became dark and confused. Instead of believing what they knew was the truth about God, they deliberately chose to believe lies. So they worshiped the things God made but not the Creator himself, who is to be praised forever. Amen. That is why God abandoned them to their shameful desires."

I am concluding that since the fall of man, selfishness and environmental surroundings lead people to commit evil actions. In addition to that, evil is inherent in all people because everybody is born with the capability to sin, for instance the Bible says;, These wicked people are born sinners; even from birth they have lied and gone their own way." Therefore as you can obviously see we live in an evil world. The only true standard of good and evil has to be something not of this world since it is evil. Because how can you make a scale to way one evil against another hoping to find the lesser evil? You cannot because everybody's perception of the extremity of a sin is different. Realizing all of that, without God there are no absolutes, just the insanity of mankind trying to be something they are not capable of being.

The Power of Kurtz in Heart of Darkness

Power has been defined as the psychological relations over another to get them to do what you want them to do. We are exposed to forms of power from the time of birth. Our parents exercise power over us to behave in a way they deem appropriate. In school, teachers use their power to help us learn. When we enter the work world the power of our boss motivates us to perform and desire to move up the corporate ladder so that we too can intimidate someone with power one day. In Joseph Conrad's Heart of Darkness Kurtz had a power over the jungle and its people that was inexplicable.

Kurtz is one of many men sent into the jungle to rape the land and its people of its natural resources. Many men have journeyed into the jungle also refereed as the heart of darkness never to return. Kurtz goes into the jungle and becomes obsessed with the people and the land. Though Kurtz has an obsession with ivory this is not the sole reason for him to overstay his welcome in the jungle.

Power this is what kept Kurtz in the jungle for such a long period of time. Determined not to become another causality he becomes allies with the natives through fear. Kurtz is a brilliant man who did not have to adapt to his environment but had it adapt to him. On top of a hill his hut is surrounded by the heads of men who have betrayed in him some sort, this serves as a reminder to anyone who contemplates going against his wish.

When Marlow finally reaches Kurtz he is in declining health. This same jungle which he loved, embraced and consumed with every ounce of his flesh had also taken its toll on him. Marlow finally meets the man whose name has haunted him on his river journey. Could this frail human be the ever so powerful Kurtz? The man who has journeyed into uncharted territories and has come back with scores of ivory and the respect of the native tribe. Yes, this was the very man and though he is weak and on his way to death his power still exudes from him.

This is where the definition of power comes in to play the "psychological relation" see even though his body was decomposing his mind was still sharp. Kurtz's voice still boomed when he spoke, he still demanded the respect he thought he deserved. Since Kurtz had terrorized the natives into fearing and respecting him even on his last legs he was still powerful. The psychological game he played with the natives was brilliant, he had them attack boats that carried people who had come to help him. There was nothing the natives would not do for him.

Kurtz does not want to return to civilization but he does not use his power to have Marlow and his crew killed either. Kurtz leaves on the steamboat leaving behind the people who have cared and worshipped him to survive on their own. He loves the feeling of the natives watching from the shores mourning his departure. He asks Marlow not the blow the whistle to frighten the natives so that he can bask in his last hour of power.

What made Kurtz so powerful? Why was he able to manipulate the natives into his puppets? Kurtz was able to do this because he preyed on the insecurities of a what was believed a less intelligent people. Rather than be the "white man" who was an enemy he portrayed himself as a friend.

This ability to play psychological games on others was a gift for Kurtz and what helped bring him into power. This same ability is what politicians posses today and inflict upon us in order for us to vote them into power. Guess we are no more intelligent than the natives.

Q.22. Discuss "White Lies" and "Whited Sepulchres" in Conrad's *Heart of Darkness*.

In his novella Heart of Darkness (1899), Joseph Conrad through his principal narrator, Marlow, reflects upon the evils of the human condition as he has experienced it in Africa and Europe. Seen from the perspective of Conrad's nameless, objective persona, the evils that Marlow encountered on the expedition to the "heart of darkness," Kurtz's Inner Station on the banks of the snake-like Congo River, fall into two categories: the petty misdemeanors and trivial lies that are common- place, and the greater evils — the grotesque acts society attributes to madmen. That the first class of malefaction is connected to the second is illustrated in the downfall of the story's secondary protagonist, the tragically deluded and hubristic Mr. Kurtz. The European idealist, believing the lies of his Company and of the economic imperialism that supports it, is unprepared for the test of character that the Congo imposes, and succumbs to the potential for the diabolical latent within every human consciousness.

Although numerous critics (including Johanna M. Smith, Peter Hyland, Herbert Klein, and Garrett Stewart) have drawn attention to how Marlow's lie to the Intended informs the whole preceding text and how that culminating scene with the Intended is connected to Marlow's initial impression of Brussels as a whited sepulchre (how appropriate in light of Belgian King Leopold II's hypocritical defence of his private company's rapacious exploitation of the ludicrously- named Congo Free State!), few have until recently focussed on how the lie affects the reader's reaction to Marlow as the protagonist and narrator of Conrad's Congo tale.

Answering questions which the dead man's Intended poses him regarding the remarkable Mr. Kurtz, Marlow does what he most despises. To protect both the integrity of Kurtz's visions and the Intended's guileless love for the quondam humanitarian Marlow acquiesces in her statements of faith ("his goodness shone in every act" prevaricates with double meaning ("His end... was in every way worthy of his life" and ultimately lies. "There is a taint of death," the death of moral integrity, "a flavour of mortality in lies — which is exactly what I hate and detest in the world — what I want to forget". Marlow has returned to Brussels "hoping to surrender to her the memory of Kurtz. She instead maneuvers him into telling her a lie: that Kurtz's last words were not 'The horror,' but her name". Ironically, Marlow finishes his story of African adventure at the point where Kurtz's career in crimes against humanity in all likelihood began, with a rationalization, a justified lie. In fact, it is the lie that renders this another of Charlie Marlow's "inconclusive experiences".

What if the Company's real objective were wealth derived from a trade in bones? — the fragile veneer of western civilisation, the great white lie of the White Man's Burden with its implicit, pseudo-altruism, must be accepted if the natives of the dark continent are to be improved, enlightened, and transformed into white people with black skins. Such a parcel of lies, exposed in their naked contumely through the course of the narrative, Marlow has found "appalling," yet he now countenances his own untruth to the Intended on similar grounds, to preserve an ideal image that should be revealed as hollow. To tell Kurtz's fiancée the truth "would have opened the bleakness of his heart to her view; and she would have known the depths to which he had sunk".

The countenancing of the greater evil, the lies like rainbow colours on the \ Company's map veiling the real motives of European imperialism in Africa, is behind both the thoughtless misbehaviour of those "jolly pioneers of progress" (24) and "emissaries of light," the ironically-dubbed "pilgrims," and the calculated reign of terror that Kurtz directs against the neighbouring tribes. Enthralled by their own money-lust the Europeans disregard both the natives' interests and their own moral well-being as they monopolize the ivory trade. The very air seems to sigh "ivory," and the only earthly reason

Europeans in the Congo can give for being out there is "To make money, of course".

However, it is not corporate profits but the welfare of the natives that Kurtz's Company has used back in Europe to justify its presence and activities in central Africa. Before he came face to face with his own base passions and atavistic drives there, Kurtz the journalist espoused those same altruistic ideals that his employers have mouthed in order to mitigate enslaving the natives to facilitate their obsessive quest for gain.

As in Conrad's "An Outpost of Progress" (1896) the manager's lofty intentions for his work at the jungle station were quickly perverted by the Darwinian ethos of the unfamiliar climate and environment, which shattered Kurtz's shallow European principles, leaving him the mere hollow shell of a civilized, rational being. "In the wilderness Kurtz's integrity collapses; only the extremes of appetite and intellect, of savagery and idealism survive". Conrad makes plain the moral bankruptcy of the system for which Kurtz stands by connecting him with Brussels, the "city of the dead" that in Marlow's reminiscence epitomizes European civilisation: "a city that always makes me think of a whited sepulchre".

In the above description Conrad alludes to Christ's characterization of his opponents, the New Testament's Pharisees, as "whited sepulchres, which indeed appear beautiful (i. e., "virtuous," in Christ's context) outwardly, but are within full of dead men's bones, and of all uncleanness" spiritually. What the Saviour found so objectionable in his sectarian adversaries is what Marlow finds so repulsive in the Belgian company: sheer hypocrisy. Just as the Pharisees maintained that they were solely concerned with the spiritual health of the people of Israel but acted out of self-interest, so the Company hides its appetite for wealth and power behind empty platitudes about advancing the light of European civilisation through the darkness of the African jungle, and "'weaning those ignorant millions from their horrid ways'".

When Marlow describes his city of departure..., white is immediately problematized for the reader. The colour acquires not only sepulchral connotations but also moral dubiousness, Marlow's description recalling the Biblical phrase for the hypocrite, the man of inner darkness whitewashed by outer manner and conventional deed.

If Brussels seems a whited sepulchre and the Company presents an enlightened façade, the interior reality is Mr. Kurtz, behind whom lurk death and desolation. The marble fireplace of the Intended's parlour possesses a "cold and monumental whiteness", connecting this particular European interior with the general exterior of the society. The white of the middle-eastern tomb's exterior is the white of the African ivory, superficially attractive (in fact, the tombs were white-washed in order to be highly visible so that orthodox Jews might avoid ritual defilement by unwittingly coming too close): the inner truth is the stench of bones. Given over to the powers of darkness, Kurtz cannot restrain himself from misusing the tools afforded him by his race's superior technology — "the thunderbolts of that pitiful Jupiter" — and assuming godhead. He becomes a savage better only in fire-power than those with whom he is in league. His sociopathic tendencies being given full play, Kurtz mercilessly murders and pillages to provide his firm with his quota of tusks — most of it, significantly, disinterred "fossil." The savagery behind the whole European commercial endeavour in Africa is symbolized by the whitened skulls which ornament the pilings of his stockade like nobs on newel posts in respectable European homes.

The closing scene of The Heart of Darkness, Marlow's interview with the dead man's white Intended (a pale figure of delusion juxtaposed against the black Athena who had usurped her place for Kurtz at the Inner Station), leaves the reader with ambivalent feelings about Conrad's chief narrator. To his male auditors aboard the 'Nellie' Marlow denies that his "trifle", his gift of unspotted memory of her beloved, was of any significance. Although he is trying to spare her further anguish, he is simultaneously denying that the evils which

Kurtz, the Company, and the pilgrims committed in the heart of darkness are still taking place. In fact, even after the follies — "the merry dance of death and trade" — he has witnessed in Africa, Marlow values European colonialism as stabilizing — "There was a vast amount of red — good to see at any time, because one knows that some real work is done in there".

Although he admits the debilitating effects of civilisation on the Congolese (even the muscles of his cannibal crew are gradually deteriorating under its influence), Marlow sees the system as setting positive constraints to individual conduct. Even in "the sepulchral city" which he loathes, Marlow sees the virtue of a system that permits people "going about their business in the assurance of perfect safety". He justifies his personal commitment to the former, unreal, idealistic and idealized Kurtz by describing his impending lie as resulting from "an impulse of unconscious loyalty, or the fulfilment of one of those ironic necessities that lurk in the facts of human existence". One must wonder if the sort of lie that Marlow tells Kurtz's Intended was the same first step that Kurtz took on the path to self-destruction at the Inner Station.

Like Willa Cather's protagonist in her psychological study "Paul's Case," Kurtz and Marlow have looked into that dark place in the human psyche and know what lies there. Buddha-like, Marlow has come back from near death on the Stygian shore to tell the world (in his mind, apparently a male construct), but feels an almost boyish reticence about revealing the horror of the darkness to the woman. Does he, as Moser has suggested, allow himself to be maneuvered into lying out of an outmoded, chivalric regard for the lady's sensibility, or does he feel that she is unworthy of (or incapable of understanding) the truth as it revealed itself to him through Kurtz at the heart of darkness? Or does he believe that someone must have his or her innocence maintained in order to sustain a worthwhile ideal that animates a workable system? "If he had told the girl the simple facts," asserts Walter F. Wright, "he would have acknowledged that the pilgrims in their cynicism had the truth, that goodness and faith were the unrealities". Or is the lie an affirmation of Marlow's fellowship and solidarity with Kurtz, whom Marlow feels that he has no right to condemn?

The answers to Marlow's motivation are to be discovered in the nature of the lie itself and in the nature of the liar. Lies, of course, have proven indispensable to fabulists ever since Cain lied to God in Genesis and Odysseus slipped out of one disguise into another in The Odyssey. But Marlow's lie is neither as wicked as Cain's (especially since it acknowledges his need to be the keeper of his spiritual brother's memory) nor as self-serving but justifiable as Odysseus's. At first glance there is neither gain to be achieved nor pain to be avoided in Marlow's lying to the Intended. Marlow's lie is neither the cowardly evasion of Cain, whose conduct evokes the reader's scorn, nor the cunning imposture of Odysseus, whose studied impersonations and self-control call forth the reader's admiration. Marlow's lie we judge as neither premeditated nor wilful. Rather, readers never doubt for a moment that, in Marlow's place, they would likewise have spared the Intended's feelings and made her a present of Kurtz's final words. And that is precisely the effect for which Conrad is striving: we would do just what Marlow did, even though, as moral, decent people, we too abhor lying and deceit. And yet we would be wrong, for in shielding her from the truth about her fiancé Marlow is also insulating her from the Darwinian reality behind not only the African jungle, but also behind Brussels' impassive façade.

If Kurtz's Intended represents bourgeois European society, then Marlow has just joined those devious political and commercial interests who are keeping the middle-class consciousness from apprehending the European exploitation of Africa for what it is: a cultural, economic, and geographical rape. "The Intended [and, by implication, European society as a whole] remains as unknowing of the truth as she always has, and remains a part of the foreboding darkness with which the story ends". As a gentleman, Marlow feels that women are to be protected and insulated from any unpleasantness; as a closet misogynist, he states that "the women are out of touch with truth", that they are an intellectually inferior, impractical species incapable of dealing with any reality, let alone the brutal reality of the Belgian fiasco in Africa. Through keeping Kurtz's Intended from the truth of his death Marlow reinforces his own chivalric image of himself: he would rather be chivalrous and lie than be cruel and tell the truth, recognizing how sustaining for her will be the illusion of a noble, sane, humane Kurtz. While Homer's epic voyager never has to lie to himself, even though he lies out of self-defence many times to others, Conrad's reflective mariner has trapped himself into doing and being what he detests, and, in doing so, has also lied to himself about his motives.

It seems an innocent, benignly-motivated deception, a mere 'white lie', but, as Rosmarin points out, in Heart of Darkness white is the "the most explicit confusion" for the reader, since it is an "off-colour," the hue of ivory (upon which the whole European economic venture rests) and of Kurtz's complexion, a muddied, sullied white that, again to quote Rosmarin, "bespeaks contamination, a mutual transference between the spheres of morality and vision, between the self one is and the self one seems to be".

As the story unfolds, Marlow reverses the normal symbology of the black-white dichotomy, so that gradually darkness comes to mean truth, whiteness falsehood. Ugly and harsh — black — as the undisguised version of Kurtz's death would have been for her, without facing "the horror" of the darkness the Intended will never be free of her illusions about the man to whose memory she has consecrated with nun-like devotion (as suggested by her mourning dress over a year after his death) the rest of her life. Conrad's subtle insistence on the whiteness of her forehead suggests that Marlow subconsciously now sees whiteness "as a symbol of all those who suffer self-deception as well as a symbol of all those who practice self-deception". The implications for the complacent, white, middle-class, and emphatically male readers of Conrad's Congo tale in the patriarchal journal Blackwood's

Edinburgh Magazine are obvious. We are brought to the realization that the pathways of the African jungle and the streets of Brussels, jungles and buildings, heat and cold, mysteries and commercial enterprise, are, as W. F. Wright remarks, mere symbols of "the larger darkness, which is in the heart of man", a darkness in which lies the potential for evil and for good.

Q.23. Is Joseph Conrad's Heart of Darkness a Literary Critique of Imperialism?

Introduction

Joseph Conrad's Heart of Darkness merits a place in any collection of literary works related to the sea and maritime law. Conrad was a seaman who sailed under several European flags before beginning his literary career, and critics of his own era often treated him as a novelist of the sea. Heart of Darkness, perhaps his best known work, does not focus on admiralty or maritime law per se, but it does cast law as one of the central features of 19th century European imperialism. Most importantly, Heart of Darkness exposes imperialism's exploitation of foreign lands and people, leaving the imperialist agents themselves empty and deranged.

From Polish Seaman To English Novelist

Joseph Conrad's origins made it highly unlikely he would one day be added to the English pantheon of literary greats. Born in 1857 in a part of Poland that had been taken over by Imperial Russia, he was christened Jozef Teodor Konrad Nalecz Korzeniowski. His parents, members of the landed aristocracy, were Polish patriots who deeply resented the way Russian, Prussian, and Austrian powers had dismantled and claimed parts of the Polish homeland. When Conrad was only four, Russian authorities arrested his father and sent him to rural Russia. Conrad and his mother accompanied his father into exile, but his mother died only three years later. Conrad's father was able to return to Poland, but he died when Conrad was 11. One of the most powerful experiences of Conrad's youth was walking behind his father's coffin in a large funeral procession in Cracow honouring a national martyr.

In a romantic novel written by a lesser novelist than Conrad, he might have picked up his father's cause and led the Polish people to freedom, but Conrad shaped his life and goals in different ways. After several years of schooling in Cracow, he decided there was no future for himself in occupied Poland and left for Marseilles and the life of a seaman. He had never even seen the sea, but like many other young men in the 19th century, he imagined the life of a seaman to be lucrative, adventuresome, and self-fulfilling. Conrad went to Marseilles and chose the French merchant marine both because his uncle had connections in the French port and because, like other educated Poles of his period, he counted French as his second language.

Conrad spent a total of four years in the French merchant marine, during which he sailed primarily to the West Indies and Latin America. According to some stories, he also fought a duel with an American over his Basque lover. Wounded in the supposed duel, Conrad was rescued by his benevolent uncle, but he then told the uncle his wounds were from an unsuccessful suicide attempt. The truth of the matter remains uncertain, but the duel and/or suicide attempt did precipitate Conrad's departure from the French merchant marine.

However, Conrad had not finished with sea adventure. Still only 21, he next joined the British merchant marine. Raw opportunity and perceptions of possible career advancement prompted the move, but it also seems Conrad took the British to be a particularly nautical people. Writing in Youth (1902), Conrad said in England "men and sea interpenetrate, so to speak—the sea entering the life of most men and the men knowing something or everything about the sea...."

Was Conrad right? Ford Madox Ford, his friend in later years and a distinguished writer in his own right, thought Conrad was misled because the Englishmen he knew best were all connected to the sea:

Most men enter London by way of Charing Cross or Victoria, railway stations about sixty miles away from the sea and its ships. Therefore, for them, London is the City of London. If you questioned them, and they were at all knowledgeable men, they might confess to a dim awareness that, somewhere in that city, there were some ships tucked away in a negligible corner, much as an inhabitant of Minneapolis coming to New York might agree that somewhere near the Battery seagoing craft would probably be found.... But Conrad first approached London from its amazing other end, going up a great silver-grey estuary between sixty miles of docks, all with seagoing ships lying shoulder to shoulder, like fish in thick shoals.

The British merchant marine served Conrad well. He sailed to Singapore, Malaysia, Borneo, other parts of the East Indies, and Australia. He passed the examinations for master mariner and was thereby able to serve in several brief instances as not a seaman but rather a first mate and even a ship's captain. He also, of course, began to refine his English, and without this important step could never have become a novelist in the English language.

For immediate purposes at hand, Conrad's most important adventure during his years of service in the British merchant marine involved special arrangements with a Belgian company in 1890. Conrad sailed to the Belgian Congo and then piloted the steamer Roi des Belges up the Congo River into the heart of the African continent. His work was disenchanting and disabling, and ill with dysentery, fever, and gout, Conrad was unable to fulfill his contractual obligations.

Not only the Congo experiences but also Conrad's larger record as a seaman were crucial resources when, in 1894, he abandoned the sea and settled in England. Using the pen name "Joseph Conrad," he began publishing stories and novels set largely in exotic places or on the sea. Conrad's great novel Nostromo (1904) drew on his experiences in the French merchant marine in Latin America. His short story, The Secret Sharer (1911), derives from British merchant marine experiences in Bangkok and the East Indies. Heart of Darkness (1902) drew on Conrad's brief experiences piloting the Belgian steamer on the Congo River.

With good reason, critics in the early 20th century (and later) saw Conrad as a novelist of the sea.3 Indeed, one of the first authors claiming to write Conrad's definitive biography used something resembling a ship's log to record the events of Conrad's life and titled the work The Sea Dreamer.

For his own part, Conrad rejected these categorizations. Yes, he had left his native Poland to become a seaman. And yes, his stories and novels in English often drew on his experiences at sea. But Conrad was troubled that the "public mind fastens on externals, on mere facts, such for instance as ships and voyages, without paying attention to any deeper significance they might have." The sea molds character, he said, "yet, in setting the conditions for shipboard drama—as to some extent it inevitably must—it reveals, like a mirror, the face of character itself." Conrad had traveled long geographical, personal, and professional distances in order to become a successful writer, and one request he made in return was that his readers not underestimate his journey

Journeying Into The Heart Of Darkness

Conrad had been settled in England for four years before publishing the installments of Heart of Darkness in Blackwood's Magazine in 1899.8 During these years he married Jessie George, welcomed the birth of his son Borys, and relocated to rustic Pent Farm near Kent. Conrad had entered the happiest stage of his life, and his writings had begun to attract critical acclaim. Yet none of the satisfaction he might have felt in his family life and budding literary career is reflected in Heart of Darkness. A brooding, unsettling work, the novella has left many unable to sleep long after turning off their reading lights.

As the story begins, the cruising yawl Nellie is at rest on the Thames, waiting for the turn of the tide. Men on board reflect on the lower reaches of the Thames, on the men and ships that had followed the river to and from England, and—most generally—on the sea. The narrator defers to a character named Charles Marlow, who will then tell the story inside the story—a device which will allow us to reflect not only on what Marlow has said but also on the degree to which Marlow has understood his own story. Marlow himself is a seaman with sunken cheeks, a yellow complexion, and an ascetic, straight back. The narrator warns us that Marlow's story will not be the average sea yarn. While most seamen tell simple stories, "the whole meaning of which lies within the shell of a cracked nut," Marlow was not typical: "to him the meaning of an episode was not inside like a kernel but outside, enveloping the tale."

The story inside the story took place several years earlier, and within this story Marlow contracts with a Belgian trading concern to pilot a steamer up a large African river, a river resembling on the map "an immense snake uncoiled, with its head in the sea, its body at rest curving afar over a vast country, and its tail lost in the depths of the land." The steamer's prior captain, it seems, had been killed by an angry African villager after the captain had beaten the villager's chief. The steamer was crucial in the transportation of ivory from the inland to the coast, and the Company was anxious to find a new pilot and put the ship back in service.

Marlow sets off as a passenger in a French ship, sailing along the western coast of Africa to the Congo region. The coast seems to Marlow an enigma—"smiling, frowning, inviting, grand, mean, insipid, or savage, and always mute with an air of whispering, Come and find out." At one point Marlow and his fellow passengers spot an anchored French man-of-war indiscriminately firing its guns into the coastal trees and vegetation. "There was a touch on insanity in the proceeding," Marlow reports.

After 30 days, Marlow reaches the mouth of the Congo River and then travels by steamer 30 miles up-river to the Company's chief station, a cluster of three wooden barracks on a rocky slope. One of the first things Marlow notices at the station is a group of six African men wearing iron collars and connected by a chain. Other severely emaciated men lounge about, and the explosions from a nearby mining venture shake the earth and fill the air with harsh, unnerving sounds. Marlow locates the Company's chief accountant, who tells Marlow of Kurtz, the Company's best agent, best obtainer of ivory, and "a very remarkable person."

Marlow then sets off with a caravan of 60 men on a 200-mile tramp to another post further up-river. African carriers die in harness, but nobody seems to pay much attention. On the 15th day, the remaining members of the caravan reach the central station, and Marlow learns that the steamer he is to pilot is stuck at the bottom of the river. Marlow, it seems, is expected to fix it. Repairs in turn take several months, during which period Marlow hears time and again of the great Kurtz. Marlow's curiosity is piqued; indeed, he becomes fixated on Kurtz, worried about the illness that has disabled Kurtz and almost desperate to meet him.

But even after the steamer has been repaired, reaching Kurtz proves to be no easy matter. Going up the Congo River to Kurtz's station, Marlow tells those listening to his tale, "was like traveling back to the earliest beginnings of the world...." The quiet along the river did not seem peaceful to Marlow. "It was the stillness of an implacable force brooding over an inscrutable intention...." Nevertheless, Marlow, his mates, and the steamer "penetrated deeper and deeper into the heart of darkness."

One morning, approximately eight miles from Kurtz's station, Marlow awakes to "a white fog, very warm and clammy, and more blinding than night." Somewhere in the fog invisible Africans are shrieking in a way that sounded to Marlow like sorrow. After the fog lifts, natives along the shore fire arrows at the steamer and its passengers. "The arrows came in swarms... but they looked as though they wouldn't kill a cat." Marlow responds by jerking the steamer's whistle and, miraculously, the shrieking and barrage of arrows stop.

The steamer continues to Kurtz's station, but Marlow and the others then learn that Kurtz has become unhinged, has taken an African lover, adopted African ways, and solicited the adoration of the tribespeople. An immense store of ivory has been accumulated, but the station is bizarre and mysterious, complete with skulls attached to the tops of poles. Kurtz himself is close to death, and Marlow feels as though he is "buried in a vast grave full of unspeakable secrets."

Marlow and the crew carry Kurtz through a mass of agitated Africans to the pilot-house on the steamer, but it is too late to save him. "The brown current ran swiftly out of the heart of darkness, bearing us downward towards the sea with twice the speed of our upward progress, and Kurtz's life was running swiftly, too, ebbing, ebbing out of his heart into the sea of inexorable time." Kurtz gives Marlow a packet of papers and a photograph. Marlow stares at him as he continues to decline, and Kurtz cries out at some image or vision: "The horror! The horror!" Shortly thereafter, Kurtz dies and is buried in a muddy hole.

Marlow interprets Kurtz's final words as a summation of his life or perhaps of life in general, and the thought of the horror the dying Kurtz perceived sticks in Marlow's mind. Marlow had been fascinated by Kurtz, even attracted to him, and this makes Kurtz's life summation even more troubling. Despite it all, Marlow continues to think of Kurtz as a remarkable man. "He had something to say," Marlow observes. "Since I had peeped over the edge myself, I understand better the meaning of his stare, that could not see the flame of the candle, but was wide enough to embrace the whole universe, piercing enough to penetrate all the hearts that beat in the darkness. He had summed up—he had judged."

Marlow then returns to Europe and, in what amounts to an epilogue of sorts for the novella, he decides to give the papers and photograph from Kurtz to Kurtz's mourning fiancee. In a tortured meeting, they compare notes on Kurtz's greatness, and the fiancee asks to know Kurtz's last words. Marlow lies, unwilling and unable to share thoughts of "the horror." "The last he pronounced," Marlow tells Kurtz's fiancee, "was—your name."

With those words, Marlow concludes his story while still aboard the Nellie anchored in the lower Thames. But recall that Marlow, formally speaking, is not the narrator of the entire Heart of Darkness. His tale consumes almost all of the novella, but the undefined narrator of Marlow's narration has the last words. Marlow stopped speaking and sat "indistinct and silent," the narrator says, "in the pose of a meditating Buddha."

A black bank of clouds stood before the Nellie and its sobred passengers. "The tranquil waterway leading to the uttermost ends of the earth flowed somber under an overcast sky—seemed to lead into the heart of an immense darkness." In the end, we are invited through the double narrative frame to know more and go even further in our thoughts than Marlow did in his.

What Does It Mean?

What is the lesson of Heart of Darkness? What meaning does the novella convey? As with almost all enduring literary works, no simple answers are available for these questions. Most certainly the work is symbolic, the symbolism is multifaceted, and the meaning is plural. One critic has seen the story as an allegory of the soul's travels through purgatory and hell to salvation, comparable to the quest for the Holy Grail or to the journey in Dante's Inferno. Another critic has interpreted the story as a comment on the agony of writing fiction and still another has suggested it is about the incompleteness of self-knowledge, both for Marlow and in general.

For purposes of this special issue of the Journal, it might be best to focus on what Eloise Knapp Hay calls "the solid soil of the story.To wit: a tale about a man employed by a European company to pilot a steamer up the Congo River to reach the company's best acquirer of African ivory. Although his thoughts do not control the interpretive enterprise, Conrad's own words seem to point to this kind of interpretation. Before the episodes of the story began appearing in Blackwood's Magazine, Conrad wrote to its editor to say the tale was about the "criminality of inefficiency and pure selfishness when tackling the civilizing work in Africa."

Put even more bluntly, Heart of Darkness is at least on one level about imperialism. Understood in the earlier 19th century as primarily a political system in which powerful nations controlled others, "imperialism" came gradually to refer to a system of economic as well as political dominance. Conrad's novella recognizes both of these dimensions. As the French man-of-war firing into coastal Africa symbolizes, European powers are seeking to establish and maintain political control over the African continent. The Belgian trading company and its agents, Kurtz notwithstanding, are extracting profitable ivory.

Law plays a role in both the political and economic aspects of imperialism, and in passing (albeit not extended) ways Heart of Darkness reinforces this point. Marlow's trip to Africa, for starters, is buoyed by law. He enters into an employment contract with the Belgian company, and this contract addresses not only salary and length of employment but also travel to the Congo region and other matters. The company also asks Marlow to sign a document promising not to disclose trade secrets and even to undergo a formal medical examination before departing.

Conrad writes at surprising length about Marlow's required visit to the company's doctor. The latter felt Marlow's pulse and also measured his head with large calipers. Why? The doctor liked to know the measurements of the crania of those heading to Africa. Marlow asks if the doctor also measures the crania of those returning, but the doctor reports he never sees them and "moreover, the changes take place inside you know." Just why is the doctor making these measurements? Why is this being done? The doctor tells Marlow, "This is my share in the advantages my country shall reap from the possession of such a magnificent dependency."

When Marlow reaches the Congo, law continues to contribute to the imperialist milieu in which he finds himself. The law's function at this point seems largely to assist imperialist control. And indeed, as Lee Lourdeaux writes regarding Apocalypse Now, Francis Ford Coppola's 1979 cinematic appropriation of Heart of Darkness, imperialists do more than merely use the law. They seize the very "right to define the law."

Time and again Marlow sees Europeans using laws which they have created to control and oppress the African natives. The ugly chain-gang Marlow encounters at the first station, for example, hardly seems to consist of criminals or enemies. However, "the outraged law" had fallen on the natives, Marlow says, like the shells from the man-of-war, like "an insoluble mystery from the sea." The poorly fed and paid African crewmen aboard the steamer, it occurs to Marlow, "still belonged to the beginnings of time," but "as long as there was a piece of paper written over in accordance with some farcical law or other made down the river, it didn't enter anybody's head to trouble how they would live." The skulls displayed on stakes at Kurtz's compound were from men who had also been judged according to European law and felt the wrath of that law. Other Africans encountered on the trip up-river had been "enemies," "criminals," and "workers," but the men at Kurtz's compound had been "rebels." However, Marlow adds wryly, "Those rebellious heads looked very subdued to me on their sticks."

Even at the end of the tale, when Marlow returns to Europe, the law continues to play a role. No "exit examination" with the previously encountered doctor awaits Marlow. No post-Congo cranial measurements are taken. But the European society and the culture of the imperialist nations disgust Marlow. "I found myself back in the sepulchral city," he says, "resenting the sight of people hurrying through the streets to filch a little money from each other, to devour their infamous cookery, to gulp their unwholesome beer, to dream their insignificant and silly dreams."

One day "a clean-shaven man, with an official manner and wearing gold-rimmed spectacles" calls on Marlow. A representative of the company that had hired Marlow in the first place, the man requests the papers Marlow had received from Kurtz. When Marlow refuses to turn them over, the man "became darkly menacing at last, and with much heat argued that the Company had the right to every bit of information about its 'territories.'" When Marlow continues to resist, the man withdraws, threatening that legal proceedings will follow. Kurtz's knowledge, Marlow muses, "did not bear upon the problems of commerce or administration."

Conclusion

Is "law" Conrad's chief target in Heart of Darkness? Does Conrad take "law" to be the key to imperialism? No, Conrad has bigger fish to fry. He takes law, as well as missionary zeal, racism, administrative efficiency, and the desire for profit, to all be components of the larger and largely despicable phenomenon of imperialism. Conrad was writing at the beginning of what one critic calls "the new imperialist crisis"—a period of emerging doubt about the imperialist venture. Heart of Darkness indicts imperialism in general more than it indicts the role law plays in imperialism.

Furthermore, Conrad's indictment of imperialism is not simple and limited but rather complex and far-reaching. In real life, Conrad had especially harsh words for the Belgian despoliation of the Congo during the reign of Leopold II. The Congo venture, he wrote, was "the vilest scramble for loot that ever disfigured the history of human conscience and geographical exploitation." In the novella, meanwhile, Conrad takes steps to generalize imperialism. Even though the company for which Marlow works is clearly Belgian, it is named the Continental Trading Company and, suggesting imperialism in general, Conrad frequently refers to it simply as "the Company." Kurtz, meanwhile, may have had a German name, but Conrad reports that Kurtz's father was half-French and his mother half-English. "All Europe contributed to the making of Kurtz," as it did to 19th century imperialism.

This grotesque political and economic phenomenon not only controlled and exploited non-European peoples but also left empty and deranged the agents of imperialism. Virtually all of the Europeans Marlow encounters in the Congo are superficial, confused, or strange. Kurtz, of course, has almost completely lost his bearings and suffers from what we would today call a nervous breakdown. "The conquest of the earth, which mostly means the taking it away from those who have a different complexion or slightly flatter noses than ourselves," Conrad has Marlow say early in Heart of Darkness, "is not a pretty thing when you look into it too much."

Q.24. What is your impression of these opening pages from Heart of Darkness? Do the Africans seem stereotyped to you? What signs are there that the narrator is sympathetic to them?

"I left in a French steamer, and she called in every blamed port they have out there, for, as far as I could see, the sole purpose of landing soldiers and custom-house officers. I watched the coast. Watching a coast as it slips by the ship is like thinking about an enigma. There it is before you— smiling, frowning, inviting, grand, mean, insipid, or savage, and always mute with an air of whispering, Come and find out. This one was almost featureless, as if still in the making, with an aspect of monotonous grimness. The edge of a colossal jungle, so dark-green as to be almost black, fringed with white surf, ran straight, like a ruled line, far, far away along a blue sea whose glitter was blurred by a creeping mist. The sun was fierce, the land seemed to glisten and drip with steam. Here and there grayish-whitish specks showed up clustered inside the white surf, with a flag flying above them perhaps. Settlements some centuries old, and still no bigger than pinheads on the untouched expanse of their background. We pounded along, stopped, landed soldiers; went on, landed custom-house clerks to levy toll in what looked like a God-forsaken wilderness, with a tin shed and a flagpole lost in it; landed more soldiers—to take care of the custom-house clerks, presumably. Some, I heard, got drowned in the surf; but whether they did or not, nobody seemed particularly to care. They were just flung out there, and on we went. Every day the coast looked the same, as though we had not moved; but we passed various places—trading places—with names like Gran' Bassam, Little Popo; names that seemed to belong to some sordid farce acted in front of a sinister back-cloth. The idleness of a passenger, my isolation amongst all these men with whom I had no point of contact, the oily and languid sea, the uniform somberness of the coast, seemed to keep me away from the truth of things, within the toil of a mournful and senseless delusion. The voice of the surf heard now and then was a positive pleasure, like the speech of a brother. It was something natural, that had its reason, that had a meaning. Now and then a boat from the shore gave one a momentary contact with reality. It was paddled by black fellows. You could see from afar the white of their eyeballs glistening.

They shouted, sang; their bodies streamed with perspiration; they had faces like grotesque masks—these chaps; but they had bone, muscle, a wild vitality, an intense energy of movement, that was as natural and true as the surf along their coast. They wanted no excuse for being there. They were a great comfort to look at. For a time I would feel I belonged still to a world of straightforward facts; but the feeling would not last long. Something would turn up to scare it away. Once, I remember, we came upon a man-of-war anchored off the coast. There wasn't even a shed there, and she was shelling the bush. It appears the French had one of their wars going on thereabouts. Her ensign (1) dropped limp like a rag; the muzzles of the long six-inch guns stuck out all over the low hull; the greasy, slimy swell swung her up lazily and let her down, swaying her thin masts. In the empty immensity of earth, sky, and water, there she was, incomprehensible, firing into a continent. Pop, would go one of the six-inch guns; a small flame would dart and vanish, a little white smoke would disappear, a tiny projectile would give a feeble screech—and nothing happened. Nothing could happen. There was a touch of insanity in the proceeding, a sense of lugubrious drollery in the sight; and it was not dissipated by somebody on board assuring me earnestly there was a camp of natives—he called them enemies!—hidden out of sight somewhere.

"We gave her her letters (I heard the men in that lonely ship were dying of fever at the rate of three a day) and went on. We called at some more places with farcical names, where the merry dance of death and trade goes on in a still and earthy atmosphere as of an overheated catacomb; all along the formless coast bordered by dangerous surf, as if Nature herself had tried to ward off intruders; in and out of rivers, streams of death in life, whose banks were rotting into mud, whose waters, thickened into slime, invaded the contorted mangroves that seemed to writhe at us in the extremity of an impotent despair. Nowhere did we stop long enough to get a particularized impression, but the general sense of vague and oppressive wonder grew upon me. It was like a weary pilgrimage amongst hints for nightmares.

"It was upward of thirty days before I saw the mouth of the big river. We anchored off the seat of the government. But my work would not begin till some two hundred miles farther on. So as soon as I could I made a start for a place thirty miles higher up.

"I had my passage on a little sea-going steamer. Her captain was a Swede, and knowing me for a seaman, invited me on the bridge. He was a young man, lean, fair, and morose, with lanky hair and a shuffling gait. As we left the miserable little wharf, he tossed his head contemptuously at the shore. 'Been living there?' he asked. I said, 'Yes.' 'Fine lot these government chaps—are they not?' he went on, speaking English with great precision and considerable bitterness. 'It is funny what some people will do for a few francs a month. I wonder what becomes of that kind when it goes up country?' I said to him I expected to see that soon. 'So-o-o!' he exclaimed. He shuffled athwart, keeping one eye ahead vigilantly. 'Don't be too sure,' he continued. 'The other day I took up a man who hanged himself on the road. He was a Swede, too.' 'Hanged himself! Why, in God's name?' I cried. He kept on looking out watchfully. 'Who knows? The sun too much for him, or the country perhaps.'

"At last we opened a reach. (2) A rocky cliff appeared, mounds of turned-up earth by the shore, houses on a hill, others with iron roofs, amongst a waste of excavations, or hanging to the declivity. A continuous noise of the rapids above hovered over this scene of inhabited devastation. A lot of people, mostly black and naked, moved about like ants. A jetty projected into the river. A blinding sunlight drowned all this at times in a sudden recrudescence of glare. 'There's your Company's station,' said the Swede, pointing to three wooden barrack-like structures on the rocky slope. 'I will send your things up. Four boxes did you say? So. Farewell.' "I came upon a boiler wallowing in the grass, then found a path leading up the hill. It turned aside for the boulders, and also for an undersized railway-truck lying there on its back with its wheels in the air. One was off. The thing looked as dead as the carcass of some animal. I came upon more pieces of decaying machinery, a stack of rusty rails. To the left a clump of trees made a shady spot, where dark things seemed to stir feebly. I blinked, the path was steep. A horn tooted to the right, and I saw the black people run. A heavy and dull detonation shook the ground, a puff of smoke came out of the cliff, and that was all. No change appeared on the face of the rock. They were building a railway. The cliff was not in the way or anything; but this objectless blasting was all the work going on.

"A slight clinking behind me made me turn my head. Six black men advanced in a file, toiling up the path. They walked erect and slow, balancing small baskets full of earth on their heads, and the clink kept time with their footsteps. Black rags were wound round their loins, and the short ends behind waggled to and fro like tails. I could see every rib, the joints of their limbs were like knots in a rope; each had an iron collar on his neck, and all were connected together with a chain whose bights swung between them, rhythmically clinking. Another report from the cliff made me think suddenly of that ship of war I had seen firing into a continent. It was the same kind of ominous voice; but these men could by no stretch of imagination be called enemies.

They were called criminals, and the outraged law, like the bursting shells had come to them, an insoluble mystery from the sea. All their meager breasts panted together, the violently dilated nostrils quivered, the eyes stared stonily up-hill. They passed me within six inches, without a glance, with that complete, deathlike indifference of unhappy savages. Behind this raw matter one of the reclaimed, the product of the new forces at work, strolled despondently, carrying a rifle by its middle. He had a uniform jacket with one button off, and seeing a white man on the path, hoisted his weapon to his shoulder with alacrity. This was simple prudence, white men being so much alike at a distance that he could not tell who I might be. He was speedily reassured, and with a large, white, rascally grin, and a glance at his charge, seemed to take me into partnership in his exalted trust. After all, I was also a part of the great cause of these high and just proceedings.

"Instead of going up, I turned and descended to the left. My idea was to let that chain-gang get out of sight before I climbed the hill. You know I am not particularly tender; I've had to strike and to fend off. I've had to resist and to attack sometimes—that's the only way of resisting—without counting the exact cost, according to the demands of such sort of life as I had blundered into. I've seen the devil of violence, and the devil of greed, and the devil of hot desire; but, by all the stars! these were strong, lusty, red-eyed devils, that swayed and drove men—men, I tell you. But as I stood on this hillside, I foresaw that in the blinding sunshine of that land I would become acquainted with a flabby, pretending, weak-eyed devil of a rapacious and pitiless folly. How insidious he could be, too, I was only to find out several months later and a thousand miles farther. For a moment I stood appalled, as though by a warning. Finally I descended the hill, obliquely, towards the trees I had seen.

Q.25. Discuss the Symbolism Motif in Heart of Darkness.

Heart of Darkness is filled with comparisons and contrasts that help to develop the plot, theme, and characters in Conrad's novel. The story opens on the tranquil Thames River aboard the cruising yawl called the Nellie. All is calm on the water as the lights of London twinkle around the boat. This river is an obvious contrast to the Congo River that Marlow navigates in Africa. The Congo is snaking, treacherous, and full of darkness, danger, and mystery at every turn. Ironically, the tranquil Thames is described similarly to the Congo. In the opening chapter of the novel, Harlow, on board the Nellie, says of the river that flows through London, "this has been one of the dark places on earth." In the closing lines of the novel, the Thames seems to be flowing "into the heart of an immense darkness." No matter where the white man exists, in civilized London or deepest Africa, he seems to bring darkness: inhumanity to his fellow man.

In contrast to the greed and cruelty of the white men in Africa, who voraciously and recklessly seize ivory at any cost to human life, Conrad depicts the black natives as having more self-control. The Manager is starving the cannibals on board Marlow's steamer to death, and although they eagerly eye the body of the dead helmsman and also the physique of the plump Russian, they restrain their native urges and do not attack the living or the dead. In a similar manner, the "savages" along the Congo do not attack the steamer bearing the greedy Europeans even though they know the intent is to be evil and destructive. It is only a white man's command, at the urging of Kurtz, that the natives attack the steamer. It is intentionally ironic that the black man in the novel has a purer (whiter) heart than the white man, whose heart is dark, cruel, and destructive (black).

There is also an obvious contrast between the vision of who Kurtz is and the reality behind the vision. Gifted with eloquence, Kurtz speaks, writes, and paints about the horrors of the ivory trade in Africa and the resulting savagery that the white men inflict on the natives. In total contrast to what he verbalizes, Kurtz's actions are totally ruthless. He proudly displays the skulls of black natives that he has conquered while seizing their ivory and makes the superstitious natives treat him like a god, crawling into his presence on all fours. The two women in Kurtz's life are also contrasted. His black mistress in Africa is very demonstrative, wearing bright clothing and jewelry and acting in a loud, wild manner, clearly displaying strong emotions.

In contrast, Kurtz's Intended in Belgium is fair, mild-tempered, and draped in black. She is the picture of calmness and patience. Despite their differences in appearance and temperament, the love they feel for Kurtz is very similar. The black mistress is devoted to her man and stretches out her arms to him in a show of great grief as he is taken away from her on the steamer. In a similar manner, the Intended is grief-stricken when Kurtz is taken away from her by death and still wears black and daily mourns his passing after more than a year.

The end for these two women in Kurtz's life, however, is a stark contrast. The departing Europeans on board the steamer needlessly gun down the beautiful black mistress in total inhumanity. The white girl, on the other hand, is brought from a seeming deathly existence to life by Marlow's lies about Kurtz. In essence, Marlow has saved her.

In a similar manner to the two women, a comparison and contrast exist between Kurtz and Marlow. They both espouse an idealistic vision behind imperialism, which is why Marlow is drawn towards Kurtz throughout the novel. Both men realise the truth, the darkness, and inhumanities behind the idealism, but their reactions are very different. Kurtz totally succumbs to the dark side, becoming more greedy and ruthless than any other agent working for the ivory company. In denying his idealism through his actions, he is so tortured by his behaviour and by his treatment by the Manager, that he seems to go insane.

Marlow also succumbs, to a much lesser degree, to the imperialist behaviour. He does not stand up and fight against the inhumanity to the Africans, as he knows he should. In fact, he usually sees the black natives as lesser beings in a typically European, inhumane manner. He also perpetrates the lie of imperialism, when he tells the Intended at the novel's end that Kurtz died pursuing noble goals in Africa and uttered her name on his deathbed. But in lying to her, he also heals her and saves her and thus, redeems himself to some degree.

The two men, Kurtz and Marlow, almost become one being — the light side (Marlow) and the dark side (Kurtz) of the same person. There are also many minor comparisons and contrasts throughout the novel. The burial of Kurtz in a muddy hole beside the Congo is a reflection of the burial of the black helmsman into the river itself. The flies that buzz over the dying agent in the accountant's office are similar to the flies that inhabit the messroom of the steamer at the time of Kurtz's death. The women at company office, dressed in black and knitting a garment that looks like a shroud, are similar in appearance to the Intended, who is dressed in black and who knits a shroud of grief around herself.

The joy that Marlow feels in finding the English book in the house by the Congo is similar to the joy that the Russian feels when he discovers his book has been found and returned to him. All of these contrasts and comparisons help to develop Conrad's well- written novel into a tightly woven tale.

Chapter 12

Further Study Questions

1. What is the point of providing a "frame narrator"? How does the presence of this kind of narrator affect your view of Marlow's authority as a narrator?
2. On 1959, what does the frame narrator say distinguishes Marlow from other sailors? How is this distinction significant with respect to the adventure that Marlow recounts?
3. What does Marlow say on 1960-61 about the Roman imperial project? How does the Roman project compare to the Belgian (and British) motivations for seeking an empire?
4. Keep track of references to maps — see, for example, 1961-62. What significance lies in Marlow's references to maps? How, for example, do they represent the novella's frequent opposition between light and "darkness"?
5. On 1963, Marlow describes a map image of the Congo River in Africa as being like a snake. What snake-like qualities does this reference transfer to the River, and how does the transference set us up for the rest of the novel's events?
6. On 1964, Marlow meets a pair of women weaving — to what Classical myths does this scene appeal, and why would such an appeal be significant in the context of the story as a whole?

7. Describe the exchange between Marlow and his idealistic Aunt on 1965. How well does Marlow's self-description as a realist hold up over the course of the story? Explain.
8. Soon Marlow sets out for Africa on a French steamship, and gets his first look at native Africans along the shore. On 1966, what qualities does he observe in them, and what seems to be his attitude about those qualities?
9. By page 1968, Marlow has reached the Company's Outer Station, and offers us some observations about it. What does he say about the reigning "Devil" in this Outer Station? How does this "Devil" differ from others with whom he has made acquaintance?
10. On 1969, what fundamental contrast or contradiction among the Outer Station inhabitants begins to appear right away, as soon as Marlow comes across dying workers and the smartly dressed Company Accountant?
11. On 1970, what is the first description we hear of Kurtz? For what quality or activity is he praised? How does the praise bring up the novella's frequent oppositions between light or whiteness and darkness?
12. On 1972 and following, Marlow reaches the Central Station. How does he describe nature's effects on the Station and its inhabitants? What power does the wilderness have over the Station, and what appears to motivate its occupants?
13. On 1975, what view of Kurtz does the Brickmaker (a favourite of the Manager) take? Why does he appear to resent Kurtz?
14. On 1977, Marlow says that he detests lies. Does this implied (and elsewhere stated) preference for truth hold constant in the novella? Does Marlow seem to understand his own character, or is he at times confused about his interests and beliefs? Explain.

15. On 1980, how do the Manager and his nephew reveal their resentment of Kurtz in spite of that agent's obvious success as an ivory collector? What effect does their resentment have upon Marlow, who has overheard their conversation?
16. On 1982-84, how does Marlow describe the Congo River and its environs? How does he describe his interaction with the River? What illusion does the River promote? What insight does it provide, at least so far as Marlow is concerned?
17. On 1984, what does Marlow imply is the basis for his ability to respond to the African natives he observes? To what extent does he here invoke the distinction often made between nature and culture, primitive and civilized? Does he accept that distinction?
18. On 1985, Marlow discovers a hut with some firewood and a book. Why does this book impress him?
19. On 1986, Marlow says that he came to an important realization as he neared Kurtz's Station. What is the realization, and to what extent does it influence or explain his behaviour in the rest of the story?
20. On 1988-89, what commentary does Marlow offer on the issue of "restraint"? What accounts for the restraint shown by the natives, and what accounts for the restraint shown by the Manager?
21. On 1993, Marlow speaks of Kurtz as "a voice." Soon thereafter, how does Marlow's manner of relating his story change? What seems to be the reason for his fascination with Kurtz' voice?
22. On 1995, how does Marlow describe the partially completed report that Kurtz penned before lapsing into his fatal illness? What effect does that report have on Marlow?
23. On 1998-2000, Marlow meets a Russian devotee of Kurtz. What view of Kurtz does the Russian set forth? How does he differ from Kurtz?

24. On 2001, Marlow sees the "symbolic" skulls lining Kurtz's hut? What reflections do those skulls lead Marlow to make regarding the nature of Kurtz' downfall in the wilderness?
25. On 2003, the travellers meet Kurtz' mistress. Does her presence affect their (or your) understanding of Kurtz? If so, how?
26. After making some less than condemnatory remarks about Kurtz, Marlow is pegged as a "fellow traveller" of Kurtz. How does Marlow react when, on 2006-09, he finally closes in upon and then encounters Kurtz?
27. On 2009-11, what does Kurtz say in his final illness? What, if anything, does Marlow learn from Kurtz? How does he interpret Kurtz's phrase "the horror, the horror"?
28. Kurtz finally passes away, and, at the text's conclusion, Marlow decides to visit Kurtz's "Intended," or fiancee. Why does Marlow lie to her about Kurtz's last words? Does his lie reflect any insight he has gained from his trip up the Congo and to "the Heart of Darkness"? Explain.

1. Discuss the narrative setting of the novel. Who is telling what to whom and under what circumstances? Is it important that this is a retrospective account?
2. Why are most of the novel's characters given only descriptive titles, and not actual names? (e.g., see the accountant, the brickmaker, etc.
3. As a related question, why is the narrator who introduces us to Marlow unnamed? Why does he appear to play such a small role in the novel?
4. What kind of a storyteller is Marlow? How does he differ from other seamen in this regard? (see 3 / 9).
5. As he begins his story, what does Marlow emphasize about England's history? (see 3-4 / 9-10).

6. Why does he refer to Brussels and/or London as a monstrous town and a "sepulchral city"? (21 / 27; 65 /70)
7. Marlow says, "The conquest of the earth, which mostly means the taking it away from those who have a different complexion or slightly flatter noses than ourselves, is not a pretty thing when you look into it too much. What redeems it is the idea only.... something you can set up, and bow down before, and offer a sacrifice to" (4 / 10). What does he mean? Is this a justification of imperialism and colonialism?
8. Comment on Marlow's discussion of maps in part one. (5 / 11) How does this relate to colonialism?
9. Before Marlow heads for Africa, he visits a doctor, who measures his head. (9 / 15) Why does the doctor do this?
10. Comment on the following: "You know I hate, detest, and can't bear a lie, not because I am straighter than the rest of us, but simply because it appalls me. There is a taint of death, a flavour of mortality in lies which is exactly what I hate and detest in the world" (23 / 29)
11. Why is this ironic? Which philosopher is mentioned earlier in part one who might help us to reflect on Marlow's attitude toward lies?
12. How is Marlow described as he narrates his story? (see especially 1 / 7 and 24 / 30)
13. What is the significance of the breaks in Marlow's narration on page 24 / 30?
14. He asks his audience if they can see Kurtz, if they can see his story, but he then says that it is impossible. Why is it impossible to convey the essence of someone's existence? He then adds that his audience can see more now than he could then. What does he mean?

15. How are the women in the novel characterized? How does Marlow feel about women?
16. What mythological and biblical elements can you find in *Heart of Darkness*?
17. How are Africans portrayed? How does Marlow feel about them? He seems not to think that skin colour is significant, but does this mean that he is not a racist? Does he feel that they have been corrupted by contact with Europeans? What does he mean when he says, "Well, you know what was the worst of it—this suspicion of their not being inhuman" (32 / 37)?
18. How does Marlow feel about colonialism? To what extent is he complicit, and to what degree does he reflect or articulate imperialist ideas?
19. Why does Marlow say that all of Europe went into the making of Kurtz? (45 / 50)
20. How does Kurtz conclude his report to the International Society for the Suppression of Savage Customs?
21. Kurtz, apparently, had hoped to conquer the wilderness. Has he succeeded?
22. Look especially at pages 53 / 57 and 63 / 67.
23. Marlow often refers to Kurtz as a voice. (43-4 / 48; 63 / 67) What does he mean?
24. If Kurtz's words are so important, why does Marlow sometimes withhold the contents of their conversation, as when he carries Kurtz back to the ship? (60-1 / 64-5)
25. How much of Kurtz's voice do we actually hear?
26. Many readers, even professorial types, have commented on the "murkiness" of Conrad's novel: the descriptions are often very hard to follow in time and space, and many of the descriptions are difficult to make out and contain an abundance of adjectives

such as "inexpressible," "invisible," "unspeakable," etc. Is Conrad simply flawed in his prose at times, or might there be a method to this style?

27. What is "the horror"? The "heart of darkness"?
28. Marlow says, "Perhaps all the wisdom, and all truth, and all sincerity, are just compressed into that inappreciable moment of time in which we step over the threshold of the invisible. Perhaps" (65 / 69). Comment on this, and on his assertion that he has been allowed to step back, whereas Kurtz had taken the last stride.
29. How is the Intended described in the final scene? Why does Marlow lie to her?
30. How does Conrad utilize opposites throughout the text, especially those relating to white/black, light/dark, inside/outside, and surface/depth?
31. Peter Brooks has written about Conrad's novel that it seems "as if someone had designed a machine to produce work far smaller than the energy put into it." Discuss this as a characterization of *Heart of Darkness*.
32. An important characteristic of storytelling is that narrators often end up telling a story different from the one they intend to tell. Does this apply to *Heart of Darkness*? If so, what is that story?

Chapter 13

Critical Essays

Gender, Race and Narrative Structure: A Reappraisal of Joseph Conrad's "Heart of Darkness".

By Carole Stone and Fawzia Afzal-Khan

Johanna Smith in her feminist reading of "Heart of Darkness", concludes, my intent has been to show that feminist criticism is a method of avoiding his detachment, of making ourselves aware of the patriarchal ideology in which he, and perhaps we too, unwittingly participate. ". Our intent here, is in some senses the opposite; it seems to us that the inherent ambiguities and contradictions in Marlow's narrative, in fact, the circularity and open-endedness of the narrative itself, as well as the high degree of self-consciousness of the narrative form, make it possible to interpret Conrad more favorably.

Although the narrative appears to follow the masculine/ patriarchal pattern of a hero who overcomes obstacles to rise to more important positions in the social, economic scheme of society, the plot vacillates in its presentation of the male journey motif. And not only does the plot vacillate, but the structure itself evades closure and judgement, as we follow Marlow, the narrator, up the serpentine river. We would like to suggest that Conrad exhibits some qualities in his writing style, in his multivocal/multi-layered depiction of the African woman, as well as in his approach to the moral dilemma of patriarchy that mark "Heart of Darkness", amongst other things, as *L'écriture Feminine,* as defined by Kristeva and other

French feminists, exhibits the quality of displacement which they see as an inherently female one; one which they associate with an androgynous, pre-oedipal phase. What Kristeva terms the semiotic is, in her opinion, a specifically pre-gendered female order of language and thought, opposed to the 'symbolic' order of patriarchal thought. By the semiotic, she means a pattern or flow of forces that we can detect within fixed' language, and which represents a residue of the pre-oedipal phase. The semiotic is the other of language, which is nonetheless intimately entwined with it.

Because it stems from the pre-oedipal phase, it is bound up in the child's contact with the mother's body, whereas the symbolic is associated with the law of the father. The semiotic, though not exclusive to women, is nevertheless closely connected to them, for it arises from a pre-oedipal, maternal phase that does not recognize distinctions of gender.

We, along with other French feminists such as Helene Cixous, believe that the semiotic is actually a bi-sexual form of writing, one which offers to deconstruct all the scrupulous binary by throwing into confusion the divisions between masculine and feminine and the oppositions — proper/improper, norm/deviation, sane/ mad, mine/yours, authority/obedience — by which societies survive. As Cixous puts it:

> Most women are like this: they do someone else's-man's-writing, and in their innocence sustain it and give it voice, and end up producing writing that's in effect masculine. Great care must be taken in working on feminist writing not to get trapped by names: to be signed with a woman's name doesn't necessarily make a piece of writing feminine. It could quite well be masculine writing, and conversely, the fact that a piece of writing is signed with a man's name does not in itself exclude femininity. It's rare but you can sometimes find femininity in writings signed by men; it does happen

Furthermore, it seems apposite to us to think through and apply judiciously to Conrad's text the concepts elaborated in Luce Irigaray's work, "Le Sexe Qui N'est Pas Une or The Sex That Is Not One" — in which the negative of the title as applied to the figure of woman signifies not only a lack, but more interestingly, an excess that rejects the other pole in the binary Man/Woman. Thus, woman is not just a lack, but more than one — hence, also, more than two, silent, yet also multivocal. Hers is the speech that cannot be contained — hence, cannot BE.

Conrad's text, we maintain, inscribes just such an excess of signification in both its libidinal narrative economy, as well as in its depiction of the African woman. To quote Irigaray: The issue is not one of elaborating a new theory of which woman would be the subject or the object, but of jamming the theoretical machinery itself, of suspending its pretension to the production of a truth and of a meaning that are excessively univocal. Of course, Irigaray is here prescribing a feminine poetics, but as we have said, this is not (or doesn't have to be) a female prerogative.

The question that women should ask according to Irigaray, then, is one that male texts such as "Heart of Darkness" can also enact if they are on the side of the feminine economy — They should not put it, then, in the way in which within discourse, the feminine finds itself as lack, deficiency, or as imitation or negative image of the subject; they should signify that with respect to this (masculinist/logocentric) logic, a disruptive excess is possible on the feminine side.

All that Kristeva terms as the semiotic, and Cixous as the feminine, seems to us, then, to apply very well both to the narrative structure as well as to the moral universe of "Heart of Darkness". We will take up our second point first. While Marlow begins his journey as a conquistador out to fill in the blank spaces on the map of Africa, his journey quickly begins to exhibit qualities that we traditionally associate with the feminine: the reliance on others, a questioning of one's motives, and the making of moral judgements that do not rely on the symbolic order of the father.

The first way in which Conrad shows Marlow's journey as linked to femaledom is by making him turn to women to secure a job. Just as a woman needed to go to a man for power during the late 1890's, when this story takes place, so Marlow must go to women. It is clear that Marlow experiences this need to ask a woman for help in getting him a position as captain of a steamer as an indignity. Then- would you believe it? I tried the women. I, Charlie Marlow, set the women to work- to get a job. Heavens! His aunt secures a job for him as a skipper of a steamboat.

Before leaving for Africa, he says goodbye to his aunt over a cup of tea, the symbol of English domestic comfort which she represents. Like those mothers who will send their sons off to the Great War, with no knowledge of trench warfare, she gives him her blessing, expecting him to return the hero, which it is his duty as a man to become. In fact, Marlow returns more domesticated than heroic, more the 'feminized male' than the 'conquering hero'.

Marlow, right from the start, is not certain that he can become the 'conquering hero', and exhibits the 'feminine' quality of self-questioning when he says I don't know why a queer feeling came to me that I was an imposter. Once at his station in Africa, Marlow again exhibits his feminized self when he overhears a conversation between the station master and his nephew, in which they seem to be plotting against Kurtz. Marlow, who is dozing on the deck of his boat, awakens in time to hear their disloyalty; yet, repulsed as he is by this, he does not protest. Powerless and marginal, he chooses to remain silent in the relative safety of his womb-like enclosure, once again exhibiting his feminine side. What we see then, in "Heart of Dark- ness" is a female subtext that threatens to pull apart the binary oppositions between male and female worlds.

With such doubts, why does Marlow undertake the journey? The ostensible answer lies in his boyhood (masculine) passion for maps where he saw the many blank spaces on earth, and one that looked particularly inviting was in the centre of Africa. By the time he grew up, it was not a blank space any more; it had rivers and lakes with names, and it had become a place of darkness, no longer virginal. Others had gone before him, filling blank space with phallic power.

Now, what is left to fascinate him is, a mighty big river... resembling an immense snake uncoiled, with its head in the sea, its body at rest, curving afar over a vast country, and its tail lost in the depth of the land. He concludes, the snake had charmed me.

Marlow sees the image of the river as snake again on a map in a Brussels office, where two women function as female guardians to the gates of Hell, the darkness dead in the centre of the map. Of this river, Marlow says, it was fascinating-deadly-like a snake-ugh! When the office door opens to admit Marlow to the chief commissioner's office, symbolically he is being admitted to the dark underworld of the serpentine river. The river represents to Marlow, the sinister, unknowable female power which he seems to need to explore, in order perhaps to expurgate the 'feminine' within himself. However, as the novel progresses, Marlow enacts, rather than expurgates, the feminine principle.

From the beginning, Conrad shows Marlow's feminine side. Firstly, he depicts Marlow as a passive man in the pose of a preaching Buddha (who is the image of peace through nirvana), which is in contrast with the role of the male conquering hero, whose tale he is ironically telling. Secondly, the ambiguities of the text — who and what is Kurtz? How does Marlow actually feel about him? What is the exact nature of Kurtz' crime? Does Marlow hate or love Kurtz? — reveal Marlow's uncertainty about himself, and the text's uncertainty about seeing everything in terms of these binary oppositions.

These binary oppositions break down even further, as Marlow's journey progresses, for his sympathies move back and forth between support for the white colonialist as the superior race, and sympathy for the blacks who have been dispossessed and robbed of their inheritance. For example, he is appalled by the dehumanization of the blacks whom he describes as moving around as ants. These people were building a railway, thus, contributing to white expansionism, while being reduced to animals. Conrad's description of the chain gang can be read at least two ways, thus contributing to the possibility of multiple interpretations:

A slight clinking behind me made me turn my head. Six black men advanced in a file, toiling up the path. They walked erect and slow, balancing small baskets full of earth on their heads, and the clink kept time with their footsteps. Black rags were wound around their loins, and the short ends waggled to and from like tails. I could see every rib, the joints of their limbs were like knots in a rope; each had an iron collar around his neck, and all were connected together with a chain, whose bights swung between them, rhythmically clinking..

A few pages later, he describes black shapes crouched...in all the attitudes of pain, abandonment and despair and further describes standing horror-struck...as one of these creatures rose to his hands and knees, and went off on all fours to the river to drink. (32) As Chinua Achebe has already pointed out in his article An Image Of Africa, Conrad in this pas sage is stereotyping the African as savage and primitive, deserving of our compassion but not our respect. However, we perceive this passage to be indicative of Marlow's identification with the subjugated 'other' and of his horror and repulsion at the cruel treatment they have received at the hands of his white male compatriots. In thus identifying with the African 'other' and against the white male, Marlow/Conrad expresses his sympathy with the unempowered female because he fears that he too will become powerless in the blank spaces of Africa, much like the natives he has seemingly come to conquer, and the disenfranchised women back home. As Brook Thomas points out, there is yet another way of looking at Conrad's presentation of the African chain-gang:

Even though Conrad had himself been there, he chose to tell his story indirectly through an idiosyncratic, first-person narrator, Marlow, whose narrative is in turn relayed by another narrator who presumably has not even been to Africa. This elaborate structure makes us aware of structure as structure; thus, the novel, doesn't pretend to offer us a perfectly clear, uncluttered, unbiased, perfectly natural view of the facts of the past.

Thomas' point of view lends credibility to our assertion that Conrad's style and structure in this novel beg to be read from a variety of perspectives. And it must be pointed out that Conrad's background as a Polish exile in England, whose second language was English reinforces the notion of multiple perspectives. For as Edward Said observes:

> Because Conrad also had an extraordinarily residual sense of his own exilic marginality, he quite carefully (some would say maddeningly) qualified Marlow's narrative with the provisionality that came from standing at the very juncture of this world with another, unspecified but different.

Michael North goes further, describing how to Conrad's friends, his Polish nationality was seen as a racial difference. North points out that Conrad's Polish accent was associated by them with the Orient, and further that his appearance and mannerisms were considered by H.G. Wells and Ford Mad Ford to be Oriental. Several critics thought he was Jewish. Another found him positively simian. This view of Conrad as racially different from his English colleagues and therefore inferior provides us with another explanation of Conrad's ambivalent attitudes in Heart of Darkness toward Africa and imperialism. For Conrad both wanted to belong to and escape from a culture that never quite accepted him.

Turning to our first point about narrative structure, then, Marlow's journey up the river is toward the realm of the semiotic, the realm of multiple perspectives suggested by the self-conscious circularity of the text. Said, in commenting upon the imperial context of Conrad's "Heart of Darkness", inadvertently addresses some points about the semiotic and female form.

> Like most of his other tales, Heart of Darkness is not just a recital of Marlow's adventures; it is also a dramatization of Marlow telling his story to a group of listeners at a particular place in a particular time... Neither Conrad nor Marlow offer us anything outside the world-conquering attitudes embodied by Kurtz and Marlow and Conrad...the circularity of the whole thing is unassailable. Except as I said a moment ago that

Conrad is self-conscious about setting and situating the narrative in a narrative moment, thus allowing us to realise after all, that far from swallowing up its own history, imperialism has in fact been placed and located by history, one that lies outside the tightly inclusive ring on the deck of the yawl Nelly.

In other words, what Said says about Conrad's self-consciousness, that implies or leads to a plurality of perspectives within the narrative construct, echoes in some ways, Kristeva's and other feminists' theories about the non-linearity, circularity, open- endedness, ambiguity and multiple perspectives inherent in a female narrative mode. 2

So Marlow, in his voyage up the river, travels toward the semiotic as seen through the disruptions and evasions of the text. Marlow evades, for example, his real feelings towards Kurtz, really fearing that if he admits how he feels to himself, he will have to recognize a part of him that is like Kurtz. Thus, he, Marlow, could end up like Kurtz. He says I think it had whispered to him [the wilderness] things about himself which he did not know, things of which he had no conception, so he took counsel with the great solitude — and the whisper had proved irresistibly fascinating.

Conrad exhibits a similar ambiguity in depicting Marlow's confrontation with the female principle embodied by Kurtz' mistress, who symbolizes both a matriarchal female goddess as well as a sensuous temptress associated in the English male mind with 'savage' races. But Conrad goes beyond conventional colonial stereotypes of 'natives' and we would agree with Marianna Torgovnick who argues that the African woman is the crux of Heart of Darkness...the representative 'native' the only one fully individualized and described in detail, except for the Helmsman, who also dies in the story. She is, the text insists, the symbol of Africa.

We would argue that Marlow's fears as represented in the text by the sensual power of Kurtz' mistress show also Conrad's fear of the female energy, the female muse within him. This female muse manifests herself in the ambiguities and omissions of the text, in the baroque, twisting style that resembles the serpentine twisting of the river. On the one hand, Conrad struggles through his narrator, Marlow, to break into a speech of triumph, of authority over the savage temptress, and yet is, finally unable to, or maybe even unwilling to block out the power of her inarticulate, gorgeous, presence. The passage that we are about to quote exhibits the text's divided attitudes toward female power: on the one hand, Conrad/ Marlow fears the savage woman's sexual mystery, on the other hand he admires and is fascinated by it.

For closely linked to this issue of female power is the power of language versus the power of silence. In this passage we see that the power to describe is one exercised through language by Marlow, Yet, in the final analysis, the silent gaze of the 'savage' woman is more articulate and powerful than Marlow's words.

And from right to left along the lighted shore moved a wild and gorgeous apparition of a woman. She walked with measured steps, draped in striped and fringed cloths, treading the earth proudly with a light jingle and flash of was done in the shape of a helmet; she had bright leggings to the knee, brass wire gauntlets to the elbow, a crimson spot on her tawny cheek, innumerable necklaces of glass beads on her neck; bizarre things, charms, gifts of witch-men, that hung about her, glittered and trembled at every step...She was savage and superb, wild-eyed and magnificent; there was something ominous and stately in her deliberate progress, and in the hush that had fallen suddenly upon the whole sorrowful land, the immense wilderness, the colossal body of the fecund and mysterious life seemed to look at her, pensive, as though it had been looking at the image of its own tenebrous and passionate soul...

Her face had a tragic and fierce aspect of wild sorrow and a dumb pain...Suddenly she opened her bare arms and threw them up rigid above her head, as though in an uncontrollable desire to touch the sky...A formidable silence hung over the scene.

Thus, the muteness, the formidable silence of Kurtz' savage/mistress, becomes emblematic of those blank spaces in the text which Conrad/Marlow wishes to inhabit and cannot. 0n the narrative level, he had wished to inhabit the 'blank spaces' of Africa, only to discover that these blank spots are a mirage; just as, on the linguistic and textual level, he acknowledges the 'muteness' of the 'other' to be a delusion. For, in fact, as his own portrayal shows, the savage mistress speaks a language as powerful as that of patriarchy and colonialism. As Gilbert and Gubar point out, she is a silent hieroglyph in the language strange that articulates both her mysterious history and her threatening hystery

Her presence suggests another silence in the text, the taboo which Conrad never addresses openly, namely her sexual liaison with Kurtz. For as Kurtz' wife, though the text never states this directly, she stands in direct opposition to Kurtz's Intended. Ironically, the text reveals Conrad's African version of womanhood and sexuality as real and potent while the Intended is a pure Victorian fantasy, a tradition of the English novel which includes such stereotypes of the fair, insipid heroine, as Amelia in Thackeray's Vanity Fair, a tradition which Conrad inherited. In a recent study of Vanity Fair, Suvendrini Perera uses the term oriental misogyny to describe the representation of gender relations in the English novel.

In Vanity Fair the males takes on the pasha role while the female, identified with the seraglio, is victim. In Heart of Darkness Conrad reproduces this cultural misogyny and racial stereotyping in Kurtz' possession of his mistress. However, like Becky Sharp, the dark figure whose racial otherness contrasts with Amelia's Englishness — described by Perera as the marginal female who manages by sacrificing her sexual respectability, to turn her unattached status murderously upon the society that excludes her, (Perera, 90) — Conrad's native woman also disrupts imperialist, racist, sexist attitudes toward women.

Torgovnick points out, Marlow clearly conceives of her as a substitute for, an inversion of Kurtz's high-minded, white 'intended.' Like the Belgian woman, she is an impressive figure, but unlike the Intended she is not 'high-minded': she is presented as all body and inchoate emotion. The novella cuts from the figure of the African woman with outstretched arms to the Intended: one woman an affianced bride, one woman all body, surely an actual bride.

If Marlow could end up like Kurtz, then he could also end up succumbing to a love which violates British codes against miscegenation. And yet the attraction of the African woman is so manifestly powerful and seductive as revealed by the text's description of her, that we cannot help feeling that she represents Conrad's real feelings about what constitutes ideal femininity.

The African woman, who, it must be noted, has no name, embodies Conrad's inherited notions of the savage female other popularized most notably by Rider Haggard in She. While she may be seductive, she is also, like Africa, deadly. To take this one step further, if Conrad is struggling with his feminine self, than to succumb to the African woman is like Kurtz, to perish. Is this then a further horror in the text? For Kurtz (and this is also a potential horror for his alter ego, Marlow) has been destroyed by a destructive femininity which fascinates but kills because it is forbidden. Like the love that has no name the African woman has no name. She is the feminine principle that Marlow must repress in order to conquer and rule. Conrad's text endeavors on the one hand to preserve the masculine principle while Marlow's identification with the African woman struggles against that principle. It is interesting to note that standard critical interpretations of "Heart of Darkness" have focused on Marlow and Kurtz as two sides of the same self, while none suggest the African woman as an aspect of Marlow's divided psyche. In fact, except for Torgovnick's and Gilbert and Gubar's, no studies of Conrad pay any attention to her as an aspect of Conrad's doubts about imperialism or his identification with her.

In our view, she is the real presence in the novella and it is she who makes Marlow confront his boyhood male passion for filling up the blank spaces he had seen on the African map

Now, instead of a blank space, he finds a human being inhabiting the African landscape. Indeed, her being betrays another multiple perspective in the novella, one suggested by the question: how can one fill up a blank space on a map in the name of culture when in actuality that space is already inhabited by a culture?

This is one of the questions which though unarticulated is raised by Conrad concerning the nexus between masculinity and femininity, between colonialism's power and colonialism's weakness, between Conrad's racism and Conrad's sympathy for the subjugated Africans. He embodies this question in the body of the African woman who is fecund and mysterious. passionate, and who belongs to the African landscape that looks at her as though it had been looking at the image of its own tenebrous and passionate soul. Is this not woman as dark continent in Kristeva's terms, which Marlow fears in himself but cannot re press? We see how the native woman embodies multiple perspectives in the text: woman as other, as African evil, and as the silent native who has no human identity.

Yet, she is never reduced to either an essence of the same (re: the European male Self) or completely exoticized (re: dehistoricized as Other). For example, Barthes, in exposing the myth of exoticism operating in the so-called documentary film, The Lost Continent writes: Faced with anything foreign, the Established Order knows only two types of behaviour, which are both mutilating: either to acknowledge it as a Punch and Judy show, or to defuse it as a pure reflection of the West. In any case, the main thing is to deprive it of its history.

The figure of the African woman in Heart of Darkness, inasmuch as she functions as a silent hieroglyph, can be reduced neither to a one-dimensional other, nor understood and hence assimilated into Marlow's world-view in the way Barthes has outlined. Furthermore, by depicting the native woman as speechless, Conrad places her at the centre of issues of colonialism. Frantz Fanon, in a somewhat different yet related context argued, I ascribe a basic importance to the phenomenon of language...one of the elements in the man of colour's comprehension of the dimension of the other. For it is implicit that to speak is to exist absolutely for the other.

Fanon argues further that Existence is language, and language is always a matter of politics. Thus, existence is a product of language and the colonized subject must learn the master's language in order to be human. By portraying the woman as mute, Conrad makes her less than human and powerless to engage in a dialogue with her master, Kurtz, except through her sexual power. So on the one hand, as representative of the native people, she possesses animal instincts and is incapable of being civilized.

But on the other hand, if she lacks speech, Kurtz loses speech. Throughout the novella he has been characterized as a voice whose eloquence has mesmerized his followers. Eric Cheyfitz points out that The conception of the orator as emperor, conquering men with the weapon of eloquence, is a classical and Renaissance commonplace, and argues that this imperial common place finds its place in the story of the orator as the first settler, that is as the first civilizer and colonizer of humans. While this story seems to be played out during Marlow's search for Kurtz, as Marlow gathers stories about Kurtz's achievements, ultimately Kurtz's power of eloquence is reduced to uttering the horror, the horror.

When, as Fanon suggests, a colonized people finds itself face to face with the language of the civilizing nation; that is with the culture of the mother country, the colonized is elevated above the jungle status in proportion to his adoption of the mother country's cultural standards. He becomes whiter as he renounces his blackness, the jungle.

With Kurtz, the reverse seems to be true; his embrace of the darkness of the jungle reveals the white lie upon which such a Manichean notion rests. For, in becoming blacker, he doesn't lose his western norms of behaviour at all, rather his hair-raising postcript exterminate all the brutes, is a fitting complement to the white civilizing mission of the International Society For The Suppression Of Savage Customs that sent him there in the first place! As Marlow gloomily observes, All

Europe contributed to the making of Kurtz. His fall from eloquence contrasts, thus, with his mistress's mute eloquence, as Conrad complicates who is conquered and who is conqueror.

As Benita Parry has also observed, Marlow hears the natives' speech as a black and incomprehensible frenzy, which echoes Fanon's sardonic observation that It is said that the Negro loves to jabber. Parry notes that It is language that draws Marlow toward Kurtz because he can speak English and its is Kurtz's voice that entices him into his orbit.

She sees Marlow's affirmation of faith over reason as connected to the natives' wild and passionate uproar. Yet, it seems to us that Conrad ultimately reverses the attitude of colonial superiority in terms of language as rationality, since the native woman's eloquent silence speaks loud and clear for the powerful other. Her merger with the jungle landscape makes clear how Africa overpowers the colonizer's language and customs.3 In a reversal of Fanon's view of the colonized adopting the colonizer's language and culture, the native woman retains her blackness, while Kurtz loses his whiteness, albeit only superficially. Furthermore, though, as previously suggested, Conrad partially dehumanizes her by making her mute, it is his text which also speaks for her; through whose gaps and ambiguities we see her silence as eloquent, and her taboo morality (outside of man's reach) as a preferable alternative against the male-signed hypocrisy of Kurtz' fiancée. In the latter's case, as the pain- fully hypocritical conversational exchange proceeds between her and Marlow, we see how Conrad's text, while on the one hand setting her up as an unbearably pathetic contrast to the vital Native Woman, on the other reveals the absurdity of its own masculine-centred discursive strand that seeks to contain her within such a Victorian construct. By refusing to even give her a name of her own, Conrad's text questions the discursive narrative strategy which renders her an object of exchange between men; an object the price of whose innocence has been paid for by a lie.

Just as Conrad's rendering of the native woman suggests a plurality of perspective rather than an either/or binary within the narrative construct, thus echoing feminist theories about the open-endedness, ambiguity and multiple perspectives inherent in a female narrative mode, so Marlow's return to England can be seen as echoing Carol Gilligan's psychological views about female moral development. Few critics have addressed Marlow's reasons for lying to the Intended, and those who do ignore the notion of female consciousness we have been elaborating. Michael Levenson, for example, argues that: Marlow never shrinks from judgement, but he judges without abstract ideals, without general principles, indeed without consistency.... He derides moral absolutes and willingly suspends universals in favor of concrete discriminations. We know that he abominates lies and that he recognizes justice as Kurtz's due, but when he meets the intended he complies with neither the maxim of honesty nor the claim of justice. Instead he acts as the practical moralist who overturns general conceptions without overturning ethics.

When Marlow describes his particular reason for lying to Kurtz's Intended, he makes no appeal to those tainted ideas: progress, pity, conduct of life. He says simply that the truth 'would have been too dark-too dark altogether.'

In Levenson's view, darkness becomes a moral sensation. which furthers our view of multiple perspectives in Conrad's ethical responses to imperial ism, racism, and colonialist corruption. However, we would further argue that the derision toward moral absolutes which Levenson points out in Marlow's decision to lie, is closer to the female-centred approach that Gilligan outlines (a possibility Levenson does not consider). What she has to say about women's moral development and moral judgement, for instance, is connected to Marlow's response to Imperialism and to Kurtz. It makes his Lie to Kurtz' Intended appear not sexist, but empathic. Because of his experiences in Africa, Marlow's moral consciousness has taken on female qualities, as described by her in her influential book, "In A Different Voice". Gilligan theorizes that women's moral reasoning is not based on abstract notions of right and wrong, like men's, but is instead, contextual, and based on perceptions of suffering and caring. Instead of using abstract rules of justice to decide whether an action was right or wrong, girls, says Gilligan, wonder who would suffer by the action:

> The reluctance to judge may itself be indicative care and concern for others that infuse the psychology of women's development and are responsible for what is generally seen as problematic in its nature.

They will usually rate as best that choice which leads to the least harm. Gilligan asks: Why should we believe that the moral sequence through which boys pass constitutes moral development *tout court* ? Perhaps the girls' abiding concern for human relatedness and personal responsibility, is not a lower form of moral reasoning, but an equally sophisticated moral point of view, complementing the masculine code of absolute right and wrong and impartial justice. Judged in the light of Gilligan's theory, Marlow's decision to lie to the Intended is not, then, taken with the intent to humiliate her (and thus all women) as Johanna Smith suggests in her essay, but to protect her from the needless suffering and hurt she would surely feel if told the Truth.

Moreover, the truth is the unsayable that Conrad has been un-saying throughout the novel. Indeed his lying to the Intended who, like the African woman, has no name, yet, unlike her, is a complete abstraction, raises further ambiguities over the Truth. Did Kurtz intend to return to his fiancée? Was his African nightmare more real than her abstract illusory drawing world? Or is Marlow's lying about Kurtz a defence against the horrific lifting of repression which rendered Kurtz impotent? It seems to us that Conrad uses the Intended to raise questions of what is real, and what is truth by suggesting that it is finally not locatable in a binary understanding of the world.

Marlow/Conrad bears witness to the horrors of imperialist oppression in Africa, as women writers have done throughout Herstory, yet does not return to report it overtly, nor does he make absolute judgements about culpability. Like Emily Dickinson, he tells the truth, but make[s] it slant. Thus, as Patricia Meyer Spacks says of women's novels, Conrad's "Heart of Dark ness" makes Marlow's journey one of subterranean challenges to absolute truths.

In this reading of "Heart of Darkness", we have argued for a perspective on Conrad's novel that allies it in many ways with an *écriture* feminine. Further, we have pointed out that Conrad's own position as racial outsider, a Polish émigré in England, contributed to his sensitivity to marginal and oppressed groups.

It can also be argued that in his maternal attachment to a pre-oedipal phase of speech (his first language, Polish) — rather than aliying himself with the symbolic father (English Imperial ism), he allies himself with the mother of an *écriture* feminine.

We do not mean to imply by this that Conrad's view of Africa is non-racist or non-imperialistic. Nor are we suggesting that women as a whole are incapable of making absolute moral judgements. We have simply desired to problematize conventional readings of the text, and to suggest that Conrad may have seen into the horror of the 'heart of darkness' in more complex and ambiguous ways than a closed or univocal interpretation allows.

An Inglorious Enterprise: Empire, Ideology and Transformation in Heart of Darkness and A Passage to India

The following is a work in progress, the first chapter in a possible thesis project. Though the actual analyses of these two fictional works is still underway and will be added soon, what follows is a brief description of the historical details that underpin the two narratives and an explanation of my critical approach. See Marlow and Mrs. Moore for an abbreviated version of the upcoming textual analysis. SG

Joseph Conrad's novella *Heart of Darkness* and E. M. Forster's novel *A Passage to India* are two examples of literature about Empire. Both works utilize Britain's Age of Empire as a backdrop for the narratives and they explore British attitudes and behaviour in the exotic locales of the imperial frontier. The two selections are also prominent in being among the most brilliant and complex of the genre. Using a Marxist critical approach, this study will compare and contrast the two works as examples of "realistic" fiction which both represents and critiques the societies in which they were produced.

HEART OF DARKNESS AND A PASSAGE TO INDIA

Distinctions and Commonalities

To compare and contrast Joseph Conrad's *Heart of Darkness* with E. M. Forster's *A Passage to India* might at first appear to be an unlikely coupling. Apart from the obvious differences in length and form, since *Heart of Darkness* is a novella of approximately one hundred pages whereas *A Passage to India* is a full-length and fully developed novel, and the differing literary approaches the two forms necessitate, (an issue that will be addressed later in this study), the two works are also separated by a generation and were produced in different periods of each artist's career. *Heart of Darkness* was published in 1902, sixteen years after Conrad began writing in 1886, as one of the three short stories contained in *Youth; A Narrative and Two Other Stories*. The story was produced midway in Conrad's writing career since he continued to write fiction until his death in 1924. That same year, 1924, Edward Morgan Forster published his sixth and final novel *A Passage to India*. Though he continued to write essays and criticism until his death in 1970, *A Passage to India* crowned the fictional phase of Forster's writing that began in 1904; it is widely considered his most mature and complex novel.

Each novelist also came from very different backgrounds and their fiction reflects their differing life experiences. Joseph Conrad was born in 1857, the only child of Polish immigrants who were exiled by the Russian government from their

Ukrainian homeland. Both of his parents died when he was a child and he lived in Poland with an uncle until he left home at age sixteen and joined the crew of a French ship in Marseilles in 1874. After twenty years at sea, (during which time he also became a British citizen in 1886), Conrad settled in England in 1894 and devoted himself to writing. Conrad drew heavily on his experiences as a seaman for material in his fiction and *Heart of Darkness* is no exception; much of the tale is loosely based on Conrad's experiences as mate of a small river steamboat in the African Congo in 1890.

E. M. Forster was born in England in 1879. His father, a middle-class English architect, died when Forster was only a year old and he, too, was an only child and was raised by his mother. His life was influenced by his great-aunt who left him eight thousand pounds in trust when she died in 1887. He was educated in English public schools and at King's College at Cambridge. His education was followed by a year of travel in Italy and Greece with his mother which provided material for his early novels. Forster travelled to India a number of times beginning in 1912 and *A Passage to India,* started prior to World War I, is considered to draw heavily on these visits.

Despite these contrasts, the two works of fiction have a number of themes in common. The action of each work takes place against the backdrop of Empire. *Heart of Darkness* is set amidst the scramble for Africa that took place among the European imperial powers in the last three decades of the 19th century and which culminated in the Boer War. *A Passage to India* takes place among the British in India following World War I when the British Empire was in its decline. In this respect both works are part of the realistic tradition in literature; they are typical in their realistic representions of the historical conditions in their respective periods and are similarly typical in their treatment of the 'culture clashes' between Europeans and the natives they encounter. These similarities make these two works of fiction especially amenable to Marxian analysis as they satisfy Marxist scholar Georg Lukacs' theory of art given in Terry Eagleton's book *Marxism and Literary Criticsim*:

"A 'realist' work is rich in a complex, comprehensive set of relations between man, nature, and history; and these relations embody and unfold what for Marxism is most 'typical' about a particular phase of history. By the 'typical' Lukacs denotes those latent forces in any society which are from a Marxist viewpoint most historically significant and progressive, which lay bare the society's inner structure and dynamic".

Much of my analysis in this study will utilize a Marxist critical approach to literature (which will be explained in more detail in the following section) and I hope to bring out in this study how the two works of fiction fulfill Lukacs's specialized definition by revealing the problems and inherent contradictions of imperialism, both of theory and practice, in the ways each work represents historical conditions.

Apart from historical setting, the most significant way *Heart of Darkness* and *A Passage to India* accomplish this "typical" representation is through their portrayal of characters. Both stories are related from the viewpoints of European characters who find themselves in foreign lands as direct representatives of a European Power or due to some connection with imperial activity, although *A Passage to India* is unusual for the fiction of the time in also featuring the viewpoint of a colonial native.

Because all of the contact between the Europeans and the natives, and for that matter between Europeans who meet within an imperial context, is influenced by the economic imperatives of imperial conquest, the relationships that develop between the various characters are to a great degree structured and determined by these conditions. Furthermore, both *Heart of Darkness* and *A Passage to India* are significant in the degree to which they closely examine the individual psychology, and the underlying ideology that informs it, of the European imperial "foot-soldier," the representative "on the ground" who carries out the imperial duties and designs of his homeland in a climate that is hostile and in a culture he does not understand and where he is not welcome. Alan

Sandison concurs in *The Wheel ofEmpire*: "Whether as administrator, trader or adventurer the imperial intruder in his embattled consciousness provides the most dramatic evidence of the moral struggle which his physical presence symbolizes". The heart of this study will be the examination of how the economic conditions of imperialism express themselves through the characters in both works in terms of ideological assumptions, cultural misunderstandings, and psychological crises and what these reveal about the imperial mission itself, as well as the culture that gave rise to it.

Following this political analysis will be an exploration of some of the aesthetic and spiritual issues suggested by the two works. The river that the protagonist Marlow travels in *Heart of Darkness* serves as a multi- level symbol in the story as do the Marabar Caves in *A Passage to India* and thus each of these "nature" symbols tie various facets within each individual work together in a uniquely organic way; each symbol represents not just one thing or idea but a number of things or ideas and yet, in some ways, they remain the ambiguous center of each work. Just as both authors exhibit an overall difference in emphasis and narrative technique, Conrad and Forster use these symbols in different ways and for different purposes, thus revealing elements of their distinctive artistic styles as well as providing comments on imperialism apart from each works' characters, setting, and plot.

There is also a spiritual or moral dimension suggested in each work that contrasts with its corresponding economic backdrop and provides insights to the more encompassing world-views of each author. Paul L. Wiley writes in *Conrad's Measure of Man*, "Conrad cares less about the state in itself as a background for his stories than about man as an individual. But he is concerned with order, or better its disappearance, in the society to which man belongs; and true order depends, finally, upon the existence of human bonds.". Similarly, while John Beer affirms that "*A Passage to India*...looks dispassionately at the phenomenon of imperialism," he quotes Forster as saying in 1960 that the novel is "really concerned with the difficulty of living in the universe.". Beer goes on to explain that while the novel indeed highlights the limitations of the ideological traditions of Empire and liberal-humanism, Forster saw a way of transcending these difficulties through "the cultivation of personal relationships [which could] nurture a core of individual resistance". Forster in particular was also attracted to the mystic traditions of Hinduism and Islam and these interests are also hinted at within the text. In various ways, both *Heart of Darkness* and *A Passage to India* make clear Conrad's and Forster's own beliefs that the moral foundations of society rest with personal relationships rather than institutions. In an imperial context this is not surprising. Brain V. Street points out in *The Savage in Literature* that "people in far-off lands communicate through various symbols and the lands no longer seem so far apart. Love and personal relationships bind those at home to those in the wilder parts of the Empire" on the limitations of the civilizing influences of industrial development.

Marxist Theory and Literary Analysis

In the Marxist tradition, works of art are analysed in terms of the historical and cultural conditions of the society in which they are produced. I feel that *Heart of Darkness* and *A Passage to India* are particularly suited to this type of approach because the set of relations between groups and classes of people that imperialism sets up, and that these two works explore, starkly reveals the contradictions within capitalism in a way that a similar piece of fiction set within one culture and dealing with characters from that culture alone cannot. Prior to the analysis however, I would like to give a brief, pertinent explanation of the Marxist approach itself and of the terms I will be using.

After years of study and research, Karl Marx published the first volume of his monumental *Das Kapital* in 1867. In it Marx presents his theory of the materialist conception of history in which the economic base of a society gives rise to and interacts in a dialectical way with the societal superstructure of culture, law, religion and art. Among other things, *Das Kapital* traces the historical development of industrial capitalism as arising out of feudalism, predicts capitalism's further evolution, and sets forth theories of class structure and class struggle. It also critiques the methods by which industrial capitalism organizes the means of production so that capital and labour are separated and held by distinct and antagonistic groups within the society. This separation overwhelmingly benefits the holders of capital, politically and economically, to the corresponding detriment of those who sell their labour. Though this is by no means an adequate summary of Marx' ideas and contributions, my aim is to provide this simple theoretical framework within which to focus on more particular elements of Marxist theory. For the purposes of this study, the Marxist views concerning imperialism, ideology, and literature will form the basis of my critical approach to the two works in question.

Marx did not use the word imperialism but he did have theories about the impact of European capitalism on non-European pre-capitalist societies and these were developed by later writers like Vladimir Lenin in his work *Imperialism: The Highest Stage of Capitalism.* Lenin describes imperialism as the "product of highly developed industrial capitalism. It consists in the striving of every industrial capitalist nation to bring under its control or to annex larger and larger areas of...territory, irrespective of what nations inhabit those regions". Though this imperial relationship between Europe and the under-developed world as defined by Lenin is certainly detectable in the historical settings of both *Heart of Darkness* and *A Passage to India,* the specific conditions, areas of the world, and historical time frames represented in each work are divergent enough to make a more specialized definition helpful. Achille Loria's article written in 1907 in which he distinguishes between two kinds of imperialism, and quoted here from Bernard Semmel's book *Imperialism and Social Reform,* is particularly useful:

> Achille Loria...drew portraits of what he called 'economic imperialism' and 'commercial imperialism.' The first he described as violent annexation on the part of old and well-

populated states of thinly populated states which because of special conditions- tropical climate, for example-cannot be colonized. This was the imperialism of the Boer War...the imperialism of capital export. 'Commercial imperialism,' on the other hand, pertained to the strengthening of bonds between the mother country and its colonies-it might mean an all-out fiscal union or simply the granting of tariff preference.

Loria's definitions of these two kinds of imperialism corresponds very well with the conditions described in each story. The economic activities described in *Heart of Darkness* are examples of "economic imperialism" in which Europeans do not settle in the area but are only there temporarily to gather and export raw materials, and the British presence in India described in *A Passage to India* more properly represents "commercial imperialism" or colonialism, in which citizens of the industrial nation actually settle in the conquered territory. The fundamental motive of both imperialisms is economic: profits are large because investment in the conquered area is minimal and native labour is cheap, and this situation is maintained by depriving the native peoples of political and economic rights. When analyzing the two works in detail, the distinction between the two forms of imperialism will help throw light on the impact these economic conditions have on the relationships of the various characters within each work.

An understanding of what ideology is and the Marxist view of its function in a capitalist society is also necessary to this study. Marx states in *The German Ideology* that "The division of labour...manifests itself also in the ruling class...so that inside this class one part appears as thinkers of the class....". The role of these thinkers is to develop and promote ideas that further solidify the power of the dominant class, which in a capitalist society is the class that controls the wealth, sometimes called the bourgeoisie. As Eagleton puts it: "The function of ideology is to legitimate the power of the ruling class in society; in the last analysis, the dominant ideas of a society are the ideas of its ruling class".

In an imperial situation, which involves an industrial state engaged with a pre-industrial society for purposes of economic gain, profit depends largely on limiting rights for the natives. James Kavanagh points out in his essay "Ideology," that such a "social situation embodies an implicit tension that can at any time erupt into open conflict, and thus every class society has certain repressive mechanisms (police, armies, courts)...to force social subjects to accept the relations of subordination and dominance between classes" (308). But ideology, defined by *Webster's Dictionary* as "the integrated assertions, theories, and aims that constitute a sociopolitical programme," is a more efficient way to manage social contradictions because it provides a comprehensive picture of the society in which social and economic inequalities are represented as natural and inevitable. The aim is to make the subordinate classes feel it would be futile to attempt to change their situation and "dominant-class subjects themselves are freer to believe that their wealth and power are after all justified".

Much of the standard British ideology regarding Empire in the late 19th and early 20th centuries conforms with two basic related themes. One body of ideological writing emphasizes Britain as the most highly developed civilization in the world and therefore asserts that the people of the regions it controls can only benefit through their exposure to Britain and its culture. A. P. Thornton, in *The Imperial Idea and Its Enemies,* encapsulates it well: "England by her traditions and institutions was the natural guardian of liberty...She must see to it that her ideas were asserted, her influence felt, and her anger feared". The other ideological theme is distinct in focusing specifically on racial and cultural differences between Europeans and native peoples. Yet Brian Street points out that racial stereotypes were already hardened before the latter half of the 19th century and "imperialism tended to use theories already worked out by scientists and which lent themselves to political manipulation". These parallel, yet interlocking, ideologies will be examined more fully in the following chapter in terms of their historical development and their prevalence in the culture and literary fiction at the time *Heart of Darkness* and *A Passage to India* were written in order to aid identification of these ideas within the texts themselves. More specifically for this study, part of my analysis will involve examining characters from both works in terms of the extent that they internalize cultural and ideological assumptions and looking at the various psychological consequences that this entails because, in this approach, individual psychology is also a social product.

The Marxist theories of literature identify it as part of a society's ideological superstructure in that literary works are "forms of perception, particular ways of seeing the world" and these, in turn, are "the products of the concrete social relations into which men enter at a particular time and place; it is the way those class-relations are experienced, legitimized, and perpetuated". But Eagleton goes on to qualify that a work of art is never "a simple reflection of a ruling class's ideas; on the contrary, it is always a complex phenomenon, which may incorporate conflicting, even contradictory views of the world". This is one reason why both *Heart of Darkness* and *A Passage to India* are so fascinating. Both works stand out as being exceptionally complex in that both present a realistic depiction of the historical circumstances in which they were written, both feature characters who espouse the ideology of the dominant culture, yet both also treat members of the "backward" countries with seriousness and sympathy as well as raising questions about the imperial mission itself in ironically drawing attention to its flaws. This all against a background of what Wendy Katz describes as "the gradually developing intensity of racism in literature [which] seems to reflect the historical shift from a relatively self-confident to a more defensive Empire". John A. McClure writes in *Kipling and Conrad* that "as the twentieth century opened, the artists and intellectuals of the age increasingly came to believe that imperial rule, if inevitable in the short run, was an inglorious enterprise that deformed both those who ruled and those who submitted". I believe that Joseph Conrad and E. M. Forster were two such artists and that the two works in question reflected their growing awareness of imperialism as an "inglorious enterprise" whether this was consciously expressed by the author(s) or not. This study will also attempt to tease out the ways in which each work both supports and subverts the imperial mission and its ideology and I will also speculate to a certain extent as to how these contradictions in the works reflected contradictions in the society in which they were written.

A Brief History of Empire

For the purposes of a Marxian analysis, which bases its analysis of literature on an understanding of the historical, political, and economic conditions in which the work is produced, it is worthwhile to give a brief historical summary of some of the major events and actual conditions of the time periods depicted in each work. Regarding *Heart of Darkness,* this will include a short history of European imperialism in Africa in the last decades of the 19th century and the effects of the Boer War. For *A Passage to India* this will include a summary of Britain's historical involvement in India and how World War I affected its position there. Both works also draw heavily on the respective authors' actual experiences, i.e. Conrad's journey to the Congo in 1890 and Forster's various travels in India before and after World War I, but this biographical information will be considered in the next chapter as an element of the critical analysis.

Ronald Hyam begins his study entitled *Britain's Imperial Century: 1815-1914* with this assertion:

British empire and expansion was a set of aspirations and activities only loosely held together, chiefly by the defining limits and overshadowing realities of the American Republic and the Indian Empire...British interests throughout the 19th century hinged upon two necessities. One was to contain or accommodate to the rival expansion generated by the Great Experiment in North America. The other was to defend the Pax Britannica in India from internal subversion and external pressure from rival European powers.

In 1815, Britain's pre-industrial empire consisted of India, Canada, the West Indies, Australia, and the Cape Colony in South Africa and as the century and the industrial revolution progressed, Britain's unique position as the only industrial power in the world gave her opportunities to develop trade without territorial possession. Not only was Britain the workshop of the world, Hyam explains, but the banker too, replacing Amsterdam as the financial capital of Europe and exporting capital in the form of investment in items necessary to expand the market like railways and mining. As "banker" of the world, Britain's activities roughly conform with Achille Loria's definition of "economic imperialism," whereas "workshop" of the world would align with Loria's "commercial imperialism." No where is the British role in "economic imperialism" seen more clearly than in the European competition over Africa in the latter part of the 19th century that resulted in its subsequent partitioning among the European imperial powers.

Hyam points out that European public attention on Africa began around 1870, though Europe had had dealings with Africa since the slave trade. By 1899, Belgium, France, Germany, Britain, Portugal, and even Italy and Spain, had carved up approximately 70 per cent of the African continent among them. British interests were scattered throughout the continent and even though Belgium controlled the Congo, the area in which *Heart of Darkness* is set, I believe Conrad's connection with Britain in his service on British ships and his naturalization as a British citizen in 1886, as well as his identification with British cultural values in his fiction and in his personal life, make his interpretation of events in Africa as British as any other English writer. British ideology regarding empire was the most developed and prevalent of any other European nation and Britain was the country Conrad chose as his adopted home. Therefore, when discussing the European presence in Africa and its portrayal in *Heart of Darkness*, I will specifically focus on Britain, especially in terms of ideology and racial attitudes, although there are many other details in the text to suggest that the story is being told from a British viewpoint. After all, the motto on the first postage stamps in the British Central Africa Protectorate was "Light in Darkness".

Hyam explains that the partition of Africa was possible because of a power vacuum in the continent left by the collapse of the Turkish Empire in North Africa and as a means to counteract the expansion of militant Islam which also had designs on African territory. Of course, Britain also had to embark on territorial acquisition to maintain her position and protect her interests in response to other countries, like France and Germany, who wanted to expand their own empires. The one widely-occuring asset that Africa had was ivory, popular since the 1820's and reaching its peak in imports into Britain in 1890, and was used for billiard balls, cutlery handles, and piano keys. London was the centre of distribution of ivory for most of the 19th century until Belgium became a competitor near the end of the century. Also by the end of the century, there was intensifying rivalry between localized European interests in Africa and rising tensions between the Europeans and natives, which resulted in a rise in atrocities against Africans and countless native revolts throughout the continent.

Inter-European rivalries came to a head in 1899 in South Africa between the British and the Boers, descendents of Dutch settlers, when it was confirmed that an area controlled by the Boers contained the largest and richest gold mine in the world. The Boers refused to grant mining rights to the British settlers and Britain was alarmed by the growing influence of German interests in the region; thus, "The question was: who was to run South Africa?".

The Anglo-Boer War lasted three years and though the British eventually triumphed, the experience heralded a rather ignominious end to Britain's imperial century. Britain's 500,000 men found it difficult to put down the 88,000 Boers in hostile and unfamiliar terrain and Britain was universally reviled for placing Boer women and children into concentration camps in which thousands died. British handling of the War and of the events leading up to it was criticized as inept, costly, and inefficient and the other imperial powers took note. Britain's reputation was damaged and many wondered if Britain could hang onto and manage its far flung territories.

These are the historical events in Africa against which *Heart of Darkness* is set. It was published during the Boer conflict and though based on an earlier trip to the Congo, Conrad could not have helped but revise his interpretation of the European presence in Africa in light of the War, as many others did in Britain. The conflict engendered a certain loss of British prestige in the international arena and a corresponding loss of self-confidence at home. A. P. Thornton writes that as a result of the war the "imperial idea...suffered a contraction, a loss of moral content, from which it never completely recovered". Britain began to seriously and publicly question its imperial mission and the reader hears an echo of this in Marlow's internal monologue. Also, native resistance was still strong and uprisings frequent as were European atrocities against the natives. All of these historical elements are present in *Heart of Darkness* making it a rich example of "realistic" fiction and a fairly typical representation of this period of European imperialism.

Britain had been present in India, through the British East India Company, since the 1600's. But when the Company lost its monopoly in 1833, the British government became more and more involved in administrating its "one piece of genuine imperial real estate". India provided Britain with cheap and mobile labour after the abolition of slavery and, from a military point of view, the Indian army made Britain a great power. India was viewed as the foundation of the British Empire, or the "jewel in the crown," and its retention was considered essential. As the 19th century progressed and the competition with other imperial powers intensified, much of British imperial policy, especially in the Middle East, centred around maintaining open trade routes with India. India differed from Africa in that the British maintained a strong and visible presence there and an entire division of the British Civil Service was devoted to its administration. Thus, India was a colony and an example of Loria's "commercial imperialism."

Though Indian uprisings occured periodically, the 1857 mutiny of the Indian Army was a turning point in Anglo-Indian relations. V. G. Kiernan characterizes it in his study *From Conquest to Collapse*: "In 1857 a war of races exploded. It was the only time in the century when a native army trained by Europe rose up against its masters". But Hyam points out that though the army mutiny was the essential trigger, it sparked a rural peasant uprising in a number of localities. Over the succeeding months, Britain was brutal in putting down the uprising, evidenced by a number of atrocities and massacres.

The Mutiny had two effects. The "native armies" were more tightly controlled and the regular British forces were increased which made British operations in India more expensive. The British government took over entirely from the East India Company and the tightening of military control also slowed political and social reform. Kiernan attests that the shadow of fear of a mutinous spirit spreading throughout the Empire lay over India for years to come and "well into the next century British soldiers coming out to India were given solemn warnings about the Mutiny, and how it might break out again". The other important result of the Mutiny-Rebellion was the "addition of hatred to indifference in the British attitude towards Indians. The 'mild Hindu' stereotype was replaced by a belief in his deceptiveness and cruelty". It was a shock for Britain to realise that their civilizing influence might not be welcomed by the Indians and the ideological veneer justifying British occupation wore off somewhat to reveal the starker realities of imperial domination.

Despite the quelling of the Mutiny, the spirit of nationalism continued to build momentum in India, evidenced by periodic and isolated uprisings, well into the early 20th century but the movement for independence was interrupted by World War I. Kiernan writes that by the time the first World War broke out in 1914 the British Empire was over-extended and vulnerable and many British were worried they would lose India but, in the end, "1,300,000 Indian soldiers were employed [in the war effort] and more than 100,000 casualities were incurred". However, after the War, native uprisings resumed and intensified as British prestige in India declined because the Indian contribution to the British war effort only increased India's aspirations for independence. This was due to one of the lessons of the War pointed out by Thornton: "Great Britain could not maintain her former world position, and therefore an overhaul of imperial strategy was necessary". India hoped that this overhaul would include eventual self-government but the 1920's wore on with no steps taken to allow India, Britain's oldest colony, to progress toward the status of other former colonies like Canada or Australia. Though it was becoming clearer to Indians and many British alike that British imperial rule of India was a 19th century concept that had no place in the new century, Britain hung on to India because it was the symbol of its might. To lose India would mean to lose its position as a major power.

A Passage to India is told against this background of political and racial turmoil in India after World War I and all the historical details mentioned above are evident or alluded to in the text. Political opinion in Britain regarding India during this time was schizophrenic, admitting home-rule for India was inevitable on the one hand and maintaining India was too backward and fragmented to govern herself on the other. Britain's anxiety at this time is explained by Thornton: "Somehow the British had to reconcile this rising nationalist spirit and the desire for self-government with the maintenance of their own power...and of imperial unity". In *A Passage to India* the British do not maintain this balancing posture with grace. Forster's treatment of the British civil servants in the novel highlights Britain's self-deception with regard to her position in India. Forster also accurately reproduces the conflicting attitudes of the Indians, especially through the characters of Aziz and his friends, who admire and resent the British at the same time. Because of the breadth of historical detail, *A Passage to India*, like *Heart of Darkness*, is a realistic representation of its time. Yet, both works not only represent but comment on historical conditions through character development, description, and plot.

Having provided some biographical and historical background for the two works in this chapter, Chapter Two will leave the "real" world and enter the "fictional" worlds created by Conrad and Forster. In this world, the reader will not only detect allusions to the actual historical conditions elucidated above, the reader will also follow the imaginative portrayals of Conrad's and Forster's fictional characters and trace how the authors represent these characters being affected and transformed by circumstances and by each other.

Cole, Sarah Conradian Alienation and Imperial Intimacy

The Johns Hopkins University Press

Sarah Cole - Conradian Alienation and Imperial Intimacy - Modern Fiction Studies 44:2 Modern Fiction Studies.Conradian Alienation and Imperial Intimacy Sarah Cole The last several decades have seen a major shift in Joseph Conrad's reputation. His status as an archetypal modernist whose fractured, convulsed narratives represent the turmoil of a literary practice at war with its past has been shaken by an assessment of the racial and gender assumptions undergirding his tales. As the language and logic of imperialism have increasingly been subjected to critical investigation, Conrad's texts have come to mark an important moment in a literary tradition defined not by its heroic break with bourgeois conventionality, but by its adherence to a Western, male world hegemony. Although literary critics on the whole have not adopted Chinua Achebe's bracing denunciation of Conrad as a "bloody racist," they nevertheless have revalued Conrad's work in the context of a discursive economy that functions in both overt and subtle ways to justify imperialism and racial hierarchy.Conversely, when Conrad is read sympathetically today, it is typically because of his modernist innovation and subsequent refusal to conform systematically to any single ideological position. In a study of Conrad's place in the adventure tradition, for instance, Andrea White concedes Conrad's problematic accession to the idea of an "imperial subject," but suggests...

Colonizers, Cannibals, and the Horror of Good Intentions in Joseph Conrad's Heart of Darkness - Critical Essay

Man can embody truth but he cannot know it." Nowhere is William Butler Yeats's adage more clearly illustrated than in the narrative of Charlie Marlow in Heart of Darkness. Throughout the text, Marlow insists upon the distinction between truth and lies; between men and women; between civilization and savagery; and, most of all, between Self and Other. Of these, the most important distinction is between Self and Other, for it is this opposition that sustains the colonial enterprise. The lure and the fear of the Other initiate the pursuit and "discovery" of colonialism; the conviction of the inferiority of the Other justifies the undertaking. Yet despite Marlow's insistence, all binary oppositions collapse in the course of his narrative: colonists prove to be conquerors, the gang of virtue is indistinguishable from the gang of greed, the illusions of women merely echo the illusions of men, and there is no clear distinction between lies and truth. Most importantly, the fundamental difference between Self and Other disappears and, with it, the unbridgeable gulf between men and women and between savage and civilized that sustains the power structure of western civilization. But this awareness offered by the text eludes Marlow for, enmeshed in his own culture, he would find this awareness "too dark—too dark altogether.

In psychological terms, the Other is but the undiscovered territory in the self. In the colonial enterprise, this territory of the unconscious is displaced onto another people who both allure and terrify. The colonizer, fearing to succumb to the Other, attempts to contain it—through subordination, suppression, or conversion. These strategies of containment are designed to preserve the opposition and inequality between Self and Other that justifies the imperialist enterprise. The central trope of imperialism is what Abdul R. JanMohamed terms "the manichean allegory" that converts racial difference "into moral and even metaphysical difference". This allegory characterizes the relationship between dominant and subordinate culture as one of ineradicable opposition. Although the opposing terms of the allegory change—good and evil, civilization and savagery, intelligence and emotion, rationality and sensuality—they are always predicated upon the assumption of the superiority of the outside evaluator and the inferiority of the native being observed.

Colonialist literature, as byproduct of the imperialist enterprise, necessarily reinscribes the manichean allegory either to confirm or to interrogate it in an effort to move beyond its limits. As a result, colonialist texts take two forms, which reflect, respectively, these two different responses: the "imaginary" and the "symbolic". These designations derive from Jacques Lacan's descriptions of sequential stages of human development. The "imaginary," according to Lacan, dates from the mirror stage of infant life, in which the child of six to eighteen months jubilantly identifies itself with its mirror image, the wholeness and integrity of which belie the internal flux and fragmentation the child experiences. Because of the unbridgeable distance of the specular image with which the child identifies, the child situates within it rivalry, opposition, and aggressivity. The relation between the self and its image, which Lacan terms "the imaginary," is one in which mirroring forestalls intersubjectivity or the interaction between two separate selves, each with its own distinct perspective.

In the "imaginary" colonialist text, JanMohamed observes, "the native functions as an image of the imperialist self in such a manner that it reveals the latter's self-alienation". This self-alienation consists in the failure to recognize as inherent within the self despised attributes the imperialist projects onto the Other. Thus, the "imaginary" colonialist text adheres to a fixed opposition between the self and the native, insisting upon the homogeneous identity of the indigenous population and taking refuge in the "superior," more "enlightened," and more "civilized" perspective of the dominant culture. Interpreted through the narrative perspective of Marlow, Heart of Darkness exemplifies the "imaginary" colonialist text.

The second type of colonialist fiction, the "symbolic," parallels the stage at which the young child, once having become convinced of its wholeness and integrity, is able to recognize and identify with an imago or subject-image as a counterpart; and is then able to enter into a dialectic that links the self or I "with socially elaborated situations". At this stage, the child is able to enter into social exchange, dialogue, and relationship. An equivalent stage in culture would make possible a dialectic encounter between Self and Other in which the dominant culture is able to bracket its own values and thus radically to question its basis for cultural inference and interpretation. Such a dialectic or exchange would aim at resolving cultural oppositions through syncretic solutions. Such, I would argue, is the larger narrative perspective of Heart of Darkness, which exposes the limitations and self-contradiction of Marlow's views to open up a complex dialogue on issues of history, culture, race, and gender. Thus the entirety of Heart of Darkness attempts to deal with the Other in symbolic terms, although Marlow is able to deal with the other only in the realm of the Imaginary.

First Descents Into The Inferno: Parallel Ideology And Experience In Conrad's 'Heart Of Darkness' And Dostoevsky's Notes From The House Of The Dead

Dr Robert Berry
English Department
University of Otago

Few critics would dispute the profoundly shaping nature of Conrad's 1890 voyage along the river Congo. Frederic R Karl assesses the episode as "momentous in Conrad's work" A letter written from Kinshasa to his aunt and confidante Marguerite Poradowska suggests the harrowing psychological impact of Conrad's 1890 journey:

> Decidedly I regret having come here. I even regret it bitterly... Everything here is repellent to me. Men and things, but men above all. (Collected Letters of Conrad 1 62).

Conrad's reaction registers not just his revulsion, but his sense of profound isolation and alienation in this thoroughly hostile environment. When nearly a decade later Conrad came to fictionalize these emotions in 'Heart of Darkness' (1899), the deep unease suggested by this earlier letter had developed into a language evoking nightmare, even supernatural experience. Marlow, narrating his voyage up the river, admits to feeling:

> Bewitched and cut off for ever from everything [he] had known once — [he is] somewhere — far away — in another existence perhaps. ('Heart of Darkness' Dent Ed. 93)

Dostoevsky, writing to his brother Mikhail in 1854, recalls a moment of similar uncertainty and isolation. As a political convict, Dostoevsky had to endure the interminable 3000 kilometre march from central European Russia to Siberia. The Ural mountains, traditionally viewed by Russians as the barrier separating a civilized West from the relative barbarism of an Asian East, marked for Dostoevsky a significant departure point into an unknown, new world:

> The moment of crossing the Urals was a sad one... There was snow and a snowstorm all around; the border of Europe, Siberia ahead and an enigmatic fate in it, all the past behind. (Dostoevsky's Letters 1 185)

Six years later, in his Memoirs from the House of the Dead (1860), Dostoevsky's fictional narrator Goryanchikov admits to feeling he has been transported, like Marlow, into another realm. The convict has left behind all that seemed familiar and reassuring, to enter a terrifying alien domain:

> unlike anything else; here were our own laws, our own dress, our own manners and customs... a life like none other upon earth, and people who were special, set apart.

It is important to note the parallel positions of each narrator here. Marlow and Goryanchikov are both perplexed, horrified and profoundly intrigued by their new environments. Like the Roman colonialists Marlow cites at the beginning of 'Heart of Darkness' (1899), living in "the midst of the incomprehensible" has a "fascination... that goes to work upon him" ('Heart of Darkness' 50). He becomes an observer trying to unravel and interpret the human (and inhuman) scenes before him, on what is a voyage of exploration in the fullest sense. Significantly, the Russian critic Konstantin Mochulsky sees Goryanchikov's narrative function in much the same way:

> A new, peculiar world had been opened before [his] astonished gaze. But he is not confined by a description of its surface; he strives to enter it inwardly, to understand the 'law' of this world, to penetrate its mystery.

In many ways, Conrad's Marlow and Dostoevsky's Goryanchikov will finally attain, in their new worlds, knowledge which lead them to draw surprisingly parallel conclusions as to the nature and evil potential of the human personality. Joseph Frank, in a passage equally applicable to Conrad, speaks of Dostoevsky's prison years bringing the writer "into firsthand contact with a terrifyingly expansive diapason of human experience" (Through the Russian Prism 126). The initial reaction of both fictional narrators, however, is not one of forthcoming illumination, but rather of profound terror. Marlow's overriding response to his journey is that it has taken him into "some lightless region of subtle horrors". Similarly Goryanchikov typifies his early experience as "a hell, a dark night of the soul" It is striking to note, in culminating passages of 'Heart of Darkness' (1899) and The House of the Dead (1860), how both Conrad and Dostoevsky make reference to an existing body of imagery to intensify the record of their individual experiences. They create their worlds, as I will now show, using a language that stongly recalls, even aligns, their narratives with an earlier literary voyage — that of Dante's underworld journey through Hell in The Divine Comedy (c. 1308 - 1321).

In the celebrated 'Bath-House' scene of The House of the Dead (1860), Dostoevsky creates arguably his most extensive nightmare vision of the convict world. Opening the door into the prison baths in Part One, Goryanchikov suspects he has walked directly into hell:

> Imagine a room about twelve paces long and roughly the same in width, into which were packed as many as one hundred, or probably at the very least eighty men at once... steam swathed one's eyes, soot, dirt, the place so crowded that

there was nowhere to stand... a mass of humanity seethed. On the whole floor area there was not a space the size of a man's palm on which the convicts were not sitting huddled splashing themselves from their tubs.

The scene here is one of unbearable human constriction. R L Jackson, writing in The Art of Dostoevsky (1981), aptly describes the passage as evoking " a veritable hell of disfigured, fragmented, compacted humanity". The visual thrust of Goryanchikov's narrative, I would argue, depends much on a body of imagery that can be traced back to Dante. Crossing the Acheron in the Third Canto, the Italian Pilgrim is awestruck at the sight of an "interminable train of/souls" tightly thronged together, trailing off towards their respective punishments. Throughout the Inferno, Dante the Pilgrim continues to encounter such scenes. In 'The Circle of the Heretics', to take one example, sinners are thrust in unthinkable numbers into cramped, burning tombs. The image of a compacted damned is one that comes to colour the entire process of the Dantean underworld experience. Although it would be laboured to insist upon any direct derivation here, it is certainly significant to note the parallel imagery and tone of Dostoevsky's own evocation.

To counterbalance his visual scene, Dostoevsky creates an accompanying nightmare world of sound. Goryanchikov, now among the convicts, tells us that:

All was yammering and cackling, accompanied by the sound of a hundred chains being dragged along the floor... Some men, wanting to get through, became entangled in the chains caught on the heads of those who were sitting lower down; they would fall cursing and dragging behind them those with whom they had become entangled. Filthy water poured everywhere. Everyone was in a kind of intoxicated, aroused state of mind; shrieks and cries reverberated. (The House of the Dead 156)

Despite its indisputable autonomous power, it is possible to see Dostoevsky being influenced here by an earlier tradition of aural imagery. Depictions of the screaming damned have been prolific in all periods of Christian literature, starting with the Bible. It is arguably the visionary legacy of the medieval imagination, however, which has shaped more recent European conceptions of Hell. Dante offers what might be claimed as a primary model. Passing through the vestibule that leads to the underworld, Dante's Pilgrim receives what Mark Musa describes as "an acoustical impression of Hell in its entirety" ('Commentary', Inferno 94):

> *Here sighs and cries and shrieks of lamentation*
> *echoed throughout the starless air of Hell;*
> *... tongues confused, a language strained in anguish*
> *with cadences of anger, shrill outcries*
> *and raucous groans... (Inferno, Canto 3 90)*

This early sound-impression develops into a recurrent image characterizing the Inferno, an image that has proved immeasurably fertile throughout Western literature. Its shaping influence on Dostoevsky's passage seems indisputable. Indeed the sights and sounds invoked in the 'Bath-House' scene strongly suggest a possibly conscious decision on Dostoevsky's part to create a world of horror that will parallel Dante's earlier, consummate example. In concluding the episode, the narrator Goryanchikov pays oblique homage to this fact:

> It occured to me that if at some later date we should all find ourselves together in hell, it would be very similar to this place. (House of the Dead)

The journey into Siberia, to cite Dante, has taken the convict into a physical, and moral, landscape of "pain and ugly anguish" (Inferno, Canto 9 151). By applying this Dantean frame of reference, Dostoevsky is able to substantially intensify the mood of horror that initially overwhelms his narrator's senses.

Leaving Europe for Africa, Marlow admits to feeling that "instead of going to the centre of a continent, I was about to set off for the centre of the earth" ('Heart of Darkness' 19). Throughout 'Heart of Darkness' (1899), he persistently reiterates the sense of "peculiar blackness" that characterizes the entire process of his journey. Like Dostoevsky, Conrad draws on the same early literature to intensify the nightmare sensation of Marlow's experience. Investigating Dante's influence on Conrad's text, one critic, Robert Evans, boldly suggests a "close structural parallel between 'Heart of Darkness' and [the] Inferno", elaborately equating the river trading posts with specific circles of Hell. Though such interpretations might seem too narrow, they do alert us to some important similarities. Nowhere, I would argue, does the conscious Dantean associations seem stonger than in Conrad's central 'Grove of Death' episode.

Exploring the chaos of the first river station in the early stages of his journey, Marlow discovers a group of dying blacks, victims of the colonialists' futile efforts at railway building. His initial response to the scene is telling:

> My purpose was to stroll into the shade for a moment; but no sooner within than it seemed to me I had stepped into the gloomy circle of some Inferno.

From the outset, Marlow draws a parallel between his forthcoming experience and Dante's model. Through this introductory reference, Conrad subtly creates a nightmarish apprehension even prior to Marlow's narrative.The debt to Dante is further in evidence in Conrad's realization of the grove:

> Black shapes crouched, lay, sat between the trees leaning against the trunks, clinging to the earth, half coming out, half effaced within the dim light, in all the attitudes of pain, abandonment, and despair.

This landspace of pain boldly recreates Dante's example. It clearly summons the visual world of prostrated bodies met with throughout the Inferno. Furthermore, it is cast in a language of hyperbole traditionally associated with epic poetry. Conrad's "black shapes" are not only lying, they are crouching, sitting, leaning, clinging: their 'attitude' is not merely one of pain, but "pain, abandonment, and despair." The literary method encountered here is regularly encountered in Dante's text. Leaving the 'Wood of Suicides" in Canto

Fourteen, to cite one contrasting passage, the Pilgrim builds a visual picture of the damned using a language that similarly compounds and reiterates diverse physical movement:

Many separate herds of naked souls I saw,
all weeping desperately...
Some souls were stretched out flat upon their backs,
others were crouched there all tightly hunched,
some wandered, never stopping, round and round.
(Inferno Canto 14 197)

It is interesting that in developing the scene, Marlow, like Dostoevsky's narrator, also focusses upon the extreme human distortion and physical dislocation of the sufferers. The appalling nightmare world, in fact, most resembles a scene of torture. Dying blacks are described as "bundles of acute angles [who] sat with their legs drawn up"; all round they are "scattered in every pose of contorted collapse". The sight, Marlow judges, is akin to "some picture of a massacre or a pestilence".With this closing reference, the narrator in effect directs us towards an unspecified, but recognizable, tradition of visual imagery, in order to more clearly define and underpin the nature of his own scene. Classical literary 'pictures' of "massacre" and "pestilence" are of course part of the normal mental furniture of the modern reader. One of the primary sources for such an imagery, and perhaps Conrad's conscious point of reference, is again Dante. Entering the 'Circle of Sorcerers' in the Twentieth Canto, in one notable instance, the Pilgrim observes a scene of human deformation that might be cited as a prototext for Conrad's' own grove of twisted humanity:

I saw people in the valley's circle,
silent, weeping, walking at a litany pace
the way processions push along in our world.
And when my gaze moved down below their faces,
I saw all were incredibly distorted,
The chin was not above the chest, the neck
was twisted — their faces looked down on their backs.
(Inferno, 20 251)

The angular disfigurement suffered by the exploited blacks and Dante's sinners are in notable accord. Indeed critics have not been slow, particularly in this episode, to note the strong parallels with the Inferno. F R Karl, to take just one example, speaks of Marlow's "Dantesque... journey underground", but does not pursue his point of contrast. For him, it is enough to say Conrad's narrator has walked" into the mouth of Hell". Though the general validity of this observation is indisputable, further investigation does profitably reveal just how close the links are between Conrad's text and the Inferno. Like Goryanchikov's Siberian world of "foul air... clanking fetters... curses and shameless laughter", Conrad's use of Dantean imagery allows him to realise an environment of complete moral horror, a world where shocking insights into the evil capacity of the human spirit will be possible. It is to the nature of these insights, won in Africa and Siberia, that I shall now turn.

Concluding a scene of intense brutality in Part Two of The House of the Dead (1860), Goryanchikov reflects with disgust and incredulity how hard it is "to imagine the degree to which human nature may become distorted". For narrator, and reader, the record of convict life is a shocking initiation into a realm where man is innately capable of the most 'bestial proclivities".Goryanchikov uncovers intrinsic moral depravity and lawlessness of spirit, a world where mankind is scrupulously observed taking the deepest pleasure in "gratuitous cruelty" Indeed Dostoevsky's vision of human perversity is extraordinary, providing studies of invididual convicts, even case histories, which chart examples of sometimes overwhelming human barbarism.

Like Goryanchikov, Marlow, in Jeremy Hawthorn's opinion, is similarly "unprepared for the levels of brutality... he is to encounter" in the Congo. Early on, he admits to feeling "secretly appalled" by the human scenes that confront him.Later on of course, the focus is turned exclusively towards an account of the "unspeakable" behaviour of Kurtz. Whereas Dostoevsky can frankly articulate the psychology and actions of the convicts, detailing their appalling homicidal and sexual drives, the delicate sensibilities of a late Victorian audience made it difficult for Conrad to employ the same degree of openness. The record of Kurtz's barbarism, therefore, is less explicit, though more subtle, in its realization. As Marlow himself admits, it is "not so much told as suggested... in desolate exclamations... in interrupted phrases, in hints". Despite this complexity, the account of Kurtz provides an alarming case study of what man can become when freed from all inhibiting social restrictions. The principal concern of Marlow, and Goryanchikov, however, is not to signal just fear, but to define the actual nature of this human barbarism, to discover some of the primary 'drives' behind such brutality. It is significant to note how both narrators isolate similar characteristics, and offer parallel explanations, to account for this human descent into primaeval savagery.

In The House of the Dead (1860), the first of Goryanchikov's close studies concentrates on the twisted nature of the convict Gazin. Introducing this "fearsome individual", Goryanchikov suspects "there could be nothing more violent and monstrous than this man". He highlights the sensual pleasure, the barbaric relish, Gazin derives from his murderous acts:

> There was... a story that he [Gazin] had been fond of murdering little children, purely for pleasure: he would take the child away to some convenient spot; first he would frighten and torture it, then, delighting in the terror and quaking of his poor little victim, he would quietly and voluptuously slit its throat.

What is perhaps the most striking feature of Gazin's murder is that it seems a routine expression, an accepted part, of the man's own nature. There can be no question of any moral guilt arising from his act; Gazin's mood is one of purely carnal and beast-like satisfaction at a kill. In a later episode, Goryanchikov turns to another convict, the bandit Korenyev, describing him as "just like a wild animal." As with Gazin, this man is motivated by the same brutal, sexual drives, but here the narrator isolates the reasons behind his disintegration.

Korenyev's "savage desire for physical pleasure, for sexual passion and carnal satisfaction" is traced to what Goryanchikov terms his shocking "spiritual indifference." He is a human example of the complete triumph of the body over the spirit — "the flesh" has gained, in Goryanchikov's words, supreme "ascendancy over all his [Korenyev's] mental qualities".

The descent into primitive savagery is linked, therefore, to the complete breakdown of an inner spiritual code. Deprived entirely of his moral dimension, Goryanchikov implies, man's regression into murderous violence and complete sexual debauch becomes a real possibility.

Though the connection is observed in Gazin and Korenyev, its clearest definition is reserved for Goryanchikov's later account of the aristocrat convict A-v. In him, the narrator depicts his "most revolting example" of human degradation; here is an individual who has become "a monster, a moral Quasimodo". Goryanchikov points to "resolute depravity" and "complete moral collapse" on a scale even he finds remarkable (104). A-v is, in fact, no longer recognizable as 'human': he is: a kind of lump of meat, with teeth and a stomach, and an insatiable craving for the coarsest, most bestial physical pleasures, to obtain the least and most whimsical of which he was capable of knifing, of cold-blooded murder.

In this study, Goryanchikov very specifically defines the cause of A-v's total moral disintegration.In his analysis, such overwhelming depravity is created when "the physical side of man" is "unrestrained by any inner norm or set of laws". Applying these observations on a more universal basis, Goryanchikov goes on to insist that within every individual there exists a "sacred limit", defined by the laws of society and personal prejudice. Should this fragile boundary be violated, man experiences the "irresistible longing to overshoot all... to delight in the most unbridled and boundless freedom". Such 'freedom' inevitably expresses itself in the form of violence. In Siberia, in effect, Goryanchikov is able to closely survey what in 'normal society' remains a submerged, but primary human drive. The convict world is, in this sense, a microcosm where Dostoevsky's narrator observes in detail man's innate capacity for barbarism in an extreme, yet entirely valid, form. The scene Dostoevsky was exposed to in Siberia, in fact, convinced the mature writer that animal savagery formed a vital part of the human condition. In his The Diary of a Writer (1873-1881), the author refers to the "alluvial barbarism" he believes is one foundation of the human spirit. The Siberian experience, in this respect, provides Dostoevsky with his first personal evidence that:

In every man... a demon lies hidden — the demon of rage, the demon of lustful heat at the screams of the tortured victim, the demon of lawlessness let off the chain.

At its bleakest, The House of the Dead(1860) is a chilling account of man's capacity to perform "superhuman inhumanities" against his fellow man. Within this broad framework, however, Dostoevsky does point to a further dimension of this primitive drive. In close analysis, his narrator isolates man's intrinsic desire to exercise power, to assert his dominating influence over other weaker individuals. In some harrowing case studies, Goryanchikov highlights what he proves to be a stongly developed faculty; he depicts individuals who derive an absolute relish from their "sense of mastery" over others. At the centre of this interest is one man given full autocratic authority, the prison lieutenant Zherebyatnikov. In his official position, he is able to exercise his instinctual urge to dominate without fear of recourse.

The brutalized Siberian environment acts as a catalyst, and encourages the emergence of powerful, primary impulses, which might ordinarily be kept in firm check. Goryanchikov shows how the human urge to power can result in truly barbaric tyranny. To support his thesis, the narrator details the unbridled sensual pleasure Zherebyatnikov derives from admininistering beatings. In his role as "executioner", the incensed lieutenant is clearly seen to revel in his power to inflict pain. In what is a compelling scene, the autocrat toys with his convict victim. At first Zherebyatnikov hints at a merciful reprieve, plainly gratified by the man's helpless pleas. Having secured his naive trust, the inevitable about-face occurs, and the convict is subjected to severe corporal punishment. The whole process records a man intoxicated by his unlimited ascendancy over another individual. At the height of the scene, Goryanchikov details the lieutenant's wild, yet profound animal satisfaction at the exercise of his power:

> 'Mangle him!' Zherebyatnikov would below at the top of his voice — 'Burn him! Thrash him, flog him! Set him alight! More, more! Hit the orphan harder, hit the villain harder! Hammer him, hammer him!' And the soldiers would lay into the man as hard as they could, the poor wretch would see sparks, he would begin to yell, and Zherebyatnikov would run along the line after him, laughing and laughing, bursting, holding his sides with laughter, unable to straighten up.

A "craving for absolute power" becomes, in Robert Jackson's opinion, a clearly defined human value in Dostoevsky's mature world picture. The validity of Jackson's observation is quickly substantiated by the important reflections which follow the Zherebyatnikov episode. Raising the argument onto a universal level, Goryanchikov suggests that "the qualities of the executioner are found in embryonic form in almost every modern person". Should these primitive dominating impulses be allowed to develop, as in Zherebyatnikov, they may entirely overwhelm "all a person's other qualities". In Goryanchikov's assessment, should any man attain "unlimited mastery over the body, blood, and spirit of another human being", or experience the "complete freedom to degrade another creature", he will, by a natural process, inevitably become "a fearsome monster". The exercise of absolute power intoxicates and stupifies the individual, leading him into a brutish despotism. Though Siberia might provide examples of this primitive urge at its most extreme, Goryanchikov nevertheless insists that, in 'normal society', there do exist people who "are like tigers, [people] who thirst for blood to lick". The lust for domination, in his final assessment, is a fundamental driving force of the human personality.

In many respects, The House of the Dead (1860) can be viewed as a major anthropological document. The insights into human psychology achieved by Goryanchikov in Omsk go to form an essential base upon which Dostoevsky builds his mature vision of man and his motivating drives. The thirst for absolute personal power becomes, to take just one instance, a central part of Raskolnikov's intellectual dilemma in Crime and Punishment (1866). He strives, by the act of murder, to prove himself an 'extraordinary man', an all-powerful Napoleon figure able, and wanting, to trample on social convention and even human life. All Dostoevsky's late novels, of course, are centred around acts of murder; man's elemental destructive energy is constantly a prime focus of the author's work.

The prototype for Rogozhin, whose violent and consuming sexual passion for Nastasya plays such a vital role in The Idiot (1869), might easily be traced back to Dostoevsky's sketches of convict figures like Gazin and Korenyev, men equally unable to restrain their native homicidal and carnal impulses. The penetrating insights into the human personality recorded in the prison memoirs are, at a fundamental level, seen to colour all Dostoevsky's mature writings. In a famous passage from his diary, the author speaks memorably of his need 'to find the man in man'. An essential aspect of the human condition — what Emile Zola called "La bete humaine" (the beast in man) — is unquestionably revealed and documented in this early prison narrative.

I shall now turn to 'Heart of Darkness' (1899), a work I feel serves a similar function to The House of the Dead (1860). For it lays the principal philosophical foundations for Conrad's own mature vision of mankind, a vision which approximates to Dostoevsky's world picture on several, important issues.

Writing in The Art of Dostoevsky (1981), Robert Jackson speaks of the "outer and inner landscapes of violence" that exist in Goryanchikov's prison narrative. In his opinion, "there is a steady descent" in The House of the Dead(1860) into "the misery and degradation" that is part of "man and human nature". On a fundamental level, Marlow's 'tale' in 'Heart of Darkness'(1899) can be seen to follow a similar formula. The attempts to define the actions and psychology of Kurtz closely chart a process Marlow himself terms as "the awakening of forgotten and brutal instincts". Indeed the process is all the more remarkable because of the seemingly extreme metamorphosis of Kurtz's personality. From the fragmentary evidence Marlow provides, one suspects a deeply cultured, 'civilized' spirit existing in pre-African Kurtz. The man's initial idealism, for example, is discussed by company agents at the first river post. Each trading station, in their record of Kurtz's early vision, was to be "like a beacon on the road towards better things, a centre for trade of course, but also for humanizing, improving, instructing". The statement, one feels, records Kurtz's genuine commitment, and cannot be equated with the "philanthropic pretence" of the other 'pilgrims'. Kurtz, futhermore, is variously described as a gifted musician, a painter, and a talented political orator. By normal Western definitions, he is a man of remarkable intellectual and spiritual refinement. Like Siberia, however, Africa proves to be an environment where "the dissolution of all controls and norms" is possible. "Out there", Marlow admits, "there were no external checks".

There exist in the Congo none of the usual restraining social forces, what the narrator whimsically refers to as the butcher and the policeman round every corner to define the boundaries of so-called permissible behaviour. Isolated from such potent symbols of order, the 'civilized' face of man soon proves to be a fragile veneer thinly disguising other dormant, but powerful, impulses. Alone and unchecked, quite a different human state begins to emerge. It is in solitude that Kurtz first begins to make discoveries about his real, inner nature. As Marlow tells us, the wilderness "had whispered to him things about himself which he did not know, things of which he had no conception". In this "region of the first ages", we are told, Kurtz discovers in himself an innate, even boundless capacity for brutal savagery. As with Goryanchikov's convicts, this urge would seem to be quantifiable as both murderous and carnal.

As I noted earlier however, Marlow's impressionistic account makes it difficult for us to define precisely the exact character of Kurtz's barbarism. Whereas Goryanchikov leaves us in little doubt as to his convict's animal depravity, Marlow tends, in Marvin Mudrick's judgment, "to persuade the reader by epithets, exclamations, ironies, by every technical obliquity — into an hallucinated awareness" of Kurtz's psychology and actions. Despite this essential difference in authorial technique, Mudrick nevertheless feels that in Kurtz Conrad does achieve a complete picture of "unplumable depravity... [of] primal unanalyzable evil".

At the Station, and during his extended sorties into the wilderness, Kurtz's "soul", in Marlow's opinion, has become "satiated with primitive emotions". In a language that remains defiantly generalized, but retains its heightened, exclamatory quality, even the numbed Marlow points to the "abominable", "monstrous", "unspeakable" quality of Kurtz's passions. Pure, unrestrained brutality is of course perfectly symbolized by the row of heads on stakes which surrounds the river compound. That this primitive drive, as in Dostoevsky, also incorporates a powerful sexual dimension is strongly implied by further remarks. Kurtz's dissolution, we are told, has reached a "colossal scale", to the point where he completely abandons himself to the "gratification of his various lusts".

He has surrendered himself entirely to base, primal instincts; he has become absolute victim to what Marlow terms "his vile desires". In an infamous snapshot vision in 'Heart of Darkness' (1899), Marlow refers to Kurtz secretly presiding "at certain midnight dances ending with unspeakable rites". Various critics, most notably Stephen Reid, have attempted to quantify the exact nature of these "rites" (45-54). Citing Sir James Frazer's study of West African civilizations in The Golden Bough (1890-1915) to support his thesis, Reid suggests these "rites" involve Kurtz in scenes of bestiality, human sacrifice, and even cannibalism. Though his investigation is unquestionably illuminating, it nevertheless ignores, even denies, the enormous suggestive quality of Conrad's image.

For without attendant detail, the image 'per se' masterfully conveys the chilling completeness of Kurtz's surrender to his native, savage impulses.

There is much compelling evidence to support the view that Marlow does not wish his listeners to consider Kurtz's degeneration as a purely isolated case. Kurtz's descent into animal barbarism (as with Dostoevsky's convicts) might represent an extreme example, but it is nevertheless indicative of a larger capacity for savagery that exists in all men. It is significant to note, in a 1903 letter to Kazimierz Waliszewski, how Conrad stresses the "great care" he took "to give Kurtz a cosmopolitan origin". Marlow, as well, reminds us that "all Europe contributed to the making of Kurtz". Indeed in this respect the figure of Kurtz assumes the role of 'Everyman'. Allayed to this is Marlow's own recognition that a latent primitive barbarism exists in himself. In his work Conrad the Novelist (1958), Albert Guerard points to Marlow as a "secret sharer" in Kurtz's violent world. In his opinion, Marlow experiences an almost psychic identification with Kurtz's mental state. Even before their meeting, I would argue, Marlow's encounter with what he calls "prehistoric man" cursing and howling at him from the banks of the river, proves him receptive to the primal savaagery present in his own nature. In a telling passage, he admits to sharing a "remote kinship" with the scene of "wild and passionate uproar". In a brief glimpse of tribal mankind, Marlow forges subtle emotional and intellectual bonds:

If you were man enough [he argues] you would admit to yourself that there was in you just the faintest trace of a response to the terrible frankness of that noise, a dim suspicion of there being a meaning in it which you — you so remote from the night of first ages — could comprehend.

Marlow's journey along the river, and his encounter with Kurtz, are truly an initiation into the dark heart of man; man who, irrespective of modern society's so-called civilizing values, still retains his essentially primitive homicidal and sexual identity. In conversation with Raskolnikov at the end of Crime and Punishment (1866), Dostoevsky's character Svidrigailov reflects on man's vast appetite for violent, sexual "'vice'". Such "'vice'", in his belief, is "'something that is founded on nature... something that is always there in your blood, like a piece of red-hot coal'". The conclusion Svidrigailov draws on this occasion, can safely be said to reflect Dostoevsky's own mature philosophy, a philosophy very much born out of the writer's passage through Siberia. Similarly, Conrad's fictionalized journey through the Congo is a learning process, what Ian Watt aptly describes as "a spiritual voyage of discovery". In this sense, it fulfills a similar function to Dostoevsky's prison narrative. Indeed Marlow himself admits that his experiences seem "somehow to throw a kind of light on everything". Like Goryanchikov's insights, Marlow's anthropological discoveries exert a profound shaping influence on Conrad's entire, mature vision of human nature.

Marlow's observations, however, also extend beyond a primary vision of innate human savagery. For Kurtz, like Dostoevsky's Zherebyatnikov, is seen to be motivated by a craving to wield absolute power. In his "unlawful soul", Marlow affirms, there exists the urge to assert a tyrannizing domination over others. It is to this aspect of Conrad's narrative that I shall now turn.

There are clear indications, in the final part of Marlow's narrative, that Kurtz has assumed the status of Man-God in the eyes of his adopted lakeside tribe. Indeed writing in his 'pamphlet', Kurtz suggests that all white men must naturally appear to these "savages" as "supernatural beings". "We approach them", he insists, "with the might as of a deity". Listening to the Harlequin's account of Kurtz's activities, Marlow comes to recognize the particular truth behind this improbable claim; in the narrator's final estimation, Kurtz has indeed achieved a "power to charm or frighten rudimentary souls into an aggravated witch-dance in his honour". Though Kurtz's 'pamphlet' envisages the use of such power for "practically unbounded... Benevolence", the reality of its exercise proves to be quite different. His "ascendancy" neither manifests itself in acts of civilizing philanthropy or altruism, to adopt Marlow's ironic paraphrasing. For here, as in Dostoevsky's universe, absolute power inevitably realises itself in tyranny.

From Marlow's oblique, yet evocative conversation with the young Russian trader, one is able to piece together a reasonable picture of Kurtz's recent conduct. The 'Harlequin' recounts that the man would disappear into the wilderness for weeks, where he would live in tribal villages. There he would "forget himself... forget himself — you know". The Russian's brief dialogue is pregnant with those "unspeakable" hints, those hidden, yet loaded meanings, which are a characteristic feature of Conrad's text. Kurtz, he continues, "could be very terrible"; his "ascendancy" over the tribe was "extraordinary". They "adored" him, they are said to "crawl" before him. The drying heads that surround the station, we are further told, are the heads of "rebels", men who have disputed Kurtz's right to absolute power. From these fleeting, but potent images, Marlow himself judges that Kurtz has indeed "taken a high seat amongst the devils of the land — I mean literally". It must be clearly stressed that Kurtz's Man-God status, through foisted upon him, is something he nevertheless accepts with profound gratification, in fact with relish. Such a thesis is supported by the 'Harlequin's' account of an argment with Kurtz over ivory. Recalling the scene for Marlow, the Russian reports:

> He [Kurtz] declared he would shoot me unless I gave him the ivory and then cleared out of the country, because he could do so, and had a fancy for it, and there was nothing on earth to prevent him killing whom he jolly well pleased. And it was true, too.

As with Dostoevsky's Zherebyatnikov, one recognizes the element of almost breathless hysteria in this paraphrase of Kurtz's words. Kurtz is clearly wildly intoxicated by the exercise of his complete, anarchistic power. For Kurtz everything and anything is now permitted, and the experience proves to be profoundly, indeed sensuously, gratifying. In remote isolation, in fact, a latent human capacity for tyranny has come to the fore, a tyranny characterized by its frenzied, animal brutality. Marlow himself admits that, in his contacts with Kurtz, he must now "deal with a being... [he cannot appeal to] in the name of anything high or low". Away from the restrictions of normal society, in the vacuum of Africa, Kurtz has been free to realise his inner, fundamental drives. Despite his genuine idealism, his belief that power might be put to purely philanthropic, civilizing ends, Kurtz's vision proves brittle and insubstantial when challenged by more rooted forces which exist as part of man's ancient psychological heritage. In many respects, the figure of Kurtz can be viewed as Conrad's first major anthropological statement; he is the prototpe for a whole Conradian universe where man shows himself to be entirely egocentric. Indeed Kurtz's image can be traced to its full fruition in later novels such as Nostromo (1904), a work in which man is consistently exposed as brutally self-seeking, once he is possessed of power. In 'Heart of Darkness'(1899), the postscriptum Marlow discovers attached to Kurtz's 'document' is itself a lasting testimony to the inevitable decline of the human spirit, should it be given the freedom to exert total dominance. Under such conditions, a brutal regime of tyranny — even Kurtz's insane call to slaughter weaker individuals, "to exterminate the brutes!" — becomes a real and horrifying possibility.

Essentially, Marlow observes in Kurtz not only one individual's fall, but a universal process of human disintegration of which all mankind is infinitely suspectible. In fact from one perspective, the whole imperialist 'adventure' recounted in 'Heart of Darkness' (1899) can be seen as the perfect collective expression of man's natural craving to dominate. Early in the text Marlow speaks of the active "conquest of the earth, which mostly means taking it away from those who have a different complexion or slightly flatter noses than ourselves". His statement, read on one level, reduces human experience to a power struggle, to a process where the strong seem almost impelled, by their very nature, to oppress weaker societies and individuals. In a famous passage from Nostromo (1904), the financier Holroyd, with facetious arrogance but perhaps also profound insight, speculates on a future world dominated by those now in power. The leaders, Holroyd suggests, will be essentially at the mercy of their own deepest instincts. Ironically, they will be powerless to prevent their own eventual supremacy in a world where the natural human order is essentially one of oppression and dominance.

As in Dostoevsky's world, the lust for power is shown to extend very deeply into man's being. Even in the most minor incidents in 'Heart of Darkness' (1899), the 'pilgrims' consistently display an almost unconscious urge to assert their dominance. On the long land trek to the Station for example, Marlow is accompanied by a sick agent being carried by natives on a stretcher. When this heavy man is abandoned by his exhausted carriers, his first cry is essentially tyrannic in character. Indeed Marlow reports that the man is "very anxious" for him "to kill somebody" at once. Similarly, following the arson attack at the Central Station, Marlow focuses our attention on a powerless black, who has been falsely accused of being the perpetrator of the fire. He is subjected to what seems an almost habitually brutal beating. Though these incidents are specifically acts of colonial aggression, they can nevertheless be regarded as entirely valid outbreaks of a larger capacity — that native urge to assert power which exists in all men.

Like The House of the Dead (1860), Conrad's novel can be regarded, finally, as a document charting the essentially violent and primitive character of man. Indeed for both writers, man remains essentially a victim of his own rooted homicidal and carnal identity. Not only this, he is seen to derive intense gratification from the brutal assertion of his own authority. From their respective observations and character studies, Conrad and Dostoevsky do distil a significantly common philosophy. It might seem surprising, in mature works particularly, to find both authors in such major ideological accord. If anything, Conrad can be said to deepen his initial responses into what is a profoundly fatalistic view of the human condition. Man, proven violent and despotic in 'Heart of Darkness' (1899), remains irretrievably corrupt in most of the later writing. The vast gallery of depraved humanity recorded by Nostromo (1904) only emphasizes this point. Figures like Sotillo and Pedro Montero are shown, as Kurtz was, to be wholly governed by their savage lust for power, by their brutally murderous capacity for greed. To the "violent men" of the Campo, to take just one example, Montero is said to appear as "little removed from a state of utter savagery". In fact Nostromo (1904) tends to augment, even darken, the quality of Conrad's earlier convictions.

Dostoevsky, similarly, continues to acknowledge the central importance of his belief in man's primitive character. In The Brothers Karamazov (1881), Dmitry Karamazov repeatedly draws attention to what he calls the "insect lust" active in himself. He knows he is irresistibly drawn to the "back alley"; that part of his nature demands that he should "sink in filth and stench at his own free will and with enjoyment". Even Aloysha Karamazov, striving for religious and spiritual purity, pays homage to the degraded sensuality he feels living in his own spirit. He senses the real truth behind his brother's accusation that, "Angel as you are, that insect lives in you, too, and will stir up a tempest in your blood". Though Dostoevsky of course insisted on the existence of a spiritual dimension in man, he nevertheless consistently paid tribute to the enormous strength of this underlying primitive personality. To further illustrate the importance of this point, it is profitable to cite Prince Myshkin. With his Idiot, Dostoevsky fought to create what would be his "wholly beautiful individual". Despite Myshkin's Christ-like purity, however, Dostoevsky was forced to acknowledge his character's identification, indeed in his dark bond, with the murderous world of Rogozhin. That Dostoevsky considered The Idiot (1869) a partial failure is perhaps attributable to this fundamental conflict between the author's attempt to realise unalloyed spiritual beauty, despite an earlier acceptance of man's latent savage identity. The discoveries made in the convict world of Siberia proved, it seems, too potent to unlearn.

As I have attempted to illustrate throughout, Siberia and Africa were, ultimately, perhaps the most important emotional and spiritual experiences in the personal lives of both writers. These private descents into the veritable hell of the human psyche were to exert a profoundly shaping influence in the later formation of both men's mature philosophies. The semi-fictionalized accounts of each writer's harrowing psychological odyssey, therefore, deserve to be recognized as major first statements of their creed. As I have shown, a parallel analysis of 'Heart of Darkness' (1899) and The House of the Dead (1860), from this perspective, does provide some revealing insights into the strikingly similar nature of both author's views on the human condition. For the literary establishment, which has long since pronounced that Conrad and Dostoevsky reside at opposing ends of a literary and ideological spectrum, there is much to suggest a major re-appraisal is long overdue. As these two early works show, there are fundamental philosophical bonds uniting both writers, bonds which seem both surprising and exciting.

Chapter 14

Critics Veiws on Conrad

Mercedes Czlapinski

Joseph Conrad's novel, Heart of Darkness, is a frame novel-the narrator writes about Charlie Marlow, who tells of his experience in the Congo from the yawl on the Thames river. Through settings, symbols, and Conrad's impressionist style, Conrad is able to illustrate the impact of Marlow's epiphany on his portrayal of humanity and on his responsibilities to mankind. Conrad's use of a frame novel helps to convey the theme of universal darkness.

In Heart of Darkness, setting helps to portray the theme of universal darkness. Conrad's descriptive passages about the "interminnable waterways" of the Congo and the Thames River show the connection between humanity and darkness. Each river flows into one another, and "lead into a heart of immense darkness". This shows that all of humanity is connected through the heart of darkness and the truth.

Conrad's use of symbolism illustrates the central theme of the novel. Kurtz himself is a major symbol in Heart of Darkness. Kurtz is considered a catalyst for change and the symbol for the whites' failure in Africa. Kurtz is unaware of his own darkness and is unable to fight it. His dying words, "the horror, the horror!" depicts the darkness of human souls. The contrast between light and dark is also very important to the theme of universal darkness. Light represents the falsehoods and corruption in the world, whereas dark is a symbol for truth. The white ivory is a symbol for the falsehood in the ivory trade as well as the failure of the commerce and that of the white man. The dark natives show the pureness and innocence of mankind, complete foils to the whites. All of mankind is connected through the darkness because everyone lies, even those who are a symbol for truth, and lies help to mask the darkness.

Conrad's impressionistic style helps to convey the theme of universal darkness. Conrad writes heart of darkness as a frame novel. The narrator is telling the story of another man who is telling his story. This allows for Marlow's digressions and for the readers to understand the horror of the darkness for themselves. Conrad's impressionist style permits the reader to experience the journey as Marlow does. As Marlow digs deeper into universal darkness, the reader follows and questions what Marlow questions. Conrad's style helps the reader to build a strong narrative alliance with Marlow because the reader can feel what he feels. This style allows the reader to understand the truth of the darkness.

Conrad's use of a frame novel helps to convey the theme of universal darkness. Through settings, symbols, and Conrad's impressionist style, Conrad is able to illustrate the impact of Marlow's epiphany on his portrayal of humanity and on his responsibilities to mankind.

Sam Awa

Going by the periods in the English literary history, Heart of Darkness can be classified as the novella of the Early Modern Period, which started in 1900 and spanned through 1939. The literature of this period was characterized by change. The change that started in Victorian era continued to the Early Modern. The change was basically in terms of permissive value and liberalism. The work is therefore, a bridge between Victorian values and the ideals of modernism. But in Africa, the novel could be classified as a colonial literature.

Over the years, the interest of many critics has always been on the psychological and mimetic features in the novella. For this reason, copious critical essays have been published on the psychological preoccupation and the racial attitude of Conrad in the novella. But a critical examination would reveal that Marxist issues are also portrayed in the work. In the light of this, we will limit the scope of this critical essay to the features of Marxist theory in Joseph Conrad's Heart of Darkness.

Heart of Darkness centres around Marlow, an introspective sailor, and his journey up the Congo River to meet Kurtz, reputed to be an idealistic man of great abilities. Marlow takes a job as a riverboat captain with the Company, a Belgian concern organized to trade in the Congo. As he travels to Africa, or better put, the Congo, Marlow encounters widespread inefficiency and brutality in the Company's stations.

The native inhabitants of the region have been forced into the Company's service, and they suffer terribly from overwork and ill treatment in the hands of the Company's agents. The cruelty and squalor of imperial enterprise contrast sharply with the impassive and majestic jungle that surrounds the white man's settlements, making them appear to be tiny islands amidst a vast darkness. Amidst difficulties in getting on with the oppressed natives, Marlow survives in the Congo but as the novella closes, he returns home in ill health.

Although there are no biographical evidences to support the notion that Joseph Conrad was a Marxist writer, there are several issues in Heart of Darkness that tend to support Marxist theory. The theory of Marxism sees the society as a divide between two classes-the rich capitalist class or the bourgeoisie and the poor exploited class or the proletariat. So, Marxists view the society as a common ground for exploitation by the so-called affluent class. For this reason, Marxist writers consciously condemn the callous exploitation of the poor class by the capitalist class and at the same time advocate a classless society. Marxists hate imperialism and interestingly, Heart of Darkness has been said to be anti-imperialist in its attack on the idea of colonization, embodied in the Belgians' ruthless quest for ivory in the Congo.

According to Michael Delahoyde, "literature reflects an author's own class or analysis of class relations, however piercing or shallow that analysis may be". A critical examination of the novella would reveal that class plays a very important role in the work, and Conrad sees the natives as constituting the oppressed class who are at the mercy of the capitalist class represented by Director of Companies, Kurtz and his cohort. In the novella, we see the bourgeoisie live in splendor with excess money to spend. They own the capital, hence the term "capitalist". A close look at the characterization would reveal the disparity between the rich class and the poor class in the novel. As the novella begins, the Director of Companies is introduced as the owner of the yacht-a pleasure merchant ship (p.5). Others are mere seamen and workers. Even Marlow has to go through a particular ritual in order to be employed. The director is in affluence. He is in control of "so many millions." From Marlow we learn that his hands are plump. This is clear evidence that he does not work. Workers do not have supple hands. There is no even distribution of wealth in the society of Heart of Darkness. Even other whites are also poor. Class disparity in the Congolese society can be said to have its root in Europe. It was poverty that drove the imperialists to Africa in the first place. Vivid evidence is the fact that Kurtz could not afford to marry beyond his class, so he left for Congo to trade in ivory so that he could get enough money to marry his Intended.

It is true that Kurtz seems to appear larger than life, cruel and greedy, but Marxists would argue that it is the lopsidedness in the society created by capitalist system that is responsible for his wanton behaviour. Other characters like General Manager, Chief Accountant, Pilgrims, Russian trader, Aunt, and Fresleven may also seem to be phlegmatic, especially to the natives, but the truth is that they simply visit their frustrations on others. Marxists are of the opinion that capitalist system can make the workers rise against one another. For the fact that they are identified by mere titles rather than their real names show that they are nameless workers whose offices are more important than their personalities. Marxism is against the capitalists' tendency to impersonalize the workers.

Another Marxist issue in the novella is education. Marxists see formal education as one of the superstructures, which tend to enslave the minds of the ordinary people in the society. The type of education the workers had is the wrong type of education that will never make the people rise against the capitalist system. Formal education is regulated by ideologies and the workers can' only be what the ideologies want them to be. There is no class-consciousness in the novella. Marxist would have wanted the people to have real education that would make them class conscious which will accelerate their revolt. It is also obvious in the novella that the natives are not educated and there is no provision for their education. They are deprived not just physically but also mentally. Because of their mental depravation, they cannot communicate with the rich capitalists. This further proves that there is a wide gap between the rich and the poor. Marxists would query the type of civilization the imperialists really brought if they do not train the natives to know what they know. So, to Marxists, the misconceived notion that imperialism is a charitable activity that brings civilization and religion to the suffering savages is nothing but a sham.

Marxists would also like to inquire about the role played by religion in the work. Like Karl Marx himself who said that religion is the opiate of the people, most Marxists do not see any saving grace from religion to stop the bourgeoisie from exploiting the masses. Most times, it is religion that makes the exploited masses accept their fate. Religion gives the people a dose of fatalism. Because of their faith in Christianity, the workers accept not only their fate but also the hypocrisy of their religious leaders. It is utter hypocrisy for the whites to preach equality but treat the blacks with disdain. Even the Bible is not in support of slavery and oppression as perpetuated by the whites. Conrad subtly makes jest of religion by using Marlow to compare the imperialistic occupation of the capitalists in Africa to that of the Roman occupation of Britain in the 5th century. As far as Christianity is concerned,

Rome or the Romans is synonymous to religion. Another religion that comes under Conrad's jest is Buddhism. Using Marlow's mouth, he describes one of the characters as having "the pose of a Buddha preaching in European clothes and without a lotus flower". From this backdrop, Conrad sees religion as nothing but a camouflage. Through his chief narrator, Conrad constantly refers to the agents of the Central Station as "pilgrims" to portray his attitude towards religion. It takes only pilgrims to suffer such difficulties in order to be appointed to a station to trade in ivory. In the novella, we are also told that the natives worship Kurtz. This also has religious connotation. Marxists believe that it is ignorance that usually drives people to religion; and ironically, the objects of their worship are usually, the source of their suffering, dehumanization and oppression. Most time, the people would worship economic structures and their fellow humans whom they believe are superior to them in order to gain their approval. Marxist would blame such mental ignominy on capitalism.

Furthermore, political issue is in the heart of Heart of Darkness. As the story begins, the narrator describes the traffic congestion in the Thames to portray the dominance of imperialism. To the Marxists, politics and political institutions are nothing but super structures that further enhance the dastardly ideologies of capitalism. It is political intrigue for the capitalists to hide under the cloak of civilizing the Congolese in order to deprive them of the only source of their wealth, which is ivory. They use brute force to get what they want.

One of the major themes of the novella is oppression. The work has a lot to say about oppression and social class conflicts not only in Congo but also in the whole of African continent. Oppression exists in the work at two levels. There is general oppression at one level and specific oppression at another level. It is an act of oppression for the Director to send the workers to get ivory for him. From the general point of view, Kurtz is an embodiment of all the evils created by free enterprise in a capitalist system. His inordinate passion for ivory in the Congo can attest to this. Everything seems to belong to him: "You should have heard him say, 'My ivory.' Oh, yes, I heard him. 'My Intended, my ivory, my station, my river, my-' everything belonged to him." Surprisingly, Marxists would excuse Kurtz's oppressiveness because it the capitalist system that gives birth to it.

Consciously or unconsciously, Conrad decries the oppressiveness of capitalism through Marlow, his chief narrator. According to Marlow, the act of imperialism in the Congo is nothing but "great demoralization of the land." The Congolese society in the novella truly portrays the oppressive occupation of capitalism, which has become the bane of the people. Resources are mismanaged; the native mercilessly exploited and in one scene reduced to slavery or forced labour. Arguably, the natives are not in any way compensated or paid for their labour. The means of production belongs to the capitalist class. There is nowhere in the novella that the natives gather ivory for themselves. They only toil day and night to enrich the oppressing bourgeoisie. There are several physical cases of oppression and victimization in the novella. A case study is the pathetic story told by the chief speaker about a native who was beaten up by one of the white imperialists Fresleven:

> Therefore he whacked the old nigger mercilessly, while a big crowd of his people watched him, thunderstruck, till some man-I was told the chief's son-in desperation at hearing the old chap yell, made a tentative jab with a spear at the white man.

Another instant of victimization is when a native is shot and is laid at Marlow's feet. He tries to talk but dies before he could get his words out. Typically of a sadist capitalist, the Chief Accountant also dismisses the cries of a dying native as annoying. Contrary to what Achebe and other critics would have us believe, the maltreatment of the natives goes beyond their skin colour. This is because we are told in the novel that the "pilgrims"-the white agents who solicit stations to trade in ivory also suffer, though not as much as the natives. Even

Conrad himself, through his narrator, believes that the white may not be better than the natives in some respect. He subtly portrays this in the statement of Marlow who metaphorically refers the white imperialists to as "whited sepulcher." Through his speaker, Conrad condemns the actions of the capitalists who capitalize on the weakness of the native:

> They were conquerors, and for that you want only brute force-nothing to boast of, when you have it, since your strength is just an accident arising from the weakness of others. They grabbed what they could get for the sake of what was to be got. It was just robbery with violence, aggravated murder on a great scale, and men going at it blind-as is very proper for those who tackle a darkness. The conquest of the earth, which mostly means the taking it away from those who have a different complexion or slightly flatter noses than ourselves, is not a pretty thing when you look into it too much.

Marx theorized that when profits are not reinvested in the workers but in creating more factories, the workers would grow poorer and poorer until no short-term patching is possible or successful. At a crisis point, revolt will lead to a restructuring of the system. For this reason, Marxists believe that there is only one solution to the oppressive tendency of the capitalist class, and that is mass revolt. Conrad subtly allows Marlow, the chief narrator to punctuate the narration with incidents of protests by the natives but this may not in any way make the novella pass for a Marxist work because there is no place in the novella where Conrad consciously educate the workers on how to revolt. Such incidents as when one of the natives makes a tentative jab with a spear at the white man cannot be said to be mass revolt against oppression and exploitation but an individual natural reaction to an act of maltreatment done to a kinsman.

Like Ikem and Chris in Achebe's Anthills of the Savannah, Marlow tries to distance himself from the oppression going on in the Congo although he is also part of the oppressing class. But Conrad fails to make him commit class suicide, which would have qualified him to be a true Marxist. Although many critics may see Marlow as merely a surrogate for the author thereby attacking Conrad for being somewhat racist, he (Marlow) genuinely identifies with the natives:

> They were dying slowly-it was clear. They were not enemies, they were not criminals, they were nothing earthly now-nothing but black shadows of disease and starvation, lying confusedly in the greenish gloom. Brought from all the recesses of the coast in all the legality of time contracts, lost in uncongenial surroundings, fed on unfamiliar food, they sickened, became inefficient, and were then allowed to crawl away and rest.

In sum, there is no doubt that Heart of Darkness seems to be a propagandistic novella that attempts to challenge the evils of capitalism in many respects. Though it may contain Marxist tendencies it is not a pro worker. At such, we may not say that the work is Marxist because it fails to educate the workers to be class conscious and how to revolt against the superstructures in the society that enslave them.

Brad Mcnally

The Heart of Darkness, a tale of how Europeans spread into the heart of Africa in the late 1800's, has been criticized in recent years as a testament to misogamy, racism, and imperialism. These types of arguments seem to have been easy to identify, citing that there are characters in the story which follow these large faults, therefore the story itself must promote those things. More specifically, it has been argued that the novel switches back and forth imperialistic and anti-imperialistic themes. This argument could be resolved with a close look at the major themes in Conrad's story instead of just single instances of behaviours. It is important to do this because readers should not be in a situation where it becomes impossible to see the forest for the trees, but one where the entire picture can be clearly seen when examined in context.

Although never expressly admitted in the story, the land they are traveling to in order to complete business is understood to be Africa, specifically as a trip up the Congo river. At the time of publication, the area known as Congo had been under the rule of Leopold II, which contributed to the atrocities taking place in the jungle. This image would have been one that was ingrained in the minds of the people of Europe. This was shown through the headline of a London paper that read "The Devil's Paradise: A British owned Congo." It seems that the people of London saw this land as an evil place, one that must be colonized to prevent this "Hell on Earth" from existing.

It could be argued that through his story Conrad attempted to contribute to this image, but that seems less than logical. One of the most important things to note in the entire work is that it presents the most evil people as the ones who are taking over the Congo in the name of imperialism. The first instance of this is the Inner Station chief, Kurtz. He is a man who happens to possess a massive amount of charisma, but, in Marlow's words, is a "hollow" man. Throughout the end of the story, Marlow meets with various relatives and close acquaintances of Kurtz, but to each one he is something different. To the cousin, he was a great musician; to the journalist, a politician and leader; to his "intended" he was a humanitarian and genius. Marlow saw the man as none of these, but this only left him questioning the validity of his memory. The way he remembers Kurtz is slightly different, basically that Kurtz was a sort of madman, almost an evil genius type of character. He does interact deeply with the native people at the station, and this draws him the criticism of many European men.

The biggest problem with the part of this that is left open to interpretation is that one could see the novel as promoting racism because the white man who interacts is attacked by other white men. Another interpretation of this is that the novel is true to life of that time period. In the expansion of the British empire, many would read this novel with a certain predefined belief. An article titled "Heart of Darkness: Out of Africa Some New Thing Never Comes" gives this the definition that the imagery of darkness in the story is portrayed in a way that is would rely on the reader's knowledge of Africa and the acceptance of certain things about the country. These things that must be accepted are that the darkness, or the African country, are primitive and savage-like, the opposite of civilization. Shetty points out that if these truths are not self-evident, then the tale becomes somewhat nonsensical. This is an interesting choice of words, specifically because in the context of the time, these truths might have been well accepted, but over time the story has become slightly nonsensical. That is not a bad thing, but merely a way of looking at it. The reason is because the story is told from memory of a memory, thus not the most reliable source, and seems to show the absurdity of the expansion of the British empire by making it a point to show how the abominations that occur in the jungle are committed by the men there to "save" the native race. This shows how nonsensical the plan of imperialism is, specifically by ousting the hypocrisy that the idea if based upon.

Another major argument that the novel attempts to promote imperialism and the marginalization of societies that are not European is the fact that at the end of the story, Marlow lies to Kurtz's intended bride. This could call into question the whole account of the tale because it makes Marlow appear to be an unreliable narrator. The first counter-argument to this is that Marlow is not the narrator, but he was a storyteller that the narrator listened to before telling the story again. This is purely textual in basis and does refute the argument, but to look at it on a deeper level, regardless of Marlow's lie, there is more going on in the story. In the beginning of the tale, Marlow is somewhat indifferent toward the the extremely important issue of expansion of the English people into other countries where they take over and eliminate the native culture. The most important fact to look at in this aspect of the story is the fact that over time, Marlow learned that the expansion movement was not a good idea by any means. This argument is made by Jerome Mechier in an article titled "The Truth About Marlow". He points out that the storytelling that is overheard from Marlow is not one that supplies him with the opportunity to lie to Kurtz's intended, but an opportunity for him to reflect on his past and make amends for the lie he once told. This idea of Marlow telling the truth about it afterwards, and making amends, enhances his overall credibility with the reader and allows him to show that he has learned to recognize absurdity in himself. The article goes on to say that it seems the lie to the intended is told with the best of intentions, and it is clearly not very serious, but the untruths used to justify Western imperialism at the time were extremely serious in comparison.

The imperialistic attitude of the England people is shown in this novella is one that is clearly rooted in hypocrisy. This is an important theme in the work and is shown by the way Marlow encounters different situations as he heads into the darkness of the African continent, specifically the way he witnesses torture, cruelty, and slavery, which all paint a rather bleak outlook for imperialism. The company that Marlow works for calls this the civilizing of the native people, but they do not treat them as any kind of civilized person. The honesty of Kurtz is at least somewhat admirable, specifically because he has no qualms about the fact that he is ruling the men through violence and intimidation. There are important issues of race at play, but also important are the issues of power and control over people of a lesser-developed country. In the context of the time, Europe would be what is now called a hyper-power nation. The world's second smallest continent in terms of area once controlled more nations than any other, and although it made point to define this action as "civilizing" the underdeveloped societies, it wiped out culture with impunity. Another important theme that could be looked at in the same vein is that madness could be a result of imperialism. This is far less prominent in the novel, but the fact that Kurtz is referred to as mad from the beginning plays an interesting role with the idea of insanity. By the middle of the story, many readers would be questioning if Kurtz was mad or not, specifically because it seems that insanity is hard to define among the culture he is presently in. Of course, this is a lesser theme for the novel, but one that still raises important questions.

Since the publishing of the story Heart of Darkness by Joseph Conrad, the themes have been given a less than flattering review. In the original publication, it raised many questions about who was right or wrong in terms of British expansion, but in later years it was argued about smaller themes that were largely irrelevant to the readers of the time. These criticisms have caused it to become a story that the forest is often lost to the trees, but if the entire work is analysed, it can be seen that the true issue being dealt with is the way the English people were taking over land that was not theirs, killing off and enslaving cultures that existed for years, and taking advantage of those who are different than them in any way possible. It is more than a story about a man who travels into a jungle and meets interesting characters, it is a story of a man who is looking back on his past mistakes and attempting to understand what he has done wrong. Marlow only wants to learn from his mistakes, and he tells the story to that others may learn from them as well.

Bob Younce

The Myth of Light: Imperialism and Paradox in Joseph Conrad's Heart of Darkness

Heart of Darkness has been a source of contention for critics since its publication. No issue within the novel has been central to this dispute more than that of imperialism in Africa. Published originally as a series in the pro-imperialism journal, Blackwood's Magazine, Heart of Darkness has been cited as unabashedly pro-imperialist and even racist on the one hand; it has been seen as scathingly anti-imperialist on the other. More than a hundred years of discussion among readers and literary critics of Conrad has failed to produce any sort of majority consensus on the issue of imperialism.

This diversity of interpretation is at least in part a result from definite tensions inherent in the text itself. Far from being an accident, Conrad seems to have juxtaposed Marlow and Kurtz specifically for the purpose of contrasting the noble precepts and ideals of imperialism with the sinister abuse of power that may accompany it. In this way Conrad takes the role of the iconoclast, destroying the constructed idols of civilization while, at the same time, demonstrating the barbarism inherent in an uncivilized world. The story becomes less an argument about civilized vs. uncivilized; rather, it seems to suggest that civilization is itself an illusion. Civilization is a human construct built for the sole purpose of justifying the evil intentions of men's hearts. Thus for Conrad the "darkness" does not refer to a geographic location, but rather to a moral condition of the human heart.

The critical approaches to interpreting notions of imperialism in Heart of Darkness fall into three camps. The first of these, promoted most notably by Chinua Achebe is that Conrad writes as a white male European and that the text demonstrates a specifically racist and imperialist point of view. McClure, as well, observes a definite admiration for imperialism on the part of Conrad. In this interpretation, it is Africa itself that corrupts Kurtz. The barbaric and uncivilized world turns a once-civilized man into a monster. Kurtz travels first to the Congo motivated by economic individualism, as "an emissary of pity, science and progress" according to the bricklayer. Only once he is deep in the uncivilized world does he become corrupted by the opportunity for raw power that is presented to him and he sets himself up as a god to the Congolese native peoples.. The problem for Conrad is then not the nature of imperialism itself. The problem with imperialism is the darkness and evil of the uncivilized world and its effect on the civilized mind. Thus, Marlow sees Kurtz's report as being a tremendously fine piece of work, but drops off the written postscript of "Exterminate all the brutes!" because it shows only Kurtz long after he has descended into darkness.

Some critics find an ardent anti-imperialism in the text. Brantlinger, for example, looks into Corad's other works, particular the story Conrad co-authored with Ford Maddox Hueffer (Ford), The Inheritors: An Extravagant Story to discover Conrad's opinion of imperialism. The Inheritors puts forth a view of imperialism which not only discounts the abuse of power in imperial situations, but rather points to imperialism itself as a terrible falsehood operating under the guise of noble motivations. The gap between the noble ideas of imperialism and Kurtz's megalomaniacal genocide is bridged by Lackey, who suggests that there is no real dissonance between Kurtz's original report and its postscript. To the contrary, the postscript flows logically from the report. For Conrad, then, the desire for power will only ever lead to the desire for more power, which in turn corrupts the soul.

There is a third sort of thought among critics regarding imperialism in Heart of Darkness. This sort of critic sees a via media between the extreme anti- and pro-imperialism positions. These critics argue that Conrad was very much behind the ideas of imperialism, but that the character of the empire would greatly inform whether expansion was performed in a just way. From this perspective, Conrad was not writing to strike against imperialism or its abuses by individuals. Instead, he was striking against the particular form of Belgian imperialism present under King Leopold that Conrad himself witnessed in the Congo, and that was making regular news in the English press around the time of his writing.

Truly, the Congo Free State had become, under Leopold, an expansive slave plantation. In contrast, Conrad sees the English implementation of imperialism as noble, just and efficient. It would be unthinkable that the Englishman, Marlow, however much he admires Kurtz, would sink into the same depths as Kurtz. According to Pericles Lewis, both Marlow and Conrad leap to the defence of England and its ideas..

The characters of Marlow and Kurtz can serve as a basis from which to interpret the text's position on imperialism. From the perspective of Marlow, there are striking differences between him and Kurtz. Kurtz serves as a sort of warning to Marlow of what Marlow may become if he were to descend into darkness. From the reader's perspective, however, the two really are different sides of the same coin. Both are possessed with their own forms or degrees of darkness. Thus a great paradox is created, both in terms of the men themselves and in terms of the consequences of their beliefs regarding imperialism.

Marlow agrees with Kurtz's basic principles, and praises his report as a beautiful piece of writing. However he fails to admire in the same fashion the brutal postscript. Marlow visits Kurtz's "intended" but cannot bring himself to be honest with her about Kurtz. When asked, he tells her that Kurtz's final words were "her name" (which we never know) rather than his actual last words of "The horror! The Horror!". Indeed, this is the Kurtz that Marlow would prefer had existed. Marlow himself cannot fully come to terms with the fact that Kurtz had done more than just gone mad; rather, he had followed the tenants of his beliefs to their ultimate, logical and horrible conclusions.

Marlow fails to recognize the darkness that has penetrated his own heart, long before he ever meets Kurtz. When he considers the cannibals employed on his ship, he cannot fathom why they would show any restraint at eating either him or the other passengers. Marlow assumes that the cannibals have no moral code or conscience and that they must be governed comletely by their basest desires. In the end he decides that the "pilgrims" traveling with them must not look very appetizing. Put into the same situation, one assumes that "Marlow the Cannibal" would have eaten his employer and his fellow travellers without a second thought. He never consideres the possibility that, even among cannibals, there are things that one does not do, such as betraying trust. Truly, Marlow is seeing his own reflection in the cannibals and reads into their psyches his own moral weaknesses.

When the black helmsman who has so faithfully served marlow for months is killed by a spear Marlow mourns him after a fashion. However, what he mourns is not the death of another human being; he mourns the breaking of one of his instruments. He referres to the helmsman as "a savage who was no more account than a grain of sand in a black Sahara". However, in the last gasp of the helmsman's breath Marlow sees something vaguely human, a "distant kinship" much like he observes earlier while watching native rituals. He is surprised by it; it seems to him to be an anomoly. Kurtz, too, seems to recognize the humanity in the Congolese natives and he uses their humanity for his own purposes just as Marlow used the helmsman. Kurtz, much like Marlow, sets his own vision of civilization and humanity above theirs.

It is perhaps Kurtz who fully realises the implications of this humanity. More than simple tools to be utilized, Kurtz sees the native Congolese as human beings in that he recognizes and manipulates a desire common among human beings: the desire to worship. He builds civilization anew in his own image, with the savages as its citizens and he as its head. It is perhaps this very image that, at the end, is so frightening to Kurtz. When he screams "The Horror! The Horror!" before he dies, it may well be the horror that he himself created. He is recognizing what Thomas Huxley recognized when considering the implications of social evolution: that social evolution, rather than removing evil, could very well create it.

It is no accident that Marlow tells his tale in a boat on the River Thames. The River Thames runs directly through London, into the very heart of English civilization. The Thames would, at first glance, appear to be the antithesis of the great Congo River. The Congo River is large and runs for more than twelve times the length of the River Thames, winding into the very heart of the uncivilized world. Conrad uses this narrative setting to draw parallels between the honest violence of Kurtz and the more subtle violence inherent in all of humanity. Referring to the River Thames, Marlow says, "And this also has been one of the dark places of the earth.". This is the same idea with which Conrad coludes the book; the Thames "seemed to lead into the heart of an immense darkness." It would seem, then, that the darkness of which Conrad speaks is not merely the darkness of uncivilized Africa; it is a human darkness, common to all.

The line bettween civilized and uncivilized is illusory for Conrad. Marlow, when he witnesses the native Congolese in their rituals, wipes away the boundary without even fully recognizing that he is doing it:

"No, they were not inhuman. Well, you know, that was the worst of it - this suspicion of their not being inhuman. It would come slowly to one. They howled and leaped, and spun, and made horrid faces; but what thrilled you was just the thought of their humanity - like yours - the the thought of your remote kinship with this wild and passionate uproar. Ugly. Yes, it was ugly enough; but if you were man enough you would admit to yourself that there was in you just the faintest trace of a response to the terrible frankness of that noise, a dim suspicion of there being a meaning in it which you - you so remote from the night of first ages - could comprehend. And why not? The mind of man is capable of anything - because everything is in it, all the past as well as all the future".

Marlow recognizes this darkness that pervades the hearts of all men. However in the end he is either unable or unwilling to protest it. He covers it up, he tries to shield his face from the horror by removing the postscript of Kurtz's report and delivering the rest intact, and by hiding the horror of Kurtz's last words from Kurtz's Intended.

In summary, Heart of Darkness does seem to make some strong arguments against imperialism, either wholesale or in its corrputed European form. At the very least it argues against the abuse of power that can occur in imperial situations. There is evidence, both in the text and in Conrad's other writings and personal letters, to support each of these positions. It is the imperialism debate upon which literary criticism has primarily focused. However, to view the work as merely a discourse on imperialism, is to miss the larger message that Conrad was trying to communicate to the reader. For Conrad, it is not merely the idea of imperialism nor the implementation of imperialism that is corrupt; it is rather the instrument of imperialism, man himself, that is possessed by darkness

Wayne Spitzer

A Prayer Against the Darkness

Near the end of Richard Wright's novel, Native Son, a defence lawyer asks the accused murderer Bigger Thomas to observe the tall buildings outside.

"See those buildings, Bigger?" he says. "Faith holds those buildings up."

He is not talking about religious faith but the faith of reason: of Euclidean geometry and of structural engineering, the faith men have in their ability to defy gravity. It would seem, even, that this faith is justified, in the sense that men and women do, indeed, defy gravity, whether in an office building or a jumbo jet, every day.

But every structure must eventually collapse of its own weight; every jet engine must eventually be scuttled. This must of necessity qualify our definition of faith, lending to it an air of transience, of illusion, even delusion. We might rightly, then, without any judgments as to its nature (be it benevolent or benign), call faith a lie.

Marlow, the protagonist of Heart of Darkness, hates a lie. Indeed, we are hardly into the narrative before he tells us:

"You know I hate, detest, and can't bear a lie, not because I am straighter than the rest of us, but simply because it appalls me. There is a taint of death, a flavour of mortality in lies - which is exactly what I hate and detest in the world - what I want to forget".

Marlow especially detests the lie of European imperialism and self-importance. He is appalled by what he sees as a mean, vain, and ultimately impotent attempt to master the un-masterable - viewing it as an absurd conceit, effete and ineffectual, and personifying it as a "flabby, pretending, weak-eyed devil of a rapacious and pitiless folly".

He stands aghast at the surreal incongruities he witnesses from the water: a French warship firing upon an unseen quarry may just as well be "firing into a continent:; a first-class agent of the Belgian Trading Company "jabbers on about himself" as the brooding wilderness looks on, "great, expectant, mute "; native workers, withered and emaciated from exposure and exhaustion, lie dying in the shadows while prim administrators "keep up appearances" - all for the acquisition of "a precious trickle of ivory".

These incongruities stand in stark contrast to the context in which Marlow sees them; i.e., the Congo River and the impenetrable world beyond its banks. It is a world which is likely to cast a spell upon its inhabitants, a world inclined to whisper in one's ear, directing the listener to look upon its depths, to gaze into the looking glass of its cold, dark waters. Writes Conrad:

"All that mysterious life of the wilderness that stirs in the forest, in the jungles, in the hearts of wild men. There's no initiation either into such mysteries. He has to live in the midst of the incomprehensible, which is also detestable. And it has a fascination, too, that goes to work upon him".

It is a faceless abyss, "this strange world of plants, and water, and silence" (30), a vacuum needing filled. It is wholly dependent upon the hearts of men for its personification; those who walk there fill it each according to their nature. The chief accountant (at the first Congo station Marlow encounters) fills this vacuum with numbers. Indeed, as we watch him etch financial runes into a ledger as unreal as it is tidy, we can't help but recall Marlow's earlier statement, that "what saves us is our efficiency - the devotion to efficiency". Writes Conrad:

"He {the chief accountant} turned to his work bent over his books making correct entries of perfectly correct transactions; and fifty feet below the doorstep I could see the still treetops of the grove of death" [where the native workers lay dying in the shadows].

His numerical runes are an incantation, a prayer against the darkness. As Marlow will observe of Kurtz, the chief accountant has "something to say," and is saying it.

Marlow, meanwhile, fills the vacuum with rivets, literally and figuratively. Work is his prayer against the darkness - his "nightmare of choice." For all his flirting about the edge of reason (an edge Kurtz has willingly stepped over), Marlow finds value in keeping his focus close at hand; indeed, in using his hands. Writes Conrad:

"What I really wanted was rivets, by heaven! Rivets. To get on with the work - to stop the hole. Rivets I wanted".

Not because there is some inherent worth to the physical product of his (Marlow's)labour, but because of the work itself: the journey, the voyage down the river under one's own steerage. Writes Conrad:

"She [his steamer] had given me a chance to come out a bit - to find out what I could do. No, I don't like work. I had rather laze about and think of all the fine things that can be done. I don't like work - no man does - but I like what is in the work, the chance to find yourself. Your own reality - for yourself, not for others-what no other man can ever know".

Unlike Kurtz, Marlow is on the river, not at its end. He has not reached its terminus, its heart, nor does he seek to. He's chosen his nightmare and he's chosen wisely. He has something to say and he's saying it. But while Marlow isn't one of the "great man's" (Kurtz) acolytes (at least, not yet) the great man is drawing closer.

And what of those acolytes, those moths crowding about Kurtz's enigmatic light? How do they fill the vacuum? It is a foregone conclusion: their "chosen nightmare," their prayer against the darkness, is Kurtz himself. Indeed, it would seem these followers have completely subjugated their own sense of self, their own light, to his. Perhaps it is because, as the company representative tells Marlow near the end, "He had faith - don't you see? - he had the faith. He could get himself to believe anything - anything".

And he could get others to believe it, too. As Kurtz's intended tells Marlow: "Who was not his friend who had heard him speak once? He drew men towards him by what was best in them But you have heard him! You know!".

By this point in the text, Marlow has done far more than hear - he has seen. Moreover, he has listened, and heard nothing, save "all the hearts that beat in the darkness".

Marlow, like Ray Milland in Roger Corman's X: The Man with the X-Ray Eyes, has seen to the core of creation and found it hollow and dark, as though he (Kurtz) WERE the natural world, the very personification of its wilderness and its waters and the vacuum in which they hang. Comments Marlow: "And this stillness of life did not in the least resemble a peace. It was the stillness of an implacable force brooding over an inscrutable intention".

Kurtz, like the world, is "an inconceivable mystery," that knows "no restraint, no faith, and no fear, yet struggling blindly with itself". He is a man who, on some level, believes himself God, and in a sense, is.

"There was nothing either above or below him," observes Marlow. "He had kicked himself loose of the earth".

Marlow has peered over the rim of things, but - unlike Kurtz - lived to tell about it. He has not thought himself out of existence. Yet the memory of Kurtz and the memory of what lie in the heart of the darkness are with him, for one cannot unsee what has been seen. Marlow expresses it as follows:

"I remained to dream the nightmare out to the end Droll thing life is - that mysterious arrangement of merciless logic for a futile purpose. The most you can hope from it is some knowledge of yourself - that comes too late - a crop of inextinguishable regrets If such is the form of ultimate wisdom, then life is a greater riddle than some of us think it to be. I was within a hair's-breadth of the last opportunity for pronouncement, and I found with humiliation that probably I would have nothing to say. This is the reason why I affirm that Kurtz was a remarkable man. He had something to say. He said it".

How and why has Marlow remained? I think it is only this: his hands are busy. He is working. Says Marlow, "I lived in an infernal mess of rust, filings, nuts, bolts, spanners, hammers, ratchet drills". Again, it is his prayer against the darkness. His lie he has come to adore - his faith. Unlike Kurtz, who had "such plans," Marlow has something to do, and he does it.

In the end, Marlow, the man who "abhors a lie," tells two of them. The first is to himself, and concerns the matters discoursed above. The second is to Kurtz's "intended," when he tells her that Kurtz's last words were the incantation of her name.

He lies to spare her and himself, "bowing [his] head before the faith that was in her, before that great and saving illusion that shone with an unearthly glow in the darkness, in the triumphant darkness from which [he] could not have defended her - from which [he] could not even defend [himself]".

In the end we all bow to something rather than face the darkness, even if we "go at it blind - as is very proper for those who tackle a darkness". Artists bow to their work; tradesmen to their trade; men to women and women to men. The British Empire bowed to the very notion of empire. Writes Conrad:

"The conquest of the earth, which mostly means the taking it away from those who have a different complexion or slightly flatter noses than ourselves, is not a pretty thing when you look into it too much. What redeems it is the idea only. An idea at the back of it; not a sentimental pretense but an idea; and an unselfish belief in the idea - something you can set up, and bow down before, and offer a sacrifice to ".

Marlow has seen. He knows that we are but "a flash of lightning in the clouds." That "We live in the flicker but darkness was here yesterday". And will be here tomorrow.

Rachel Heng

" For Marlow (and Conrad) civilisation is a varnish which wears off as soon as man is cut of from the conditions that created it." The statement implies that civilisation is merely a veneer which man is easily stripped of. The concept of civilisation is dealt with in the novel, and this concept is juxtaposed against that of the primitive state of man. In Heart of Darkness, civilisation is associated with light, and the lack of it with darkness. Throughout the novel, this metaphor is used to convey the overwhelming power of the darkness and by implication, the fragility of civilisation's veneer.

One way in which this is conveyed is through the constant insinuation that civilised white man is no different from the "savage" natives surrounding him in Africa. Marlow says of Europe "darkness was here yesterday", that is, only too recently were the Europeans as uncivilised as the African natives. He then goes on to describe the Roman conquerors' experience, "[living] in the midst of the incomprehensible, which is also detestable". Despite then going on to differentiate the Roman conquerors from the European colonists, the parallel between the African natives and the Europeans is clear. He calls the Europeans of the past "wild men", just as the Europeans call the African natives as such. This parallel suggests that civilised white man is no different from the uncivilised African native, that, after all, they merely "live in the flicker". The fragility of civilisation is clearly implied. Civilisation is seen as a temporary, foolish notion which though on the surface differentiates men; in actuality does nothing of the sort because men at the heart are all alike, just as the Europeans are no different from the Africans.

This idea is also brought out in the description of the African drums, "a sound weird, appealing, suggestive, and wild and perhaps with as profound a meaning as the sound of bells in a Christian country." Once again, Marlow draws a parallel between Africa and Europe, comparing the African drums to European church bells. Though on the surface he seems to be making a casual statement, in actual fact he links the Africans closely with the Europeans, suggesting once again that they are no different. This is further emphasized by the language used to describe the drumbeats, "appealing" and "suggestive", implying that though white man does not recognise it, he, in some way, identifies with the drumbeats and therefore with the savage natives. This is an example of Conrad's narrative technique which he uses to deal with the theme of civilisations fragility.

This narrative technique is also evident early on in the novel. His description of Fresleven and Belgium are very similar. He first describes the scene of Fresleven's death as "grass growing through his ribs [being] tall enough to hide his bones", then describes the streets of Belgium: "[there was] a dead silence, grass sprouting between the stones." The similarities between these two descriptions are evident. The stones in the streets of Belgium are described as dead Fresleven's bones are, a morbidly vivid image bringing to mind death. Once again, a parallel is drawn between what happens in African and in Europe, that is, death, greed, corruption and darkness. The village was "deserted, the huts gaped black, rotting, all askew within the fallen enclosures"; here, death, greed, corruption and darkness is obvious, just as the decay of the village is in plain sight. In Europe however, these things are all inconspicuous but nevertheless still there in the "white sepulchre". This suggests once again that civilisation is merely a veneer, easily stripped from man.

Another way in which Conrad establishes that "civilisation is a varnish which wears off as soon as man is cut of from the conditions that created it" is through the depiction of Europeans in Africa whom Marlow encounters along his journey down the Congo. At the first station he alights at, Marlow meets the Company's chief accountant. The accountant is "a white man, in such an unexpected elegance of get-up" that he is described as "a sort of vision". The detailed description of his dressing ("high starched collar, white cuffs, a light alpaca jacket") emphasises the attention the accountant pays to his appearance, so much so that it is slightly absurd, as conveyed by Marlow in the slightly humourous comment: "and had a penholder behind his ear." The accountant's appearance is described as being "unexpected" and "amazing", suggesting the incredulity Marlow feels upon seeing him for the first time. Such attention to appearance is hardly what one expects to find in uncivilised Africa. For this fact, Marlow "respected the fellow", as "in the great demoralisation of the land he kept up his appearance". The accountant maintains the veneer of civilisation despite having "been out nearly three years".

Further down the river at the Central Station, Marlow meets the manager. The manager is portrayed as power hungry and petty. He remarks in a calculative and thoughtful manner "Ah! So they talk of [Kurtz] down there", displaying his competitive attitude. He is clearly jealous of Kurtz and wants him out of the picture. Despite the surface niceties the manager utters, the reader is made to doubt his words through Marlow's cynical attitude and effective narrative technique. "He could not wait. Had to start without me." This is an example of Marlow undermining what the manager says. He mockingly paraphrases what the manager says, casting doubt on his insincere words. Hence though the manager says that the "chief, Mr Kurtz, was ill. Hoped it was not true", the reader is led to believe otherwise, that is, that the manager hopes something will happen to Kurtz so that he has one less contender in the fight for power, wealth and fame. The manager seems far less civilised than the impeccable accountant further up the river. The manager, though not consumed by darkness as Kurtz is, does exhibit certain qualities that suggest he has fallen prey to it. He is presented to the reader as greedy, power hungry, hypocritical and insincere, an all in all dislikeable character.

Finally at the Inner Station, Marlow meets Kurtz. Kurtz is seen to be completely consumed by darkness, the veneer of civilisation completely thrown off. He is savage, brutal and completely uncivilised. Marlow remarks "The thing was to know what he belonged to, how many powers of darkness claimed him for their own." Kurtz is crazed by his desire for power, status, wealth and hence, ivory. This is clearly reflected in his claim "My Intended my ivory, my station, my river, my -". So consumed is he by his atavistic lusts that his brutality and capacity for violence is unbounded; the harlequin reveals that Kurtz "came to [the natives] with thunder and lightning" and that "he could be very terrible". This is also evident in "those heads drying on the stakes under Mr Kurtz's windows", a clear expression of power. His "ascendancy was extraordinary. The camps of these people surrounded the place, and the chiefs came every day to see him. They would crawl" This suggests the complete indulgence Kurtz took in the power he wielded as a result of his capacity for being "terrible".

Hence as Marlow goes further down the river, he meets people who are increasingly less civilised. This illustrates Conrad's point that the further man is "from the conditions that created [civilisation]", the more uncivilised he becomes. Civilisation is portrayed as a fragile veneer that man loses once he is removed from the trappings of civilisation, once "no warning voice of a kind neighbour can be heard whispering of public opinion." Marlow astutely observes that "Acquisitions, clothes, pretty rags rags that would fly off at the first good shake" are hardly enough to protect one from descending into darkness as Kurtz does, that is, the veneer of civilisation is completely inconsequential once man is removed from a civilised setting.

Cody Franklin

On the surface, Joseph Conrad's Heart of Darkness may be about a perilous adventure through the heart of Africa, though the journey may be more adequately surmised as a journey through the heart of the human mind and conscience. Every aspect of the book covers up a hidden meaning. The prime example of this is the character of Kurtz. Disliked by competitors yet portrayed as a hero and even divine, Kurtz seems the perfect person. Yet, evidence proves he is the most flawed character within the story, although he actually participates very slightly within the plot. Each character has their unique view of him as a different person with a different personality and characteristics. Through this, Conrad grasps the problems of human nature and pursuit of self interests. Furthermore, Conrad addresses problems with imperialization, the treatment of others less fortunate, and the eventual result the two have on an individual. Through Marlow's observant eyes, we, as readers, are given a view of seemingly insignificant story, yet produce from it a much deeper meaning. Eventually, one begins to wonder just what, if anything, makes the jungle cause insanity.

Adrian Miller

"The horror. The horror." falls off Kurtz's dying lips, but his final words, seemingly a plea for an extension of life, represent far more. The words separate Kurtz into two separate beings, the idealistic politician seeking in his self-righteous superiority to civilize the natives of the Dark Continent, and the god of the wilderness removed by Marlow from the power he covets, committing far more horrendous acts against the native tribesman than the mandates his original agenda set forth. These are not the perspectives of two radically dissimilar men sharing one body, but multiple facets of the same man. Kurtz's actions, choices, and experiences refine him of the impurity of the altruism Christianity believes inherent in the conversion of barbarian infidels, burning away the allusion to the divine impetus of the cause and leaving the oppressive nature that is beneath it. Kurtz's deathbed epiphany mocks the European need to shape and mold those the West deems inferior, proving that it is no more than a smoke screen to inflict savage indignities on a noble and worthy people as the means to a despicable end. Frances B. Singh, who wrote "The Colonialistic Bias of Heart of Darkness," asserts, "the horror being referred to is the blackness of Kurtz's soul.". The white men who penetrate the heart of Africa are the real darkness, dispensing with Christian idealism and perverting the conversion of the African savages with greed and ignorance. Kurtz's fear and loathing in that last moment demonstrates the ability of every human, light and dark, to wrestle with and even kill themselves in order to save themselves from what they do not understand or want to admit.

In Robert LaBrasca's essay "Two Visions of The horror!'," Kurtz is portrayed as the quintessential European. LaBrasca claims the story's "darkness illuminates the grim emptiness at the limit of personal and national ambition, the vanity of power's claim to civilization, and the frail evil that lurks in even the best of its emissaries.". Marlow describes Kurtz's pamphlet for the International Society for the Suppression of Savage Customs as "vibrating with eloquence," but the writings scrawled in Kurtz's own handwriting as "luminous and terrifying.". Kurtz entrusts his pamphlet to Marlow because the two men share a confidence he is unwilling to impart on other Europeans. According to Frances Singh:

> Certainly from the point of view of the African tribesman Kurtz has done nothing abominable in recognizing the virtues of his way of life. And from the point of some modern anthropologists, who believe that only by becoming part of another culture can one understand and appreciate it, Kurtz is an enlightened individual, far more advanced than his contemporaries in his thinking about primitive societies..

Kurtz initially faces the dark frontier as an intrepid social missionary with the dream of molding the native Africans into a state more compatible with "Caucasian" interests, but his compatriots stain the pristine image of his society while he abandons it. Chinua Achebe's critical piece "An Image of Africa: Racism in Conrad's Heart of Darkness" places the blame for Kurtz, indeed for every European in the story squarely upon the shoulders of Conrad himself, illuminating the relationship of Africa to Europe as that of "a carrier onto whom the master unloads his physical and moral deformities so that he may go forward, erect and immaculate." He goes on to show that Kurtz entered the jungle "foolishly exposed [] to the wild irresistible allure of the jungle and lo! The darkness found him out.". There is a sense in all of these works that Kurtz entered the jungle with much more than when he left it. The jungle stripped the agenda of his pamphlet of falsity until its true worth, or lack-thereof, could be clearly determined.

Conrad dramaticizes the change in Kurtz with the expectations of the character Marlow, and the tales told to him of Kurtz by the other Europeans. LaBrasca reaches the conclusion that "Amid the grotesque oppression of the mysterious, defeated natives, the flies, the heat, and the jackals bearing the flag of progress, Kurtz becomes a vestige of hope.". In the hope of reaching Kurtz, denial selectively oblivious to the harshness of European dominance over the African tribes lingers beneath the surface. As Marlow approaches his goal, however, the jungle and its fearful occupants distort the prize. Singh explains:

The problem with Kurtz, which Marlow doesn't realise, is not that Kurtz went native, but that he did not go native enough, for Kurtz perverted the customs of the tribe, making them a means to a deplorable endnamely, keeping ivory flowing and colonialism a profitable venture for his employersand he never assumes the positive virtues of the tribe..

The empty shack with its offering of wood foreshadows the emptiness within Kurtz's plan for the natives. Achebe gives Conrad some charity by suggesting that he "saw and condemned the evil of imperial exploitation but was strangely unaware of the racism on which it sharpened its iron tooth.". Achebe does not mention Marlow's affection for the barbarian tending to the steamer's engine. Despite their differences, he feels the native's death more severely than he would have any of the white men aboard his ship, even Kurtz. Kurtz, in like fashion, enters the jungle with the intention of standing over the natives exerting god-like influence to change their nature to suit his vision. Kurtz not only fails to rebuild them, but he allows their cultural values to sink into him, such as adopting their brutal methods for dealing with malcontents. His corruptive assimilation into African culture as a would-be God highlights the ignorance of any plan to separate men and women from their culture.

Achebe describes Marlow as a true Englishman "holding those advanced and humane views appropriate to the English liberal tradition which required all Englishmen of decency to be deeply shocked by atrocities in Bulgaria or the Congo of King Leopold". Marlow, in this light, is little less than an oppressor himself. He does not enslave Africans, but he watches as others do it and takes no action to stop it. In the jungle, Marlow is the captain of a vessel that floats like a speck of civilization on an ocean of lawlessness and chaos. He watches the shore with dire apprehension, likening it to a primeval man threatening to crush them with his bestial humanity. LaBrasca reminds us that Kurtz does have another agenda for being in the jungle other than social reform, stating that he "was at least driven by greed for ivory and the ambition to have kings meet him at railway stations,'". While it is true that Kurtz continues to pour ivory out of his dilapidated station, the return from that investment never materializes into anything obvious or useful to his cause. In Singh's more resolute opinion:

> I have just argued that Kurtz's depravity consisted not in giving in too much to the tribal way of life but in not giving in enough. If that is the case I would suggest that contrary to Marlow's implication the "horror" refers first to what Kurtz has done to the blacks and only secondarily to what he has done to himself, since the latter is only the effect, and not the cause of the former. Consequently the full application of Kurtz's last words would not only be to himself but also to men like Marlow who seemed to hate colonialism but really lived by its values and associated the practices of the blacks with the road to perdition.".

Kurtz's Ivory is intended more to appease the civilized men prowling on the outskirts of Kurtz's empire ready to rip it asunder than to make him rich and famous. "I was on the threshold of great things,' he pleaded in a voice of longing []. And now for this stupid scoundrel.' Your success in Europe is assured in any case,' I affirmed steadily.". Kurtz does not care about ivory. His pamphlet's original agenda is primary in his thoughts, even though its original spirit has long since evaporated. The sinewy tether of control he exerts on the natives replaced that spirit, the only part of the agenda that remains intact throughout.

The power to govern one's own life while curtailing the rights of others is the greatest measure of dominance one society can have over another. Through gunpowder, the ignorance and fear of the natives, and the vein tapped by an ivory-addicted nation, the Europeans obtained power in Africa. Achebe clues us in on the primary tactic in obtaining this power, "Africa as setting and backdrop which eliminates the African as human factor.". In other words, Conrad placing Kurtz and Marlow in the centre of Kentucky may not have had the devastating impact of Kurtz's plans and actions on the reader, but the Kentuckians would have suffered just as dehumanizing a degradation as the Africans, in that their suffering is immaterial to the all-important mental break-down of the protagonist. Conrad's special consideration of Africans as the denigrated is Achebe's point in criticizing "Heart of Darkness." In a more human outlook, LaBrasca takes a look at Conrad's life and suggests that his story is "a journey Conrad had made eight years before up the Congo River.". Of Kurtz's deathbed utterance, Marlow says that, "It was an affirmation, a moral victory paid for by innumerable defeats, by abominable terrors, by abdominal satisfactions. But it was a victory.". Marlow comes back from the Congo a man changed by Kurtz's having stepped over the edge into a kind of revelation. Singh writes about this remarkable transition, stating, "Kurtz's tribalization, therefore, can be seen as a rejection of the materialism of the West in favor of a more honest way of life.". Marlow does not make as dramatic a change. He is able to stay in the safety of his position in life, but he sees what Kurtz discovers in the darkness, the need for the European society to impress its values upon its neighbours while at the same time defying those values by robbing Africa of precious commodities. Kurtz does not change from one man to another from Europe to Africa, but discovers within himself the horrifying truth. The monster he has become has always been there, dormant but undeniably real.

Conrad illustrates through the words of Marlow a man larger than life, a man with the power to command the deaths of the ship's crew. Kurtz is at once gentle and violent; he craves justice and is blind to the unjust. He enters the jungle full of diverse and tangible goals that the jungle tears away piece by piece until only the foundation, ultimate control, remains. Kurtz is idealized by Marlow not for his methods or his reasoning, but because his becomes a path to final clarity. Kurtz sees what he is, what he wanted to do, and what he has done, and comes to a conclusion not many men in his time could bear. Marlow is taken for a moment onto that path, leaving off the suffering of travel just far enough to tell where the road leads. Because of this insight, Marlow finds it difficult to return to Europe and see as he once saw, feel what he once felt about himself and his society. Conrad sympathizes with Kurtz through Marlow only so far as to say he set out in a direction, and through adversity stayed true to the course.

Dustin Blechschmidt

The Docks

While at the docks, Marlow has already taken the remnants of Kurtz's spirit into himself. Before reading Heart of Darkness to the end, it is near impossible to realise the foreshadowing that occurs at the docks. Many of the Kurtzisms' that Marlow tells of are ones he currently embodies. The narrator points out subtly one of Marlow's Kurtz like characteristics, "His remark did not seem at all surprising. It was just like Marlow. It was accepted in silence. No one took the trouble to grunt even...". This is one of Kurtz characteristics that Marlow is notified of later in the novella, that people do not have conversations with Kurtz, they listen to him. It is also noticeable that the narrator speaks of Marlow's tale as one of his inconclusive experiences. This in a way is also factual if considering that Marlow does not enter the heart of darkness along with Kurtz.

The Outer Station

The scene at the Outer Station is horrifying. Marlow makes it out to be as severe as one of the levels of hell, and judging by the river it could likely be the fifth level. The fifth level of hell is where the wrathful and gloomy are condemned, and the river Styx runs through it. Since this is a journey to the heart of darkness it is likely that Joseph Conrad wrote it this way on purpose. Everything has dark overtones, from Marlow's realization that the black shapes around him, " were dying slowly," and that, "The were not enemies, they were not criminals, they were nothing earthly now nothing but black shadows of disease and starvation, lying confusedly in the greenish gloom," to the demonic appearance of the chief accountant.

The Central Station

When Marlow and the boiler-maker get together in the Central Station, interesting incidents happen. The main aspect of the Central Station is the false hope that both Marlow and the boiler-maker have in getting rivets in three weeks time. It causes the two grown men to act in a highly sporadic manner, "I don't know why we behaved like lunatics. I put my finger on the side of my nose and nodded mysteriously[he] snapped his fingers above his head, lifting one foot. I tried a jig. We capered on the iron deck,". The hope is later shattered when instead of rivets arriving, the Eldorado Exploring Expedition came through instead, a band of individuals which represent the greed of man. Marlow recalls that the men talked like buccaneers, that their speech was, "reckless without hardihood, greedy without audacity, and cruel without courage,". The transition from hope to greed being the main focal point of the Central Station is a strong mark in the journey to the heart of darkness.

The Inner Station

The Inner Station is the throne of Kurtz much like the ninth level of hell, Cocytus. Marlow talks about his possessiveness of the Inner Station, as well as other people, places, and things, "You should have heard him say, My ivory.' Oh, yes, I heard him. My Intended, my ivory, my station, my river, my' everything belonged to himbut that was a trifle. The thing was to know what he belonged to, how many powers of darkness claimed him for their own,". Much like the ninth level of hell being the furthest from any light, the Inner Station is the furthest point from civilization. From later in the text Marlow talks about the heads surrounding the station house of rebels and traitors. Cocytus is the final resting place of traitors and mutineers, where all is frozen from Satan's massive wings and the traitors are frozen in solid ice up to their necks, their eyes and mouths frozen shut.

The Sepulchral City

The Sepulchral City and Kurtz's Intended who resides there are nave to who Kurtz really was, or the entire situation that led up to his death. Only Marlow knows Kurtz at this point, and Marlow has taken part of Kurtz with him as he died. The Intended makes a remark about Kurtz words never dying, and Marlow says, "His words will remain,". For the rest of the Marlow's conversation with Kurtz's Intended he takes on one of Kurtz's habits the sentence fragment. As they talk about Kurtz's dying words, Marlow begins to sound more like him, until he pulls himself together and makes up some last words for Kurtz that would favor the Intended's naivety, "The last word he pronounced was your name,". The Intended fell for it like a polar bear wearing roller skates chasing a baby seal.

Kaylie Mack

Wickedness is disillusionment. Innocence is believing in lies. Experience is always corruption.

Conrad makes this point in the Heart of Darkness. Marlowe's journey towards discovery (Kurtz) is a dark and corrupting one, leading to knowledge he is even now trying to escape. Kurtz has achieved absolute knowledge. The wilderness has called to him and made him stand face to face with himself. As a result, "his soul had gone mad". He was sane (knowledge is sane) but his soul was mad with experience and disillusionment. Who would not cry out in horror?

There is and obscurity and remoteness in Conrad which is only approached by the style of his contemporary, Henry

James. Conrad is the master of suggestion. The hero (Kurtz) appears in the second half of the book and dies, having committed some awful crime which is never clearly related. The nameless heroine appears only in the last scene.

The darkness cannot touch Kurtz's Intended. She is innocent in her lack of experience and pure in her faith in a downright falsehood. She believes that the man who was cheating on her with the other nameless, silent female of this masculine novella loved her as she loved him, with absolute conviction. She also believes that Kurtz was a great man and that great men are necessarily good. She is living in a time of naivete and idealism.

Marlowe describes his meeting with the Intended. She is the light in a room where the darkness of Kurtz's charismatic soul is, unperceived by her, closing in. She is worshiping the memory of a satanist with perfect innocence. She asks to know her lover's last words. As the darkness swoops in upon them, Marlowe saves her by a lie. "The last words he pronounced were...your name."

The irony of the fact that she does not even have a name is lost on on one, but her cry of triumph drives back the darkness. She has conquered. The righteous have prevailed.

Camelot did not fall because Lancelot and Guinevere committed adultery. It fell because Mordant told everyone that the perfect city was corrupt. If Marlowe had told the girl the truth, it would have been, as he says, "too dark...too dark altogether". Safe in her illusions, she can live a life of peace. He must journey on into the heart of darkness.

Asil Rekue

Kurtz's dying words, "The horror! The horror!" fill the reader with a rush of juxtaposing emotions: confusion and enlightenment, disappointment and pleasure,disgust and admiration. Yet no matter what the reader feels or does not feel for Kurtz, his death scene is incredibly powerful. His death brings the audience to a peak of curiosity about who Kurtz truly is and whether or not he came to Africa with any morals.

Although the answers to these questions are open to interpretation, they finalize various themes explored throughout the book. Conrad concludes the prevalent theme of Heart of Darkness, how people react in situations when they have no internal or external checks, by including the recurring elements of hollow men who have nothing inside of them, the darkness which pulls men toward temptation, and the restraint/ moral victory that holds them back from giving in to that temptation.

The hollow man idea is the part of the theme that determines whether men will have the soul and conscience needed to prevent them from acting destructively in a place that has no law. At Kurtz's death, this concept is present because Marlow is still not positive whether or not Kurtz is a hollow man. Up to the point when Kurtz utters his last words, Marlow still believes that Kurtz is the ultimate hollow man. When Marlow arrives at the Inner Station, he learns from the Russian that Kurtz became addicted to the power, causing him to act irrationally. Kurtz used the guns to assemble a tribe of natives to raid villages and acquire ivory. He also killed natives, which is apparent from the heads on stakes. All of this leads Marlow to believe that Kurtz is the ultimate hollow man, and every other hollow man in the novel has just been leading up to Kurtz. So, either Kurtz's "emissary of light" intentions were never genuine in the first place, or something about the wilderness stripped him of those qualities. These revelations help give the rest of the book greater meaning where the hollow man is concerned. Conrad introduces the concept of the hollow man with the accountant, and from there, every successive European introduced can also be deemed as hollow. Marlow describes the accountant as a "hairdresser's dummy" because he has a perfect exterior, but there is nothing on the inside. The next hollow man is the manager. Marlow wonders if there is anything inside of him because he would ruthlessly do anything to benefit himself. Marlow also alludes to the brickmaker's hollowness by giving him an epithet. He calls the brickmaker a "papier-mache Mephistopheles" with nothing inside of him except a little dirt." So, when Marlow walks into the cabin where Kurtz lies dying, the hollow man aspect of the scene unifies the rest of the novel where the hollow man is mentioned. The hollow man component of the theme signifies that all men have the potential for evil. When people are stripped of the veneer of civilization, they are all hollow at the core if they have no real principles.

Another element of the overall theme of Heart of Darkness is the darkness that consumes people and brings out their inner corruption. The darkness is a broad category for all that is wrong in Africa including corruption, death, deceit, disease, and insanity. From the very first page, Conrad's diction establishes the dark mood that foreshadow the theme. For example, on the first and second pages, Conrad uses the phrase "brooding gloom" in some form four times. From then on, basically every single character, object, and place has dark imagery. The knitters wear black dresses, Fresleven stole black hens, Kurtz's painting has a dark background, and the European's souls are black with corruption. When Marlow travels through Africa, he feels as though the darkness consumes him, and he obsesses over reality versus unreality. By the time Marlow arrives at the Inner Station, he sees that all of the other places of darkness have led up to Kurtz's station. This station has the most darkness of all because of Kurtz. Kurtz gave in to his inner darkness because he became addicted to the power. The darkness consumed Kurtz when he killed people and put their heads on stakes. All of the darkness through the entire novel, though, leads to the point of Kurtz's death. In the scene, Kurtz lies in a dark cabin. Marlow brings in a candle; however, Kurtz cannot see the light of the candle which is only a couple inches away from his face. This represents the darkness part of the theme that dictates all men will eventually relent to the corruption or madness or death after living in a place of complete and total darkness.

The last component to the theme is restraint. Marlow discovers that the only way for people to cope with the darkness is to finds some kind of restraint. For example, Marlow's restraint is work and the manager's restraint is the preservation of appearance. Yet, Kurtz seems to possess no restraint. Marlow sees the heads on stakes as a symbol for Kurtz's lack of restraint. Kurtz was drawn to the darkness, and he gave in to the powers of the various temptations he faced such as the ivory, the power, and th mistress. Even when Kurtz is too weak to walk, he feels an overwhelming need to return to the jungle, and he crawls back to the natives. But, at the death scene, Kurtz's last words change everything. Marlow believes that Kurtz has a moral victory when he says, "The horror ! The horror!". Marlow accepts that at the instant before Kurtz dies, he has a complete knowledge of the darkness inside his soul and is able to place judgment on himself. Even though there are various explanations for Kurtz's dying words, Marlow believes that in the final moment before death, Kurtz relived "ever detail of desire [and] temptation, and surrender[ed] during that supreme moment of complete knowledge."

This leads Marlow to believe that in the end Kurtz does have some restraint, conscience, or soul inside of him, which shows that the other examples of restraint, or lack of restraint in Heart of Darkness are different from Kurtz. For instance, the pilgrims show no restraint when they eagerly fetch their guns and shoot at the harmless natives. The helmsman displays a lack of restraint when he impulsively opens the shutter of the cabin. In the end, Kurtz does not qualify as a hollow man after all. As a result, Marlow's previous idea that everybody is internally hollow in a place of external savagery, changes. The overall theme of the book in relation to Kurtz's moral victory now main that people are not completely hollow if at their dying moments they are able to look inside their souls and pronounce judgment upon themselves.

The single major theme in Heart of Darkness is how people succumb to evil when they have no internal checks as well as no external checks. The parts of this theme, the hollow man, the tempting darkness, and the necessary restraint to resist, are all explored at Kurtz's death scene which in turn helps to illuminate the meaning of the work as a whole. The hollow man sub theme dictates that when man is removed from civilization, he will lose all decency and concern for anything except himself. The darkness aspect of the theme means that when people live in an uncivilized society for a certain amount of time, they will eventually give in to the darkness. Furthermore, the restraint part of the theme adds that the way for people to remain somewhat decent and sane, is to find a restraint that will allow them to be free from the contamination of the darkness. Finally, the theme at Kurtz's death reveals the overall human lesson of Heart of Darkness: all people at some point must find a restraint, so that it is possible to remain mentally sound with internal checks when the point comes when it is necessary to tolerate "breathing dead hippo."

Brent

Conrad uses shadows and hollowness to reinforce his theme that the essence of human beings is hollow and dark. He does this throughout the novel by making subtle connections between people and the dark, shadowy areas in which they find themselves. He also makes more overt statements when he calls people hollow or full of shadow. The subtle intimations about the true nature of humans begin almost at the very beginning of Marlow's tale, when he walks through "A narrow and deserted street in deep shadow." References like this could be dismissed as coincidence, if not for the fact that they are so prevalent throughout the novel. Later, when Marlow is piloting up the river, he says that the river "Ran on, deserted, into the gloom of over-shadowed distances." Here the river is said to be running into the darkness of the jungle, but the reader also understands it to be a subtle reference to the journey into shadowy heart of mankind. When Marlow is talking with the Russian prior to meeting Kurtz, he describes the changes that had taken place while they talked.

"The long shadows of the forest had slipped downhill while we talked." During the discussion they day had progressed, but Marlow had also seen deeper into the darkness of the human soul. Aside from these subtle references, Conrad makes many overt statements about the hollow darkness inside the human soul. Upon seeing several Africans lying despondently under a tree, Marlow describes them as "they were nothing earthly now - nothing but black shadows." Marlow says outright that there is nothing left to these people, just the shadows within them that are finally visible. Marlow describes Kurtz in much the same way upon first seeing him, "This shadow looked satiated and calm." Kurtz, like the despondent blacks, has lost everything but the very essence of himself, the shadow that lives within us all. When he is leaving to stop Kurtz from escaping from the boat, Marlow says, "I was anxious to deal with this shadow." He is comparing Kurtz to a shadow again, but he is also talking about the shadow that he knows is within himself and that he wanted to confront. Aside from just being shadowy, Conrad also tells us that the human soul is hollow, very clearly in most cases. When describing Kurtz at he says "He was hollow at the core." Marlow is speaking about Kurtz, but also humanity as a whole. While Kurtz is dying, Marlow once again calls him hollow. "The original Kurtz frequented the bedside of the hollow sham." He is speaking about the wasted state of the man before him, but also at the damage that has been done to his soul. The true nature of the human soul was released in this man, and its true hollowness has been revealed. Conrad's reference to shadows and hollowness, both subtle and overt, help to reinforce his theme that all humans are dark and hollow at heart.

Curtis J. Smothers

In his introduction to Conrad's "Heart of Darkness," Franklin Walker quotes Conrad as having once said, "A work of art is very seldom limited to one exclusive meaning and not necessarily tending to a definite conclusion" (viii). This article examines Conrad's statement from the points of view of three scholar critics - Hilton, Cole, and Barry - each of whom find separate "exclusive meanings" as well as attribute their own unique "symbolic character" to the novella.

The critic N. Hilton looks at Conrad as an author "obsessed with ambiguity, hypocrisy, and lies". In his article

Hilton offers a somewhat Freudian explanation of Conrad's continual use of the ambiguous and obscure. He cites Conrad's statement that "one's own personality is only a ridiculous and aimless masquerade of something hopelessly unknown" as both a reflection and a result of Conrad's childhood experiences and his unfortunate loss of both his parents at an early age.

Hilton develops his thesis with an almost psychoanalytic approach to Conrad's writing and again relies of Conrad's own words. For example, in one conversation with an old friend, Conrad provided insight on his writing technique: "(B)efore anything," Conrad confided, "switch off the critical current of your mind and work in darkness the creative darkness which no ghost of responsibility will haunt". Moreover, Conrad writes, "all my work is produced unconsciously". (The foregoing might explain why I had so much difficulty in reading "Heart of Darkness.")

Continuing along the Freudian vein, Hilton points out that after the death of Conrad's parents, Conrad felt that "their deaths emphatically cancelled all hope of security, stripping off my simple trust in the government of the universe'". Hilton develops this notion of the loss of trust to Conrad's early conclusion "that someone was not telling the truth or that no one was or perhaps, finally that there was no truth".

In the remainder of his article, Hilton evaluates Marlow's journey from the "light" of civilization to the "darkness" of Africa in search of Kurtz and his ultimate discovery of the essential hollowness of a soul teetering on emptiness and ambiguity. Hilton ends his article with what could be the most exquisite ambiguity of all, i.e., Marlow's "lie" to Kurtz's fianc. Marlow tells her that the last thing on Kurtz's lips was "your name." In fact, the last thing on Kurtz's lips was the famous exclamation, "The horror! The horror!" Perhaps the real horror was The Intended's continual living of the lie of ordered, albeit meaningless, existence.

Hilton's critique was, to me, an enlightening dissertation on "The Heart Of Darkness," a work of fiction that I originally found somewhat difficult to understand. The article was informative, well documented, and gave me an insight into Conrad, which in turn greatly assisted in my deeper understanding of the novella.

The second critic, Sara Cole, writes from a historical and feminist perspective. Her theme is "alienation and imperial intimacy." The "alienation" she addresses is Marlow's disconnection from the masculine community of the imperial experience. She builds a credible case that the "imperial experience" is the Victorian legacy of "intense masculine relations" that become entrenched in "nineteenth-century ideological superstructures"

To illustrate her point, Cole describes the quintessential Victorian "travel narrative and the adventure quest" of Stanley and Livingstone, "which rapidly achieved the status of a culture icon in both England and America". Stanley meets Livingstone after a search in the "Dark Continent." After their meeting the two men bond and become great friends in a milieu of white men bringing the "light" of European patriarchal culture to Africa.

Cole further focuses on nineteenth century Europe as a pervading conglomerate of patriarchal institutions. Men dictated cultural mores, defined relationships within the context of men's values, and considered places like Asia and Africa as dark, female places whose inhabitants were "children". Cole describes Marlow's relentless quest to meet and bond with Kurtz in as the central struggle in the novella. She supports her argument with examples where "Marlow's energies are directed exclusively towards Kurtz".

Cole also interprets Marlow's trek towards Kurtz as a singie-minded journey towards an ideal self-knowledge, which is only directed inward because of "a collapse in a trajectory towards intimacy with another man". While recognizing Marlow's "tendency to maintain an ironic distance from Kurtz's behaviour in Africa" she contends that this "distance is repeatedly eclipsed by Marlow's insistence on the power and permanence of their bond"

In an interesting twist on Marlow's encounter with The Intended, Cole continues with her thesis on male imperial bonding. "Clearly," Cole contends, "Marlow and the mourning woman compete for Kurtz's memoryand Marlow's decision to lie to her is as much in his own interest as it is an act of generosity."

I found Cole's article very interesting and a fascinating interpretation of Conrad's work. In contrast to Hilton's strictly Freudian interpretation, Cole never wavered from her contention that the central conflict in Heart of Darkness was the search for relief alienation from the comfort of male camaraderie in the world of Victorian imperialism. I felt that Cole either glossed over or completely ignored many of the important psychological permutations that were an important element of Conrad's work, but Cole's article, to me, was one way of looking at "Heart of Darkness" that I had not considered.

The third scholar critic was Dr. Robert Berry, an English professor in New Zealand. Berry also discusses Conrad's "sense of profound isolation and alienation in (a) thoroughly hostile environment". In contrast to Hilton and Cole, however, Berry develops his theme by paralleling Conrad's novella with Dostoevsky's "Notes From the House of the Dead," and he compares them both with Dante's Inferno. Although Berry's article focuses on interesting similarities between Conrad and Dostoevsky, I will confine my final discussion to his treatment of Conrad's novella.

In the context of Dante's Inferno, Berry describes Marlow as finally attaining knowledge, which leads him "to drawconclusions as to the nature and evil potential of the human personality". He even quotes one critic, Robert Evans, as suggesting a "close structural parallel between Heart of Darkness' and (the) Inferno, elaborately equating the river trading posts with specific circles of Hell".

Berry further uses quotes from Dante to draw uncanny comparisons to Conrad's descriptions in the novella. He demonstrates "Conrad's use of Dantean imagery," which "allows him to realise an environment of complete moral horror, a world where shocking insights into the evil capacity of the human spirit will be possible." In what he describes as a "Dantesquejourney underground," Marlow has walked "into the mouth of Hell". Kurtz's descent into the hell of "animal barbarismis...indicative of a larger capacity for savagery that exists in all men".

The savagery in Kurtz is seen "to be motivated by a craving to wield absolute power" and "the urge to assert a tyrannizing domination over others". The imagery continues when Kurtz creates minions (the "savages") to dominate and becomes the "Man-God' in the eyes of his adopted lakeside tribe". In short, "absolute power inevitably realises itself in tyranny". In a particularly revealing description, Berry says, "Marlow himself judges that Kurtz has indeed taken a high seat amongst the devils of the land'".

Building on the theme of Kurtz's lust for and unfettered exercise of power, Berry describes Kurtz as "wildly intoxicatedEverything and anything is now permitted". Isolated, remote and separated "from the restrictions of normal societyKurtz has been free to realise his inner, fundamental drives". Significantly, these forces "exist as a part of man's ancient psychological heritage," and Kurtz is "the prototype" for a universe where "man shows himself to be entirely egocentric".

I particularly enjoyed Berry's interpretation of Marlow's work. His critique was, to me, highly insightful and provided a clear and well-documented interpretation of Marlow's dark work. With what I thought was a forthright summation, Berry states, "Conrad's novel can be regarded, finally, as a document charting the essentially violent and primitive character of man." The foregoing statement was typical of Dr. Barry's clarity and readability.

In summary, each critic described above provided different, and often contrasting views of Heart of Darkness. Hilton stressed the deep psychological meanings underlying Conrad's writing. Cole provided another perspective from the point of view of a feminist. Finally, Berry's more conventional evaluation of the Novella was, in my opinion, the best of the three.

Nevertheless, these writers clearly uphold Conrad's assertion alluded to in the first paragraph of this article that a "work of art is very seldom limited to one exclusive meaning"

Michelle Kasdano

Common Characteristics between "Heart of Darkness" and the 20th Century.

"Heart of Darkness", the work of 20th century writer Joseph Conrad, has succeeded throughout the past few decades to gain classical recognition, hence carving its reputation as an outstandingly deep portrayal of human nature, and modern thought. In spite of being published in the twentieth century, this novel has raised confusion and controversy regarding the literary period it belonged to. While many still believe and insist upon its being a part of Victorian literature, numerous aspects shared between this novel and 20th century principles point out its modernist lineament. Features such as post-colonialism, psychological delving, alienation, meta-narration, impressionism, imagism, symbolism, and many others confirm the appropriateness of such a classification.

Following the colonial period, during which England managed to morph the world into an empire of its own, cracks were beginning to appear in this system of rule due to wars, riots, and upheavals in European-governed colonies. From here, "Heart of Darkness" seems to have been a scathing critic of the deterioration of man's morale brought about by colonialism, harshly attacking it, and hence adopting post-colonial ideology. Such a system of belief was clearly portrayed in Conrad's novel, revealing the ways in which power over other human beings can lead to the corruption of the conqueror on one side, and the suffering of the conquered on the other. This brutality was embodied perfectly by Kurtz's character, his broken noble-mindedness, the cruel treatment of the natives, the pilgrims' avarice, as well as the violent attack by the natives on Marlow's crew, and the killing of his helmsman. All this chaos contributed somehow in the rise of a pessimistic view, and skeptic thoughts regarding the building of British empires, leading to questioning the real intents of colonialism. The author's doubt explicitly seeps through when Marlowe states: "The conquest of the earth, which mostly means the taking it away from those who have a different complexion or slightly flatter noses than ourselves, is not a pretty thing when you look into it too much." Plus, this attitude is enforced through adopting a highly sarcastic and cynical tone throughout the whole story, hence indirectly criticizing all that had accompanied imperialism.

Another striking feature in this novel is the exploring of the inner psychology of man, and the stress on the messy, chaotic, gloomy, and confusing ambiguity of our experiences. Marlow attempts at creating a halo surrounding what he had been through in Congo, reshaping his adventure through an intermingling of events and feelings, allowing the readers to explore the dark corners of the human mind, and somewhat reconciling good and evil. This duality is portrayed through a contrast between his character, still not tinged by the malignant hues of colonialism, versus the manager's or Mr Kurtz's weakening immunity in the face of this bitter plague. Another feature stemming from Marlow's musing is his alienation, which is also a characteristic of 20th century art. Not only is this character a unique, autonomous, and "not typical" being, but he is also unable to communicate clearly his genuine feelings with the listeners while narrating his story, and hence stops at times exclaiming for instance: " It is impossible to convey the life sensation of any given epoch of one's existenceit is impossible. We live as we dream- alone".

Moving from like themes, to common forms, styles, and language, one is bound to notice how "Heart of Darkness" earned its classification as part of the modernist literary tradition. This frame narrative- in which Kurtz' story is enveloped within Marlow's tale, itself recounted by the narrator- is somehow self conscious and thus a meta-narrative, seeing that it comments on itself oftentimes. Marlow stops his narration three times in the course of the novel, making way for the outer narrator to give a certain remark, such as "I knew there was at least one listener awake besides myself." The use of a narrator taking part in the action of the story in "Heart of Darkness" is another aspect shared with 20th century literature. In addition, Conrad's work pertains to "Imagism" and "symbolism" prevailing in modern writing, both shaping what is known as "Impressionism". At several points in the story, the imagism is so strong it lingers in our minds, appealing to our mental senses. This is clear when Marlow describes the smell of the "hippo-meat" on board, and we can somehow smell it ourselves. Another good example would be the endless detailed depiction of the harlequin look-alike. Symbolism also permeates the whole of the novel, and is used at several occasions to give the reader an impression of something missing, where he is supposed to fill out the parts, or make out the full picture. An example would be Marlow's "flinging overboard a pair of new shoes" while he is actually alluding to the tipping of the helmsman overboard! A faint trace of "stream of consciousness" could also be experienced in the narrative, where reality of experience is presented as layered, disconnected, fragmented, and seems like a flow of events and emotions all juxtaposed within no clear frame of time. Oftentimes, Marlow appears to indulge in temporary digressions, monologues, and confession-like meditations, jumping from one time period to the other. This confuses the reader, and makes it harder to see when Marlow really meets Kurtz for example, seeing that he is always flashing forward to their meeting then going back to imagining what the man would be like in reality!

Finally, all of the mentioned traits serve as a proof to the modernism of such a piece of art. This novel thus discards the "art for art's sake" outlook on creation, but rather aims for higher truths, through shedding light on historical facts, while embellishing and rendering them even more exciting through mixing with them the most crucial of all experiencesthe human experience!

Regina Mouser

In Joseph Conrad's novella, "Heart of Darkness", one can plainly see the relationship between the title and the actual events portrayed within. The "Heart of Darkness" can be attributed to different facets, including: man's darkness within himself', the darkness of civilization'; the darkness of non-civilized peoples'; the darkness' of the climate and atmosphere of the areas described, etc. Conrad's style of writing, through Marlowe's narrative, also portrays the general darkness and gloominess of the journey. The abuses of other individuals, monopolization of territories that have been inhabited by others for centuries, and even murder, or at least death by neglect are all of these topics covered in this novella.

The landscape, climate, and environment of the entire area that Marlowe speaks of is portrayed as being very drab and dreary, with references made often of fog, dark nights, extreme temperatures, etc. The environment itself is foreboding and dangerous, because of the native inhabitants, wild animals, and unknown terrain of the river and land. These are also allusions to a "heart of darkness", symbolizing the fear and terror one would feel, if not familiar with this geographical area.

Both Marlowe and Kurtz (the "head man") relate to the heart of darkness', albeit in different ways; Marlowe in witnessing just how dark and terrifying it can be, and Kurtz, as the "ringleader" of the evil that is ongoing within the storyline. In some ways, Kurtz symbolizes Satan, or a demon, who is the "prince of darkness", thus, his taking up residency and reigning over those he feels are beneath him would be acceptable to him and those like him. Marlowe, on the other hand, is not used to this type of behaviour, so he receives a rude awakening. He begins to realise that what expectations he had for this journey are not realistic at all and as he witnesses the terrible circumstances and environment, he is very well aware that he is indeed in the heart of darkness.'

As one can tell by Marlowe's narrative to his crew members, he still has enough of his own conscience left to be sympathetic to the natives' plight. Unfortunately, he witnessed enough of the evils of society within that short time period to scar him for life. The events that he speaks of will probably remain within his memory forever, causing his view of the world to be stained. It is in this that one sees that he has truly been to the "heart of darkness."

Meaning in Heart of Darkness by Joseph Conrad

A search for meaning in Heart of Darkness by Joseph Conrad. Finds a thread of social commentary and work ethic to unite this novel and gives it meaning, instead of being merely an exercise in cynicism.

Searching for continuity in Heart of Darkness can be a challenging task. One wonders whether Conrad is a social critic, scrutinizing western civilization, or merely a vivid pessimist, condemning mankind to a helpless dichotomy of facade and brutality. Upon close inspection, one recurring idea seems to sew a common thread through the darkness of Kurtz and Africa and the ignorance of the Intended and the European facade. This motif lies in Marlowe's work ethic. Although Marlowe often seems to contradict his own analysis of his story, these contradictions arrive at a consistent value emphasizing integrity, frankness, and intelligence.

Conrad uses Marlowe's imagery and objective observation to establish a criticism of "civilized" society. The very opening paragraphs create a dark image of London, the centre of civilization during Conrad's time. "A haze rested on the low shores that ran out to sea in vanishing flatness. The air was dark above Gravesend, and farther back still seemed condensed into mournful gloom, brooding motionless over the biggest, and the greatest, town on earth" (Conrad 65). The dichotomy of dark imagery paired with the implication of "light" which civilization and London represent begin an extended Blakian contrary of light and dark with civilization and brutality. After further explication of the gloominess and "lurid glare" of London, Marlowe speaks his first words. "'And this also has been one of the dark places of the earth'" (67).

Although it does not seem obvious at first, corroborative descriptions of civilization create a distasteful and critical depiction of it. The sun changes from "glowing white" to "dull red without rays and without heat, as if about to go out suddenly, stricken to death by the touch of that gloom brooding over a crowd of men" (66). Here again the contrary of light and dark surfaces as London, which typically spreads the "light" of civilization, extinguishes the light of the sun in a fit of darkness. Although this continually contradicting imagery of light and dark seems somewhat erratic at first, it serves to perpetuate the connected idea that civilization, or light, contains an intrinsic element of the savage, or the dark.

The French ship at war with a camp of natives in the jungle produces the first example of this extension to the savagery of civilized society. Marlowe describes the situation as follows: "In the empty immensity of earth, sky, and water, there she was, incomprehensible, firing into a continent". Indeed, the random shelling of a few natives armed with spears and arrows with mortars from a man-of-war certainly seems to be overkill. The treatment of the natives at the Company's station increases the barbarity of the "civilized" whites. First Marlowe sees a chain gang of several natives who seem starved and nearly worked to death. As they pass by, they seem to have the blank stare of death, unconscious to Marlowe's presence even though they pass within six inches of him. Again in the grove of death, Marlowe sees the effect of the civilizing light of Europe upon the natives. "They were dying slowly... nothing but black shadows of disease and starvation... lost in uncongenial surroundings, fed on unfamiliar food, they sickened, became inefficient, and were then allowed to crawl away and rest". Marlowe implies in this passage that the natives were abused, used relentlessly for labour until they were spent, at which point they were "allowed" by the civilized whites to crawl into the grove of death to die. Truly a barbaric and dehumanizing view, using the natives only for their labour power, with no concern for their health or even their existence.

The comparison between the pilgrims and the cannibals on Marlowe's ship yields another example of the savagery of civilization. The pilgrims parallel the French man-of-war by "simply squirting lead into that bush". In an amazing lack of intelligence, the pilgrims attack the jungle, creating a cloud of smoke which blinds Marlowe's navigation. In another incident, the pilgrims throw the cannibals' only source of food overboard in what "looked like a high-handed proceeding." The cannibals, however, maintain a measure of self-restraint, facing the pangs of hunger rather than eating the whites who they outnumbered thirty to five. Marlowe strikes down possibility after possibility in trying to comprehend the restraint of the cannibals.

"No fear can stand up to hunger, no patience can wear it out, disgust simply does not exist where hunger is; and as to superstition, beliefs, and what you may call principles, they are less than chaff in a breeze. Don't you know the devilry of lingering starvation, its exasperating torment, its black thoughts, its sombre and brooding ferocity? Well I do. It takes a man all his inborn strength to fight hunger properly. It's really easier to face bereavement, dishonour, and the perdition of ones soul...".

Here Marlowe not only emphasizes the savagery of the pilgrims by comparison with the "nobility" of the cannibals, extending the contrary of light/dark and civilization/savagery, but he also begins to indicate what it is that deserves some measure of respect. The nearly impossible feat of withstanding hunger is accomplished by the savage cannibals through some inexplicable integrity. Although this integrity has no moral, religious, or philosophical foundation, Marlowe seems to emphasize the importance of integrity as an end in itself.

When Marlowe meets the Company's chief accountant, he expresses his immediate respect for the man. Even here, in the dark places of the earth, the accountant manages to keep his hair oiled, his collar starched, and his boots varnished, despite the unnecessary inconvenience it causes. In a place where everything else is in a muddle, dusty, splayed with rubbish, "this man had verily accomplished something". Marlowe's respect for the accountant derives from this accomplishment, this integrity. When faced with the repair of his ship, Marlowe goes to work immediately, stating, "[i]n that way only it seemed to me I could keep hold on the redeeming facts of life". Here Marlowe begins to explicate his emphasis on work and integrity as having value in themselves. In order to prevent becoming a part of the dusty muddle of the station, Marlowe decides that he must rely on physical labour. The other men in the station "[strolled] aimlessly about in the sunshine of the yard." Marlowe continues to scrutinize the meaning of this apparent vagrancy, with their "absurd long staves" and the "taint of imbecile rapacity" accompanying the word 'ivory'. Marlowe's extended call for rivets so he could "get on with the work," again emphasizes his priorities. After an extended conversation with the brickmaker of the Central Station about Kurtz and the "gang of virtue," the only real question on Marlowe's mind is when he will get his rivets. Marlowe then expands upon his philosophy about work. "I like what is in the work — the chance to find yourself. Your own reality — for yourself, not for others — what no other man can ever know. They can only see the mere show, and never can tell what it really means". Paired with the aspects of other men in the novel which Marlowe identifies with, this element in the work is a kind of work ethic or integrity — a sense of accomplishment and a testament to oneself that defines existence on another level than the dusty, aimless vagrancy of the company men.

Marlowe also exhibits a resolution of frankness and truth. Throughout the novel he emphasizes his contempt for shallow, materialistic men (and "civilized" society) and his value on honesty. When confronted with the primal beating of the drums in the jungle, Marlowe discusses the facade of inhumanity attributed to the natives by the whites as a deceptive self-defence mechanism. "No, [the natives] were not inhuman. Well, you know, that was the worst of it — suspicion of their not being inhuman... but what thrilled you was just the thought of your remote kinship with this wild and passionate uproar". Marlowe condemns the dishonesty of attributing the natives with an inhuman savagery simply as a means of self-deception. "Ugly. Yes, it was ugly enough; but if you were man enough you would admit to yourself that there was in you the faintest trace of a response to the terrible frankness of that noise". Marlowe even criticizes the professions of his friends to whom he is narrating, implying the futility of self-deception and even civilized behaviour itself. "I felt often [the inner truth's] mysterious stillness watching me at my monkey tricks, just as it watches you fellows performing on your respective tight-ropes for — what is it? half-a-crown a tumble". In response to the protestations of one of his listeners, Marlowe replies: "I beg your pardon. I forgot the heartache which makes up the rest of the price. And indeed what does the price matter, if the trick be well done?".

Here we come to the heart of Marlowe's philosophy. He realises the futility of any "purpose." Why is he boating down the river into the heart of Africa? To get rich? To civilize the brutes with a civilization he sees as corrupt? No, Marlowe simply captains the boat because the boat needs a captain, and, as a captain, Marlowe needs a boat. This is not to say that Marlowe in any way accepts separatism, pessimism, or a selfish rejection of society. The very fact that Marlowe continues a path of struggle disproves these assertions. Marlowe chooses a strenuous philosophy by choosing to realise his own "heart of darkness" and the brutality of civilization. Ignorance could have provided him a paved road, but Marlowe rejects this option; it provides no integrity. At the same time, Marlowe could have rejected society and its facades by following in the path of Kurtz. Kurtz has rejected the facades and deceptions of society in favor of not only a recognition of his "heart of darkness," but a surrender to those dark temptations. In Kurtz' final moments, Marlowe describes the changes that came over him. "It was as though a veil had been rent. I saw on that ivory face the expression of sombre pride, of ruthless power, of craven terror — of an intense and hopeless despair. Did he live his life again in every detail of desire, temptation, and surrender during that supreme moment of complete knowledge?". Kurtz then proceeds to judge his life, unrestrained violence, rampant greed, unconditional surrender to his "heart of darkness," in his final phrase, "The horror! The horror!" Marlowe meets the penultimate example of the deceptive facade of society, embodied in the Intended, and the extreme rejection of civilization, Kurtz. Marlowe rejects both of these paths, the Intended's being too smooth in ignorance, and Kurtz' being too smooth in complete surrender to primal urges. Marlowe's path, one of realization, acceptance, and a constant struggle to maintain integrity, provides a real continuity within Heart of Darkness.

Bibliography

Achebe, Chinua. " 'An Image of Africa': Racism in Conrad's 'HEART OF DARKNESS.' " In HEART OF DARKNESS: *An Authoritative Text, Backgrounds and Sources, Criticism,* ed. Robert Kimbrough. New York: Norton, 1988.

Bloom, Harold, ed. *Marlow.* New York: Chelsea House Publishers, 1992.

Cheng, Yuan-Jung. *Heralds of the Postmodern: Madness and Fiction in Conrad, Woolf, and Lessing.* New York: Peter Lang, 1999.

Conrad, Joseph. Heart of Darkness. New York: W. W. Norton & Co., 1963.

Eagleton, Terry. *Criticism and Ideology: A Study in Marxist Literary Theory.* London: Verso, 1976.

Firchow, Peter Edgerly. *Envisioning Africa: Racism and Imperialism in Conrad's* HEART OF DARKNESS. Lexington: University of Kentucky Press, 2000.

Guetti, James L. *The Limits of Metaphor: A Study of Melville, Conrad, and Faulkner.* Ithaca, New York: Cornell University Press, 1967.

Navarette, Susan J. *The Shape of Fear: Horror and the Fin-de-Siecle Culture of Decadence.* Lexington: University of Kentucky Press, 1998.

Stape, J. H., ed. *The Cambridge Companion to Joseph Conrad.* Cambridge: Cambridge University Press, 1996.